JOHN GRIERSON

# JOHN GRIERSON

## Life, Contributions, Influence

❯ JACK C. ELLIS

Southern Illinois University Press
Carbondale and Edwardsville

03 02 01 00    4 3 2 1

*Frontispiece:* John Grierson, Hyderabad, India, May 1971. Photo by Len Chatwin
© Photothèque National Film Board of Canada.

*Library of Congress Cataloging-in-Publication Data*
Ellis, Jack C., 1922–
    John Grierson : life, contributions, influence / Jack C. Ellis.
       p. cm.
    Includes bibliographical references and index.
    1. Grierson, John, 1898–1972. 2. Motion picture producers and directors—Great Britain Biography. 3. Documentary films—History and criticism.  I. Title.
    PN1998.3.G75E44   2000
    791.43'0232'092—dc21                           99-36971
    ISBN 0-8093-2242-0 (cloth : alk. paper)            CIP

# ➻ CONTENTS

# ➽ PREFACE

More than any one other person, John Grierson, a Scot, is responsible for the documentary film as it has developed in the English-speaking countries. He first applied the term *documentary* to Robert Flaherty's *Moana* while in the States in the 1920s. In 1927 Grierson took the word and his evolving conception of a new kind and use of film back to Britain with him. There he was hired by Stephen Tallents, secretary of the Empire Marketing Board, a unique government public relations agency intended to promote the products of the British Empire.

The first practical application of Grierson's ideas at the E.M.B. was *Drifters* in 1929, a short feature about herring fishing in the North Sea. Following its success, Grierson established, with the full support of Tallents, the Empire Marketing Board Film Unit instead of pursuing a career as an individual filmmaker. He staffed the unit with young people, mostly middle class and well educated (many from Cambridge University). The training at the E.M.B. Film Unit and subsequently the General Post Office Film Unit was ideological as well as technical and aesthetic. The young filmmakers exposed to it came to share Grierson's broad social purposes and developed an extraordinary loyalty to him and to his goals. It was in this way that the British documentary movement was given shape and impetus.

What Grierson wanted documentary to do was to inform the public about their nation and involve them emotionally with the workings of their government. He assumed that if people at work in one part of the Empire were shown to people in the other parts, and if a government service was presented to the population at large, an understanding and appreciation of the interrelatedness of the modern world and of our dependency on each other would develop, and everyone would contribute his or her share to the better functioning of the whole. On these assumptions was based the first phase in Grierson's lifelong activity on behalf of citizenship education. Phase one included some of the most original, lovely, and lasting of the British documentaries: *Drifters, Industrial Britain, Granton Trawler, The Song of Ceylon, Coal Face,* and *Night Mail.*

Phase two, which began in the mid-1930s, consisted of calling public attention to pressing problems faced by the nation. Since these matters may have involved differing political positions and in any case did not relate directly to the concerns of the sponsoring General Post Office, Grierson stepped outside the G.P.O. to enlist sponsorship from private industry. Big oil and gas concerns were especially responsive to his persuasion. The subjects dealt with in this new kind of documentary included unemployment *(Workers and Jobs)*, slums *(Housing Problems)*, malnutrition among the poor *(Enough to Eat?)*, smog *(The Smoke Menace)*, and education *(Children at School)*. Unlike the earlier British documentaries, these films were journalistic rather than poetic and seemed quite inartistic. Yet they incorporated formal and technical experiments. Most notable among these was the direct interview, with slum dwellers in *Housing Problems*, for example, presaging the much later cinéma vérité method, and a standard technique of television documentary today.

The use of institutional sponsorship, public and private, to pay for his kind of filmmaking, rather than dependence upon returns from the box office, was a key Grierson innovation in the development of the documentary. A second innovation, complementing the first, was nontheatrical distribution and exhibition: going outside the movie theaters to reach audiences in schools and factories, union halls, and church basements.

During the ten years between *Drifters* and Grierson's departure for Canada, in 1939, the sixty or so filmmakers who comprised the British documentary movement made over three hundred films. These films and the system they came out of became models for other countries. Paul Rotha, one of Grierson's principal lieutenants, went on a six-month missionary expedition to the United States in 1937, and film people from America and other countries visited the documentary units in Britain. Grierson carried his ideas himself not only to Canada, where he drafted legislation for the National Film Board and became its first head, but to New Zealand, Australia, and later South Africa, all of which established national film boards.

The National Film Board of Canada stands as the largest and most impressive monument to Grierson's concepts and actions relating to the use of film by governments in communicating with their citizens. During his Canadian years he moved beyond national concerns to global ones. The Film Board's "The World in Action," a monthly series for the theaters along "The March of Time" lines, expressed some of these concerns. His ideas regarding the education of citizens required in a world at war, and the new world to follow, were expressed in major essays that have inspired many. My reading of them started this biography, in a way.

I first encountered Grierson when I was working on a doctorate at Teachers College, Columbia University, from 1950 to 1953. The Citizenship Education Project, funded by the Carnegie Corporation, gave a lot of graduate students employment at the time. Its mission was to develop curriculum materials for junior and senior high schools that would fit into courses in history, social studies, and even language arts. We annotated books and pamphlets, articles and short stories, audio recordings and, in my case, films and filmstrips which dealt with concepts of U.S. citizenship as related to the Declaration of Independence, the Bill of Rights, and the Constitution. I thought my work pretty dull stuff, for the most part, until I came across the collection of writings entitled *Grierson on Documentary*, edited by Forsyth Hardy. Grierson's conception of citizenship education—to which his whole life was mainly devoted—gave me a totally new view of the possibilities. This was due not only to his ideas, which were unfamiliar to me, but also, maybe especially, to the way he expressed them. I first became interested in Grierson, I suspect, solely on the basis of his writing. I think him a fine prose stylist.

Some while after leaving Columbia I managed to get a job teaching the first film courses at Northwestern University. In my second year there I introduced a course in the theory and history of documentary film. A little later, when it seemed to me I should develop a research area of some sort, I thought, why not documentary, which interested me, and with which I was familiar? And if documentary, why not John Grierson, who could lay claim to having invented the term itself as applied to film and to laying the basis for documentary theory?

At that time, around 1960, however, there were no scholarly biographies of filmmakers except for several on Chaplin that might qualify and Marie Seton's biography of Eisenstein, so I had no models. I read what I could find about the nature of biographical writing and started to comb Northwestern's library, using research techniques remembered from graduate courses in the history of literature. I searched all the standard bibliographical and biographical resources for every mention of Grierson as well as related topics, persons, and institutions. (There was an early brief confusion with a John Grierson who occupied a place of importance in the history of aviation; since my Grierson seemed so protean in his activities, and to be turning up everywhere, I wondered for a time if he might have taken on flying as well.) The 3x5 and 5x8 note cards began to accumulate in large quantities.

Having found out everything I could from library research, the next step was to interview people who knew Grierson and had worked with him and, of course, Grierson himself. The interviewing led to two trips: one in 1962, for two weeks, as I recall, to Montreal and the National Film Board; the other, in 1966, for six weeks, to England and Scotland. I spent my last full day in England with Grierson at his home near Calne, Wiltshire.

My sources thus became published materials of all sorts, plus interviews with some forty or more persons. I don't think there were relevant archives available at the time—if there were it didn't occur to me to seek them out, and no one suggested I do so. In any case, it wasn't until later that freedom of information acts in Great Britain, Canada, and the United States fully opened up government records as additional sources of information. It was fortunate for me that Grierson had been so much in the public eye that a great deal could be learned about him and verified by playing off press coverage against interviewees' recollections.

I wrote the bulk of a book-length manuscript in a milk shed on a deserted farm in Wisconsin during the summer of 1967, and a little more in the summer of 1968—got to midpoint in the penultimate chapter, on his television career. Then I put that work aside to deal with other, what seemed at the time, more pressing professional matters. Before I got back to it, Forsyth Hardy, who had gotten out a second edition of *Grierson on Documentary*, announced, following Grierson's death, that he had agreed to undertake a biography (though he had assured me he never would) at the request of Mrs. Grierson. Since he had known Grierson much longer and better than I, it seemed courteous, and perhaps politic, to wait and see what he had to say.

In my own biographical explorations I was taking a line a bit more critical of Grierson than the standard line—and, believe me, there was a standard line—and I felt deeply indebted to his friends and former colleagues who had been so very helpful. They had provided me with insights, clippings, access to correspondence, and pretty elegant room and board on occasion. All were so closely involved with Grierson emotionally, so protective of him, that I was smothered by their kindness, it now seems to me. Sir Arthur and Lady Margaret Ann Elton, at Clevedon Court, Somerset, for example, or Basil Wright, sitting beneath his original Rouaults in Little Adam Farm near Henley-on-Thames, and others, were all very seductive, let me tell you. At the time, between my uneasiness about being disrespectful of Grierson and the solidity of Hardy's biography, my book seemed ungenerous and unneeded.

What I had tried to do, as well as learning in detail what Grierson had achieved, was to get at the complexities of his personality and the motivations for his actions, which contained some implications that made me uneasy. There were things he wanted to do for the common good that I didn't think would work, or even should work; and certainly there were episodes, even periods, in his career that Hardy waltzed around or skated over, or, in some instances, ignored altogether.

When I finally returned to the project, I could see that Hardy's biography, while thoroughly researched, acknowledged sources very sparingly and limited the amount of detail in order to heighten the drama of Grierson's advance through life. My manuscript had a substantial scholarly foundation and emphasized differences of opinion rather than synthesizing or reducing them. I sensed the opportunity to produce a new biography that would be both comprehensive and detailed. It could be of interest to those who wanted to know a lot about Grierson and the people and institutions he worked with as all this fitted into a larger film history.

As I continued to pore over the manuscript, a plan evolved: that, in addition to the biography itself, there would be an added section addressing the various understandings of Grierson that have appeared since my own research and writing. Rather than trying to deal with these bit by bit throughout the text, breaking up the form I had tried to achieve, I would end with an elucidation of Hardy and the main-line Griersonians and, especially, of the recent revisionists, some of whom take very different views from the traditional ones.

So, that's what's to follow, beginning with Grierson's beginning.

# ➻ ACKNOWLEDGMENTS

I am much indebted to Alan Rosenthal, Hebrew University, Jerusalem, and hugely indebted to John Huntington, University of Illinois, Chicago, and Carolyn Anderson, University of Massachusetts, Amherst, for helping make this a better work than it was when they first saw it. My thanks to all three. Thanks, too, to Haseenah Ebrahim, Northwestern University, for her computer smarts, without which the manuscript would have been at considerable risk.

The frontispiece photo of Grierson was taken by Len Chatwin and provided by Ken McReady, both of the National Film Board of Canada. I am obliged to them as well. Permission for its reproduction was granted by the N.F.B.

Parts of this biography have appeared earlier in slightly different form in the following books and articles by the author: *The Documentary Idea: A Critical History of English-Language Documentary Film and Video* (Englewood Cliffs, N.J.: Prentice Hall, 1989), 75–76, 130–31. "The Final Years of British Documentary as the Grierson Movement," *The Journal of Film and Video* 36, no. 4 (fall 1984): 41–49. "Grierson, John," *International Dictionary of Films and Filmmakers*, 3d ed., (Detroit: St. James Press, 1997), 2: 396–99. "John Grierson's Relations with British Documentary During World War Two," John Grierson Project, McGill University, *John Grierson and the NFB* (Toronto: ECW Press, 1984), 62–76 (used by permission of ECW Press, Toronto). "Changing of the Guard: From the Grierson Documentary to Free Cinema," *Quarterly Review of Film Studies* 7 (winter 1982): 24–35 (used by permission of Harwood Academic Publishers GmbH). "The Young Grierson in America" from *Cinema Journal* 8, no. 1 (fall 1968): 12–21; "John Grierson's First Years at the National Film Board" from *Cinema Journal* 10, no. 1 (fall 1970): 2–14; and "Grierson at University" from *Cinema Journal* 12, no. 2 (spring 1973): 24–35 (used by permission of the University of Texas Press).

✦ JOHN GRIERSON

# 1 ⇻ SCOTLAND (1898–1924)

## Deanston and Cambusbarron (1898–1915)

Eighteen-ninety-eight was a good year for babies who would grow up to become filmmakers. Born in that year were René Clair (in France), Sergei Eisenstein (in Russia), Joris Ivens (in Holland), Rouben Mamoulian (in Armenia), Preston Sturges, Leo McCarey, and Walter Lang (in the United States), and—in the tiny village of Deanston, in Stirlingshire, Scotland—John Grierson, on April 26. Deanston is a hamlet of no more than a dozen houses lined up alongside a stream in a narrow valley. Its inhabitants were supported by a cloth mill, a large two-story brick structure at the end of the single street. The physician who officiated at the birth may have come from Doune (known for Doune Castle), a small town less than a mile away. The child's mother was Jane Anthony Grierson; the father Robert Morrison Grierson. John was the fourth child and first son.

The earlier Griersons had been lighthouse keepers. John's father was born on the lighthouse at Rhu Vaal, on the tip of the Isle of Islay, the southernmost of the Hebrides, and his predecessors were all lighthouse men back to the first keeper on Bell Rock (or Inchape) in the North Sea. His mother came from an Ayrshire family said to be well known for its radical outlook.[1] His father was a Calvinist and his mother a free thinker, though neither his religion nor her agnosticism seems to have been strong enough to lead to any particular conflict. They were of opposing political persuasions as well—he describing himself as a conservative—and this may have caused a bit more tension, with Mrs. Grierson sitting on the speaker's platform of one candidate and Mr. Grierson on his opponent's.

Robert Grierson was a schoolmaster, "a good dominie of the old school" his son would later characterize him. John Grierson pointed out, on that later occasion, that "Conservative as he was, this village schoolmaster . . . was something of a pioneer in the teaching of the social amenities." He pioneered school gardens and domestic science for girls, for example, and showed educational films "long before the big towns like Edinburgh and Glasgow knew anything about them. These, too, were documentaries," wrote his son, "and the first film I saw was none other than Opus 2 in the history of cinema—the Lumière boy eating his apple [cereal, surely]."[2] The father also helped to build a village institute, "so that his fellow citizens would have more literary papers on this and that. . . ."[3] He taught to within a year or so of his death, in 1928, dying just before the completion of his son's first film, *Drifters*. That film, because it was about the sea and fishing, came out of a "family emotion," John said. "My father and I myself grew up with the passion for the herring fishermen, so when I got the chance of making a film, one of my first instincts was to do something about this that was near and dear not only to me, but for my old man, and, you know, it's always a satisfaction if you can pay some tribute to the people you owe so much to."[4]

In later life John Grierson came to feel increasingly that his role was also that of an educator. In an article quoted above, he described his father's educational theory and how it came to seem lacking for the new century. "He called himself a Conservative," wrote John, "but his operative philosophy in education was a good sample of what a liberal Scottish education meant. He believed in the democratic process as Burns and all Scotsmen naturally and natively do. A man was a man for a' that." Grierson went on to say that the basis of his father's educational philosophy was "according to the eternal verities."

> It was deeply rooted in Carlyle and Ruskin and the natural rights of man. The wind of the French revolution still blew behind it. But it was strictly individualist. Education gave men a chance in the world. . . .

. . . the prevailing idea was as always that the individual might be more enlightened. One suspected that the end of it all was to make every workman a gentleman in a library—perhaps without too much leisure to be a gentleman and not too much of a library, but still as good as any man alive in the deep pursuit of truth and beauty.

The smashing of that idyllic viewpoint has been probably the greatest educational fact of our time; and I saw it smashed right there in my village and I saw the deep doubt creep into the mind of that schoolmaster that everything he stood for and strove for was somewhere wrong.[5]

The village to which Grierson referred was Cambusbarron, a few miles from Deanston and close to (and now a suburb of) Stirling. The family moved there when John was two. In that part-mining community, prompted by increasing economic hardships and labor unrest, "the miners themselves and the economists among them" were taking his father's place as an educational force. "They read their Blatchford and Keir Hardie and Bob Smillie; they attended their trade union meetings; and the day came when they elected their first Labour member of parliament, and, with so many other villages in Scotland, joined in the great drive for a socialist Britain."[6]

Grierson claimed to have drawn two conclusions from that village story. The first, that "education can only, at its peril, detach itself from the economic processes and what is happening in the world. In that sense," he wrote, "if official education does not give realistic leadership in terms of what is happening and what is most deeply needed in the world, be assured the people will find other more realistic leadership." The second lesson was that "the individualist dream in education is over and done with in a world which operates in terms of large integrated forces. There is nothing I can think of so cynical today as to teach a boy that the world is his personal oyster for the opening or talk, as Lord Birkenhead did, of the glittering prizes that fall to a flashing sword."[7]

Though serious about his work, Grierson's father was a gentle man, respected and no doubt loved by his children, but less forceful than their mother. The conclusions John said he arrived at may have had something to do with her as well as with his own early observations of his father's philosophy. Certainly one can infer that the tough liberal-mindedness with which his ideas were phrased was part of her legacy. A story told by Lady Margaret Ann Elton, which presumably she got from Grierson himself, was of the young Johnnie running in tears to his mother because the other boys were teasing him about there being beetles in the soup of the soup kitchen his mother administered. "That will teach you how hard it is to be a socialist," she is said to have replied.[8] She was a suffragette early and later became active in the Independent Labour Party. The latter, founded in 1893, was left of the present Labour Party; it advocated extreme political changes, was pacifist, and totally anti-capitalist but not communist. Its subsequent strength grew out of the effects of the post–World War I depression on the working-class area of Glasgow along the River Clyde—the Clydeside.

It was Grierson's mother who pushed for the children and probably pushed them as well. She had been a lecturer in a teachers' training college in Glasgow before her marriage and after it collected bright children around her and tutored them in the evenings. She worked alongside her husband in this, and again Grierson recalls of his father that "it didn't matter where the boys came from. If they were lads of parts, he felt it his God-given mission to put them on their way . . . intensifying on the bright ones, so that they could win scholarships and go to high school and on to the university. . . . It is still pleasant to think how he would trudge off miles into the country to prevail on stubborn ploughmen, who needed the extra money coming in, to give their boys a chance and not put them to work at fourteen."[9] The Cambusbarron school was reputed to have produced the highest percentage of university graduates of any school in Scotland, and one boy even managed to get into Oxford.[10] Mrs. Grierson helped in all of this in addition to mothering eight children. She died in 1937.

Forsyth Hardy has suggested that the large Grierson family "delighted in the argument characteristic of many Scottish homes of the period" and conjectured that "perhaps Grierson's ability in debate owes something to the grounding of these lively family discussions."[11] At any rate, the family was close as well as large and continued to be so with much visiting and communication back and forth. The children were Janet (who became a teacher at a Glasgow high school for girls), Agnes (who also taught high school), Margaret, called Madge (who died at the age of ten, before the diagnosis of appendicitis was known), John (who, by general account, more or less ran the family after he became an adult), Anthony (an M.D.

who later lived near John in Wiltshire), Dorothy (who became a masseuse), Ruby (who died in the torpedoing of a refugee ship early in World War II), and Marion (who eventually became a youth worker in Glasgow). All of them went through their father's school, and all went on to Glasgow University except Dorothy. John brought into film with him Ruby, who became a director of some distinction before her death (e.g., *Today We Live*, with Ralph Bond, 1937; *They Also Serve*, 1940), and Marion, who became a competent one (e.g., *Key to Scotland*, 1935, and *For All Eternity*, 1937), as well as editor of the periodical *World Film News* from 1936 to 1938. Marion stayed with John in London just after his return, in 1927, from three years in America. The two boys, John and Anthony, were in the service together in World War I; both were wireless operators on mine sweepers in the North Sea. According to Margaret Grierson, John's wife, the brothers' deep and lasting fondness for each other was expressed chiefly through friendly bullying and teasing.[12] John was called Jack by the family and by almost no one else.

Cambusbarron remained the family home during John's growing up. Situated in an agricultural valley, it was a lovely place during the mild seasons of the year, with the Highlands beginning to the north and the mines nearby to the south. The village population was composed half of farmers and half of miners. The region was rural and sparsely populated, as was most of Scotland. Agriculture consisted of the raising of cows and sheep mostly, with light farming. Stirling, however, was a town of some grandeur, with its imposing castle cresting the great rock, the scene of ancient Scottish glories. Before Scotland became part of England, the Scottish parliament used to meet in Stirling. Today it is the county seat of Stirlingshire and a market town. This area on the Stirlingshire-Perthshire boundary was the field of the Battle of Bannockburn, where the Scots held off the English, with the near-sacred Gillies Hill close by. (Grierson's ancestors are buried in a churchyard beside Bannockburn.) The now fertile valley, through which the River Forth runs, was formerly an impassable morass that served as a strategic border between Lowlands and Highlands. The wild, romantic country of Loch Katrine and Loch Lomond is not very far away. Grierson would eventually write the script for a film on Stirlingshire called *The Heart of Scotland* (1961).

This spot, though about equidistant from Glasgow and Edinburgh, was under the cultural sway of Glasgow. Rather than the arts, traditions, and architectural beauty of dignified Edinburgh, the semianarchist world of Glasgow's Clydeside, with its squalor and ugliness but great vitality, exerted the polar attraction. The violence of politics in Scotland was half associated with the nationalist movement; because of English domination, the nationalist fervor could only be expressed in political discussion, and there were great debates, formal and informal. Five or six organized political points of view would be represented in the local tavern. By the time he was twelve Grierson was listening to political speeches.

He began school, his father's, at the age of five. He was, of course, a "lad o' pairts," one of the boys of obvious and early talent whom schoolmasters sought out and developed when they found them. Grierson later said, "They were looking for bloody geniuses under every bush."[13] School started at 8:00 A.M. for the lads of parts (for everyone else at 9:00). They stayed on after 4:00 P.M., with his mother coaching them. At the age of ten he began high school at Stirling. (The usual entrance age was eleven or twelve.) Though he and his brother both played football (soccer), he was at his books from 6:30 P.M. until midnight from the age of thirteen on, with an hour or two a day minimum study during summer vacation.[14] For holidays as a boy he went to the Isle of Islay.

Grierson's intensive schooling would condition his outlook for the rest of his life; though his activities had international scope and he lived and traveled in far-flung places, like many of his countrymen he managed to remain profoundly a Scot. In fact his upbringing was not unique—different more in degree than in kind from that of other boys in Scotland at the time. To his Scottish friends who complained later in his life that he talked like an American gangster, one can only say that his Scottish burr seemed ultimately to predominate. Referring to Grierson's own statements on the subject, Forsyth Hardy has said that "the Scotland he knows in his heart . . . is the Scotland of fifty years ago, when the Church was still strong and the Calvinistic disciplines still counted for something. On the other hand, Clydeside was wild with the new Socialism. It was a stirring period in which the old self-disciplined, sensible Scottish tradition was lit up with wild new hopes and new rhetoric and new poetry of expectation."[15]

Grierson accounted for his pioneering in documentary film as a result of trying to combine three influences that stemmed from his youth. First, his educational drive from his father, being born into a schoolhouse, as he said. Second, his attraction to politics and public service, coming from his mother's side. And last, his interest in the arts, which he developed largely on his own—an interest uncharacteristic of the family. That the combining of "these three fundamental interests" should have taken place in film he accounted for as part of a national tradition.[16] Speaking of his early exposure to films he would later write: "The significant thing to me now was that our elders accepted this cinema as essentially different from the theatre. Sin still, somehow, attached to play-acting, but, in this fresh new art of observation and reality, they saw no evil. I was confirmed in cinema at six because it had nothing to do with the theatre, and I have remained so confirmed."[17]

This Calvinist tradition, respect for education, the poverty and dependency of the country, the fierce nationalism leading into a special kind of socialism were all closely linked. The excellent Scottish schools (an educational system superior to as well as more democratic than the English system) were introduced by John Knox himself, who decreed that there would be a church in every parish and in every parish a school. The first education enactment in Scotland attached a school to each of the church communities, and they remained in continuous existence from the late sixteenth century on. The schoolmaster became a key figure, the hub of the community, along with the minister. Often farmers would put one child into teaching and another into the ministry, and the Scots admired a boy who escaped the labor of the fields or the mines. The gifted boy of his school or year was respected in every community as a star athlete might be elsewhere. When a boy did break through to success, it was usually with the help of the dominie. Robert Burns, for example, was very well educated; he knew Greek by the age of ten. By the 1880s there were village libraries, and the woman who cleaned Robert Grierson's schoolhouse was a great reader.

In a poor country, with few natural resources and little fully productive land, it is hard work to make a living. Not only was learning considered power but education was a kind of investment in the future. By the nineteenth century, promising sons of laborers, like David Livingston, the African explorer, did not go into commerce; that would have been thought as lacking concern for the public good.

Instead, they trained to be doctors, lawyers, or professors. When Grierson announced that he was going into film, his father, thinking of Hollywood daydreams no doubt, expressed the old Scottish fear that he was pursuing the shadow instead of the substance.[18] Because of the inadequate opportunities offered in his own country, it was thought at least natural that a bright boy should fix his gaze on the horizon. Education equipped him to go abroad and to rise to a point of eminence and command.

The rigorousness of that academic discipline marked Grierson's career: he would always feel the need to be fully informed on any subject he touched upon and, in the particular case of films with which he was connected, always insisted on the most thorough investigation of the material dealt with. The intellectual effort in his youth was very strenuous, he conceded in his old age in a tone combining pride with an undercurrent of resentment.[19] The prodigious amount of work accomplished and self-discipline imposed that so strongly characterized the mature man were characteristics of the mold that formed him.

Also, as a Scot prepared to go out into the world—he once described himself as "a good cosmopolitan Scotsman"[20]—Grierson would later be particularly sensitive to the "cultural validity, however small, and cultural dependence, always so great" of all other small and dependent countries.[21] (This attribute would equip him admirably for his role of interpreting Canada to the Canadians through the production of the National Film Board.) Speaking at Montevideo, Uruguay, on an occasion during his UNESCO days, he allied himself with the Uruguayans' inferiority complex. And he pointed out that when Uruguay had beaten Scotland seven to one in a recent international football contest, it was a greater loss to Scotsmen than the loss of India.[22] He would share in a highly complex form his countrymen's respect for and resentment of the dominant English. It was as a young Scot that Grierson scaled the walls of the British establishment and dealt with its civil servants on their home ground of public administration, his admiration for their organizational abilities always at war with a dislike of mandarin ways and Scottish mistrust of English deviousness. Furthermore, as a government film officer, he early seized many opportunities to introduce Scottish themes into British cinema, from his initial film,

*Drifters*, on through *O'er Hill and Dale*, *Upstream*, *Fishing Banks of Skye*, *Granton Trawler*, and others to follow.

## North Sea (1916–19)

In 1915, at the age of seventeen, Grierson made what was described by one of his professors as a brilliant entry into Glasgow University.[23] In the Bursary Competition—a nationwide test—he became the first entrant who was not a classical scholar and who didn't know Greek to take a major (second) prize.[24] The result was that he received a scholarship to the university as a Clark Scholar.

By then, however, the country was a year into World War I. Grierson later recalled that on August 4, 1914, the date of Britain's entry, he had been on the coast of the Scottish Hebrides. The war seemed very near as he "spent the whole day watching the trawlers and the drifters breasting the tide, puffing their way back in hundreds to become minesweepers and anti-submarine patrols."[25] With classes barely under way he left the university to enlist in the Royal Naval Volunteer Reserve (illegally it would seem, since nineteen was the minimum age). His period of service would last three and a half years. Though he once growled to a companion that he had spent the war cleaning latrines,[26] he was, as mentioned before, a wireless operator on mine sweepers in the North Sea. His ships were mostly converted whalers; cross-channel boats and trawlers were also used as sweepers. *White Whale* was the ship he was on most and Storaway was the home port for much of the time, though he would write: "I have been in and out of every sea loch from Cape Wrath to the Mull of Kintyre and in every sheltering harbour east and west from the Butt of Lewis to Barra Head. Nor can there be many islands in the great highland galaxies that I haven't been to, and that includes St. Kilda and the Flannans, North Rona and the Monachs. I have been on ships the world over but there have never been ships again for me like the highland and island ships."[27]

Still, one doesn't quite know what effects this experience had on the young sailor. A photo of him at the time, in Navy uniform, shows him handsome, with bright eyes, a smooth heavy face, sturdy neck and chest. From this picture one wouldn't guess him to be the small man he was. Hardy said he never spoke about the Navy experience with any regret and suggested that "It confirmed him in his love of ships and the sea and in other respects it was inevitably a toughening process."[28] Grierson himself remembered that these boats were totally without comfort;[29] cramped quarters and the dirty weather of the North Sea must have been continuing banes to the sailor's existence.

While in the Navy, the intellectual preparation was continued on his own with unabated vigor. Each day, he said, he did four hours of reading and wrote a thousand words, in various forms—light verse, short stories, essays—to learn to be a writer. It was a matter of discipline, self-imposed. (He began to publish as soon as he returned to the university—in the university magazine and occasionally in a London paper.)[30] His two most personal films, *Drifters* and *Granton Trawler*, would surely draw on this experience, and they manifest a strong feeling for sea and ships and the men who sail them. His writings are sprinkled lightly with nautical phrases and imagery, and his marvelous review of the 1937 Hollywood film *Captains Courageous* brings him head-on into what is clearly familiar and favorite subject matter. It had everything he had asked for thirty years ago, he wrote. "I confess I have been fortunate since. I have gone to sea as I vowed and fished cod one after the other with hand lines one after the other, and there isn't a whip of wind or water, or a hull heeling over so it didn't seem it would come back, that I couldn't match; and the reality was as good as the dream, as all realities are when you look into them."[31] His knowledge of the sea, along with his boyhood in Stirlingshire and university days in Glasgow, would form a steady romantic point of self-reference in his speeches and articles. He was to say "I spent something like ten years in universities; but the things I prize today are what I learned in the village I came from, and the time I have spent with fishermen, sailors, farmers and miners."[32]

The transition back to civilian life was of course difficult. Twenty-five years later Grierson wrote:

> I remember still that I did not leave my port of demobilization for days. I hung around and wandered disconsolately along the harbour front taking a last look at the ship that had been my home for years. I had become accustomed to life on shipboard. I knew my neighbours. Perhaps, looking back, I was scared to leave the disciplined, co-ordinated,

harmonious life of the navy, where you knew exactly where you stood, and what you had to do, and for your well-ordered duty received in return a well-ordered security.

I remember how clumsy were some of my own attempts to exchange this systematic and disciplined life for the individual and unprotected free-for-all which civilian life suddenly appeared. I cannot remember that the welcome home meant anything at all. I thought, foolishly, that I had lost four years of my life and that I had a great deal of leeway to make up. I came back, as I thought, to an alien world of dreary people who were still doing the same old things, teaching the same old things in the same old way, as though this war of ours had made no essential difference to the world. I resented their complacency. . . .

We were not wise enough to know that we had not lost those four years as we thought. We had learned skills; we had acquired experience of people and events beyond our years; but none was wise enough to confirm us in this thought and strengthen our sense of confidence. We had learned at an early age, some of us, to organize and to lead and to hold our own in the tough company of men; but people were stupid enough to hold us at arm's length and say, more or less, these attainments may have been all very well in the war, but are less than useless in the civilian world you now enter; it is the certificates of merit we want and the paper qualifications and the smooth ways and, first and last, your accommodation to the old patterns. To tell the truth, these were the very things for a long time that we were not very good at.[33]

## Glasgow (and Newcastle-on-Tyne) (1919–24)

But to accommodate himself he returned to Glasgow University. At first, he continued,

We could not concentrate; we could not learn; and the boys who had not left for the war were skating rings around us for awhile, and we knew it. It was not perhaps for a couple of years or more that we quietened our anxieties and cooled our heads and began to fit in. I am still appalled when I look back at the lack of imagination on the part of the professors to whom we reported. . . . With only a rare exception, they gave no indication of any understanding whatever of the psychological gulf a life on active service can create between a service man and civilian life.[34]

Nonetheless, Glasgow University was an exciting place on his return in 1919 and, much more than most universities, particularly

European ones, was firmly attached to the life of the people, and to social reform. The university was also very political in its orientation at a time when Glasgow's river was called "The Red Clyde," in reference to the socialist ferment in the working-class section along its banks. Out of the extreme poverty of the post–World War I years grew the intense feelings expressed through the Independent Labour Party.

Grierson later offered his own view of these stirrings and commented on their relationship to his subsequent activity:

> The Clydeside cult was the most humanist in the early Socialist movement. This was its deep political weakness, as Lenin himself pointed out, and men like James Maxton came practically to demonstrate. But while recognizing this, as one must, the over-riding humanist factor did not thereby lose its ultimate validity as the harder forces of political organisation have taken control of the thoughts we had and the sympathies we urged. For myself, I shall only say that what I may have given to documentary—with the working man on the screen and all that—was simply what I owed to my masters, Keir Hardie, Bob Smillie, and John Wheatley; and no one will understand me better in this than the Rt. Hon. Walter Elliot who calls himself a Tory.[35]

The returning veterans, a bumper crop of unusually talented as well as mature students (Grierson was 21 after military service), entered into the ferment, added some leadership and much discussion. James Bridie, the playwright, and Walter Elliot, the public official mentioned above, had been in the generation preceding; Grierson's class lived under their shadow.[36] During his own time, in addition to his brother Anthony, there were Charles Dand, who would also work in films in the government service; William Barclay, who would become chief political writer of the London *Daily Express*; and Alexander Werth, later a brilliant political analyst. Grierson acknowledged that he owed a lot to Werth,[37] and the debt was probably mutual. Werth was a Russian emigré who had lived in Paris. When he arrived in Glasgow, Grierson "adopted him more or less"[38] and developed from him a consciousness of the artistic avant-garde in France. Together they published in the university magazine some Russian poetry which Werth translated and Grierson edited.[39] Werth also had an interest in film; at least he wrote movie reviews during university days until fired after giving a bad notice to an American film which was promoted in a paid advertisement in the paper.[40] Grierson claimed to have written his first movie piece in 1919, about a "certain 2-reel comic called Chaplin."[41] The film under discussion was *A Dog's Life*.[42] His review was published in the university magazine, presumably, but no one has been able to track it down. Perhaps Forsyth Hardy had it right when he observed that, while at the university, Grierson was a regular contributor to the university magazine, and "although these contributions did not include formal film criticism, several of them revealed his interest in the cinema, particularly in Chaplin."[43]

Much closer to Grierson's eventual interest in cinema would have been Robert Flaherty's *Nanook of the North*, which arrived in Glasgow "around 1922. The whole aspect of it was so fresh and curious," he recalled, "that, though I had no reason at the time to concentrate on films, I must have seen it half a dozen times over." There was an early equivalent to a film society "in a little drinking group led by an Armenian girl from the Art School," to whom Grierson said he would always be obliged.[44] He also claimed to have been the art critic for the *Evening Citizen*, a Glasgow paper, while at the university. He told the editor he knew everything about painting, in order to get the job, then "went home and boned up on it." His (considerable) interest in art dated from that time, he said.[45]

Grierson's academic progress led him from an early pursuit of literature on to philosophy (he was always most interested in *political* philosophy, he said),[46] and finally to what might be called political science. Bertrand Russell's *Social Reconstruction* (1919) exerted an acknowledged influence, but it seems likely that of more lasting use was the university custom of debating all issues from the three prevailing political positions—conservative, liberal, and socialist. In developing arguments as skillfully as possible for each of these three political stances, the student of course came to understand their logic dynamically as well as deeply. It was a strong start on the kind of broad social-political-economic analysis at which Grierson would become adept. His analytical thinking would become so deeply ingrained as to be automatic: he couldn't turn it off (not that he should have), and it would occupy much of his informal conversation and personal letters as well as his published writing and public addresses. The ability to understand the Tory position, for example, better than most Tories, and to argue how it might be most effectively implemented, would give him an enormous professional resource in the many years and millions of dollars spent in producing films under government sponsorship. The trick then became merely one of finding where his own social-political-economic motives coincided with those of the party with the purse.

Another influential experience of his university days is worthy of comment. For two years Grierson was a preacher for two small Highlands churches—until he gave a radical sermon and was defrocked.[47] Any senior in philosophy at the university could enter his name with the divinity school and be assigned a church. He could not officiate at sacraments, of course—baptism or the Lord's Supper—but could preach sermons to his heart's content. Grierson did this only partly for the added income; he looked upon it as practice in standing up and speaking, and he clearly relished the tradition of great speechifying in Scotland at the time.[48] Much later Grierson discovered in New Zealand a custom he thought worthy of wide export. The speaker would be given a staff of honor, and Grierson enjoyed striding back and forth on the stage emphasizing his remarks with loud thumps. Basil Wright once wrote, ". . . when Grierson talks you can't stop him, even if you want to (he is the worst listener I have ever met)."[49] A great talker he was to become, surely, and always a lay preacher.

He was also a teacher. He himself recalled:

> When I was pretty young myself, I had to teach a night school in Scotland to young people who worked all day in the local coal mines. They were poor tired characters and I was supposed to teach them literature or something, and the subject was Shakespeare's "Midsummer Night's Dream." That is what they called adult education in my early days. If you know coal mines and know "Midsummer Night's Dream," you know it was pretty silly calling this adult education or anything else. Young as I was, I thought it silly myself, so I went to the movies they went to and to the local theatre where they ran melodramas like Sappho, the Worst Girl in Paris, and we talked the pictures and the plays over and all about the theatre. We were getting along fine and I have no doubt we would sooner or later have taken Shakespeare in our melodramatic stride, when the Inspector came along, and they knew a lot about the theatre but not a thing about "Midsummer Night's Dream," and I was promptly retired.[50]

He also recalled that part of his student experience included observing the wards of an insane asylum once a week,[51] which may not be unrelated.

Charles Dand, who was with Grierson at the university, filled in from his recollections personal details to flesh out some of the lines already established. He set forth a portrait of the man Grierson had become and, in many significant respects, would remain.

When I enrolled as a student at Glasgow University the first thing I did was to set about becoming a member of the University Fabian Society. . . . The meetings of the Society were held in the women students' union and when I turned up to the first one of the term there were about a dozen men and women present in a small room with a large fireplace and only one comfortable chair which no one seemed to want to occupy, contenting themselves with upright wooden chairs arranged in a semicircle facing the comfortable chair. For about fifteen minutes nothing happened. It wasn't the chairman they were waiting for since she had spoken to me. Suddenly the door was thrown open and there strode in a small man in a bowler hat, a military trenchcoat rather too large for him and reaching right down to his ankles, and wearing a small mustache. One's first thought was of the suggestion of Charlie Chaplin in the size, the hat, the moustache and something in the gait as he crossed the room, threw off the coat, and sank deep into the comfortable chair. The expression on his face was grim and he spoke no word, gave nobody a greeting, merely settled back in the chair and stared fixedly at the ceiling.

There was no doubt it was he we had all been waiting for. Hastily the chairwoman introduced the subject of the evening and somebody began to speak. I have no recollection of the subject and probably paid it scant attention, being fascinated by the figure in the chair who in the course of the talk swung himself round, elevated his feet to the mantlepiece, and closed his eyes. His expression relaxed and I wondered if he had gone to sleep. When the speaker had finished the chairwoman asked for discussion and some desultory talk began. There wasn't much heart in it, however, and I got the feeling that the participants were addressing their remarks primarily to the recumbent figure in the chair and hoping it would come to life. Suddenly it did. It rose to its feet, took a long churchwarden clay pipe from the mantleshelf, filled it with tobacco, applied a long wax taper to the fire, and puffed clouds of smoke into the air. The talk languished into an expectant silence. The figure sank down into the chair again and began to speak.

I sat transfixed, as did we all. Never in my schoolboy life had I encountered anything like that flow of analysis and authoritative exposition. It was not just the eloquence. A great new light was being shed. Man and subject had blended into an effulgence at which I gazed in rapt admiration and wonder. He spoke for perhaps fifteen or twenty minutes and stopped, resuming his pipe. An animated discussion ensued. There was no deference about it. Everybody spoke freely and not all were in agreement with the man in the chair who debated with vigour and a skill that stunned me. I left the meeting feeling that I had had the most exhilarating experience of my young life. . . .

My open-mouthed admiration continued for three or four meetings until one day I was browsing in the library and picked up a copy of *New Age*, a periodical edited by A. R. Orage, a brilliant left-wing journalist of those days but up to then outside my ken. I started to read an article by Orage on the Middle East Crisis of the day in which (if I remember rightly) British gunboat diplomacy was being threatened against Turkey. Words, phrases, arguments sounded familiar. Then I realised with shock. It was these words and arguments Grierson had been so impressive with in the last Fabian discussion. So this was where it all came from. I hunted through back numbers. Yes, there it all was. My venerated oracle was an echo. But not, as I happily had the sense to appreciate, on that account a sham. . . .

I have not related this anecdote to suggest that there was nothing original about Grierson in those days. On the contrary, wherever he got his facts and whoever influenced his opinions, the personality of the man which gave him such persuasive and dominating influence in the documentary film world was already highly developed. We waited for his views in the Fabian Society because we recognised him as a leader. It might be Orage he was giving us but it was Orage presented with the racy speech, the analytical penetration, the thrusting logic, and the visionary enthusiasm of Grierson. . . .

Grierson worked [equally] hard and brilliantly on the academic side. His industry was prodigious. He seemed to read everything. . . . He was a great admirer of Lenin and Trotsky, more of the latter. He was more interested than most of us in the tremendous social experiment then starting in Russia. None of us, however, ever thought of labelling him as a Communist. He was too individual, too catholic in his interests. It was not the methods of organisation and government that seemed to draw him but the hopes the Russian experiment raised of a power-house of reconstruction, a new release and orientation of human energies. It was this conception of revolutionary possibilities that he found in Trotsky and it was one of the inspirations of his approach to documentary film. Another was his feeling of kinship with the miners and farm-workers among whom he had grown up as a boy and the sailors and fishermen with whom he had lived and worked during his war service and which was also evident in his student days. An intellectual himself, he was fascinated by the rhythms, skills and wisdoms of the men who worked with their hands and drew its harvests out of the earth. These men deserved a new respect from us, a life worthy of their own integrities and it was by them and for them that whatever revolution was needed to release suppressed and depressed human energies should be organized. Add to these his interest in all experiments in expression and communication, verbal and visual, and you have Grierson the revolutionary, at least as far as I understood him.

Grierson was popular and respected, however, among a wider circle than the intellectuals and political left-wingers. He seemed to share all the robuster human interests. He was a football fan—rugby and association. He fished and shot and could drink with anybody, professor or dustman. He had humour, a delight in the grotesque and eccentric, on occasion an impish sense of fun. He had friends even among the divinity students to whom he must have been something of a puzzle. His Presbyterian heritage, his love of language, and his interest in all manifestations of the human spirit, enabled him to talk their jargon better than they could themselves and to debate them into the ground. . . .

With all these talents it was inevitable that he should be something of a *poseur*. I mentioned the bowler hat and the trench-coat. It was not the things themselves but the *panache* with which they were worn. They made him a familiar character to hundreds of his fellow-students who never knew his name. There was his walk. It was the rolling gait acquired on the decks of mine-sweepers and retained because he loved to be thought of as a sailor. There were many ways in which he played to his galleries. But we who were close to him readily forgave him for them. They were Grierson.[52]

In 1923 Grierson received an M.A. from the university with distinctions in English and Moral Philosophy. Thereupon he lectured at Armstrong College in Newcastle-on-Tyne in the northern English county of Northumberland. Although fourteen miles from Durham, Armstrong (later renamed King's College) was one of the constituent colleges of the University of Durham. (In 1963 it gained autonomy and became known as the University of Newcastle-on-Tyne.) Of his stay there Grierson recorded that, "it consisted of teaching Plato to a lot of old clerks and spinsters . . . who evidently wanted to know about Plato, but would have been better occupied raising hell about the slums of the city, the malnutrition of its children and its horrible schools."[53]

Nonetheless he not only "survived" the experience, as he put it, he was lifted out of it rather quickly with the award of a Rockefeller Research Fellowship in Social Science. In 1924 he left for study in America[54] and the start of his life work with film and other media more appropriate to the needs of mass adult education, as he envisaged it, than Plato's dialogues. To his use of the newer means of communication, however, he brought the superb intellectual equipment assembled at Glasgow University and would draw upon it constantly over the years.

# 2 ❧ UNITED STATES (1924–27)

## Chicago

Although it is not certain how precise Grierson's research goals were at the time he left for the United States, they may already have been centered on the role of mass communication in shaping public opinion. In any case, by then he had become aware, as Forsyth Hardy put it, that "The power to tap the springs of action had slipped away from the schools and churches and had come to reside in the popular media, the movies, the press, the new instrument of radio, and all the forms of advertising and propaganda."[1] Eventually he came to concentrate on "the dramatic and emotional techniques by which these media had been able to command the sentiments and loyalties of the people where many of the instruments of education and religion had failed."[2]

The selection of the University of Chicago (as a base to operate out of, as it would prove) may have been somewhat arbitrary. He chose Chicago, Grierson would say years later, partly because of Sherwood Anderson, Ben Hecht, and Carl Sandburg, who had lived and written there.[3] It was "a pioneering act," he felt, being one of the first of the British intellectuals to "come West." Harvard and the Eastern schools he regarded as second-rate Oxfords. He wanted the vitality of Chicago and saw it as a direct extension of Glasgow, which he had chosen over the English universities.[4] Even if, as he asserted, he might have gone to any university, it happened that he went to one with a distinguished social science faculty (as the Rockefeller Foundation would have known if Grierson himself didn't yet). He came as a bootlegger, he liked to say, crossing on a ship carrying thirty thousand cases of Scotch whiskey. ("'Give us your poor,' you asked on the Statue of Liberty. I brought you the whiskey," he once told an American audience.)[5] Landing at Halifax, Nova Scotia, he moved "in stages" to Boston, then to New York, and finally to Chicago.[6] Once enrolled in the university, as a visiting postgraduate scholar, he attached himself to Charles Merriam, the brilliant pioneering political scientist. Robert Park, the eminent sociologist who pioneered the field of media studies, was there at the time; also a young instructor who would later distinguish himself in intellectual enquiry into communication and the mass media, Harold Lasswell.

Though Grierson remained formally connected with the university throughout his three-year sojourn in the United States (a requirement of the foundation no doubt), he never took a degree or wrote a thesis. He did do research for Merriam, however, and the first assignment was a study of the "criminal drop outs" among the children of Chicago's foreign-born population. This investigation began with records of the criminal courts, but the notion of the "drop out" extended more widely to include other manifestations of social restiveness and deviation—among members of the I.W.W. (Industrial Workers of the World, the "Wobblies," whose national headquarters was in Chicago), alcoholics, and drug addicts. He spent a lot of time on West Madison Street, he said, Chicago's skid row.[7] A common characteristic was discovered—these were people who had been driven from their homes or, at any rate, had lost contact with their families.

The strain between generations—the parents trying to hang onto the old world; the young attempting to become part of the new—was evident in (both eased and exacerbated by) the then-powerful press. For the foreign-born there were six thousand foreign-language newspapers in the country at the time. For the first generation there was the Hearst press, like Chicago's *Herald Examiner*, and its imitators. This was the newspaper scene portrayed in *The Front Page* (1928), the play by Ben Hecht and Charles MacArthur, both reporters on popular dailies in the twenties. Grierson noted that, with their headlines and photos, their simplifications and dramatizations, these papers served as informal but nonetheless compelling means of leading young Lithuanians and Poles, Germans and Italians, Irish and Czechs away from their parents and the old country and into an Americanization of one sort or another. The news *report* of the European press had been shaped into the news *story*. The active verb was the key: something does something to something; someone does something to someone. This approach seemed to him to reflect the way the American mind worked, and the documentary film, as it would develop, came in part out of his understanding of this dramatic, active strategy.[8]

Grierson's interest in newspapers, which would remain constant throughout his life, began with this respect for their ability to assist in the conversion into United States citizens of the children of immigrants who read them. In fact, he became more interested in the melting-pot process occurring on Halsted Street than in the lectures being delivered in the classrooms on the Midway. The lessons he learned as a result of that interest he would always regard as the most important part of his Chicago experience.[9]

At about the same time Walter Lippmann, in New York, was expressing his grave concern over the practicability of Jeffersonian democracy in a large, highly complex modern state. His extraordinarily farseeing *Public Opinion* had been published in 1922. In it he argued that the democratic procedures formulated when Virginia gentlemen kept themselves adequately (if somewhat tardily) informed by reading Philadelphia newspapers, then went to the polls to express their opinions on issues through votes for candidates, had broken down. They had broken down, Lippmann felt, largely because the ordinary citizen could not be expected to amass enough ever-changing information to make intelligent decisions about, for example, government regulation of business by an Interstate Commerce Commission, the effect of gold reserves on international trade, or the entrance into and prosecution of a world war. As a result, modern citizens, now in massive numbers, had become apathetic, indifferently or grudgingly allowing themselves to be governed by increasingly large, specialized, and powerful administrative machinery over which they had no control. They clearly lacked both the understanding and interest to try to exert control, he felt. What Lippmann was saying was not unlike what Grierson had come to believe about his schoolmaster father's theories of education—that the gentleman in the library had lost its validity, and certainly vitality, as a goal. The collective complexity of the problems being faced seemed to both Lippmann and Grierson to demand a kind of democratic education that went beyond the individual stuffing himself with knowledge.

Though Lippmann's assessment of the possibilities of remedying the situation in time and on an adequate scale remained a discouraging one, he did point the way that Grierson was to follow, even the means he was at that time groping toward. Grierson was able to fuse the two analyses, his own and Lippmann's, during 1925 and 1926, leading to the activity to which he would become dedicated. As he later wrote, succinctly enough to defy paraphrase,

> The idea of documentary in its present form came originally not from the film people at all, but from the Political Science school in Chicago University round about the early twenties. It came because some of us noted Mr. Lippmann's argument closely and set ourselves to study what, constructively, we could do to fill the gap in educational practice which he demonstrated. At first, I must confess, we did not think so much about film or about radio. We were concerned with the influence of modern newspapers and were highly admiring of the dramatic approach implicit in the journalism of Mr. Hearst. Behind the sensationalizing of news we thought we recognized a deeper principle, and I think Mr. Luce [Henry Luce, publisher of *Time* magazine] at very much the same time was recognizing it too. We thought, indeed, that even so complex a world as ours could be patterned for all to appreciate if we only got away from the servile accumulation of fact and struck for the story which held the facts in living organic relationship together.
>
> It was Mr. Lippmann himself who turned this educational research in the direction of film. I talked to him one day of the labor involved in following the development of the yellow press through the evanescent drama of local politics. He mentioned that we would do better to follow the dramatic patterns of the film through the changing character of our time, and that the box office records of success and failure were on file.[10]

While in Chicago, Grierson lived on the Near North Side, an area roughly equivalent to New York's Greenwich Village. At first he was on Ontario Street next door to a Schofield Company florist, co-owned by Dion O'Banion, gangster chief. In November, about the time Grierson moved in, O'Banion was gunned down in his shop while clipping chrysanthemums by three members of the rival Johnny Torrio–Al Capone gang. Grierson would remember O'Banion's impressive funeral with thousands of mourners and often referred to the $10,000 silver casket in his recollections of Chicago. Subsequently he moved to a little room at the corner of Schiller and Clark. He was living there when he began a lifelong friendship with the Chicago painter Rudolph Weisenborn and his wife Alfreda ("Fritzie"), who lived nearby on La Salle Street.

Early in their acquaintanceship Grierson impressed Rudolph by establishing the chronological order of eighteen or twenty of his charcoal drawings, which Weisenborn characterized as "a remarkable feat." As their friendship ripened, Grierson proposed that the Weisenborns feed him and he would furnish booze and take them to the movies and theater. (He was receiving $150 a month from the Rockefeller Foundation, a quite comfortable sum then.) Fritzie claimed that it was Rudolph who first got Grierson seriously interested in films; Rudolph responded to everything visual, she said. They saw *Greed* together and *Battleship Potemkin* (later), over and over. When attending movies Fritzie said she sat separately because Rudolph and Grierson would make constant observations to each other about what was on the screen.

After these outings, if Rudolph's and Grierson's discussions became unduly heated, Grierson would leave. The next day Fritzie would go to Grierson's room and ask him to come back. His reply sometimes was that he wasn't sure he wanted to talk to *Mr.* Weisenborn again. (Richard Griffith told much the same story about Grierson's stormy relationship with Robert Flaherty, with Griffith in that case acting as envoy and peacemaker.) Mrs. Weisenborn suggested that Grierson was attracted to creative personalities—wanted to see what made them tick. Though not essentially creative himself, she felt, he was fascinated by and perhaps envious of this quality in others, especially when it appeared in its natural state.

Grierson was interested in and supportive of an art movement that Rudolph founded called Neo-Arlimusc—new-art/literature/music—and credited Weisenborn with teaching him an appreciation of American architecture through climbs up and down Chicago skyscrapers. He also became a great jazz fan and went with the Weisenborns often to Negro cafes, the black-and-tan clubs as they were called, to listen to Louis Armstrong, Bessie Smith, and others, before jazz was widely appreciated.[11] Grierson would maintain his interest in jazz and in popular performers generally. In 1966 he observed that the most sensible thing the State Department might do to improve the abysmal public relations of the United States abroad was to send Bob Dylan on a world tour![12]

Grierson's writing for the press burgeoned in Chicago. In the course of analyzing newspapers he wrote for them. (He would always insist that analysis be followed by doing—that investigation be conducted for the sake of action.) At first, as in his earlier writing at Glasgow University, he did not concentrate exclusively on film. One effort was a regular column on painting for the *Chicago Evening Post*. In the course of championing modern art and abstractionism, Grierson at one point invoked Plato. Another art critic of the *Post*, Samuel Putnam, in a published letter, accused Grierson good-humoredly of misreading the philosopher, and went on to say that he suspected Grierson, though he had resolutely favored form over content, of "a lurking sociological bias"—a prescient observation. Putnam was answered by an informed and perceptive explication of Plato's aesthetic position. In another issue, the *Post* reproduced a charcoal "Study of John Grierson by Rudolph Weisenborn." Its caption read: "A Vorticistic portrait of the young Scotch newspaper man and art writer who, within less than a year, has made a place for himself in bohemian circles of Chicago."[13] (Grierson would continue to write art criticism in England well into the thirties.) He also did art and movie reviewing for *The Chicagoan*, a little journal. For Grierson beauty equalled vigor. In the course of this journalistic activity he got to know newspaper people. Before he departed from Chicago, he left his first-edition copy of *Ulysses* with Fritzie Weisenborn to be sent on to Elsie Robinson, a columnist for Hearst. Fritzie kept it instead.[14] (During his Glasgow days Grierson had subscribed £5 out of his meager resources towards the Paris publication of Joyce's masterpiece.)[15]

## Hollywood

Though his respect for Merriam continued, Grierson had become increasingly restless at the university and began moving about the country. At the same time, he started to follow Lippmann's advice that he investigate the patterns of American film forms and contents and the responses at the box office which provoked and supported the changes in them. He managed to gain access to box office records of a major Hollywood studio covering a considerable period of time—Famous Players–Lasky Corporation, which subsequently became Paramount Pictures; "a young man named Walter Wanger opened the necessary files,"[16] Grierson said. Using this data as indication of popular appeal, he analyzed the movies in terms of the changing personalities of screen stars, the shifting values manifest in the films, and, more specifically, the evolution from western to epic-western.[17] (Paramount's *The Covered Wagon* [1923] would be one of the key films screened by the staff at the Empire Marketing Board.) Some of Grierson's findings appeared in a series of six articles published in *Motion Picture News* in November and December of 1926. Following the publication of this series, he was taken "round the houses, and very rightly" by another trade journal, *Variety*, for offering as general industry news what was actually "inside stuff" from Paramount. His conclusion from this affair was, "In a film critic, concentration is liable to be misunderstood, and is best avoided."[18]

This research was intended to be applied as well as academic—a projection of the next star trend as part of it—and Grierson recalled phoning Jesse Lasky to report excitedly: "I've seen her"—the young, hopeful Thelma Todd, who seemed to have the requisite sociological characteristics for the upcoming star type.[19] She was trained in Paramount's school for aspiring actors at its Astoria, Long Island, studio and went on to a modest stardom.

Though the insights he gained during this investigation into the functioning of motion picture power, and the personal contacts he made, especially with Wanger, would be of lasting value to him, Grierson's economic sense told him that if he could not control the essential process of star-making, there was no way to finance films through the established industry and its forms. In short, what would become documentary film would have to be modeled on other precedents and to look elsewhere for its support.

While in Hollywood, observing film production firsthand, he came to know a number of celebrated filmmakers. His early writings carry numerous references to this experience and to these men: "I knew [Josef von] Sternberg just after his *Salvation Hunters* and liked him immensely. . . . I watched Sternberg make still another picture, *The Woman of the Sea*, for Chaplin" (the latter never released). It was in this same review, of *Shanghai Express*, that Grierson hung the famous epigrammatical albatross around von Sternberg's neck: "When a director dies, he becomes a photographer."[20] Of Erich von Stroheim's *Wedding March* he wrote: "I saw great slices of it shot and great hunks of financiers' hair torn from the roots in the process." Of Stroheim playing a film director in *The Lost Squadron* he recalled: "I have seen him go off the hoop as he does subsequently, and be very much the blood-curdling creature of temperament he demonstrates."[21] And, again, "I have heard [Raymond] Griffith and [Harry] Langdon and Chaplin all discuss the [screen] figures they attempted to be . . . in the Hollywood I knew. . . ."[22] Apparently the writer Donald Ogden Stewart was in on this same discussion, and Grierson came to know and admire him, as he did the poet e. e. cummings, a friend of Stewart's.[23] Grierson also wrote that he "saw something of" King Vidor "and liked him for that seriousness"[24] and seems to have become acquainted with F. W. Murnau and Ernst Lubitsch as well.[25]

## New York City

The main scenes of Grierson's American stay were Chicago, Hollywood, and New York City, but not in that strict order, since he appears to have shuttled back and forth among them. In many ways the New York experience would prove more decisive than the Hollywood one. Journalism was his entree into New York, stemming from the interest newspaper editors and film critics took in his evolving ideas about film. He was invited to write as guest critic for several papers, notably the *New York Sun*.[26] For the *Sun* he did a column in which he was "supposed to be a bit more highbrow than Cohen [John S., Jr.], the ranking film-editor, and the sort of odd body who looked after lost causes, including, as I remember, most of the people who happened to be good."[27] (To people Grierson didn't approve of he was said to apply the phrase "That guy's no good.")[28] Richard Watts Jr., then film critic for the *New York Herald Tribune* and subsequently drama critic for the *New York Post* until 1976, was one of the few other reviewers to take film seriously. Grierson has acknowledged an influence from Watts, and Watts has recalled the conversations that he and Cohen and Grierson had about film at the time.[29] It was in his *New York Sun* column that names like Flaherty and Eisenstein were first exalted and words like *tempo* first articulated.

In one instance at least the lost causes he was supposed to look after included religious films. Ten years later he was still sufficiently upset by the experience to write: "I have seen these pictures of Jesus. . . . I reviewed a batch of them for a New York paper, and wrote one of the rudest articles of my life: and no wonder. If I did not head it 'Jesus in a Nightgown' I should have done, for the preposterous array of nightgowns, wigs and false beards was a travesty of every reality the Gospels could possibly intend."[30] Confronting another sort of faith and another kind of reality he was much more sympathetic. In an evaluation of the Soviet cinema, he found it instinctual with an artistic force capable of reaching into all fields of inquiry and imagination. He stressed the fluidity of its dramatic movement, the robustness of its approach, and the social reality of its content. The article was documented with references to many Russian films of the period.[31]

Surely the major outcome of his reviewing for the *Sun* was that it brought him into close relationship with Robert Flaherty, which formed one more link in the chain leading to the British documentary film movement.[32] He had seen Flaherty's earlier *Nanook of the North* (1922), as already noted; at some point he even saw the preceding version whose negative had burned up while Flaherty was editing it in Toronto. There was at least one positive print, however, which Flaherty showed around a good deal. Grierson had this to say of it later: "By an odd chance, I once saw a good part of the original lost *Nanook*, and if I never mentioned it to Flaherty it was because it was not in his thought or memory that anything survived. . . . In his first version, Flaherty was still with the old travelogue of Hale's Tours and planning learning from the ground up, not to mention the backs and fronts of sledges."[33]

Among the lavish reviews by well-known reviewers of Flaherty's second film, *Moana*, after its premiere at the Rialto Theatre on Broadway, February 7, 1926, the most important from historical perspective was the one appearing in the *Sun* the next morning under the pseudonym "The Moviegoer." Many years later, at the time of Flaherty's death, Grierson explained how he came to write that famous piece: "I first met Robert Flaherty around 1925. He had just come back from British Samoa with *Moana*, and he was having the difficulties he was always to have in the last stage of production. In this case it was Paramount that did not see it his way. There was talk of a grass-skirted dancing troupe . . . and a marquee offering of 'The Love Life of a South Sea Siren.'. . . I took Flaherty's case like a sort of critical attorney."[34]

The critical attorney's brief had been presented in part as follows:

> Moana deserves to rank with those few works of the screen that have the right to last, to live. It could only have been produced by a man with an artistic conscience and an intense poetic feeling which, in this case, finds an outlet through nature worship.
>
> Of course Moana, being a visual account of events in the daily life of a Polynesian youth, has documentary value. But that, I believe, is secondary to its value as a soft breath from a sunlit island, washed by a marvelous sea, as warm as the balmy air. Moana is first of all beautiful as nature is beautiful. . . .
>
> And therefore I think Moana achieves greatness primarily through its poetic feeling for natural elements. It should be placed on the idyllic shelf that includes all those poems which sing of the loveliness of sea and land and air—and of man when he is a part of beautiful surroundings, a figment of nature, an innocent primitive rather than a so-called intelligent being cooped up in the mire of so-called intelligent civilization.[35]

This is thought to be the first public use of the word *documentary* as applied to film. Note that it is being used in the sense of *document*. (French critics had already coined the term *documentaire* to denote serious travel and expedition films, as distinct from travelogues.) Curiously, the word document (which comes from the Latin *docere*, to teach) as late as 1800 meant "a lesson; an admonition, a warning"—evidently somewhat in the sense we would now call indoctrination or propaganda—according to the *Oxford English Dictionary*. Documentary would achieve its later meaning, not too far from that earlier one, through practice—through the hundreds of British films of the thirties which proudly bore that label.

Another interesting aspect of Grierson's review is the implicit laying out of the two lines of his lifelong argument with Flaherty: (1) profound respect and sensitive praise for the beauty created by poetic genius—no one appreciated Flaherty's films more fully than did Grierson, and (2) final relegation of them to the "idyllic shelf"—as the work of the modern world was gotten on with. In Flaherty's case, as Grierson first put it in that review, the documentary value was secondary to the poetic value. Grierson's *single* reservation about *Moana* was that it didn't tell the whole story—that through its omissions it was less than authentic and hence less relevant to Samoan life than it should have been: "Lacking in the film was the pictorial transcription of the sex-life of these people. It is rarely referred to. Its absence mars its completeness."

Flaherty was also, though marginally, involved with a second film event during Grierson's New York period which would leave a deep imprint on Grierson and the British documentary movement to come. Towards the end of 1926, Flaherty helped in the launching of the first Soviet masterpiece to be shown in America: *Battleship Potemkin*. It was given a spectacular premiere in December, at the Biltmore Theatre, with seats at $5.00.[36] But it was Grierson who helped Cohen, the film critic of the *New York Sun*, do the titles.[37] The events leading to this assignment Grierson narrated as follows: "Douglas Fairbanks came back from a triumphant tour of the Soviet Union, and with him came the first print of a film that was to change a good many concepts of film-making. . . . Somehow the rumour of this great new experiment in the dialectics of imagery reached us in New York, and somehow we found ourselves called upon to take it apart and put it together again for the American market."[38]

The effect Grierson's close familiarity with *Potemkin* must have had upon him (he became acquainted with Eisenstein later) may account for an only half-facetious observation floating around England in the thirties that the whole British documentary movement was born out of the last reel of *Potemkin* (especially the engine room scenes). As if to confirm *Potemkin*'s importance in his development, Grierson chose to double-bill the premiere of his own first film, *Drifters*, with the first English showing of *Battleship Potemkin* at the London Film Society, almost exactly three years after the latter's New York opening. The version screened was the one he had helped title in New York.[39]

By the end of his American stay, Grierson's preparation seems to have been complete: citizenship education was the broad necessity, film the chosen medium, documentary its special mode. Or, as Grierson put it on his return to Britain, not realizing, possibly, that he was refining the final years of his American experience: "What I know of cinema I have learned partly from the Russians, partly from the American westerns, and partly from Flaherty, of *Nanook*. The westerns give you some notion of the energies. The Russians give you the energies and the intimacies both. And Flaherty is a poet."[40] The preparation over, the career proper was about to begin.

# 3 ⇻ EMPIRE MARKETING BOARD
# FILM UNIT (1927–33)

## Society and Film in Britain

The United States Grierson left in 1927 was well into its international ascendancy following World War I, the bustle and boom of the Roaring Twenties much in evidence. The Britain he returned to was beginning its decline from the heights of imperial power. It had suffered terribly in the war, not only in loss of lives; as a result of the enormous costs, its economy was in serious trouble. Exports were below the prewar figure; at the same time imports increased, leading to a sustained deficit trade balance. These factors led to persistent, widespread unemployment.[1] The Conservative Party remained in office through most of the twenties, but economic unrest and militancy of the trade unions, especially among the coal miners, increased, leading to the General Strike of 1926. Overall the social-economic outlook was dour: a sort of stasis existed that would become more severe during the Depression years of the 1930s.

As for British cinema, it too suffered from the effects of the war and the new importance of the United States on the world scene. Michael Balcon, later head of Ealing Studios, succinctly summarized the situation in his memoirs: "the war had virtually killed off British production and the Americans, quite properly, had taken full advantage of this to provide all the films that British cinemas required."[2] In the enormous expansion of movies as popular entertainment in this period, the products of Hollywood dominated the British market. Rudolph Valentino, Mary Pickford, and Charlie Chaplin became the movie stars of Britain, as they were of much of the world. Further, little of quality was being made in British studios.

In 1926 no more than five percent of the films shown on British screens were British. In the following year, the government introduced legislation to protect British producers. The Cinematograph Films Bill contained regulations to insure that all cinemas showed an increasing proportion of British films, but the lack of a clause to foster quality had unexpectedly disastrous consequences. The Quota Act, as it was called, stimulated production only in the sense that many producers made numerous cheap and shoddy films which were guaranteed an outlet, if not a profit, by the regulations. Production rose sharply but the "quota quickies" were unpopular with both audiences and exhibitors and merely brought British filmmaking into further disrepute.[3]

Apropos contemporary reality as portrayed in British films, "'the General Strike of 1926 never took place, trade unions did not exist and when sympathy was expressed for the poor it was not for the unemployed but for those struggling along on a fixed income.' Film makers . . . ignored the changes occurring in the society around them and described a world where the social order was 'as fixed and mechanical as that of the Incas,'" according to Julian Symons.[4] Thus was the film situation in Britain when Grierson arrived in London.

## Beginnings of the E.M.B.

While Grierson was in America, there had been established in London, in May 1926, the Empire Marketing Board, a department of the Dominions Office. This unique government agency was created specifically to "promote all the major researches across the world which affect the production or preservation or transport of the British Empire's food supplies."[5] A million pounds had been budgeted by the government for that purpose. The man behind the creation of the board was L. S. Amery, Dominions Secretary, a farsighted member of the Conservative Party who, along with Lionel Curtis and others, had grasped the real significance of the Commonwealth and Empire relationship, and was seeking to give it human meaning. Amery was at the Dominions Office not as a "blimp" but as an idealist in terms of imperialism. Concerning the formation of the E.M.B., he wrote in his autobiography, "What we wanted to sell was the idea of Empire production and purchase; of the Empire as a co-operative venture. Above all as a co-operative venture between living persons interested in each other's work and each other's welfare. Our task was not to glorify the power or the wealth of the Empire but to make it live as a society for mutual help, a picture of vivid human interest, as well as of practical promise."[6]

The broader purpose implicit from the outset, then, was an enlightened effort to substitute for the decaying military and political ties of Empire the economic ones of Commonwealth. To achieve this goal, the E.M.B. had necessarily to inform public opinion about the Commonwealth and Empire and thus became the first government body in Britain to undertake public relations work on a large scale and to make wide use of all sorts of publicity media: newspapers, posters, radio, exhibitions, films.[7]

Secretary of the Empire Marketing Board was the creative and effective Stephen Tallents, who had been in charge of food rationing during World War I.[8] Even before the arrival of Grierson, Tallents had started to involve the E.M.B. in the use of films. As for the origin of the film idea, he recalled:

> One summer afternoon in 1926—the first summer of our work—I had driven to lunch with Mr. Rudyard Kipling in his house at Burwash. Mr. Kipling, who had so far fought shy of films, confirmed our belief in the possibilities of cinema and held out hopes that he would himself guide the making of a film for us. This seemed to me a magnificent opening. I had little difficulty in persuading my Board to pursue it. I had much more difficulty in selling the idea to an extremely sceptical Treasury. In the end, however, I got leave to employ a man named by Mr. Kipling as particularly suited to work with him. . . .[9]

The man was Walter Creighton, known for his staging of pageants and tattoos, especially the Aldershot Military Tattoo, and the film would eventually become *One Family*.

Tallents continued the story: "The adventure began with the arrival from the Treasury in October 1926 of Mr. J. S. Fletcher, whose courage in joining us, as well as his long and admirable service in the organisation of Government Film work, deserves to be put on record. Then Creighton came in and set himself to prepare, to some extent in consultation with Kipling, the scenario of a film that was nominally based on the Empire plum-pudding, but was in fact an ambitious excursion in fantasy."[10]

## Consulting and Early Activities

Shortly thereafter Grierson, who had just returned from the United States and was now in London, obtained a letter of introduction to Tallents from a mutual acquaintance, Robert Nichols, a minor English poet. When Grierson had left Britain in 1924, film had been merely one aspect of his manifold interests in the arts and society and in their interconnection. When he returned in 1927, he was deeply absorbed in the possibilities of using film as a medium of education and persuasion.[11] In the Empire Marketing Board, already launched along similar lines, he must have thought he saw the sort of backing he had already decided was necessary for the uses he wanted to make of that medium. Nichols also, apparently, recognized that Grierson's ideas were not unlike those of Tallents, and said so in his introductory note. Tallents said of that February 1927 interview, "I took to Grierson at once, and felt that here was a man that we needed and must enlist in the service of the E.M.B."[12]

As for Grierson's *ideas*, however, Tallents recalled,

> I cannot say with equal truth that I fully grasped at that first interview the theories which he expounded to me. . . . But I think I can briefly summarize what Grierson was thinking at that time. He was shocked at the meagre content of community life everywhere. Its enrichment depended, he thought, on a better understanding of the stuff of which it was compounded. That better understanding could not be secured by the orthodox methods of academic education. "Education," he was to say of the public a few years ago, "has given them facts but has not sufficiently given them faith." It was necessary to touch the imaginations of the people—not merely to impart facts to them; and their imaginations could best be touched by eliciting and presenting to them in dramatized form the exciting material which he found in the real life around him.[13]

In a general way, Tallents concluded,

> His line of approach fitted in with ours. The E.M.B. had determined, before he joined it, to bring the Empire alive [an E.M.B. slogan] to the minds of its citizens, and in doing so to substitute for talk and theories about it a vivid and exciting representation of its infinitely various lives and occupations. For that purpose we needed to employ, in

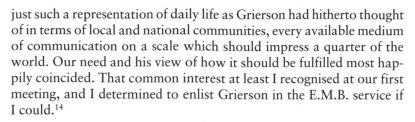

just such a representation of daily life as Grierson had hitherto thought of in terms of local and national communities, every available medium of communication on a scale which should impress a quarter of the world. Our need and his view of how it should be fulfilled most happily coincided. That common interest at least I recognised at our first meeting, and I determined to enlist Grierson in the E.M.B. service if I could.[14]

Grierson, for his part, observed:

In Sir Stephen Tallents' book on the *Projection of England* [first published in 1932] he used a sentence from Mill which said a good deal of what some of us were thinking round about 1928. "It is the artist alone in whose hands truth becomes impressive and a living principle of action." Yet Tallents had not the same slant on the matter as some of us, and it is important to note the distinction. For my part, the approach was almost completely academic. I was an educationist born and bred and I was interested in the dramatic levels of apprehension. I was sure, as I am now, that the dramatic level of apprehension is the only one that relates a man to his Maker, his neighbor or himself. I set it over against the informational level on which the poor liberal theory of education had been humourlessly insisting for half a century. I had noted in ten years of universities, as so many have done in less, that the facts are many and the professors have a habit of being beside the point of them. I was inclined to raise the sense of smell to among the highest of virtues.[15]

The relationship between Tallents and Grierson was to be long-lasting and fruitful. Grierson's feelings of indebtedness are acknowledged throughout his writings, and the dedication to the first edition of *Grierson on Documentary*, in 1946, reads, "For Stephen Tallents." Let Grierson, then, have the last word on the subject:

It was no wonder, looking back on it, that we found our first sponsorship outside the trade and in a Government department, for the Empire Marketing Board had, from a governmental point of view, come to realise the same issue. Simplifying and dramatizing the concerns of citizenship. Set to bring the Empire alive in contemporary terms, as a commonwealth of nations and as an international combine of industrial, commercial and scientific forces, it, too, was finding a need for dramatic methods. For the imaginative mind of Sir Stephen Tallents, head of that department, it was a quick step to the documentary cinema.[16]

When he began work, Grierson said, "The only conditions laid down were that we should have the good sense to explore a few

35

preliminary avenues, work for a period experimentally, and remember the sensitive nerves of Treasury officials. . . . I cannot say we succeeded at first with this neurological aspect of our work. . . . Whitehall [government civil service offices], we discovered, was longer by a bittock than the road to Damascus, and sky splitting an even more valuable art than cinema. But we did, and for two long years, explore the avenues."[17] To Basil Wright, Grierson once said that his first job in films was to learn to be a good civil servant. "And the fact that he had a good many enemies in Whitehall in his time," added Wright, "is probably due to his having learnt civil service technique so well that he can out-minute a permanent civil servant with very little difficulty."[18]

Whatever discouragement he was feeling, Grierson seized this entree with characteristic vigor. He produced memoranda on a scale to please the most tireless bureaucrat, with particular emphasis on how the production of informational films and their nontheatrical distribution were going ahead in France and Germany.[19] But beyond this, he initiated a series of screenings in a theater the E.M.B. had installed at Grierson's suggestion at the Imperial Institute in South Kensington. These showings would become an adjunct to the training of young documentary filmmakers, providing texts for study, as it were; but before that, they helped Grierson shape his own ideas on documentary films and served to interest and inform government officials in the uses of film—cabinet members who would have to approve his undertakings among them. As Grierson put it,

> we must have seen every propaganda film in existence between Moscow and Washington. We certainly prepared the first surveys of the propaganda and educational services of the principal Governments. We ran, too, a school of cinema where all the films we thought had a bearing on our problem were brought together and demonstrated in whole or part, for the instruction of Whitehall. . . . we had all the documentaries and epics worth a damn; though, in calculation of our audience, we had perforce to change a few endings and consider some of the close-ups among the less forceful arguments.[20]

In the choice of the films, which reveals the trend of his thoughts at the time, Grierson cast his net wide and deep: films of various kinds and from several countries were shown. Tallents recalled those screenings in considerable detail. He wrote that Grierson proposed that we should . . . view once a month for our own instruction a series of films, and especially films made in other countries, that might have a bearing on our own needs. These showings caught on at once. Members of the Board and its Film Committee came to them and brought their friends. Each display began with a short introductory talk, given, so far as I can remember, either by Grierson himself or by me with previous coaching from him. By this means we were enabled to explore not only what was being done already in the simpler forms of direct propaganda but certain lines of approach by other countries to the screen from which, as Grierson saw the problem, our own course might derive valuable guidance.[21]

The aesthetic origins of British documentary grew out of these screenings and lay in the work of (1) Robert Flaherty (*Nanook of the North* [1922] and *Moana* [1926]); (2) Alberto Cavalcanti (*Rien que les heures* [1926]) and Walter Ruttmann (*Berlin: Symphony of a Great City* [1927]); and (3) the Russians (Sergei Eisenstein, *Battleship Potemkin* [1925], V. I. Pudovkin, *The End of St. Petersburg* [1927] and *Storm Over Asia* [1928], Victor Turin, *Turksib* [1929], Alexander Dovzhenko, *Earth* [1930]).[22]

It was the Russian films, as Tallents remembered it, "that made the deepest impression upon those small evening audiences. Eisenstein's *Potemkin* was the first of them to come upon our screen— that grim story of mutiny in a ship-of-war in the Black Sea with its unforgettable sequence of the Cossacks advancing down the harbour steps of Odessa and shooting impassively men, women and babies as they go." Turin's *Turksib* followed, an epic about the building of the railway between Siberia and Turkestan; shown more than once were the two reels "which depict the harnessing of the water, from its distant trickle in the mountains to the building of the great dam." Tallents also vividly remembered Pudovkin's *Storm over Asia* and Dovzhenko's *Earth*. "Through these films we came to appreciate the need for concentrated work in the editing of the raw material. Their 'massing of detail,' one of our programmes of that time noted, 'the distribution of detail and sequences of rising or falling tempo, the enthusiasm for dramatising working types and working gestures, combine to make their films of work as exciting as any in the world.'"[23]

Tallents's enthusiasms apparently were not universally shared, however. Grierson subsequently recalled that:

When the posters of the Buy British Campaign carried for the first time the figure of a working-man as a national symbol, we were astonished at the Empire Marketing Board to hear from half a hundred Blimps that we were "going Bolshevik." The thought of making work an honoured theme, and a workman, of whatever kind, an honourable figure, is still liable to the charge of subversion. The documentary group has learned freely from Russian film technique; the nature of the material has forced it to what, from an inexpert point of view, may seem violent technical developments. These factors have encouraged this reactionary criticism; but, fundamentally, the sin has been to make cinema face life; and this must invariably be unwelcome to the complacent elements in society.[24]

Though these internal screenings deserve the weight they have been given, even during the two pre-*Drifters* years Grierson was at the E.M.B. there were efforts to reach out to the public through the exhibition of films. For example, the E.M.B. installed a small automatic daylight projector in Victoria Station and ran some short films for the benefit of travelers. With the help of the Department of Agriculture for Scotland they staged some film demonstrations for farmers on market days in Scottish towns and loaned the Leicestershire County Council a projector and some films for use in a traveling van.[25] One day, when the members of the Imperial Agricultural Research Conference were traveling down by special train from Edinburgh to London, the travelers were accompanied by a film show in a guard's van. With the help of the local education authority and the local branch of the Cinematograph Exhibitors' Association, the E.M.B. arranged film showings for forty-five thousand children in Newcastle and Gateshead. Films were also provided for displays connected with Empire Shopping Weeks. At the same time they experimented with a talking film designed for the education of native African producers.[26]

## Drifters

Considering the making of his own film for the E.M.B., Grierson and Tallents arrived at herring as its subject. There were several reasons for this. They wanted to do something for the home fishing industry and, because of his naval experience, Grierson knew the sea. In addition, and not incidentally, the Financial Secretary to the Treasury, Arthur Samuel, was an authority on the English herring fisheries, and in fact had written a book on the subject. So the film on herring was added to the Creighton/Kipling project. "The E.M.B. considered and approved this programme at their meeting in March 1928. Mr. Samuel was not present; but the Treasury disclosed their opposition after the meeting, and the issue had to be carried to the Ministerial level."[27]

As for that crucial meeting,

> The British documentary came to birth on 27th April 1928 [the day after Grierson's thirtieth birthday], and the maternity home in which it first saw the light was Mr. Amery's room at the Dominions Office. . . . There came together at the bedside Mr. Amery [L. S. Amery, Dominions Secretary], Major Walter Elliot (then chairman of the [E.M.B.] Film Committee), Mr. Samuel, Mr. Craig of the Treasury . . . and I. None of those present at this meeting can have had a full sense of the significance of the accouchement at which they were attending. Yet some of us must have had a subconscious sense of its importance. For I remember the gathering as vividly as any that I ever attended—and I have attended a multitude of meetings in my time and have forgotten what happened at practically all of them. I preserved, too, as I was glad to discover the other day—and that again was quite contrary to my usual practice—a note of what took place at it.
>
> After the usual pleasantries and preliminaries, the meeting began with a salvo from Samuel. Based on experience he had had in advertizing, he thought it a waste of money "to think of increasing the sale of Empire products by means of the cinema." Elliot countered by saying that they were not proposing to advertize particular products but to show "interesting aspects of English life and character"—that "England herself was the subject"—and that from such an advertisement demand for particular products might well follow. That so powerful a medium as the screen should not be neglected. Amery supported Elliot's argument, while Craig observed that if such an end were desired there were many commercial companies which might be expected to achieve it effectively. Amery then pointed out that, "though he welcomed the advice of the Financial Secretary and of the Treasury on points of financial propriety, the responsibility rested with the E.M.B. and himself." Following that forceful statement, accompanied by a skillful compliment, Samuel responded by saying that "he could probably give some help with the herring fishery material and would be happy to do so."[28]

And so, *Drifters* was born and *One Family* continued on its way. Begun almost three years before *Drifters*, *One Family* was not released until July 7, 1930. Subtitled "A Dream of Real Things," it featured a small boy who dreams his way into the throne room of Buckingham Palace and is met by the Yeoman of the Guard and a bevy of six titled beauties representing the United Kingdom and the Dominions. He has a vision from the windows of the Palace (a sort of dream within a dream) of the daily work at home and overseas by which the various ingredients of the King's pudding were produced.

"But in spite of all its regal, military, social and animal supports," Tallents ruefully admitted (the animal support being Mickey Mouse in *Barnyard Concert*, which accompanied *One Family* on its first showing),

> it failed to make a hit. It ran for a week to wilting houses at the Palace, but thereafter commanded next to no theatrical circulation. Pieces of it were used freely for non-theatrical circulation about the country; and I remember laboriously calculating the number of people who had viewed some part of it and trotting out the imposing figure that resulted to a sceptical but, as I felt at the time, unexpectedly generous Public Accounts Committee. But its fate seemed to prove that fantasy was not the right line of film approach to Empire problems, and we went no more a-roving by the light of that moon.[29]

Of Creighton's seven-reel theatrical venture, produced through British Instructional Films, Basil Wright would observe a bit more bluntly that it was "Based on outmoded conceptions of propaganda, entertainment, and indeed the British Empire[;] the . . . film (which cost twice as much as *Drifters*) failed completely."[30] Grierson himself wrote of it as sympathetically as he could manage (courtesy to a colleague and loyalty to his employer, no doubt), but the film's lack of success precluded the necessity for sharper criticism: it fell of its own weight.

The contrast between the purposes and contents of *One Family* and *Drifters* was as clear and much more significant than the differences in their popular reception. Creighton stood in the line of traditional pageantry and tourist-attraction pictures of Merrie Olde England; Grierson was striking out for the here and now of work done to feed the nation. Creighton's line would only go underground, not disappear, during the high-water days of British documentary. It reappeared strongly before the end of the thirties in a brouhaha over the choice of films to represent Britain at the New York World's Fair.

For the production of *Drifters*, Grierson was appointed "Assistant Film Officer" to the E.M.B. and a contract with New Era Productions was signed for the making of it. Tallents testified, however, that all the real work was done by Grierson himself.

Because of his experience at sea, he got along well enough during the shooting, but about his crew he wrote: "Of my cameramen one also was an ex-seaman [Grierson himself, who shot a considerable amount of the footage]. The other, for all his bravery, was mostly unconscious [Basil Emmott, presumably, the cameraman provided by New Era]." By the end of the shooting there had still been no storm and Grierson desperately wanted one for the film: "a real storm, an intimate storm, and if possible a rather noble storm." He waited in Lowestoft for weeks until the gale signal went up and then put to sea for the last time.[31]

The editing of the film was done mostly in a basement Grierson had rented in London (Belsize Park) in which he lived as well. It was one large room with a tiny bathroom and a kitchenette.

> There was an old-fashioned projector at one end, a screen at the other, a cutting-bench, numerous bins and lines of wire from wall to wall from which hung a forest of pieces of film. In a corner was a bed and there was a mantlepiece which did duty as a dining-table, high stools providing the seating accommodation. At the foot of the bed was a large notice: "Eventually—why not now?" This was Grierson's exhortation to himself to get up in the morning. He had a pot, a kettle, a frying-pan, two or three plates and a number of jam-jars which he used as cups or beer mugs. He lived almost entirely on eggs which he boasted he could cook in 57 different ways.[32]

Subsequently, he obtained another basement which he used just for editing. "In 1929, the British documentary film movement, insofar as it was a deliberate movement, was represented by one cellar in the Charing Cross Road at 7 shillings."[33]

It was through the editing of *Drifters* that Grierson met and married Margaret Taylor, a native Londoner whose family lived in Kentish Town. She worked for New Era as an editing assistant and negative cutter on *Drifters*. New Era had been contracted to provide a sort of umbrella for the unit—there was as yet no administrative machinery for government filmmaking—and to provide equipment and technical personnel. New Era was essentially a producer of entertainment features—*The Co-optimists*, from a popular stage production, and *Q Ships* were two of them at about that time. Before joining New Era, Margaret Taylor had worked as a secretary for the London Musical Company, one of the few musical companies still left in the East End. She was also a manager of a movie theater for a while, then worked for Blunt and McCormack, producers of short films (one was about the *Daily Telegram*).[34] The story had it that Grierson couldn't afford to pay her wages so he married her (in 1930). Even so, given the fashion among artistic types at the time, he pretended to some of his associates that he was living with Margaret in unmarried sin—in spite of an occasional embarrassment with government officials nosing about.[35]

Tallents continued:

> Grierson's film was completed . . . in the late summer of 1929. Then came the news that the London Film Society had asked leave to include it in one of their monthly programmes. On a 10th November Sunday afternoon, Grierson and I sat together in the Tivoli Theatre to see what reception it would get. We watched the drifter leaving harbour and facing the open sea; the crew in their cabin and on deck, the captain on the bridge; the herring shoals pursued by dogfish below the surface; the shooting of the nets and the pause from labour which followed it; toiling men hauling the nets inboard on a rough sea, under threat of a gathering storm; the silver fish pouring on to the deck, into the hold; the drifter's return to port through the storm; the unloading of its catch at the quayside. The film was shown before *Potemkin* and was at least as warmly applauded as that Russian classic. The more discerning critics endorsed the Society's verdict. It was plain that, whatever happened to it in the commercial market, *Drifters* had scored a remarkable *succes d'estime* in discerning eyes. I had not known such a relief from official anxiety since the day in February 1918 which had shown that rationing would cure the food queues.[36]

What a canny and chancy move it was for Grierson to open *Drifters* in the company of *Potemkin* (which had long been held back by the censor). It was typical of his flair for showmanship, perhaps, but think of the standard of comparison he put himself up against. In any case, half of intellectual London and all of the national Press were at this thirty-third performance of the Film Society (which had been founded in 1925, while Grierson was in America) to see the much-heralded Eisenstein film. Happily, *Drifters* was an immediate success, as Tallents indicated, both with the audience that day and the critics the next morning—even somewhat at *Potemkin*'s expense. Grierson later recalled that Eisenstein, who was in England at the time and attended the performance, "was very disturbed by the English reviewers who answered the question 'What have we got to learn from the Russians?' with 'Why one of our unknown young fellows has this montage business all sewn up.'"[37] Incidentally, since *Drifters* was a silent film (already anachronistic in 1929 in that respect), at this performance Grierson had it accompanied by a nonsynchronized recording of Mendelssohn's "Fingal's Cave," which Paul Rotha and Basil Wright remember as being "played over and over again with great nostalgic success."[38] *Drifters* was shown shortly thereafter by the Film Society of Glasgow, which had begun in November 1929.[39]

This first E.M.B. documentary was distributed to the theaters by New Era, as second feature with their (apparently not very good) *Co-optimists*, and it managed to make a respectable showing at the box office. The E.M.B. was glad of the revenue, but even happier that the film was being widely seen by the public. As Tallents put it, "That fact alone justified this film venture of ours against those who had counted on its failure. It indicated, too, that here was a medium of publicity that could be made in part at least self-supporting. If *Drifters* had done no more than that, it would have been amply justified."[40]

Of course it did much more than that. Of his own film, Grierson—with his usual perspicacity and ability to home in on essentials—reflected in 1937 that,

> Though each chapter was a deliberate study in movement, the film took good care to lead up to and stage an event. More important still, as I have come to consider, it had a theme—the ardour and bravery of common labour—and simple themes of the same sociological bearing have served us ever since. . . . *Drifters* seems simple and easy now, though I remember the effort it took to convince showmen of the time that an industrialised fishing fleet might be as brave to the sight as the brown sails of sentiment and that the rigours of work were worth the emphasis of detail. . . .
>
> This explains why *Drifters*, simple film as it was, was so much of a *succes d'estime*, and why it so quickly became more of a myth than a film. It had the rarity value of opening for Britain a new vista of film reference.[41]

Allowing Tallents his pride of place among the many evaluators of the film, fully earned by the close and contributory relationship he bore to the project, here is his evaluation of the full importance and special qualities it possessed:

> *Drifters* was a real pioneer . . . it rejected the escapist approach of the ordinary box office film. It did not seek to spirit its audience away from real everyday life to dreams. It had no snob appeal, making falsely glamorous and desirable to humble people the fundamentally common-place and vulgar luxuries of the rich. It took as its raw material the day-to-day life of ordinary men and from that neglected vein won interest, dignity and beauty. These qualities it presented with drama indeed but also with truth. It thus threw open to British film produc-tion new sources of material limited only by the borders of life itself. It differed from Flaherty's work in that it did not go to the Far North or the South Sea Islands in search of the remote or the exotic. It dif-fered from the work of the Russians in that it was harnessed to no political theme. Owing much to those two sources, it yet enjoyed a greater liberty and struck a more universal note than *Nanook* or *Turksib*. So this modest and cheaply produced film, in spite of weak-nesses which any documentary producer of today would avoid, caught at the time both the attention of qualified critics and the interest of unreflecting audiences. By virtue of its original and pioneering qual-ity, it has since become a legend.[42]

Paul Rotha, historian of the movement, wrote ecstatically of it in the 1930 edition of his *The Film Till Now* (just before he would go to work for the E.M.B.). He compared it with *Potemkin*, find-ing that, though alike in some ways, much was to be said for *Drift-ers*.[43] Later, in the 1939 edition of *Documentary Film*, he dropped the comparison and reduced the importance of *Drifters*: "In that *Drifters* is Grierson's only personally directed film, it has come to be regarded as being more important than it actually is, or was, for that matter, intended to be." Nonetheless, he somewhat grudgingly goes on to give the film its due:

> It humbly brought to the screen the labour of the North Sea herring catch from such an approach that the ordinary person was made to realise, probably for the first time, that a herring on his plate was no mere accepted thing but the result of other men's physical toil and possibly courage. It "brought alive" . . . not just the routine of the catch but the whole drama of emotional values that underlay the task, in-terpreting in its stride the unconscious beauty of physical labour in the face of work done for a livelihood. Moreover, there was brought to the conception all the poetic qualities of ships, sea and weather. In other words, Grierson took a simple theme (there for the taking), took ac-

tually existing material (there for the shooting), and built a dramatised film by interpreting the relationships of his theme and material in the sphere of daily existence.[44]

If it has become a "myth" and a "legend," "regarded as being more important than it actually is," it was nonetheless the final, fully formed prototype for what we have come to know as the documentary film.

## Establishing the Unit, Hiring and Training Staff

The success of *Drifters* meant that Grierson could plan a next move. There was the possibility of his going on to make further personal films, of course, as his friend Flaherty had done, and other filmmakers before and after him. He began to talk about a film, in fact, and in 1930, Associated Sound Film Industries announced that Grierson was going to direct a film for them about "the spirit of youth and comradeship in British industry."[45] But that project was never completed, at least not by Grierson. He did direct a couple of marionette films at the Wembley studios,[46] and later shot considerable footage for a film about the Port of London Authority (working title "P.L.A.") which was never completed. Much of the latter material found its way into other E.M.B. films, however, including *Industrial Britain*.[47]

Instead of attempting to pursue this sort of individual success, however, he decided to try to build a movement:

> With one theatrical film you hit or miss; with a machine, if it is reasonably run, the preliminary results may not be immediately notable or important, but they tend to pile up. Piling up they create a freedom impossible on any other policy. . . . The problem was not so much to repeat the relative success of *Drifters* but to guarantee that, with time, we should turn out good documentaries as a matter of certainty. It was a case of learning the job, not on the basis of one director, one location, and one film at a time, but on the basis of half a dozen directors with complementary talents, and a hundred and one subjects along the line.[48]

To advance a program of this scope meant that he had to secure an administrative niche within the E.M.B. structure, hire a staff, and begin a steady flow of films.

In support of his plans, the E.M.B. had fortified itself with an impressive Film Committee, of which Walter Elliot was the first chairman. Tallents remembered that

Its roll during the next few years included such distinguished personages as Mr. Hore-Belisha, Sir William Furse, Lord Pethick-Lawrence, Mrs. Alfred Lyttleton, Sir Edward Marsh and Mr. Malcolm MacDonald. The function of this high-powered instrument was to guide an expenditure upon film production and distribution which began with £1,217 in 1926 and reached its peak at £17,748 in 1929. . . . As so often happens with advisory committees, its real value lay elsewhere. The E.M.B. staff derived much encouragement from the lively interest which most members took in the work, and they were valuable ambassadors to the outside world of a good but struggling cause.[49]

Struggling indeed. As Grierson wrote later,

In official records you would find the E.M.B. Film Unit tucked away in a long and imposing list of E.M.B. Departments and Sub-Departments, forty-five all told. The Film Unit was number forty-five. "Research and Development" interests accounted for the first twenty-four. . . . "Marketing Economic Investigation and Intelligence" . . . Then "Publicity," banner-heading the departments of newspaper advertisement, posters, recipes, leaflets, lectures, broadcasts, exhibitions, shopping weeks, and trade meetings. After trade meetings, cinema.[50]

In spite of that apparent lack of priority, Grierson's proposals for the future E.M.B. film production were farsighted. They should aim, as Tallents recalled,

at building up a school of young producers, selecting carefully for the purpose young men (or women) of first-class ability and intelligence but without requiring of them previous film experience. We should, however, require hard and concentrated work from them, and put them through a severe apprenticeship in the basic craftsmanship of filmmaking. Then we should employ those of them who showed promise, according to their aptitudes, on the production of a considerable number of films of different types. In so doing, we must keep strictly within our E.M.B. commission; but we must provide room for experiments. We must expect, too, a percentage of failures.[51]

"You can no more contract for the quality of a film than you can contract for the character of a baby," Grierson was to write Tallents in later days.

No difficulty was found in recruiting staff for the new unit. On the contrary. Tallents remarked that "Youth, fired by the success of *Drifters*, and thwarted in its search for a self-respecting way of access to the screen, at first in its tens and later in its hundreds, wrote to Grierson and asked to join him. An advertisement which he inserted in the 'Agony Column' of *The Times* brought a spate of answers."[52] Grierson himself gave an entertaining account of the rush a few years later. "Of the fifteen hundred tyros who have applied for jobs in the E.M.B. unit, fifteen hundred exactly have expressed their enthusiasm for cinema, for art, for self-expression and the other beautiful what-nots of a youthful or simply vague existence." Not one of them, he declared, understood that the E.M.B. was working within the terms of a definite commission with financial resources limited to that commission.[53] Nevertheless, by careful selection he enlisted between September 1929 and the autumn of 1930 a handful of apprentices, and most of the men and women he thus picked became mainstays of the British documentary school.[54]

Some came from the ranks of amateur filmmakers, some from those who felt frustrated in the commercial studios, while others had no film experience at all. In order of joining the unit, they were: J. D. Davidson, Basil Wright, John Taylor, Paul Rotha, Evelyn Spice, Donald Taylor, Arthur Elton, Edgar Anstey, and Stuart Legg.

The hiring of Legg would complete the first principal trio of documentary directors in England. Grierson would say of them, "Together they put a distinctive mark on Documentary development: Arthur Elton with the wonderful lucidity of his technical and scientific films, Basil Wright with his excursions into the poetry of the screen, and Stuart Legg with his studious and intelligent analyses of public event. . . ."[55] These lads of parts had the brightness and talent that would have been demanded by Grierson's father. They also had other qualities that would prove of lifelong value to Grierson and the movement: they were upper class, public school and university educated (all three from Cambridge, whose undergraduates seem to have had a special interest in film), and therefore were used to being listened to. With them, he gained "a tremendous reverberation"—they powered his ideas and pushed them through the establishment in a way that might not have been possible otherwise.[56] In addition, they had substantial private incomes which would be put to use on behalf of the public in backing some of Grierson's many projects. Along with Anstey, whose background was middle class, this group would develop a powerful traction, because of their sustained loyalty and because of the complementary capabilities which each of them possessed.

J. Norris Davidson, an Irishman, fresh from editing the Cambridge student paper, *Granta*, joined the unit at about the same time as Legg; and Harry Watt, who would distinguish himself from the subsequent General Post Office Film Unit period on, arrived a little later. By this time Margaret Taylor was Margaret Taylor Grierson; she continued film editing for the E.M.B. Marion Grierson, John's youngest sister, in her early twenties, came to the E.M.B. after working as a journalist for two years in Canada. Initially she was a sort of production manager at the unit.[57] Shortly thereafter she made a series of films for the Travel and Industrial Development Association of Great Britain and Ireland. Another of John's sisters, R. I. (Ruby) Grierson, came to the field from teaching a little later. Between January 1930 and July 1933 the E.M.B. Film Unit grew from two to over thirty.[58]

These young people, because of the special faith in cinema they were developing, were not tempted back into the regular commercial film world (with the exception of Donald Taylor), and their singular loyalty to Grierson and his idea began here. They came to prefer, as he put it, "the dog biscuits of E.M.B. production to the flesh pots of Elstree and Shepherd's Bush," the centers of British feature production. Certainly they came to work for the E.M.B. at rates and under conditions which Wardour Street, center of film distribution, mocked. (The documentary workers were called the "literati" in the trade press.) Wright, for example, was paid £4 a week as director of his first film, *The Country Comes to Town*. He had to employ an outside cameraman, James Burger, at £10 a week. "From time to time," Tallents admitted, there was "a measure of their underpayment when one of them was released to work for awhile with a commercial company. For these engagements . . . they always earned at least double and sometimes three times the salaries which [the E.M.B.] was able to pay them."[59]

They were most inadequately housed and equipped as well. From Grierson's basement, as the unit began to form, it was moved to a midget-sized cutting-room in Dansey Yard (now Dansey Place), off the lower end of Wardour Street, which Anstey described as "comparative squalor."[60] The whole unit was housed in this eight-foot-square room, where all office work and cutting was done, including projection onto a lavatory wall with a hand-turn projector.[61] Rotha recalled young John Taylor's pride in projecting *Turksib* on that lavatory wall during the summer of 1930. "The copy, with Russian flash-titles before Grierson's dynamic titling, had just arrived."[62] Anstey said that veterans of the even earlier days talked of "a dignified official table into which two long nails had been driven so that film could be wound from one waste-paper basket into another."[63] After the move to an attic at 179 Wardour Street, in October 1930, there was an office and a cutting room. The latter was also the projection theater, however, so that the cutters had to stop work when anyone wanted to screen a film. At nights the cutting room was also turned into a studio for shooting poster films (brief commercials), in defiance of local fire regulations.[64]

At this point they rigged up a theater in a small room, unfit for normal uses, in the basement of the main E.M.B. offices at Queen Anne's Buildings.[65] In May of the next year, 1931, the film unit moved again into larger, regular, office-like premises in an upper story at 37 Oxford Street, opposite the old Frascati's Restaurant.[66] Of the combination of "sweated labour and slum conditions," Tallents said, they "contrasted comically with the imposing arrangements which the E.M.B. made to guide it in the disbursement of the pittance which it devoted to its cinematic enterprises."[67] His reference was to the E.M.B. Film Committee and the Treasury.

Perhaps in part because of the hardships and limitations, Grierson's young men and women became imbued with a spirit and were trained into a skill that marked him, to use a phrase he once applied to Flaherty, as one of the great film teachers. This could be argued to have been the most valuable of his many roles. Part of his educational method, dictated by necessity, was to put novices to work immediately—often allowing them considerable latitude and demanding that they assume commensurate responsibility. Basil Wright, for example, with only amateur films behind him, was assigned the task of making, out of a long film sponsored by Cadbury's, the food company, a 400-foot (4 minute) item on empire cocoa production. This became the prototype for a series of E.M.B. poster films.[68]

Grierson didn't hold back his criticism of his students' efforts. Forsyth Hardy, for his part, remembered vividly the red-headed Anglo-Saxon giant Arthur Elton standing wordlessly like a schoolboy with head down as Grierson raked over him at one of these sessions. As Edgar Anstey remembered it,

> Grierson's particular *forte* was the analysis of rushes. Individual shots often became the subject of hours of discussion and a badly composed shot or a bad camera angle would be sufficient to drive Grierson roaring from the theatre—but never before the precise word had been spoken which would point the way to better work next time. I shall

never forget how a simple incidental scene I had shot of a final cop-
ing-stone being laid on a building job aroused such wrath that I had
to spend almost a week tramping the streets and telephoning building
contractors to find locations where I could repeat a similar episode.
Several attempts had to be made at different places before Grierson
was satisfied that I had chosen a camera angle and movement which
expressed fully the purpose and feeling of this simple operation. It
would have been easy to dispense with the scene altogether, but this
was not the point. Documentary accepted without question none of
the film-making conventions of the day and was busy evolving its own.

On the other hand, Anstey concluded, "To see Grierson himself at
work on location or in the cutting room was the best training of all.
The speed with which he grasped the essentials of any production
or editing situation is something which I am afraid none of his pupils have succeeded in equalling."[69]

Of this training, Grierson himself said simply, marking the year
1930, "In the three years that followed we gathered together, and
in a sense created, Basil Wright, Arthur Elton, Stuart Legg, and a half
a dozen others."[70] Tallents, somewhat more completely observed that

> Grierson fused and welded his eager and miscellaneous team—inter-
> nally often an argumentative crew but in their outward front united—
> into an enthusiastic, hard-working and single-minded company. Of
> their enthusiasm we used laughingly to recall as symbolic a night on
> which their eagerness to project their films put such a load on the light-
> ing resources of the Imperial Institute as to reduce to temporary dark-
> ness a large reception at which the principal guest was H.R.H. the
> Prince of Wales. There were hot debates about the cause of the break-
> down, but we were content to accept responsibility for it. Of their hard
> work, lights burning late in the windows of 37 Oxford Street were the
> outward token.[71]

Hardy summed up: "There was, at the E.M.B. Film Unit during those
early thirties, an energizing and inspiriting atmosphere which affected everyone who made contact with it. One was aware both of
an unselfish devotion to an ideal and a sense of vital urgency in the
effort towards its realization."[72]

## Production

Still working through New Era (as the unit did until 1931, when it
became sufficiently established to have a separate annual budget),[73]

the next major film to follow *Drifters* was completely different from it—in technique, purpose, and the audience for which it was intended. Entitled *Conquest,* it was about the settling of the American West, commercial conquest being presented as more meaningful than military conquest. It was entirely a compilation film, with its bits and pieces drawn largely from Paramount super-westerns— *The Covered Wagon, The Thundering Herd,* and *The Iron Horse* (the latter Fox)—and from the pioneering Canadian Government Motion Picture Bureau. Put together by Grierson and Wright as a three reeler (30 minutes), it emphasized transportation, from covered wagons to modern trains. It was press-shown in September 1930, where it was well-received by several critics, and was presented at the (London) Film Society. As an experimental "illumination" film, it was intended for school use (even if one observer thought that, although "admirable . . . the technique and treatment were more suited to the theatre than to the school hall").[74] Also, it was a test, in comparison with the methods of *Drifters,* in which cost was measured against effectiveness. Since there was no important successor, one may assume that Grierson felt the compilation method could not compete with the control possible in original shooting for his more ambitious projects.[75] Tallents felt, however, that it did "a serviceable job" in the schools, until the expiration of contracts for use of *Covered Wagon* and other footage required its withdrawal.[76] The next production of the E.M.B. Film Unit would be much more enduring and influential.

The project began to coalesce one summer evening in 1931 in a pub when the small band of E.M.B. film people were chatting about the day's work (a custom basic to Grierson's curriculum). The unit had only recently moved from its attic offices on Oxford Street, and the pub frequented at the time was the Coronet, in Soho Street just off Soho Square. Jimmy Davidson, the cameraman, who had been working late, came into the bar and said to Grierson, "There's a Mrs. Flaherty calling you from Berlin up in the joint." Grierson dashed out.[77] When Frances Flaherty phoned she already had been in Berlin for some time with her three daughters—she approved of German education—while Robert Flaherty was working on *Tabu.* At the beginning of 1931 he joined them. As Grierson recalled—in a letter to Tallents written at the time of Flaherty's death, twenty years later—when Frances phoned that evening she reported that "Bob was exhausting the family fortune—hers—in Berlin, waiting for an invitation to go to Russia to make a film of the Russian woman. It sounds crazy, but that was the tale at the time. The key-word, as I remember, was 'valuta' [exchange value of currency]."[78]

At that point the E.M.B., though there were numerous poster films and modest compilations, had only two productions of any real weight to its name: *Drifters*, now eighteen months old, and *Conquest*, released the preceding fall. As Rotha and Wright put it, "In his inimitable quick way, Grierson at once grasped the fact that to have Robert Flaherty working with the EMB film unit would not only add lustre but it would also give a unique chance for the young tiros to learn something at first-hand of his instinctive handling of a movie camera and of his wonderful sense of observation."[79]

Of this scheme, Grierson recalled to Tallents:

> You on your side were at first pretty dim about bringing in an alien, for we were in the quicksands anyway. Then again you thought it would be permissable if he came in as a "schoolmaster": your word. So the whole business of making *Industrial Britain* was a bit phoney from the start. Bob was to demonstrate to the youth how to shoot in smokey Birmingham, etc. With the other half of our mind, of course, we wanted a picture, because you were playing C—— of the D.o.T. [presumably Craig (an official) of the Department of Treasury] on the line at the time and the agreed theme was craftsmanship.[80]

Tallents's way was eased by the widened mandate given the E.M.B. by the Imperial Conference of 1930. Formerly the enforced concentration had been on empire goods to be consumed within Britain; now the E.M.B.'s terms of reference included empire markets overseas as well as inside Britain.

Within a few days of the phone conversation between Frances Flaherty and Grierson, the Flahertys had checked into the York Hotel, Berners Street, only a short distance from the unit's offices. Rotha and Wright wrote that they recalled "vividly" the Flahertys being conducted by Grierson through their first tour of the unit's by-then two-floor premises.[81] Flaherty liked London and the young documentary group. In the first days he often spent the early evenings with them in the Coronet.[82]

It was agreed among Tallents, Grierson, and Flaherty (Rotha and Wright reported) that Flaherty should go off and "produce a film which would reveal the craftsmanship which persisted in even the most modern of British industries, even behind the smoke and steam and grime of the industrial Midlands."[83]

As for script,

Grierson had explained to Flaherty that someone down in Whitehall—meaning the top people at the EMB—would want a script of the film he was going to make. At first, Flaherty point blank refused. He had never written a script before and he wasn't going to start now for some civil servant. Grierson was polite but firm. Flaherty retired sulkily to the York Hotel and remained there hermit-like for several days. Then he appeared at the unit and gave Grierson a thick wedge of paper. On the top sheet were the words in Flaherty's heavy hand, INDUSTRIAL BRITAIN: a film about craftsmen: A SCENARIO; and underneath, Scenes of Industrial Britain. If anyone in Whitehall ever read a script for the unit's new production before money was sanctioned for its making that script was certainly not written by the maker of *Nanook* and *Moana*.[84]

Nonetheless, Flaherty and J. P. R. Golightly, whom Grierson had hired as production manager for the film, set out with what was for the E.M.B. a generous amount of raw stock. Mrs. Flaherty remained in London. When the first rushes started coming back, "what shocked Grierson (and others)," Rotha and Wright recalled, "was the amount of footage shot on things which for the most part could not remotely be related to the subject of the film being made. Matters were not made easier when, courteously cautioned by Grierson over the telephone about the amount of film stock he was blazing away, Flaherty, no doubt rather hurt, explained that the rushes were only 'tests' he had made to get 'the feel of things.'"[85]

After this first shooting, Flaherty and Golightly returned to base, and no doubt a serious and probably stormy conversation took place between Flaherty and Grierson. Be that as it may, the two-man unit quickly set out again, this time headed for the industrial Midlands. When it became clear that even a man of Golightly's resourcefulness could not cope with the multitude of tasks now assigned him, John Taylor was dispatched from London to join them at Stoke-on-Trent as "dogsbody no. 2."[86]

At the end of one day, when Flaherty had been out shooting at a steel plant near Birmingham, Grierson and Jimmy Davidson turned up unexpectedly at the hotel in Birmingham. Grierson was in high spirits because he and Davidson had shot some splendid steel mill footage on their way up. As his description waxed increasingly lyrical, Flaherty's countenance darkened. It became evident that Grierson had shot, without permission, at the very plant which had denied Flaherty permission earlier in the day. Flaherty's rage became towering because, as he saw it, he had been outwitted by Grierson, perhaps on purpose. "Didn't these goddamned steel people, didn't these goddamned civil servants in Whitehall, didn't he—John Grierson—realise that Robert Flaherty couldn't be treated like this?" According to Golightly's recollection, "Grierson gave a characteristic goading reply, 'Why, Bob, in Whitehall they just think you're a bloody beach-photographer.' Flaherty drew himself up to his full height and size [he was a bear of a man], raised his clenched fists to the ceiling of the crowded hotel-lounge, and bawled in best Anglo-Saxon, 'F—— them! F—— them! F—— them!' They were all requested to leave the hotel."[87]

Shortly thereafter the Flaherty-Golightly-Taylor crew moved over to Northern Ireland, where they were to shoot some shipyards at Belfast. It was in Belfast that the money finally ran dry. Golightly sent telegram after telegram to the unit in London, from which came no reply. Finally Flaherty became very angry and phoned Grierson that unless some money was put in the next mail he would sell their Newman-Sinclair camera. The money came.[88]

Flaherty finished shooting only when the supply of film stock was used up. On his return to London, as the footage was reviewed, it became clear that though it contained some superb scenes they did not add up to a coherent picture. In some way an agreement was reached that Grierson (with Anstey's help, as it turned out) would edit the film.

According to Anstey, about twelve thousand feet of the Flaherty material was turned over to him. (Compared to the more than two hundred thousand feet shot for *Moana* this is a tribute to the ability of Grierson and Golightly to keep Flaherty within governmental means.) Not only was there no script, Anstey stated that at no point did he have anything on paper to work from. During part of that time, Grierson was home ill in bed and would edit the film by eye. It was completed as a silent film, two reels in length, with much the same shape as we know it in *Industrial Britain*.

After the editing was completed, however, it lay on the shelf all of the next year, 1932, waiting for an arrangement to be concluded with Gaumont-British Distributors for the theatrical distribution of six short pictures that came to be known as the "Imperial Six." Part of the deal was that Gaumont-British would provide sound-recording facilities so that music and commentaries could be added to the films, under E.M.B. supervision. The release of the "Imperial Six" was held up until all of them had been synchronized. As a result, *Industrial Britain* did not have its first showing until the summer of 1933, two years after it had been begun. Its screen credits read: "Produced by John Grierson and Robert Flaherty for the Empire Marketing Board."[89]

A great deal of the Flaherty footage was used, of course, and it, along with the Grierson-shot steel sequence, forms the backbone of the film. But Grierson, in his letter to Tallents already quoted, after granting that Flaherty had provided the sort of demonstration they had hired him for, acknowledged that "Wright, Elton and I constructed what there was of a picture." He felt that "*Industrial Britain* is still the best of its sort but [for] the poor *s'ecoute parler* [self-conscious speech]."[90] There is too much commentary (Grierson himself had written it) and it is read in a stilted radio announcer's voice, accompanied by stock music.

The visuals and editing are much superior to the track; in fact, more than acceptable, granted the style, with some flashes of brilliance. The pull between Grierson (industry of the modern world) and Flaherty (disappearing crafts from the past) results in a fuzzing of the approach, however, rather than the dramatic tension that seems to have been intended. Perhaps because it represents neither purely, both Grierson and Flaherty have tended to underrate the film. In his letter to Tallents, Grierson wrote of *Industrial Britain* as a sort of key, however: "I wonder if it will give you a guide to the good Bob? It was made in spite of him. Its manner and mood were not his. On the other hand, it is true that it was the combination of Flaherty's approach and ours—different as they eventually proved to be—that set the line for a decade of documentary-film-making here and abroad."[91]

Along with *Drifters*, *Industrial Britain* was the most successful and generally liked film to come out of the entire E.M.B. output. It played with popular success at one of London's main West End movie theaters. The worker—a comic stock figure in English entertainment films—had at last been given his dignity. Grierson recalled that ". . . the workers' portraits of *Industrial Britain* were cheered in the West End. The strange fact was that the West End had never seen workmen's portraits before—certainly not on the screen. *Industrial Britain*, significantly, was hailed as a patriotic picture. . . ."[92] It was still being circulated by British Information Services in countries outside Britain years after World War II.[93]

Flaherty's withdrawal from the E.M.B. after he had done the *Industrial Britain* shooting was not without concern to Grierson. On the other hand, Flaherty had set his heart on making a film about the people of the Aran Islands, off the western coast of Ireland. To help move that hope towards realization, Grierson got in touch with Angus McPhail, then head of the story department at Gaumont-British Picture Corporation.[94] Through the persistent efforts of McPhail and Cedric Belfrage, film critic of the B.B.C., and the "supporting courage" of Michael (later Sir Michael) Balcon, who was in charge of production for Gaumont-British, Flaherty was given his chance to make *Man of Aran*.[95]

Grierson continued to hover over and encourage its production in one way and another, including trips up to Inishmore, the largest of the three Aran Islands, where the film was being shot. On one visit Grierson "was nearly harpooned by Tiger King [the man of Aran of the picture] after a tactless remark during an alcoholic expedition. . . ."[96] John Taylor was loaned to assist, and Harry Watt, who had just come on at the E.M.B., spent some time with the Aran crew during the autumn of 1932. Watt, a twenty-six-year-old Scot who had gotten his education at Edinburgh University, was a later hero of the G.P.O. and Crown units.

As for the other films among the "Imperial Six," *The Country Comes to Town* (1931–32, one reel), Basil Wright's debut as a director, has already been touched upon. Elton's *Upstream* (1931, one reel), about the salmon fisheries in Scotland, included a slow-motion sequence of salmon leaping the Falls of Shin. Tallents well-remembered ". . . the frantic daily telegrams which passed between [Elton] and Oxford Street while he sat idly by the waters of Shin, waiting for weather and for fish."[97] *O'er Hill and Dale* (1932, one reel) was Wright's second film. An account of a day in the life of a shepherd on the border of Scotland and England, it "admirably described the lambing season in the Cheviots [the hills which range along the English-Scottish border]."[98] *Shadow on the Mountain* (1931, one reel), Elton's second film, was about Professor Stapledon's pasture experiments at Aberystwyth in Wales. At the Plant Breeding Station, Elton shot the processes by which new strains of grasses were bred. On the mountains of Plynlimmon he found material to demonstrate that scientific research and practical energy could quadruple the sheep-carrying capacity of unpromising pastures. Tallents regarded it "a beautiful little film."[99] *Big Timber* seems to be the least well-remembered of the six—seems, in fact, to have faded completely from memory and record.

During the four years from the release of *Drifters* to the closing down of the Empire Marketing Board, Grierson supervised the production of over a hundred films—sometimes as many as twenty productions at a time.[100] He thought of this output as falling into distinct types. First were the documentaries for the theaters (e.g., *Drifters* and the "Imperial Six" series). Next were short-interest films for nontheatrical audiences—the compilation films (e.g., *Conquest* and *Lumber*) and those made from outtakes of other productions (e.g., *The English Potter*, which Marion Grierson edited from Flaherty footage not used in *Industrial Britain*). Third were classroom films for use in conjunction with curriculum units. These dealt exclusively with the economic geography of the empire. Fourth were poster films for advertising. These seem to be a particularly original experiment, foreshadowing the strategies and techniques of the television commercial some twenty-five years in advance. Rotha, who worked on them, wrote about the poster films fully and glowingly in his 1931 book, *Celluloid*.[101] Only two to three minutes long and running on continuous-loop daylight projectors at railway stations, exhibitions, and so on, they were often abstract designs with a simple sales push, for National Mark Eggs or Home Grown Tomatoes, for instance—decorative and interesting. According to Tallents, the foreign correspondent of the *New York Evening Post* once called them "England's best contribution to the cinema so far"![102] The sheer number of the E.M.B. productions precludes anything approaching individual evaluation, but, in addition to the films already mentioned, there were some noteworthy contributions to documentary practice from these earliest years, and, since there were no precedents, all of the films were to one degree or another experimental. Few of them are extant, but, judging from contemporary writing about them, among the most significant were *The Voice of the World*, *The New Generation*, *Cargo from Jamaica*, *Windmill in Barbados*, *Aero-Engine*, and *Lancashire at Work and Play*.

Many of these films involved outside sponsorship in various arrangements. Often the directors would go off salary and return to the E.M.B. when they had finished the outside assignments—a practice Grierson would continue to encourage in order to bring new young replacements to his own unit and thus present a broader front.

*The Voice of the World* (1932–33, four reels) was produced by Grierson and directed by Elton for the Gramophone Company. It detailed the processes of radio manufacturing and broadcasting. For the Chesterfield Local Education Authority, Legg made *The New Generation* (1932, two reels) at about the same time, recording the operation of a modern educational system, with incidental glimpses of the industrial and social life of the town. *Cargo from Jamaica* (one reel, 1933), an impressionistic study of the banana industry, and *Windmill in Barbados* (1933, one reel) were both directed by Wright on a journey to the West Indies. (His *Liner Cruising South* [two reels] was made for the Orient Line to pay for the ticket!) Elton's *Aero-Engine* (1932, five reels) was produced with Air Ministry help. It dwelt on the research and the careful and accurate processes which underlay the making of airplane engines. *Lancashire at Work and Play* (1933–34, four reels) was made by Donald Taylor for the Travel Association.

In retrospect it does seem that, in spite of his anti-"aestheticky" position (to be spelled out later), the films which Grierson himself was most closely associated with were the loveliest of the lot and have been the most lasting: *Drifters, Industrial Britain,* and *Granton Trawler* (1934, one reel). The latter was a sort of remake of *Drifters,* a condensation of it, an essence. Grierson shot it while on holiday in Scotland and turned over the footage to Anstey for editing on his return. An account of trawling in rough weather on the Viking Bank, it goes beyond its subject material, with lyrical imagery of men and sea, and clearly involved a sort of aesthetic experimentation with the shifting horizon and the ever-present sense of disorientation. The track, suggesting sounds aboard the trawler—a thumping engine, mumbled words, whistling, wind noise, and the like—is extraordinarily elegant in its simplicity and contrapuntal effectiveness. Though shot during the E.M.B. days, it was finished after the unit had been transferred to the General Post Office. It has not dated and is still in active nontheatrical distribution.

## Distribution and Exhibition

While E.M.B. production was going ahead at a prolific rate, there were equally ambitious innovations in distribution and exhibition.

In fact, Grierson's major contributions all began during this period: the development of the purpose and form of documentary film, an economic base for production in institutional sponsorship, and the establishment of nontheatrical distribution and exhibition for the completed films. The latter was no doubt suggested by his earlier researches into German and French nontheatrical film use, as well as by his realization "that there was more seating capacity outside the commercial cinemas than inside them."[103]

Since nontheatrical channels were primitive, almost nonexistent to begin with (this was before the widespread use of 16 mm film), commercial theaters initially were the main outlet. Largely through his salesmanship, Grierson managed from *Drifters* on to push E.M.B. films into theatrical distribution. Even when industrial, working-class, and social themes were supposed to be death among the exhibitors, most of the films intended for the theaters got there— generally in groups of six and usually two reelers—and most of them did fairly well.[104] The "Imperial Six" series played with popular success in London's West End and later throughout the United Kingdom and overseas.[105]

But experience showed that theatrical distribution was neither the easiest nor the best outlet for documentaries. The trade was unaccustomed to marketing this type of film and regarded shorts as "fillers," with little financial value and limited appeal. The comparative success of *Drifters* and the "Imperial Six" did little to change that attitude. General adoption of double-feature programs early in the 1930s further limited the openings for shorts.[106] With this situation clearly before it, the Empire Marketing Board set up an alternative scheme of exhibition and then of distribution. It was only shortly after Grierson was hired that he succeeded in installing a movie theater in the Imperial Institute.

Founded in 1887 and opened in 1893, the Institute was housed in a huge building erected in South Kensington. In 1926, the year the E.M.B. was established, it was reorganized to increase its educational value, particularly for children. Its four great galleries, running east, west, south, and north, were divided into Empire Courts, and each court contained photographs, dioramas, specimens, and other exhibits which illustrated the life, scenery, and industries of some part of the empire.[107] According to Lt. Gen. Sir William Furse (director of the Institute and member of the E.M.B. Film Committee), though those at the Institute had longed for moving pictures as well as still, it was the Empire Marketing Board that came to their aid. At the E.M.B.'s expense, a pavilion attached to the galleries was converted into a movie theater which, from July 1927 until July 1933, presented twenty-six showings weekly, four each weekday and two on Sundays. The total attendance was over 1,603,000; roughly half the audience were boys and girls from 1,477 different schools. Funds necessary to operate the theater continued to be provided by the E.M.B. until its demise.[108] Similar E.M.B. showings were sponsored at various exhibitions—the British Industries Fair and the North-East Coast Exhibition, for example.[109]

In the autumn of 1931 the E.M.B. established, in a small building detached from but quite close to the Institute theater, the Empire Film Library, a lending collection of 16 mm films for nontheatrical distribution to the provinces. During the first six months of its operation, 350 schools and institutes made repeated use of the library's films. The E.M.B.'s slender production up to that time was supplemented by films drawn from other sources and by films the E.M.B. editors made from outtakes and from stock footage obtained elsewhere, notably from Canada's Motion Picture Bureau and the Canadian National Railways. Forty such films went into circulation in the single year 1932–33.[110] By August 1932, when an enlarged catalogue of available titles was published, the number of users had swelled to 650. In 1932 alone, over six thousand films were booked from the library and were seen by an estimated audience of eight hundred thousand[111]—a not inconsiderable number. "The increase during 1933 has continued," wrote Sir William. "At the present time we are sending films to 800 different schools and institutes."[112]

The Empire Film Library would long outlive its parent organization; it was carried first to the General Post Office after the dissolution of the Empire Marketing Board. In 1934 this library, together with the G.P.O. documentaries, was transferred (back, in a sense) to the Imperial Institute, which continued to give daily film shows and to circulate films throughout the country. In that way the Institute became an important channel of documentary distribution. At the outbreak of World War II, its film section became part of the Central Film Library of the Ministry of Information (M.O.I.),[113] which handled the E.M.B. and G.P.O. films plus the M.O.I. productions.

The decision to concentrate on nontheatrical distribution came to seem a logical, if only partial, solution to the problems presented by theatrical distribution. It opened up new ways of reaching the public outside the movie houses and helped documentary producers secure their independence from the ordinary commercial channels. It was also a logical step in the development of the documentary, because the nontheatrical audiences, gathered in schools and at meetings of societies and trade unions, could be appealed to along the lines of their special interests, unlike the heterogeneous Friday night audience in the theater.[114] What the documentary gave up in mass appeal it gained in social utility and precision-tooled effectiveness.

## Promotion

Preceding, paralleling, and in some measure supporting film activity at the E.M.B. were a series of Imperial Conference recommendations. They began when the Conference of 1926 (the year the E.M.B. was established) passed a resolution aimed at stimulating the production and distribution of films within the empire—i.e., commercial entertainment films. The following year, the Imperial Studies Committee of the Colonial Office went a considerable step further by asking for the kinds of films that would make the empire "a real and living thing to the world by means of the screen"[115]— which sounds a lot like Tallents, with or without Grierson. The Imperial Conference of 1930 added to this growing body of resolutions: "The Conference, recognising the value of films for propaganda purposes, whether direct or indirect, in connection with Imperial trade, as well as for other purposes . . . recommends that attention should be devoted to establishing and maintaining contact between the different parts of the Empire in relation to film production with a view to the sharing of experience and the promotion of the production of such films as will best serve the interests of the several parts of the Commonwealth."[116]

As a result of that resolution Grierson visited Canada briefly at the beginning of 1931 to make firsthand acquaintance with the most substantial government film enterprise in the empire, Canada's Motion Picture Bureau.

"It was a fruitful trip," Tallents recalled. "He began by sending me back from New York, in the best E.M.B. tradition, a note of some practical tips he had gleaned on his outward voyage in the kitchens of his Cunarder. The eggs came from France; the vegetables, fruits and canned goods came from the United States. The ship's cooks told him that other countries put their rhubarb aboard, bundled and dressed, and their carrots properly washed. Wasn't there an opening for us here?"[117] Once in America, the potential of 16 mm film, especially for schools in Britain, came strongly to his attention, and he wrote back to Basil Wright urging that he look into the matter.[118]

On his arrival in Ottawa, Grierson got to work immediately with Captain Frank Badgley, head of the Motion Picture Bureau, who had visited England and the E.M.B. in 1928. The Bureau was a pioneer organization. Established in 1917 as a branch of the Department of Trade and Commerce, its films promoted tourism especially. ("Every pine tree, I find," Grierson wrote Tallents, "between here and Vancouver is set against a sunset, and every horse against a horizon.") Its equipment and organization were what impressed Grierson, rather than the excellence of its films. "In cinema qualities we have not so much to learn on this side, but on the equipment side and in the creation and management of circulation we have almost everything."[119]

As a result of his visit, seventeen new negatives were added to the Empire Film Library, and fifteen thousand feet of positive film were sent from Canada to the E.M.B. unit for editing in whatever form it chose.[120] And, of course, this trip would become the background for a later trip and for the establishment of the National Film Board of Canada, with Grierson as its first head.

Accompanying this protean activity (Grierson's career at any given time always looks as if five men were bearing his name), and tenderly nursed by him, was a growing support of documentary film by the press and by people in high places. The attention and praise offered by press and radio was, in fact, far out of proportion to the size or exhibition value of the pictures. Grierson enlisted the active backing of journalists and critics, not only in London but also in English provincial cities and in Scotland. There was a special coterie of half a dozen or so interpreters of his ideas scattered about the country whom he would take pains to keep informed and to look up during his travels. Forsyth Hardy in Edinburgh, himself one of these critic-journalists, who had met Grierson shortly after the release of *Drifters*, explained this press response:

> Some of us who were writing regularly about films at that time were often impatient of their meagre mental standard and were always on the alert for anything that would push the cinema a little nearer to its

unrealized potential. Documentary provided one proof that the medium could be used with intelligence and imagination on a more demanding mental wave-length than trivial escapism. The result was that each new film as it appeared was responsibly analysed, each change in the direction of the movement noted. Thus the articles . . . were more than film reviews: they stimulated and, I imagine, on occasion guided Grierson; and they kept the achievements of the movement before the public.[121]

As an example of the sort of writing being done, here is C. A. Lejeune, in the London *Observer* of March 27, 1931; surely she had been listening attentively to Grierson's ambitious plans, and even tried with him to salvage that much-abused word "propaganda."

What we want from the British cinema is *real* films. We want pictures of real life, of plain facts, of industries and expeditions as adventurous as the wildest tales of the woolly West. We want our own country put on the map, our cities, our pasturage, our machinery, our railways, our fisheries, our workers, our traditions, gnarled and rooted in the soil as grand old forest trees. It is time that we began to be country-proud and empire-proud in the cinema, to boast a bit, to be a little swaggering for once. God knows we have plenty to swagger about. The Port of London has movie in it [and Grierson had started on it] as exciting as anything that came out of Russia. We have tractors too, doing giant's work on the mountain sides, though we have never made film heroes out of them yet. Russia has turned her raw materials to magnificent movie purpose in *Turksib* and *Earth* and *The General Line* [aka *Old and New*]. America has long ago discovered how to make movie and propaganda synonymous. Propaganda is a grand word for a nation with spirit, but we have made a bogey of it. To our ears it means insidious discontent. It should mean strength for Britain, through propaganda's most powerful instrument, the screen.

On June 6, 1931, in the *Observer*, Lejeune added: "At the moment there is practically no other workshop than the E.M.B. in which a film apprentice can learn his job with a mixture of imagination and hard common-sense." Later she abruptly changed her mind, however, and shocked the documentary people in what Rotha and Wright labeled "a notorious piece." Appearing in the *Observer* of August 21, 1932, it was headed "This Documentary Fetish"![122] Even this negative commentary shows tribute to the power of the genie that had been uncorked. There can be no question of what Grierson felt about the key role played in the movement by the marching companions of the press. He frequently acknowledged their help.

Regarding the personages who lent their individual support to the movement, and were frequently visitors at 37 Oxford Street, H. G. Wells, Julian Huxley, and Walter Elliot were among the most distinguished as well as the most helpful. One of Wells's comments on *Turksib*—"I do not like your epileptic technique"—was preserved in fond memory by the E.M.B. Unit.[123] A few years afterwards, at the G.P.O., Wells "confessed" that he was still learning from the filmmakers.[124] Grierson would later work under Huxley at UNESCO. Elliot was chairman of that first E.M.B. Film Committee. All three men would remain Grierson's lifelong friends.

## Speaking and Writing

With press and individual backing, Grierson himself took the lead in the promotional effort. He lectured tirelessly all over the country—to learned bodies, film societies, discussion groups, at universities, conferences, schools.[125] He wrote, and he wrote, though he would later affect a tone of diffidence about it: "Writing has no doubt helped us clear our heads and renew our spirits as we went along, but the most important point about the ideas on which we have speculated is that we have worked them out in practice. In fact, one must see the writing of the documentary group as somewhat strictly related to action."[126] Like those prefaces to George Bernard Shaw's plays which have outlasted the plays themselves, however, the writing has outlived those first films. Surely Grierson must have realized its full importance.

The most brilliant of the articles were addressed to colleagues and sympathizers and appeared in *Cinema Quarterly*, founded in Edinburgh by Norman Wilson and Forsyth Hardy and more or less commandeered by the documentary group. The first issue, Autumn 1932, lists Wilson as editor, Hardy as review editor, and Basil Wright as London correspondent. (This house organ, as it almost was, metamorphosed into *World Film News* in 1935 and then into *Documentary News Letter* in 1940, which lasted until 1948. From 1935 on publication was out of London and editorial supervision, firm if informal, was exercised by Grierson.) Of the regular contributions of Grierson and his young filmmakers, Tallents, allowing that they wrote "perhaps, a little over-generously of each other's productions; sometimes, perhaps, a little too severely of the productions of the commercial world," concluded fairly enough: "But they always wrote intelligently."[127] At a time when film criticism, at least in periodical literature, was scarcely formed, they began to build out of this printed discussion a coherent body of theory that still makes inspiriting reading.

Grierson's "First Principles of Documentary," begun in the *Cinema Quarterly* of winter 1932 and continued in the spring 1933 and spring 1934 issues, have a Kantian majesty and lasting validity:

> (1) We believe that the cinema's capacity for getting around, for observing and selecting from life itself, can be exploited in a new and vital art form. . . . the living scene and the living story. (2) We believe that the original (or native) actor, and the original (or native) scene, are better guides to a screen interpretation of the modern world. . . . (3) We believe that the materials and the stories thus taken from the raw can be finer (more real in the philosophic sense) than the acted article . . . the movement which tradition has formed or time worn smooth.[128]

Of the young documentary makers' understanding of the central issue involved in this aesthetic he wrote:

> The best of the tyros know . . . that beauty will come in good time to inhabit the statement which is honest and lucid and deeply felt and which fulfills the best ends of citizenship. They are sensible enough to conceive of art as the by-product of a job of work done. The opposite effort to capture the by-product first (the self-conscious pursuit of beauty, the pursuit of art for art's sake to the exclusion of jobs of work and other pedestrian beginnings), was always a reflection of selfish wealth, selfish leisure and aesthetic decadence.[129]

It would surely, as Forsyth Hardy observed in 1947,

> be interesting to assess just how much Grierson's lucid and compelling exposition of its aims has contributed to the development of documentary. Certainly they have been a source of stimulus and enrichment for those who were outside the immediate range of his personal influence. Individually they have enunciated principles which have conditioned the whole trend of the movement and set a pace for it. Together they constitute the most solid and penetrating analysis yet made of the film as an instrument affecting public opinion.[130]

In addition, during these years and almost as a hobby it would seem, resting from his labors, Grierson continued the stream of reviews he had begun in the United States. (He came to regard his American writing as "journalism," unworthy of republication.)[131]

Art criticism quickly gave way to a concentration on film. He chose largely popular American movies, especially comedies (e.g., *Animal Crackers, City Lights, Laughing Gas, Monkey Business, The Passionate Plumber, I'm No Angel*), the gangster cycle (e.g., *Quick Millions, The Public Enemy*), and westerns (e.g., *Cimarron*). Of course there was a review for each of the Soviet masterworks as it appeared (e.g., *Earth, The Man with a Movie Camera, Thunder Over Mexico, Enthusiasm*) and other major films with realist tendencies (e.g., *All Quiet on the Western Front, Street Scene, Kamerad-schaft, M*) or special quality (e.g., *Sous les toits de Paris, Tabu, Frankenstein, Le Million, The Lost Squadron*).

He seems to have been particularly attentive to certain directors and to have sought out their work, even some that was less than important; e.g., Cecil B. De Mille *(Dynamite)*, King Vidor *(The Champ)*, William Wyler *(A House Divided)*, John Ford *(Arrowsmith)*, Josef von Sternberg *(Shanghai Express)*, Ernst Lubitsch *(The Man I Killed)*, G. W. Pabst *(Don Quixote)*. And, understandably, he supported the best two directors at work in England at the time: Alfred Hitchcock *(Murder, The Skin Game, Rich and Strange)* and Anthony Asquith *(Tell England, Dance Pretty Lady)*.

Grierson published at least fifty movie reviews while at the E.M.B.—the first (of Vidor's *Hallelujah!*) appearing in the *Clarion* of February 1930; the last (of Gregory La Cava's *Gabriel Over the White House*) in June of 1933 in the *New Britain*, just a month before the E.M.B. closed. He wrote for the *Clarion* (later titled *New Clarion*), *Everyman*, and *Art Work* on a regular basis, and also for *New Britain* and the *Spectator*. Thanks to Forsyth Hardy's diligence, at least a fair selection has been preserved in *Grierson on Documentary*.

Since samples are in evidence, there is no need for a review of the reviews; but it is necessary to present Grierson's general critical position and to give a few examples of its application. "Of every film and of every film talent," he wrote, "I ask a modicum of revelation."

> It may be a novelty of fact, or an angle of beauty, or an efficiency of technical demonstration. These will serve in the absence of better things: the sort of greatness that comes with Chaplin and Pudovkin, and every now and again from people like Hitchcock and Asquith and Lachman and Vidor and Sternberg and Flaherty and Roland Brown. It is my old-fashioned opinion that nothing less will serve us finally in

our attendance on cinema. It would be foolish to expect a lot of it, for revelation will remain, as ever, a difficult and rare experience; but, consciously or not, we do ask a little of it every so often. Even a medium of professedly popular entertainment cannot quite escape that demand.

As I understand it, the first job of a critic is to stand as sensory instrument to the world of creation, and register this revelation as it comes along, and point people to it and, it may even be, do something to underline and elucidate it.

I look to register what actually moves, what hits the spectator in the midriff, what yanks him up by the hair of the head or the plain bootstraps to the plane of decent seeing. I see no reason why, because a film is made for the populace and made for money, we should exempt it from the ordinary duties of art.

But it is never a question, this criticism, of our seeing all things alike. If I am a Scotsman with origin in the Black Sabbaths of the North, my judgment is bound to be more hardbitten and even ruder on certain issues than that of an Englander. But the Englander, on the other hand, will be a far better guide to the metropolitan graces. This sort of thing you must expect from any critic. The asses' ears of particular, and sometimes indefensible, predilections, haunt even the philosopher.

Cinema is, by permission of our queer lopsided and undisciplined system of society, a very haphazard affair, the effects and achievements of which are almost always dictated by the mind of the profit-monger. To any body of men interested in the better shaping of the world, its influence is a serious matter. By romanticizing and dramatizing the issues of life, even by choosing the issues it will dramatize, it creates or crystallizes the loyalties on which people make their decisions. This, in turn, has a great deal to do with public opinions.

I do not mean that the critic must examine in every film its social implication or lack of it. It is enough if a critic is conscious of the general question and does his utmost to have the honors of life decently distributed. . . .

But as for the ordinary commercial film, it so often hides mere cheap showman's intention behind its excitement and spectacle, that the critic must stand ready at all times to pass a scalpel (or a dollop of carbolic) over it. I am not sure how much we effect by so doing, but there is one consolation. The decent intention is the only one that can be publicized, and even the most commercial showman may yet hear of it.[132]

As may be inferred from the above, Grierson's approach was a bit like American movie critics James Agee and Robert Warshow of the 1940s (more like the former than the latter) but he prefigured both. Here's some Grierson, pre-Warshow, suggesting Warshow's seminal essays on the western and the gangster film:

The world [the western] rules may be a simple world, where the principles of law are understood even by cow-punchers, and I am not sure that the technique of lying and deceit in which all of us so proudly graduate is not better suited to the particular villainies we fight, but the other has dignity.

It is this quality more than any other that the Cagney [i.e., gangster] heroes lack. They are bravos in their own way, though obviously the world has become too deep for them. The Western's straight to the mark solution for bandits and bad men has become a posturing protest . . . [in the gangster film]. I notice that our metropolitan toughs roll into action only on the more orthodox occasions. They will push a moll in the face, smack her garter a yard high, tip a drink down her blouse, and square up on all possible personal occasions.[133]

Grierson also preceded film theorist Siegfried Kracauer's *Theory of Film* in insights into the camera's capacity for redeeming physical reality:

The camera-eye is in effect a magical instrument. . . . [Its magic] lies . . . in the manner of its observation, in the strange innocence with which, in a mindtangled world, it sees things for what they are. This is not simply to say that the camera, on its single observations, is free from the trammels of the subjective, for it is patent that it will not follow the director in his enthusiasms any more than it will follow him in the wide-angled vision of his eyes. The magical fact of the camera is that it picks out what the director does not see at all, that it gives emphasis where he did not think emphasis existed.

The camera is in a measure both the discoverer of an unknown world and the re-discoverer of a lost one. There are, as everyone knows, strange moments of beauty that leap out of most ordinary news reels. It may be some accidental pose of character or some spontaneous gesture which radiates simply because it is spontaneous.[134]

He valued Alfred Hitchcock and his work for some of the same reasons the later *auteur* critics would. "A Hitchcock film is a Hitchcock film—and never a bad one—and this, if you will believe me, is an achievement of character where so many hands, grubby and otherwise, contribute to the final result of a film."[135] And a year later he wrote: "Hitchcock has a personal style of his own direction, which can be recognized. . . . He is known to have a freer hand than most in direction and to have odd thoughts of greatness. It is no wonder, therefore, if in criticism we exalt him a trifle. . . . we need strong and individual directors more than anything else. Financiers and impressarios you can buy two a penny. Directors who have something to say and the power to say it, you can only close your fingers and wish for."[136]

He was drawn to the vigorous, the lively, and the real with an ever-present sensitivity to the truly poetic. The writing is always incisive, and marvelously witty when the occasion offers; above all, it is beautifully in keeping with the spirit in which the films were produced and in which the audience responded to them. C. A. Lejeune, of the *Observer*, wrote that it was Grierson who taught her "how to look at films and see them whole; how to judge each one on its own merits; not seeking in it for some quality that was not intended to be there. He was a sharp and brilliant critic."[137]

Those judgments made on the firing line have a very high score in terms of his evaluation of the lasting qualities of the films and of the people who made them. If he was wrong anywhere by present standards, it may have been in overpraising Chaplin at Keaton's expense—but not without giving his reasons:

> When comedy is merely a matter of artificial situation and expert gags, as in the case of Harold Lloyd and, to some extent, in the case of Buster Keaton, you laugh and are done with it. They are clever fellows to work their way through such amusing scrapes, but they mean no more. Keaton shows admirably the distinction between the higher and the lower comedy. His mask is a very significant thing with its dumb registration of things felt. It might pass through life registering a heap of things most deeply felt. But it does not. In every Keaton story the action whoops in reel five to allow Buster Keaton the clown to become Mr. Keaton the romantic achiever of all things, and the fun of his face sums up nothing but a temporary pretence.[138]

Hardy makes a case for Grierson's reviews fitting into an overall strategy designed to advance the documentary cause, but their *brio* suggests as well a love of film viewing and critical writing for their own sakes—for the fun of it. He himself remarked that "A social sense is a good slave but a bad master when it comes to the measurement of art and the difference probably is a sense of humour."[139] And ten years after that, looking back over his critical writing, "It appears that I have spent my life walking a tightrope. I have been lecturing the film industry like a sociological Dutch uncle on the one hand; yet, on the other, I have done something to celebrate the basic vitalities and vulgarities of the medium, and no one,

I know, with greater native affection. I confess I have not worked out a solution to that paradox. Thanks, I imagine, to Fred Astaire and Jimmy Cagney, I am not yet old enough."[140]

After the E.M.B. period, with ever-increased responsibilities, he gradually (but very gradually—the reviews continued throughout the 1930s) confined himself to writing chiefly about documentary and its political, social, and educational ramifications, and about the problems of the British film industry generally.

## End of the E.M.B.

For a while during the summer of 1933 it appeared that Grierson's production, teaching, and leadership of the fledgling documentary movement might be discontinued—under government sponsorship at least. After the Ottawa Commonwealth Conference of 1933, the Imperial Committee on Economic Consultation and Cooperation recommended that the Empire Marketing Board be disbanded. The arguments were that, on the one hand, it had already done its job of encouraging empire trade sufficiently well, and, on the other, that the sort of public relations undertaking it represented was a luxury the government could no longer afford. Happily, just at this time Sir Kingsley Wood, who had succeeded Clement Attlee as postmaster general, was taking steps to reorganize the General Post Office and to improve its image in the eyes of the public and of its own employees. When he invited Tallents to join his staff, the latter replied that he would be happy to accept but would "come with a much better heart" if he could bring with him the E.M.B. Film Unit and the Empire Film Library. There was a certain logic to this request since the unit had already begun several films for the Post Office, under the direction of Stuart Legg, and the G.P.O. had purchased sound recording equipment to further its anticipated production. Wood agreed to take on the unit and the library, subject to Treasury consent, and Tallents became the first G.P.O. public relations officer. He recalled that he "forewent [his] summer holiday in order to get that transfer through." The Empire Marketing Board ended officially in July of 1933 (the film work was the only part of it to survive) and the G.P.O. Film Unit came into being.[141]

As far as finding harbor for the library, however, Tallents wasn't yet through the shoals. In the introduction to a new catalogue, hastily produced after his arrival at the G.P.O., he attempted to justify its operation by the Post Office. "With its pictures of life in Great Britain and in so many overseas parts of the Empire," he argued, the library "afforded the best possible setting for a special series of films depicting those postal, air mail, telegraphic and telephonic resources [all the responsibility of the G.P.O.] by which communications are maintained within the United Kingdom and between the United Kingdom and the rest of the Empire."[142] The Select Committee on Estimates remained unimpressed by his reasoning, however, and recommended against the G.P.O. maintaining a library with films unrelated to its immediate concerns. "At that point," Tallents conceded, "the library came near to being dissolved." But he appealed to Sir Harry Lindsay, who had succeeded Sir William Furse as director of the Imperial Institute, to take over the library and save it. At first Lindsay was "apprehensive," and Tallents wrote that he well remembered the lunch at which he pleaded with him to assume paternity. In the end Lindsay agreed and the E.M.B. films were permitted to live their full life of nontheatrical usefulness. They were, as already mentioned, greatly supplemented by the productions of the G.P.O. Film Unit, and then by those of the Ministry of Information after the outbreak of war.[143]

Throughout these years it was true, as Grierson repeatedly acknowledged, that "the initiative lay with Tallents. Without him we would have been driven exhausted . . . into the arms of Hollywood or into the practice of less expensive art. Tallents marked out the habitation and the place for our new teaching of citizenship and gave it a chance to expand. In relating it to the art so variously called 'cultural relations,' 'public relations,' and 'propaganda,' he joined it to one of the actual driving forces of the time and guaranteed it patronage."[144]

What, finally, had Grierson achieved under Tallents's aegis by the end of those E.M.B. years? He had taken the scattered bits and pieces of realistic cinematic possibility that existed before and around him, given it the term "documentary," provided it with a theory of education and a concept of public duty, built it as an instrument of civic revelation, and made a school and a movement out of it. He had carefully avoided what he thought to be the escapism of Flaherty, the arty-symphonics of Ruttmann, the dramatics of the Soviets. Instead he had discovered and invented simple functional forms for dealing with the workaday everyday, insisting on (1) the ordinary on the doorstep, (2) the social necessity of patterning the terms of present-day life, and (3) the semi-journalistic semi-dramatic approach to changes of the modern state. Throughout this first period, the films produced under him emphasized work, and especially workers in industry.[145]

To start a movement such as this in virgin and not altogether fertile soil was desperately difficult—constantly and nigglingly hard—and the films that resulted, it must be admitted, frequently showed the strain of bureaucratic limitations as well as of creative inexperience. In comparing the situations in Britain with those in the Soviet Union, and the resulting films, Grierson wrote, in a tone of complaint so rare for him as to be almost unique, that in Britain ". . . there was no such grouping of directors . . . and no such grouping of dramatic loyalties where the cinema of public affairs [was] concerned. Any one of us," he said, "who starts in on the job, starts in at scratch." Furthermore, "the difficulty of our art, the size and life-giving power of our art [is] ignored by the classes who have Power of the Militia (financial and all else) in this ribald State of England. We work ignominiously, half artists and half, for our living, errand-boys to the dickering doddering half-witted old Status Quo. It would take a giant in such circumstances to produce anything comparable with the Russian films (and they are fools who expect it), for there would be no public thought or public urging behind the job."[146]

Giant or no, as his early student, later friend, and always comrade-in-arms Paul Rotha pointed out, from those humble beginnings there evolved a film unit that sowed in Britain the seeds of documentary, which became that country's most important contribution to cinema as a whole. Whatever its shortcomings, the E.M.B. Film Unit was the only group outside the Soviet Union to have a real understanding of the documentary purpose, bringing "certain aspects of modern Britain to life on the screen with a sincerity and skill unapproached by any commercially operating company, at the same time bringing into existence a co-operative method of working and a spirit of loyalty which is notably absent in most other centres of film manufacture." Finally, Rotha said, "the E.M.B. also represented the first attempt to portray the working-class of Britain as a human, vital factor in present-day existence, to throw on the screen the rough labour of the industrial worker, the skill of the trained craftsman and the toil of the agricultural labourer."[147]

As to the long-range power of this propaganda which had broken free from the established requirements of the box office, let Grierson have the final word: "Quick takings are a guarantee of immediate public interest and are therefore important, but the persistence of a film's effect over a period of years is more important still. To command, and cumulatively command, the mind of a generation is more important than by novelty or sensation to knock a Saturday night audience cold; and the 'hang-over' effect of a film is everything."[148]

# 4 ⇻ GENERAL POST OFFICE FILM UNIT (1933–37)

## Mandate

If the Empire Marketing Board had been the launching pad of British documentary, the General Post Office would serve as a substantial refueling station in the newly expanded space. By July of 1933, though documentary was still a relatively small and uncertain impulse, members of the E.M.B. unit already had made films, under Grierson's guidance, for several other government departments and a number of businesses and industries. But it was vital that the seminal government unit continue as clearinghouse for documentary theory, training school for documentary practice, and laboratory for increasing experimentation.[1] Grierson himself felt that

> With our new found relationship between film making and public affairs, there were so many fields open to us beyond the E.M.B. that the disappointment [over its demise] could only be momentary. The first one that offered itself was the G.P.O. We grasped it eagerly, for the story of communications was as good as any other and in one sense it was better. When the E.M.B. Film Unit was invited to go with Tallents to the Post Office—or Tallents insisted on it—we had at least the assurance of imaginative backing.[2]

After the grandeurs of empire, however, the subject matter presented by the post office seemed limiting to the point of discourage-

74

ment. "One remembers looking at a sorting office for the first time and thinking that when you had seen one letter you had seen the lot," wrote Grierson.[3] Even before he arrived, however, the G.P.O. had been taking steps to expand and enliven its public relations practices. In 1931, with Clement Attlee still postmaster general, a Telephone Publicity Committee had been appointed, which Tallents sat on during his E.M.B. days. But the problems of the G.P.O. differed from those of the E.M.B. As Tallents saw it, the need now was ". . . to bring alive, to the eyes of the public and its own staff, an immense organisation."[4]

Though Tallents had been a bit apprehensive about a possible collision between the "rather unorthodox Film Unit and staffs deep-dyed in the Post Office tradition,"[5] the chief difficulties arose from the outside. In those beginning G.P.O. days, the unit was still a modest enough enterprise. Its staff in February of 1934 numbered eighteen and its expenditures for the first six months at the G.P.O. had totaled £4,219 5s. Still, filmmaking continued to be regarded in some important quarters as a hardly respectable way for the Treasury to use public funds. Later, after he had left the G.P.O., Grierson wrote that "obstacle after obstacle was put in the way of the documentary film whenever it set itself to the adult task of performing a public service. Sometimes it came in the cry of the Censor that the screen was to be kept free of what was called 'controversy'. More often it was in the whispered obstruction emanating from Conservative Party politicians."[6] And the film trade attacked more openly, on grounds of unfair competition to private enterprise and inefficient expenditure of government money.

A manifestation of this obstruction and criticism would officially limit the mandate of the filmmakers within their first year at the G.P.O. Witnesses of the Film Industries Department of the Federation of British Industries stated, before the 1934 Select Committee on Estimates, that the industry objected in principle to the making and distribution of films by government departments. They objected particularly to the activities of the post office in making and distributing educational and instructional films and in giving advice to other government and public and semi-public bodies.[7] Though Tallents and Grierson provided figures to show that the post office was producing films no more expensively than commercial firms, the committee reported on July 2 that they were not convinced that all expenditures incurred by the post office had been included in its figures. They recommended that, without wishing to restrict what they conceived to be the legitimate activities of the post office for increasing its business, the policy for the film unit should be confined within the limits of advertising post office services and, if so determined by Parliament, to the technical instruction of post office staff.[8]

## Expansion in Technique and Staff

While pushed a step backward on the field of policy, on the technical and aesthetic side the unit was able to surge ahead in that summer of 1934. It had acquired a new headquarters at 21 Soho Square and, just recently and much more importantly, its first studio in a ramshackle building at Blackheath, in southeast London. Basil Wright became the first studio manager. There they installed a sound recording system which, Tallents remarked, would have been of much better quality if they hadn't had to consider "the parsimonies of government."[9] In any case, the unit which had started with one young filmmaker who had admittedly made its first silent film "without knowing one lens from another,"[10] was now not only trained but minimally equipped to take on all comers.

That summer, in a piece exuberantly entitled "The G.P.O. Gets Sound," Grierson wrote:

> We waited five years for sound at the E.M.B. We saw our first film fall in the gulf between silence and sound, and our subsequent films pile up in silence on a fading market. Our solitary access to sound last year was bound to be a disappointing one, for . . . we were reduced to attendant orchestra and attendant commentator. Under such conditions responsibility passed out of our hands and experiment was plainly impossible. The result—in *Industrial Britain, O'er Hill and Dale, Up-Stream* and the others—was, I suppose, competent. From any considered point of view it represented no contribution whatever to the art and practice of sound.[11]

It wasn't until the acquisition of the Blackheath studio that sound began to play an important part in their films.

The cadre of E.M.B. veterans would be augmented in numbers and advanced in distinction during Grierson's four years at the G.P.O. It was in 1934 that one of the most important of these recruits, Alberto Cavalcanti, came to fill the sort of position Flaherty had for a time occupied as principal teacher and inspirer alongside

Grierson. Stuart Legg jokingly suggested that Grierson invited Cavalcanti over to have someone his own age and with comparable sophistication to talk with—that all his co-workers were younger and he himself had taught them whatever they knew.[12] Cavalcanti would have been thirty-seven to Grierson's thirty-six when he arrived. Born in Rio de Janeiro, educated in Geneva, Cavalcanti had been working in Paris since the early twenties. He made a living from commercial features—first as art director (e.g., *The Late Matthew Pascal* [1924]) and then as director (e.g., *Le Capitaine Fracasse* [1928])—and made a name as producer-director in the avant-garde (e.g., *Rien que les heures* [1926], *En rade* [1927]). Whereas Flaherty's contribution had been along the lines of the interpretive power of the camera and of putting ordinary people onto the screen, Cavalcanti was responsible for inspiring a great deal of the technical experimentation, particularly in the use of sound, which would mark the G.P.O. films. "His technical virtuosity [was] great, and everyone profited and [was] grateful for his skill as a craftsman, critic and teacher," said Arthur Elton.[13] Usually he signed himself somewhat imperiously on the screen as "Cavalcanti," like a French painter, but his colleagues called him "Cav." Hired as a "guest producer," he stayed on at the unit after Grierson left until 1940, when he joined Ealing Studios as director and producer.

R. H. (Harry) Watt, though he had joined the unit during the late days of the E.M.B., as earlier noted, became a star at the G.P.O. After a year and a half as an assistant at E.M.B.–G.P.O., he made *Radio Interference*, a simple and successful instructional film, and went on to the major work that will be discussed later.[14] He also directed a number of English items for the American "The March of Time" series and, like Cavalcanti, he later turned to Ealing and features. *Nine Men*, the first of these, which he wrote and directed in 1942, brought to the studios the kind of story-documentary he had pioneered first at the G.P.O. (*The Saving of Bill Blewitt* [1936], and *North Sea* [1938]) and then at Crown (*Target for Tonight* [1941]). (Incidentally, the great Danish feature director Carl Dreyer, who also had a considerable documentary output to his name, came over to help on the script of *North Sea* in its early stages, though his contributions were slight and he received no screen credit.)[15] Of *Nine Men*—and Watt, and Grierson—Lejeune observed "Harry Watt was trained by John Grierson and when Grierson trains anyone they stay trained."[16]

Len Lye originated the animation technique of painting directly on film that another Grierson protégé, Norman McLaren, continued to perfect at the National Film Board of Canada. (McLaren, though he too began at the G.P.O., worked initially on live-action films rather than animation. He was first apprenticed to Evelyn Spice as cutting assistant and assistant director, under Cavalcanti's supervision.) Lye was born in Christchurch, New Zealand, in 1901. In 1928 he came to London with a friend, a musician and expert on jazz—Lye also loved jazz. Together they made *Tusilava* in 1929, "an abstract film which few people saw and fewer remember," but which must have been the first film ever to be made by drawing directly on celluloid.[17] During the early thirties his paintings were exhibited, at the Seven and Five Society at the Leicester Galleries for example, though Cavalcanti, for one, admitted liking Lye's films better than his paintings. At any rate, it was in 1935, Cavalcanti recalled, "that Len Lye came to see us and said that he wanted to make a film without a camera. It took a lot of his personal charm to make us listen to him, but when he had explained what he wanted to do, both Grierson and myself were convinced that he could do it. Grierson, that King of Showmen, wouldn't miss this opportunity. Furthermore, it sounded frightfully simple."[18] It took some effort on Grierson's part, however, to mold both the inflexibilities of the Savings Bank and Lye's artistic aspirations so that each could contribute to the joint affair which culminated in *Colour Box* and the series of brief abstract delights to be discussed.

Humphrey Jennings, whose great achievements would come during the years of World War II, joined the G.P.O. unit in 1934. He had been born in Suffolk in 1907, educated at Perse School and, like Wright, Elton, and Legg, Cambridge University (Pembroke College). Before and while making films he was also a surrealist painter. Elton recalled that Jennings's first film at the G.P.O.—not listed in most filmographies of his work—was a short one on the history of railways.[19] Grierson evidently viewed Jennings's particular combination of English intellectual distinction and aesthetic sensibility with some wariness. Gerald Noxon, who worked on distribution at the G.P.O. along with Thomas Baird, told a story of Grierson with visitors at Blackheath while Jennings was in production. After showing them part of the premises, Grierson said, "Now let's go back and see Humphrey being good with the common people."[20] It may not be merely coincidental that his ascendancy occurred after Grierson's departure; Jennings's great strengths would, in any case, be quite different from Grierson's.

Raymond Spottiswoode, who had written *A Grammar of the Film*, published in 1935 when he was just out of Oxford, also came on at the G.P.O. Grierson had read that important book of exalted theory and minute classification (had reviewed it severely, in fact)[21] and ordained, as a result, that Spottiswoode should begin his training as a tea boy. After six months Grierson felt he still wasn't humble enough.[22] Spottiswoode would continue to work with Grierson at the Film Board in Ottawa and at the World Today in New York City.

Alexander Shaw, born in 1910, had started work at the E.M.B. and continued on at the G.P.O. He would have an important career as a director and producer in the main English units, and especially as a sort of international missionary for documentary. Pat Jackson, born in London in 1916, joined the unit in 1936. Before switching to features, he was in documentary for a good many years as an editor then director. In 1937 he codirected *Big Money* with Harry Watt. J. B. (Jack) Holmes, born at Bickley, Kent, in 1901, stayed on as head of the unit, with Cavalcanti as chief producer, after Grierson left. Before that he had directed some important educational films for Gaumont-British Instructional (e.g., *The Mine* [1935], and *Medieval Village* [1936]). *The Islanders* (1939) was one of his films for the G.P.O. Winifred Holmes, his wife, had been born in London and educated in India, England, and Australia. Formerly interested in education, she entered films by writing the commentary for *Cover to Cover*, directed by Alexander Shaw at Strand in 1936, and then worked in various capacities at the G.P.O. Ralph Bond, director and producer, was born in London in 1904. In 1928 he founded Atlas Film Company to import and distribute Continental productions and organized film societies in London and provincial towns. He had joined the E.M.B. in 1931, working first as a unit production manager and then as director. At the G.P.O. he produced and directed. Max Anderson, educated at Sloane School, Chelsea, and Cambridge, was twenty-two when he joined the unit in 1936. He became a director and remained there until 1940, when he joined Realist Film Unit.

Grierson also recruited outside filmmakers and would-be filmmakers, most notably among musicians. Music is an important part of certain documentary styles—for instance, the epic and the lyric. Composers have fewer limitations placed on them by the documentary form than by the plot and dialogue of feature films; and they work in greater equality with the other creative members of the crew. As a result, many composers of front rank have been attracted to documentaries—especially in Britain. By 1935 Walter Leigh and Clarence Raybould had already composed documentary scores. Leigh would become a principal contributor, in a dozen or more films, to the experimentation being conducted at Blackheath with sounds (including some new noises he created himself) as well as music. The last two scores he composed before he volunteered for the Tank Corps were for Rotha's *The Fourth Estate* and G.P.O.'s *Squadron 992* (both 1940). He was killed in action during the Germans' last push for Alexandria.

In 1936 Benjamin Britten, twenty-three years old and at the beginning of his career, joined the staff of the G.P.O. to score *Coal Face* and *Night Mail* and many subsequent post office pictures. Britten had been born in Lowestoft (where *Drifters* was shot) and educated at Gresham's School, Norfolk, and the Royal College of Music. Other scores of his for the G.P.O. during Grierson's period included *The Calendar of the Year*, *The Saving of Bill Blewitt*, and *The Tocher*. In 1937 he wrote the score for his first feature, *Love from a Stranger*.

William Alwyn, born in Northampton in 1905, had studied at the Royal Academy of Music. His first film music was composed in 1936, too. Years later he wrote:

> What days they were. . . . the cutting-rooms were alive with new sounds and strange noises. My own career in documentary began by blowing a flute in the odd little orchestras that gathered for recording, but soon I was busy, stop-watch in hand, scribbling, conducting and playing— and always stimulated—stimulated by new ideas; a new approach; always the search for something new. We did not want the large lush orchestra of the feature film and in any case we could not afford it; we had to rely on our modest resources, which meant experiment, experiment and again experiment.[23]

His first score was for *The Future's in the Air* (produced for the Strand Film Company by Rotha and directed by Alexander Shaw). For the G.P.O. he scored *Wings Over Empire*, and he continued to be one of Britain's most prolific composers for documentaries and features.

It is worth noting, as Rotha did, that the British documentary movement "led the way in using outstanding composers"—Sir Arnold Bax, Alan Rawsthorne, Vaughan Williams, Clifton Parker, and Brian Easdale he adds to the above-named—"all of whom *subsequently* worked on feature films."[24] The brilliant young Maurice Jaubert, who composed scores for many of the most famous of the French features of its "Golden Age" in the late 1930s and was killed fighting in 1940 when the Germans invaded France, was also invited over.

As for the other arts, Grierson had his eye on the poets as well. Wystan Hugh Auden joined the unit as a script writer in 1935—he would have been twenty-eight years old. Born in York, he had attended Christ Church College, Oxford, after which he taught school. He wrote the verse featured in *Coal Face*, *Night Mail*, *The Way to the Sea*, *The Londoners*, and many others. (Later Dylan Thomas worked as a script writer for documentaries during the war, *New Towns for Old* [1942], *These Are the Men* [1942], *Wales—Green Mountain, Black Mountain* [1942], *Our Country* [1944].) J. B. Priestley, the novelist, wrote much of the script for the film on international communications which eventually became *We Live in Two Worlds* (1937). And the artist William Coldstream (subsequently head of the Slade School of Art and chairman of the Board of Governors of the British Film Institute) was one of the workers at the G.P.O., his painter's eye and individual sense of humor evident in *The Fairy on the 'Phone* (1935), for example. John Skeaping, the sculptor, had also served since first building a set for *Drifters*.

It may have seemed less remarkable than it does now that Grierson should be able to bring into his unit those young men already clearly destined to make their reputations in other fields, especially since the production method called for collectivity and anonymity in the public service. Grierson was firmly of the opinion that "only an idiot will pretend of any film that he has been the 'onlie begetter'. The creative force lies in the unity, and those personal credits which flutter across the opening of a film, though they may comfort the wives and mothers of the individual filmmakers, give no picture of the process. I never saw a good film happen except that three or four heads were devoted commonly to it, with personal nonsense out. I never saw personal nonsense come in and a film prosper."[25]

## Production

Before joining the G.P.O., Raymond Spottiswoode observed that "Production in this unit is co-operative: that is to say, a great part of its personnel is engaged upon each stage, preparing the script, shooting the material and cutting sight and sound to make the final film." He added, however: "Thus Mr. Grierson's work informs not only each production, but every part of each; and it is much more misleading in this unit to credit the director with the whole excellence of a good film than in the majority of . . . instances. . . . The example of Soviet Russia has been followed in making the director *primus inter pares*, a leader among colleagues instead of a personality dominating the actions of a number of assistants."[26]

Stuart Legg confirmed Spottiswoode's impression of Grierson's omnipresent influence,[27] but there is also considerable evidence of the freedom and control offered to particularly gifted directors. Grierson himself wrote: "only one thing gives the producer importance: the fact that he makes directors and, through directors, makes art. It is the only thing worth an artist's making: money not excepted."[28] And elsewhere he wrote: "The documentary idea, after all, demands no more than that the affairs of our time shall be brought to the screen in any fashion which strikes the imagination and makes observation a little richer than it was. At one level, the vision may be journalistic, at another it may rise to poetry and drama. At another level again, its aesthetic quality may lie in the mere lucidity of its exposition."[29] The degree of Grierson's involvement with any given film seemed to depend largely on the strategic importance he placed on the project and his own feelings of affinity for its subject and style—plus, of course, the number of other productions he was overseeing at the time.

The experimental quality of much of the G.P.O. production is not suggested by bald explanations of its working methods. Though not individual creation to the extent of the French avant-garde of the 1920s (the loyalty and selflessness of group effort was part of the British documentary ethos), it was unlike the commercial studios with their extreme departmentalization. The expense and complexity of sound, anyway, had ended the possibility of the young painter or poet borrowing a camera and making his cine-poem or his painting in motion. Also, the attention given art for the sake of art had shifted to a concern with art for society's sake. While conceding that documentaries represented a "runaway from the synthetic world of contemporary cinema," Grierson also recalled it as

a reaction from the art world of the early and middle twenties—Bloomsbury, Left Bank, T. S. Eliot, Clive Bell and all—by people with every reason to know it well. Likewise, if it was a return to "reality" it was a return not unconnected with Clydeside movements, I.L.P.'s, the Great Depression. . . . Documentary was born and nurtured on the bandwagon of uprising social democracy everywhere: in Western Europe and the United States, as well as in Britain. That is to say, it had an uprising majority social movement, which is to say a logical sponsorship of public money, behind it.[30]

Cavalcanti supplied a unique symbolic link between the avant-garde of the twenties and documentary of the thirties in opting for that public money. His former French colleagues either retreated to the commercial cinema (René Clair, Luis Buñuel, Jean Vigo) or returned to "the practice of less expensive art" (Man Ray, Fernand Leger, Salvador Dali) as Grierson had foreseen. Cavalcanti, perhaps, was able to advance most freely their earlier absorption with the film experiment by putting his artistic technique to new social uses.

"Within the G.P.O. Unit 'experiment' was the watchword," wrote Roger Manvell, and added that that word "acted like magic in the mid-thirties. You were just nowhere if the film you had just made or the film you were planning was not an experiment in something."[31] The formal experimentation moved along three main lines, represented by the preoccupations of Cavalcanti, Lye, and Watt already alluded to: sound, animation, story and characterization. During the years 1933–37 there was also movement away from the simple description of work and workers to a broader sociological analysis of the underlying and surrounding human conditions. This latter tendency would often have a chance to work itself out more fully in the increasing production being industrially sponsored than in the government unit itself, which in part accounted for Grierson's decision to withdraw from government service in 1937.

At the G.P.O. veterans of the E.M.B. were first into the field, of course. In fact, Legg had directed his series for the post office while the unit was still at the Board in 1932–33: *The New Operator, Telephone Workers, The Coming of the Dial*, and *Telephone Service*. Of these, the middle two (three reels and two reels, respectively) were regarded as the most important. More notable, however, was Legg's and Shaw's *Cable Ship* (1933). By using the voices of the workers themselves to describe their jobs, it may be said to have begun the experimentation with sound. (Rotha wrote that Arthur Elton's *The Voice of the World*, also of 1933, was "the first documentary, at any rate in Britain, which used sound at all imaginatively.")[32] Legg's

*B.B.C.—The Voice of Britain*, started in 1934 and completed in 1935, was even more ambitious: a short feature at five reels. It was awarded a medal of honor at the International Film Festival held during the Brussels Exhibition of 1935.

Of Legg's work during this period, Raymond Spottiswoode wrote that it was "marked by a scrupulous attention to camera angle, which, when it does not wholly fix the mind on qualities of pure design, conveys a very precise and powerful sense of atmosphere. It leads also to a concentration on static effects which might not appeal to a public educated in the rush and movement of the American cinema."[33] Anstey later added a note about this static quality, a general characteristic of the early E.M.B.–G.P.O. productions. "It will be observed," he wrote,

> that most of the film-makers whose work we admired in 1930 [he has cited Ruttmann, Cavalcanti, Eisenstein, Pudovkin, Dziga Vertov, Kuleshov, and Turin] tended to be concerned with composition within the static frame and with creation by 'montage' at the editing bench. Form was everything. Narrative was merely an aspect of the form in which the visuals were composed—visuals which might be stylized almost to the point of abstraction.
>
> Grierson made an absolute rule that no scene was ever to be photographed except from a tripod. More than that, it was only after Flaherty had joined the unit to make *Industrial Britain* . . . that movement of the camera on a tripod head was accepted as a permissable technique (the smooth, slow, *revealing* pan or tilt). In viewing rushes—always a frightening occasion, for Grierson would speak vigorously and with a healthy disregard for our artistic sensitivities—scenes were individually and ruthlessly assessed with little regard to their relation to the line of the film, let alone to the script—if any existed.[34]

As for Legg's use of sound, even in those early films Spottiswoode observed that he had "experimented successfully with speech which, starting from an alliance with the speaker, continues over a divergent picture and imparts a greater openness as well as a greater contrastive force to a basically orthodox system of dialogue."[35] The qualities Spottiswoode singled out, particularly Legg's play with word in relation to picture, would also mark his later, highly successful "The World in Action" series, made at the National Film Board of Canada during the war.

*Under the City* (1934), another of the early sound films, was directed by Alexander Shaw under Elton's guidance. The same team made *Airmail* in 1935. *Weather Forecast,* of 1934, was Evelyn Spice's most considerable achievement. Around a well-defined central event—the prediction and eventual onset of a storm—she ingeniously arranged the accessory phenomena of meteorology, the telegraph, and the telephone.[36] In this "symphonic" form, sounds associated with the gathering storm are used contrapuntally. It was shown at the (London) Film Society and became the most famous of the 1934 group of G.P.O. films. It was long afterwards distributed in the United States by the Museum of Modern Art Film Library.

Basil Wright in 1934 completed what, along with *Granton Trawler* and *Night Mail,* is the loveliest and most enduring of all the E.M.B.–G.P.O. films: *The Song of Ceylon.* It was one of a series sponsored by the Ceylon Tea Propaganda Board. Wright got this commission partly because of his E.M.B. West Indian experience making *Cargo from Jamaica* and *Windmill in Barbados.* He was said to have taken the assignment so seriously that "one doubts if a director ever went better equipped in knowledge of the region he was to visit."[37] Accompanying him as production assistant was the young John Taylor, just finished with his work on *Man of Aran.* Taylor took a remarkable set of production stills of Ceylon (with a superbly equipped Leica Flaherty had given him after Aran),[38] but the lyrically beautiful cinematography is almost entirely Wright's. On his return he was assisted by Cavalcanti and, especially, by the composer Walter Leigh—the sound track is unquestionably Leigh's finest film work. Grierson produced, of course. Running approximately thirty-five minutes, it was first shown to the Film Society.

Its theme is the contrast between contemporary Singhalese life and what it was before "civilization"—or, more precisely put, the survival of a traditional way of life side by side with the modern complexity of commerce and labor[39]—which is conveyed by a mounting counterpoint between what is heard and what is seen. On the track there is the use of market-price quotations against scenes of tea-gathering and transport, temple gongs rising to an almost unbearable climax of sound, Singhalese poetry, and commentary from a book on Ceylon written by a Scottish traveler in 1680.[40] It carried off first prize as the best documentary at the Brussels Festival and the *Prix du Gouvernment Belge* as well. Graham Greene, then a film critic, wrote that it was "possibly the greatest British-produced film in any category up to 1935, and for sustained beauty probably unequalled anywhere outside Russia."[41] A decade after its release,

*Time* magazine described it as "extraordinarily beautiful": "The film bears about the same relation to ordinary travelogues that Keats's *Ode on a Grecian Urn* bears to a cheap pottery catalogue . . ."[42] It is still in wide and active distribution.

Wright went on to codirect with Harry Watt the second G.P.O. masterwork, *Night Mail*, the following year. Camera was by Jonah Jones and H. E. Fowle, sound by Cavalcanti, verse by Auden, music by Britten; it was produced for the G.P.O. by Grierson. The script was Wright's, "though the shooting detail of Watt was out of his rough, rich self, and the cutting was Wright's though Cavalcanti in a burst of inventive quality gave it its sound line."[43] One of the most effective and innovative aspects of the film is the verse by Auden, much of which had been planned to match the rhythm of the mail train and was spoken by Legg, up to the moving culmination read by Grierson himself.[44] Twenty minutes in length, it followed the nightly run of the Postal Special from London to Glasgow. Watt's handling of people here becomes more than surface description— as exemplified by his treatment of the young trainee and the short sequences of postsynchronized dialogue from workers on the train— and starts a development in his work that will be discussed later. It is a film that has been universally liked by all kinds of audiences and is so generally known and readily available that not much more need be written about it here.

Years after its release Grierson was told by a Yugoslav filmmaker that he had been part of a group of partisans who discovered a 35 mm print of it left by the retreating Germans. Since the partisans had no projector, they sat on the ground and viewed it by hand, just as Grierson had studied the Soviet films frame by frame to understand their technique. In some small way this was the beginning of a distinguished Yugoslavian documentary movement, thought Grierson.[45] *Night Mail* and the earlier *Coalface* were called by Roger Manvell

> the last great films of . . . industrial romanticism. Grierson described *Night Mail* . . . as a kick in the belly. He was a philosopher and preferred *Coalface*. The public, and there was a public by now, preferred, however, to take the kick. What Wright had done for East and West in Ceylon, Watt with Wright to help him, did on a lesser scale for the G.P.O. and the railway. . . . It stood to the public as *Drifters* did to the documentary directors themselves. They saw the light where hitherto had been some darkness.[46]

Watt had earlier directed *6:30 Collection* (1934) with Anstey, a film about the G.P.O.'s West End sorting office. It was Anstey's, and possibly the unit's, first use of sound recording equipment on location. He recalled their being "more interested in sounds than in speech. We turned our ears to every machine, to every audible process, hoping to isolate sounds which would communicate the essence of our subject-matter. We were not interested in recording dialogue or commentary, both of which we regarded as non-filmic."[47] Grierson acknowledged that it was "probably the first documentary made entirely with authentic sound."[48]

*B.B.C.—Droitwich*, Watt's next film, a one-and-a-half reeler, was completed in 1935. Of it, Spottiswoode wrote that it was "valuable as a faithful as well as an imaginative record of the construction of a giant broadcasting station, from the choice of the site to the issue of the first programme."[49] *The Saving of Bill Blewitt* (1937), directed by Watt, followed *Night Mail* and will be discussed later.

Cavalcanti, while assisting importantly on most of the unit's production, also had films for which he was mainly responsible. *Coalface* (1935) was the second and perhaps most important of these. (*Pett and Pott* [1934], the first, will be discussed later.) The crew was a distinguished one and much the same as *Night Mail's*, which were: producer, John Grierson; direction and script, Alberto Cavalcanti; editing, William Coldstream; music, Benjamin Britten; verse, W. H. Auden.[50] In it they used the sound track in a new way, a way which was to be developed with even greater success in *Night Mail*. It was, wrote Manvell, "an oratorio of mining." He added, however, that "oratorios are not popular with film-goers. The visuals were good but not exceptional. What mattered was the sound."[51] Orchestra, chorus, and natural sound were cut rhythmically in counterpoint with the images. For the track Auden wrote a poem, which was sung by female voices on the return of the miners to the surface; choral chants were set to the score by Britten. Anstey suggested that it anticipated Britten's later operatic work, in *Peter Grimes*, for example. It won a medal of honor at the Brussels Festival. The film has been out of general circulation for some time, but, in the same article, Anstey reported that a later viewing showed it to be "remarkably undated."[52]

Cavalcanti exerted artistic control over five films the G.P.O. Film Unit coproduced with Pro Telephon, Zürich, in 1937: *Message from Geneva, Line to Tschierva Hut, We Live in Two Worlds, Four Bar-*

*riers*, and *Men of the Alps*. The creative personnel were largely the same for all five; that is, Grierson as producer, Cavalcanti as director, John Taylor as cinematographer. J. B. Priestley wrote the script for and narrated one of them; Maurice Jaubert, the eminent French film composer, conceived the music for a couple of them. About two of this series Rotha observed: "Of all the films of this period . . . *We Live in Two Worlds*, was perhaps the most technically mature. With its by-product, *Line to Tschierva Hut*, it was a model of shooting, editing and imaginative use of sound. Both films require several viewings to appreciate their subtle technique, which, at first sight, appears so simple."[53]

For a summary of the experimentation with sound, which had Cavalcanti at its center, let Anstey offer a final bit of insight and tribute. "It was not entirely because we seldom worked with synchronous equipment that we thought from the first in terms of the free use of sound. The slavish linking of sound with its actually correspondent picture seemed quite unnecessary to those of us who had followed—sometimes rather enviously—the B.B.C.'s experiments in radio documentary. We had also in the mid-thirties the advice, indeed the inspiration of Alberto Cavalcanti."[54]

Meanwhile, Len Lye was pursuing his own experimental way in animation. It was here that the freedom for technical experiment at the G.P.O. was illustrated most strikingly. *Colour Box* (1935), as already mentioned, was the first in the series, a painting directly on film. Synchronization of sight and sound was done by Jack Ellit, as it would be on most of Lye's animated films; it ran three minutes. Of it Paul Nash wrote, "Len Lye conceives colour film as a direct vehicle for colour sensation. . . . I consider *Colour Box* to be a unique achievement, neat and finished. It was made by painting literally to music. The features of the musical form [a beguine] dictated, more or less, the pattern of the colour arabesque."[55] Cavalcanti, for his part, said, "To me *Colour Box* is a very important film, not only because of its successful use of colour, but also because it is a demonstration of the rhythm created on the screen by the succession of lines composing each individual image or frame, or each group of frames."[56] It was shown at the Brussels Exhibition, along with the G.P.O. documentaries, but, since "It could be accommodated in no category . . . one was made to fit it and it was awarded a special prize."[57]

*Kaleidoscope* (1935) followed, using the same technique. It was made outside the G.P.O. unit, for P.W.P. Productions, and was sponsored by Churchman Cigarettes. The music, "Beguine d'Amour," was played by Don Baretto and his Cuban Orchestra. It was shown at the Film Society on October 27. On Lye's next film, *Birth of a Robot*, begun in 1935 but released in 1936, he was back at the G.P.O. and working with Humphrey Jennings. In it they attempted, apparently without great success, to use puppets.

In *Rainbow Dance* (1936), Lye tackled the human figure and produced what was perhaps the first essay into film-ballet.[58] Rupert Doone was the dancer. "The amount of technical knowledge of colour shown in this film," wrote Cavalcanti, "and in [Lye's] next, *Trade Tattoo* (1937), is formidable."[59] Music was by Rico's Creole Band and the color process, as it had been for the others, was the primitive Gasparcolor, which preceded three-color Technicolor. Both *Colour Box* and *Rainbow Dance* publicized the G.P.O. Savings Bank; *Trade Tattoo* inter-dominion trade. In *Rainbow Dance* and *Trade Tattoo*, especially, Lye experimented not only with abstract patterns but also with the application of artificial color to subjects originally photographed in black and white.[60]

*N. or N.W.* (1937) was Lye's first direction of a documentary. It warned the public of the risks of addressing letters inadequately. From then on and during the war Lye worked largely in live action and black and white. He was hired by March of Time and left for America in 1944.

As Cavalcanti has summarized Lye's achievements, "Perhaps the greatest . . . experiments were with colour. But rhythm came very close nearby. And there were many other items such as camera angles, and a very personal way of pursuing pure filmic expression."[61] What is extraordinary about this experimentation and "pure filmic expression," apart from the landmark creative contributions represented and a joyousness as infectious today as it was in the mid-thirties, is that it began and continued under a roof of the staid British civil service. "It was not," as Elton pointed out, "until Len Lye had an opportunity to use his great talents for public information that he made films of real experimental or artistic value."[62]

In addition to the animation work at the G.P.O., there were at least two attempts at nonrealistic comedy. Not particularly successful in themselves they at least widened the scope of experimentation and revealed a substratum impulse to enliven documentary's sobriety and warm up its austerity—an impulse which would not begin to come successfully into the open until the story-documentary developments of Grierson's last eighteen months at the unit. A comic fantasy was, in fact, Cavalcanti's initial directorial assignment after his arrival in England, an at least partially white elephant named *Pett and Pott* (1934). Of it Tallents wrote, "I forget its story, but not the disappointment with which I saw on my first view of it the fruits of much hectic overtime work by its producers."[63] What Tallents was gently hinting was that this experiment, as well as being inconclusive (at best), was expensive. Because of the resources poured into the film, Grierson always defended it publicly and privately, and presented it at its first press screening as a masterpiece.[64] He himself rushed into print, pointing to the complex intertwining of image and sound (which Cavalcanti had composed first, cutting the picture to it). Grierson's position was that *Pett and Pott* must be "regarded as of historic importance in the development of sound film."

> For certainly no sound film before depended so little on stage example. The music was written to create the mood of the theme. The sound strip invaded the silent strip and turned a woman's cry into an engine whistle. Recitative was used in the train scene instead of the usual sound of the wheels on the rail. The film illustrated how a commentator—a voice of God in the last instance—might be used effectively even in a story film. Other effects included the joining of a drum and fife band with a domestic quarrel, and the film showed the dramatic point that can be achieved by cutting from one sound sequence to another.[65]

He even managed to enlist some support from Herbert Read (Sir Herbert later), the distinguished author and critic, who wrote that "this new counterpoint of sight and sound may lead to a completely new kind of film."[66] Its newness may have been unarguable, but Tallents regarded it as a "curious film" and a vagary,[67] and Elton, flatly, as a failure.[68]

Apparently more successful, if slight, was another humorous fantasy, *The Daily Round* (1937). Directed by Richard Massingham and using an actor, it dealt with a country postman's sorrows and joys. Rather than comedy, however, it was drama that would bring the documentary a warmth and intensity, and new and larger audiences, in a hybrid form called, somewhat helplessly, the semi-documentary.

Anstey, thinking back on the prevailing technique and resultant style of the documentaries up to the mid-thirties, wrote:

> whilst our films were often artistically satisfying as compositions (more akin to music than to literature) they had little to say about the people who appeared in them. Characterisation was formal and heroic in the early Soviet manner. The worker would be shown magnificent against the sky from a low angle, symbolising proletarian virtue. Sometimes there might be a little humour but characterisation was never more than skin deep.
>
> It is, of course, true that Flaherty had reminded us that a warmer and more intimate representation was possible. At the same time we remained wary of romanticism which might lead to sentimentality, the gravest sin of all.[69]

And in certain ways a line of development from 1936 on, pursued most resolutely by Harry Watt, represented a return to Flaherty. From *Night Mail*'s suggestion of melodrama (Will the Hollyhead arrive in time for the Postal Special?), characterization and mild humor among the men in the sorting-car, and an overall chronological (i.e., narrative) line, Watt moved on to *The Saving of Bill Blewitt* (1937). Here clearly was a new type of story film, set in a Cornish fishing village and using real fisher-people in their own characters. Furthermore, and this is the difficult part in terms of sound technology and directorial technique, natural direct-recorded speech was substituted for the postsynchronized voice-over commentator. Not that the film was a complete success: it suffered from its partial strength. Rotha wrote of it that, though it was the best handling of natural actors up to that time, "the plugged publicity angle of the Savings Bank was so incongruous beside the honesty of the people themselves that despite its subtle introduction, the audience was resentful at being fooled. For all the natural quality of the acting and the technical skill of Cavalcanti and Harry Watt's production, the film never got beyond being a publicity film as did *Night Mail* and *The Song of Ceylon*."[70]

*North Sea* (1938), again with Watt directing and Cavalcanti producing, was more nearly a total success. It took story and characterization a step further, with a dialogue script written around and for a group of people working in the ship-to-shore radio service and the crew of a trawler experiencing difficulties in a gale off the east coast of Scotland. Of it Rotha wrote at the time:

Whereas two years ago it would have been a film primarily about a storm, today it is a film primarily about human beings and their reactions in a moment of emergency. Acted throughout by real people, it is a remarkable example of how ordinary persons can be directed for the screen. So natural are these fishermen and their families and the radio-operators at the Wick Radio Station that it is difficult to imagine professional actors doing the job better or even as well. Like a director of a feature story-film, Mr. Watt made "tests" of his "actors", used careful discrimination in "casting" and recruited some of his players from the local Employment Exchange. Not all the characters played their real parts. The skipper of the *John Gillman*, for example, is played by the bosun; the skipper's "wife" by the wife of a local baker. Thus, although the main incident of the film is based on fact, the characters and details are wholly fictional. As in a story-film, dialogue is used throughout. The ubiquitous commentary of many documentary films is happily relegated to a twenty-word sentence at the end.

*North Sea* may well claim to be considered as the most progressive step in British documentary films since Basil Wright, Watt and Cavalcanti made their by-now internationally famous . . . *Night Mail*, in 1936. It would be wrong, however, to estimate *North Sea* in terms of documentary perspective alone. By its fictional element as well as by its characterization and in spite of its relatively small cost of production, it claims to be measured against the story-films of the studios. Its place of showing should be the cinemas, not the lecture-halls of the country.[71]

Rotha's assessment of the importance of the production method and emergent narrative/dramatic form of *North Sea* was exact. It would lead directly to Watt's *Target for Tonight* (1941), that remarkable prototype for the cycle of wartime feature-length semi-documentaries that fitted so naturally into the beginning-middle-end and conflict inherent in military action. Grierson was perhaps less interested in this development of narrative than were Cavalcanti and Watt, as he was less interested in lyrical screen poetry than was Jennings. He may well have regarded both as somewhat "aestheticky"—his own wartime work in Canada was determinedly journalistic. The expository was the mode of expression he tended to insist on (and perhaps felt most at home in, judging from the relative lack of success of his feature productions at the ill-fated Group 3 years later). Given his own social-aesthetic formulations he would have seen, too, that the story form (increasingly attractive to Cavalcanti and Watt, who, as has been noted, moved into the studios during the war), though it might work very well for the natural excitements of a train speeding across the countryside, a storm at sea, and battle, it wasn't adaptable to the broader and more basic education in citizenship which preoccupied him. His own *Drifters*, growing out of Flaherty and the Soviets as it did, had been a precedent for the later line, of course, but the main thrust of his production throughout his life, though it might allow for narrative, was an effort to find new nonfictional forms for subjects and purposes that didn't yield themselves to storytelling. Teacher and preacher that he was, how could he give up the commentator's words to point his meaning or the possibility of images freed from the unities and cut precisely to illustrate it?

"I look on cinema as a pulpit, and use it as a propagandist," he pronounced in a manifesto written shortly after his arrival at the G.P.O.,

> and this I put unashamedly because, in the still unshaven philosophies of cinema, broad distinctions are necessary. Art is one matter, and the wise, as I suggest, had better seek it where there is elbow room for its creation; entertainment is another matter; education, in so far as it concerns the classroom pedagogue, another; propaganda another; and the cinema is to be conceived as a medium like writing, capable of many forms and many functions. A professional propagandist may well be specially interested in it. It gives generous access to the public. It is capable of direct description, simple analysis and commanding conclusion, and may, by its tempo'd and imagistic powers, be made easily persuasive. It lends itself to rhetoric, for no form of description can add nobility to a simple observation so readily as a camera set low, or a sequence cut to a time-beat. But principally there is this thought that a single say-so can be repeated a thousand times a night to millions of eyes. That seven-leagued fact opens a new perspective, a new hope, to public persuasion.[72]

Of course the story-documentary did shift the emphasis from work to workers and thus helped to carry along the richer and more detailed exploration of human conditions which Rotha had been urging in his book *Documentary Film* (1935) as had Grierson in his own way. In other documentary styles as well, description of industrial processes began to give way to sociological analysis and also to a reaching out to international concerns.

Though the unit was confined to the subject matter of the post office, Grierson nonetheless succeeded in widening the field to include the whole story of communications, national and international.[73] "We gradually began to see, behind the infernal penny-in-the-slot detail in which the Post Office is so symbolic of our metropolitan civilization, something of the magic of modern communications," he wrote. "We saw the gale warning behind the Central Telegraph Office, the paradox of nationalism and internationalism behind the cable service, the choral beauty of the night mail, and the drama tucked away in the files of the ship-to-shore radio service. Most significant of all, in a film called *Big Money*, Cavalcanti achieved the singular feat of getting under the skin of the Accountant-General's department and bringing the routine clerk in most human terms to the screen."[74]

As summarized in the Arts Enquiry's *The Factual Film*,

> Social and economic issues, no more than implied in earlier films such as *Drifters* and *Industrial Britain*, became increasingly the main concerns of the makers of documentary films, politically and socially conscious of the disturbing events of the 'thirties. They came to regard their immediate task as not merely to describe and dramatise industry and labour and the everyday world, but to present a cross-section of modern society in this country, exploring its weaknesses, reporting progress, dramatising issues.[75]

Though this trend was apparent in the G.P.O. productions—*We Live in Two Worlds* and *Forty Million People* were apparently among the clearest examples—it was more obvious in the work done outside the unit from 1935 on by the Grierson-trained directors who, "as soon as they were really good," he "tended to loose on the world."[76] During the second half of the thirties the documentary filmmakers together covered progressively most of the aspects of what was regarded by Grierson as necessary material for the civic imagination in relation to contemporary surroundings, confirmed and enriched documentary film's aesthetic potential, and advanced it as an international movement.[77]

## Distribution and Exhibition

As for distribution, always in the forefront of Grierson's thinking, it was expanded far beyond the early efforts at the E.M.B., especially nontheatrical distribution. By the time he left the G.P.O., the distribution staff had come almost to equal the production staff in size,[78] and its leadership and supervision consumed a great deal of his energies.

The more outstanding productions continued to be theatrically released, through Associated British Film Distributors, and were seen in theaters throughout the country. Still, documentary could not use the commercial system easily or fully. Of the small proportion of films distributed commercially, few of them made enough from theater bookings to cover costs, far less to make a profit.[79] It wasn't that they didn't get bookings—*Night Mail* and *North Sea*, for example, were well booked—it was that the average rental paid by exhibitors for short films was so low.[80] The Arts Enquiry explained the situation:

> The average pre-war rental paid by the exhibitor for a documentary film was as little as 15/- to £1 per cinema booking. The usual trade practice was to sell a short together with a feature film for a joint sum, the renter deciding what percentage of the takings should be allotted to the short. The renter deducted approximately 40 per cent. of the gross revenue for handling the film, after which the cost of copies and of publicity still had to be deducted. Thus producers needed a very large distribution to recover costs.[81]

Only newsreels booked by contract over a period, a cartoon, or an American entertainment short, often handed out with the main feature, were viable commodities.[82] As a result, as Rotha strongly put it, "At no time in the 'thirties was a British documentary film ever produced on the normal footing of making back its production cost, plus a profit, from showings in the public cinemas."[83] The economic base of the documentary remained with the sponsor, and nontheatrical distribution and exhibition had to be expanded even further to reach a truly significant audience.

This was hardly a handicap, as it turned out. In a later memo written at the National Film Board of Canada (by Grierson himself, judging from the style), three benefits of nontheatrical distribution/exhibition were listed: "(a) there is more seating capacity outside the theaters than there is in them, (b) everyone has two moods: the one in which he seeks escape and entertainment, and the other in which he is professionally or otherwise personally interested and is prepared to take his civic perspectives seriously, (c) better to play top bill in a village or town hall, than be a throw-away in an Abbott and Costello program."[84] At the G.P.O., the nontheatrical campaign moved ahead on three fronts, two already established and one new.

First, the showings at the Imperial Institute and at exhibitions throughout the country continued. By 1935, three-quarters of a million people a year, the great majority of them children, attended the daily showings of E.M.B. and G.P.O. films at the Imperial Institute.[85] At big trade exhibitions (e.g., Olympia; Belle Vue, Manchester; Kelvin Hall, Glasgow), theaters were installed for continuous screening of G.P.O. films, and the same procedure was followed in conjunction with special post office exhibitions organized in various cities throughout the country every winter.[86]

In addition, traveling projection vans began to criss-cross the countryside from 1935 on, tapping an outlying public of considerable size and enthusiasm—an intensive method which Grierson admitted he had borrowed from Germany, and which would later be exploited on a large scale in Canada.[87] The van units carried projectors, screens, and films and were capable of projecting in almost any sort of premises. Providing screening in schools, in collaboration with Directors of Education, they reached an audience of half a million children by 1936–37.[88] In that year there were four units on the road: two 35 mm and two 16 mm. A unit stayed at least a week in each place visited, making it possible for film programs to be presented in the evenings to local film societies and to adult education and similar organizations. The programs for that year were made up of *Weather Forecast, Post Haste* or *Savings Bank, Travelling Post Office* or *Night Mail, Granton Trawler* or *Spring on the Farm, Upstream* or *6:30 Collection.*[89] By 1937–38 six units were at work, visiting schools controlled by seventy-two local education authorities.[90]

Finally, the Empire Film Library, which had been passed from the E.M.B. to the G.P.O. to the Imperial Institute, in 1935 was reinaugurated, as it were (by H.R.H. the duke of Gloucester, who was presented by Lt. Col. J. Colville, MP and president of the Institute's Board of Governors). The policy of free-loan distribution continued unchanged and the E.M.B. films were steadily added to as the G.P.O. films were released. In 1936–37, an audience of an estimated million persons saw these borrowed films. All told, through its several means of nontheatrical distribution and exhibition, the G.P.O. reckoned its audiences in Great Britain at two and a half million persons by 1937–38.

## Outside Sponsorship, Independent Units, Organizations

At the E.M.B., as earlier noted, Grierson had encouraged his young filmmakers to take assignments from outside sponsors, but with only a few exceptions they had returned to base between those commissions. At the G.P.O., however, a stream of permanent departures started (with no visible loss in the effectiveness of the parent organization, it must be added), culminating in Grierson's own resignation in June 1937. The reason for this spreading out was twofold. Through the precedent of the G.P.O. Film Unit and Grierson's tireless proselytizing on behalf of documentary film, there were now enough institutions outside the government eager to use film in public relations to support substantially increased production. Secondly, the range of subjects and the approach taken to them were of course restricted in a unit supported by the taxpayers. It was time to move on from showing one part of the empire to another (E.M.B.) or the activities of one government department to the public at large (G.P.O.), to tackle specific social and economic problems of employment, housing, health, or education. The withdrawal from the parent unit and the establishment of new units was a policy intended to increase the breadth and strength of documentaries as an instrument for social progress. Experiments with form would continue— the most important journalistic rather than poetic or narrative—but would be geared more closely to the job at hand.

Paul Rotha had pioneered this independent production earlier when he left the E.M.B. unit after a brief apprenticeship in 1931, and by the mid-thirties was already well-established in the field. Even his first film, *Contact* (1932, four reels), had been a considerable success. It dealt with the transcontinental air routes of British Imperial Airways, was sponsored by the Shell-Mex Company, and made with facilities acquired from British Instructional Films. It was first shown in 1933 and in all secured some 1,500 theater bookings, repeating the commercial success of *Drifters*.[91] Of it and its maker, though, Grierson observed: "The trouble with Rotha is that he doesn't think about cinema (like Eisenstein), nor does he patently enjoy making it (like Elton): he worries about it. If in his next, he forgets half of what he knows, doesn't care much about the other half, and sets out to enjoy his material as well as shoot it, he will do something very exciting indeed."[92]

Rotha didn't exactly follow Grierson's instruction for his next film (*Roadwards*, sponsored by Daimler autos), nor his third (*Rising Tide*, sponsored by the Southern Railway), but in his fourth, *Shipyard* (sponsored by the Orient Shipping Line and Vickers-Armstrong in 1934–35), he arrived at a good measure of excitement. Using an impressionistic style, his subject was the building of the S.S. *Orion* and the socio-economic effects on the life of the English shipbuilding town. All three productions were made with facilities obtained through the newly formed Gaumont-British Instructional (G.B.I.). His *Face of Britain* (1934–35) was financed by G.B.I. and was awarded a medal of honor at the Brussels Exhibition. After that Rotha joined the Strand Film Company as director of production, and went on to produce *To-day We Live* (1936) and *The Future's in the Air* (1937). The former was directed by Ruby Grierson and Ralph Bond, the latter by Alexander Shaw.

Like Rotha, Donald Taylor also left the unit. In 1933 he became editor for Associated Sound-Film Industries-Tobis, at Wembley Studios, and then directed for the "Ideal Cine-Magazine" and "Gaumont Mirror" in 1934. The following year he made *Citizen of the Future* for G.B.I. Late in 1935 it was he, in collaboration with Ralph Keene, who acquired Strand Film Company, then a feature film concern, and reorganized it as the first of the independent units designed to make sponsored documentaries. Donald Taylor's title was managing director. In January 1936 Strand began work with films for the Ministry of Labour. Incidentally, Ralph Keene, former painter, illustrator, and picture dealer, was one of the few important documentary people who was not an E.M.B./G.P.O. alumnus; his first direction at Strand was *Rooftops of London* (1936), made with Paul Burnford. Donald Alexander also joined Strand in 1936. During that first year of operation Strand produced fourteen films, including *Cover to Cover*, which, like *Night Mail*, opened at the Carlton, Paramount's first-run London theater. The following year a "zoo series" of twelve films was started in collaboration with Julian Huxley.

Edgar Anstey moved off of the production of *6:30 Collection* and out of the G.P.O. early in 1934 to establish what would become the famous Shell Film Unit. He planned and equipped premises, selected staff, and undertook production. The Shell Marketing and Refining Company had taken this step on the basis of a report prepared by Grierson in 1933; it was the first unit to be formed directly by an industry. At about that time Arthur Elton (who would later take charge at Shell) produced independently for the Ministry of

Labour *Workers and Jobs* (1935). Early in 1935 the British Commercial Gas Association commissioned Elton and Anstey to produce a series of five films, inviting their collaboration on the choice of subjects. (Roy Lockwood succeeded Anstey at Shell.)

This second commissioning of a complete production program came about because the gas industry was beginning to suffer from comparison with electricity, being regarded by the public as an outdated and rather Victorian affair. The documentary solution to the problem was to relate the function of the gas industry to the whole area of public well-being.[93] Elton and Anstey hired studio facilities, since no documentary company was yet in existence, and assumed complete responsibility. *Housing Problems* (1935–36) was one of the first of the series.[94] *Workers and Jobs* and *Housing Problems* together marked out a new area in the use of sound and anticipated the television documentary and cinéma vérité with their interview technique.

As Anstey put it, what he and Elton discovered in those two films was that "Men and women, stimulated by the atmosphere of a casual conversation . . . spoke to their fellow citizens about what it meant to be on the industrial scrap-heap, to see their children attacked by a rat or by armies of bedbugs, to have not a scrap of food in the cupboard and little prospect of getting any until the weekly Public Assistance fell due next day."[95]

As for the production techniques employed,

To begin with there was the problem of getting the unwieldy 35 mm. equipment and the necessary lighting into rooms perhaps twelve feet square. (Much of the equipment stayed inevitably in the doorway and lights were often shone in through a window.) Then it might be necessary, for example, to persuade a formidable Cockney lady (who had never even seen a film) to give what turned out to be a classic account of the successful battle she had fought in her living room with a large and ferocious rat. Self-consciousness was overcome by developing conversations alongside the camera. For cutting material we would hope to get sections repeated, or overlapped on a second lens. Spontaneity precluded exact repetition and editing often needed to be ingenious. . . . The result was powerful enough to give rise to whole-page illustrated reviews in two national newspapers and leading editorial articles in two others.[96]

Of these two modest films Grierson acknowledged that "They took the documentary film into the field of social problems, and keyed it to the task of describing not only industrial and commercial spectacle but social truth as well."[97] John Taylor worked on both films as cameraman, and Ruby Grierson was responsible for the direction of the South London slum dwellers in *Housing Problems*. About her work on that film, Rotha observed, "Ruby Grierson's ability to win people's confidence gave a spontaneity and an honesty to the 'interviews' that contrasted sharply with the previous, romantic handling of people."[98] She herself was reported to have said at the time to her brother John, "You see everything like a gold fish in a bowl; I'm going to break the bowl."[99] Forsyth Hardy later commented that "after *Housing Problems* the films were never again quite so detached and impersonal."[100]

The series sponsored by the gas industry, which remained annual up to the outbreak of war, continued the innovations in screen sociology and reportage. Elton made *Party Dish* and Anstey *Enough to Eat?* both for the London Gas, Light, and Coke Company, in 1936. The latter, on malnutrition, was scripted, directed, and edited by Anstey, with a narration read by Julian Huxley. It included statistical diagrams, controversial discussion, and statements to the camera: "the victims of social conditions were cross-cut with scientists, doctors and men of affairs," wrote Anstey. "Julian Huxley was used as a kind of expert chairman, a compere, an 'anchor man' as television would now say."[101] Attesting to the film's bite, Grierson revealed that, "Though the Minister of Health expressed publicly his gratitude . . . it was branded by political busybodies as 'subversive.'"[102] *Children at School* (1937), which followed in the series, was directed by Basil Wright. *Smoke Menace*, also 1937, was produced by Grierson (by then at Film Centre) and directed by Wright and John Taylor for the newly established Realist Film Unit. Both the latter two films were sponsored by the Gas Association.

As a result of his success with *Enough to Eat?* Anstey became the first production director of the March of Time's London unit in 1936. (Grierson acted as consultant for a period.) Though Anstey remained with the M.O.T. until 1938, first directing films in England and then joining the headquarters staff in New York City in October 1937 as editor of foreign editions, he was not altogether at ease within the rigid "March of Time" format. Influential though they were on the British documentary, particularly on Rotha's wartime production and Grierson's and Legg's Canadian work, the M.O.T. films were "journalistic first and last," having developed from newsreels into screen feature stories, news-cum-editorial, like the cover stories of their parent *Time* magazine. Grierson felt that Louis de Rochemont, who began producing the M.O.T. series in 1935, unlike himself, ultimately was not concerned with aesthetic or educational theory, or with social or international problems except as material for journalistic features.[103]

Basil Wright left the G.P.O. in January 1937 to found the Realist Film Unit. John Taylor, who had left the G.P.O. to direct his first film at Strand, would join him there. He worked as a director initially but eventually was more or less in charge of Realist until 1947. Then he returned to the government unit, which had become the Crown Film Unit, as its head. Ralph Bond, another alum from the government unit, also directed films for Realist. Evelyn Spice left the G.P.O. (after completing *A Job in a Million*) when Grierson did, in the summer of 1937. She went to Strand, where she followed Donald Alexander into the zoo series. (Paul Burnford, Ruby Grierson, and Stanley Hawes directed films for that series as well.) Stuart Legg also left with Grierson and, after a six-month stop at Film Centre, became chief producer at Strand when Paul Rotha left on a trip to America. William Coldstream joined Legg, and they co-directed *Roadways* in 1937. Marion Grierson the previous year had become editor of *World Film News*, published by the documentary group, and was also directing for Strand (e.g., *Beside the Seaside, Key to Scotland, Heart of an Empire, For All Eternity*—a series sponsored by the Travel Association).

While initially there had been only one documentary unit, by 1937 there were four major units in addition to the G.P.O. Gaumont-British Instructional (previously British Instructional Films) was under the leadership of Bruce Woolfe, Percy Smith, and Mary Field, and was best known for its popular science–nature series "Secrets of Life" (which had been preceded by the pioneering "Secrets of Nature," 1919–33). Though they specialized in educational films, they produced many documentaries as well, as has been noted. The Shell Film Unit was under the direction of Elton. These two sponsored units were paralleled by the Strand Film Company (Donald Taylor and Ralph Keene) and the Realist Film Unit (Basil Wright and John Taylor), which operated independently. There were other smaller units and independent producers as well.

Where there had been only one sustained sponsorship, that of the government, there was now a host of sponsoring commercial and institutional enterprises. Of these, oil (Shell Marketing and Refining Company, Shell-Mex, British Petroleum, and the Anglo-Iranian Oil Company), gas (British Commercial Gas Association, London Gas, Light, and Coke Company), shipping (Orient Shipping Line), and airlines (British Imperial Airways) were the most important. But there was also the Ceylon Tea Propaganda Board, the National Book Council, the National Council for Social Service, the Zoological Society, the League of Nations, and others. In most cases the documentary filmmakers found a sympathetic and enlightened understanding in the public relations departments they served.[104] Particularly attuned to the uses of film was John Louis (Jack) Beddington. From 1930 to 1940 Beddington was with Shell-Mex Ltd. as publicity director and assistant general manager, and during the war he became director of the Films Division of the Ministry of Information.

In addition to sponsoring production, some of the major firms set up their own systems of distribution and exhibition in imitation of the G.P.O. Film Unit and the Empire Film Library. For example, Shell-Mex and the Gas Association had their own lending libraries. The manufacturers of 16 mm projectors—notably Gaumont-British Equipments (British Acoustic), Sound Services (Western Electric), and Pathé—offered to provide sponsors with mobile projectors to give road shows, and a number of commercial lending libraries were founded.[105]

This burgeoning activity created a need for further organization among the now numerous documentary filmmakers themselves, and for coordination and liaison between sponsors wanting to have films made and producers wanting to make them. Earlier, in 1933, the British Film Institute had been established to "encourage the use and development of the cinema as a means of entertainment and instruction."[106] At first it gave considerable attention to the educational film, and later it concentrated on the entertainment film. Though its work became extremely valuable, it was never a strong force in the development of British documentaries; Grierson once wrote of someone's plan for improving the British film industry, "Why, it sounds like another damned panel of the Film Institute."[107] Also in 1933 an Independent Film-Makers Association was formed "To coordinate the efforts of those who are seriously engaged in the production of experimental, documentary, and educational films." Grierson was among its board of advisors, as were Stuart Legg, Paul

Rotha, and Basil Wright, but it seems to have been designed mostly to assist amateurs—individuals and film clubs.[108]

It was not until late 1935 that a group was created, Associated Realist Film Producers Ltd., which would truly represent the documentary movement. At first its membership consisted of about a dozen of the senior producers and directors. From it developed Film Centre Ltd., to be discussed at length later, with which it continued to work in close cooperation when that organization was set up in 1937. Directors of the A.R.F.P. were Edgar Anstey, Arthur Elton, Paul Rotha, and Donald Taylor, and it proposed to offer the following services: "i) Advice to bodies desiring to have films made; ii) Preparation of scenarios; iii) Drawing up complete programmes; iv) Provision of Film Officers to handle complete production programmes; v) The taking of responsibility for the production of films by qualified units." Its "Associate Film Directors" were Andrew Buchanan, William Coldstream, Marion Grierson, J. B. Holmes, Stuart Legg, Alexander Shaw, Evelyn Spice, Harry Watt, and Basil Wright. "Consultants" were Alberto Cavalcanti, John Grierson, Professor J. B. S. Haldane, Professor Lancelot Hogben, Julian Huxley, E. McKnight Kauffer, Walter Leigh, and Basil Wright.[109]

By 1939 it had over fifty members.[110] According to Rotha, the general secretary,

> Almost every person in the British documentary film field—whether producer, director, educational officer, cameraman or distribution manager—was a member, irrespective of what company he or she worked for. The aim was to unify the movement and to preserve its democratic relationships, to eliminate unnecessary competition and to act as a public relations front for the whole documentary film movement. Associated with the Society as honorary members were leading men of science, art, music and architecture, as well as documentary producers and educationalists overseas.[111]

In the spring of 1940 the A.R.F.P. was suspended, however, when most of its membership was scattered by the war. While it was never revived, an analogous organization, Federation of Documentary Film Units, was formed at the end of the war in 1945.[112]

## Speaking and Writing

Along with his work at the G.P.O., and his hand in the guidance and organization of the documentary movement as a whole, Grierson continued to write and speak, reaching out for converts and a broader understanding of his cause. As for his writing, he explained when he arrived at the G.P.O.: "Documentary, or the creative treatment of actuality, is a new art with no such background in the story and the stage as the studio product so glibly possesses. Theory is important, experiment is important; and every development of technique or new mastery of theme has to be brought quickly into criticism. In that respect it is well that the producer should be a theorist."[113] The extent of his theoretical and critical writing has already been suggested.

In the spring of 1934 he gave a series of ten lectures on "The Art of Cinema and Its Social Relationships" at the University of Leicester. During the same 1933–34 season, at the Glasgow Film Society—whose membership had grown from the 80 who saw *Drifters* to 670—he gave a lecture illustrated by a 16 mm screening.[114] For the Scottish Educational Cinema Society, also in Glasgow, he organized a matinee for school children. Shown on the latter occasion were films drawn from the E.M.B.–G.P.O. collection, including *Drifters* and *Industrial Britain*, and Grierson talked to the three thousand children about his own filmmaking.[115] He also served as judge in the Scottish Amateur Film Festivals, which started in 1934, and discovered the talent of a young Norman McLaren in this way. McLaren and Stewart McAllister, as members of a small student film production group at the Glasgow School of Art, had produced a fanciful documentary entitled *Art School Ball*. Though very critical of it—seeing sexual symbolism where none was intended—Grierson hired both of its makers.[116] The former would become a world-renowned animator at the National Film Board of Canada; the latter editor of some of the finest of the British wartime documentaries, notably those of Humphrey Jennings.

Other speaking engagements occurred at the first summer school of the Independent Film-Makers Association (August 1934)—"I think I am justified in saying that John Grierson was our star turn," wrote one attendant;[117] the Manchester Film Institute Society during a conference hosted by the G.P.O. (December 1935)—"Mr. John Grierson afterwards delivered a fascinating address on the possibilities of publicity films of the type made by the G.P.O.";[118] the second film school organized by the British Film Institute at the University of London (July–August 1936);[119] and a series of classes, lectures, and screenings conducted by *World Film News* (beginning November 1936).[120]

Addressing the English-speaking Union in April 1937, at which a number of American documentaries were shown, Grierson described the documentary as "the essay and pamphlet form of the film art." Presiding at that meeting was Edward R. Murrow, then European director of the Columbia Broadcasting System, later a distinguished documentary filmmaker himself. Murrow stressed the danger of the documentary film if it got into the wrong hands—"If the mirror [held up to life] was one which reflected a distorted image"[121]—but it is not clear whether the hands he was thinking of belonged to Pare Lorentz of the United States, Leni Riefenstahl of Nazi Germany, John Grierson of Great Britain, or to others.

As for publication, aside from his steady flow of articles and reviews, he engineered the replacement of *Cinema Quarterly* (out of Edinburgh) by the monthly *World Film News* (out of London). *WFN*'s first policy statement explained that "*Cinema Quarterly* had, of necessity, to rely on theory. *WFN* has more information, less theory. In the film world there is an excellent service of commercial and trade news and an excellent service for fans. There is no news service which reports on creative people and creative efforts in the many branches of cinema. *WFN* is, in this sense, a necessary paper." The editorial went on to state that "Its promoters are working film people—producers, directors, writers. All that interests them is a monthly survey of progress. To this exclusively *WFN* will remain devoted."[122] Its "Controllers" were John Grierson, Alberto Cavalcanti, Forsyth Hardy, G. D. Robinson, Norman Wilson, and Basil Wright. Marion Grierson became editor in July 1936. She was assigned the job because of her earlier journalistic experience in Canada. Esmond Romilly, a nephew of Winston Churchill, worked on it; and Alistair Cooke was a regular contributor.[123]

The publication was as good as its word. The format was large and newspaperish, like a trade journal. Less attention was given to documentary and to Grierson's work and ideas. This effort to reach out to a wider readership by embedding documentary in a general survey of film entertainment and art didn't really catch on, however. It was subsidized heavily by Basil Wright, his father Charles, and brother Lawrence (the latter also one of the directors of the Realist Film Unit); but in the face of competition from *Sight and Sound*, underwritten even more fully by the British Film Institute, and the onset of war, retrenchment was eventually necessary. In 1938 Marion Grierson left and was succeeded as editor by Reginald Groves. With the January 1940 issue *World Film News* was reconverted into the much more modest and parochial *Documentary News Letter*, owned and published by the Film Centre, edited by Ronald Horton, with an editorial board composed of Edgar Anstey, John Grierson, Donald Taylor, John Taylor, and Basil Wright. Grierson's public thanks to Charles and Lawrence Wright in his later writing had mainly to do with their support of the failed cause.

## Other Activities

One other aspect of Grierson's avocational campaigning during the G.P.O. years deserves attention. In 1936 the government appointed a committee, under the chairmanship of Lord Moyne, "to consider the position of British films, having in mind the approaching expiry of the Films Act of 1927," and to advise the Board of Trade on new legislation.[124] Grierson and Bruce Woolfe, of Gaumont-British Instructional, gave evidence before the committee in support of the inclusion for quota of certain types of short films, including most documentaries, which were excluded under the 1927 Act. Apparently they were sufficiently persuasive. Among the Moyne committee's recommendations incorporated into the 1938 Cinematograph Films Act were reenacted quota requirements including for the first time protection for short films.[125]

Grierson's personal life during the G.P.O. days continued on its usual gregarious round. After Flaherty finished shooting *Man of Aran* he returned to London to headquarter there until 1939, except for a period on location in India for *Elephant Boy* (1937). Grierson saw much of him and rushed to the defense of *Man of Aran* (1934) to counter the criticism being leveled at it by some of his own documentary-trained people.

Ralph Bond, a doctrinaire Marxist, launched the attack in the summer 1934 *Cinema Quarterly*. He charged escapism, sensationalism (two storms and a shark hunt), and avoidance of the class struggle. Now, it must be admitted that the Grierson of the winter 1932 *Cinema Quarterly* (while Flaherty was actually shooting in Aran) had sounded not so unlike the Bond of the summer of 1934, even if more elegant of phrase. It was in those "First Principles of Documentary," in fact, that Grierson claimed to have invented the very word "escapism" as a stick with which to beat his old friend: "I hope the Neo-Rousseauism implicit in Flaherty's work dies with his exceptional self. Theory of naturals apart, it represents an escapism, a wan and distant eye, which tends in lesser hands to sentimentalism."[126] If he had coined the word (as he had "documentary," also to characterize Flaherty's work), *he* would decide when and where it applied. Flaherty's self-appointed "critical attorney" then began a statesmanlike defense.

For his first blow he bypassed Bond and singled out another detractor: "David Schire's article puts the principal objections: that Flaherty is a romantic escapist and that the film is only so much idyllic fudge. As I originally, I think, invented the word 'escapism' . . . it may seem scurvy in me to double-cross a supporter. But I do not agree with his estimate either of Flaherty or *Man of Aran*. In the first place one may not—whatever one's difference in theory—be disrespectful of a great artist and a great teacher." Here, it seems, is the crux, but Grierson continued the argument. Flaherty was an explorer—his subjects were natural to him. "It would be foolish, as Professor Saintsbury once remarked, to complain of a pear that it lacks the virtue of the pomegranate. I call it futile, too, to ask of Flaherty an article which cannot under commercial conditions be possible. His methods need the larger basking of the commercial industry and he must obey its rules." This accounts for the sensational and the spectacular.

Grierson then urged, "But rather than complain of the result, I wonder that so much was done within commercial limitations. No English film has done so much. . . . I am all for congratulating Flaherty on pushing the commercial film brilliantly to its limit. I am all for commending his fortitude in yet another sickening encounter with commercialism." But then gently back to the central distinction between his own work and Flaherty's, now put with proper respect.

> Seen as the story of mankind over a period of a thousand years, the story of the Arans is very much this story of man against the sea and woman against the skyline. It is a simple story, but it is an essential story, for nothing emerges out of time except bravery. If I part company with Flaherty at that point, it is because I like my braveries to

emerge otherwise than from the sea, and stand otherwise than against the sky. I imagine they shine as bravely in the pursuit of Irish landlords as in the pursuit of Irish sharks.[127]

After the hullabaloo Flaherty's relations with the documentary group became a bit strained, and he spent less time with them in the Coronet. He and Grierson continued their lifelong dialectic over a glass, however. Rotha and Wright wrote of their Olympian contest: "It is said that only two people could ever get the better of Flaherty in a talking-match. One was Oliver St. John Gogarty; the other was John Grierson. But then Grierson better than most knew Flaherty's weaknesses and could not resist the gentle art of goading, at which he is adept. Their verbal quarrels are fabulous."[128] In a letter written years after her husband's death, Frances Flaherty recalled: "What passed between Grierson and Bob was verbal fireworks. Grierson loved to provoke them; Bob could never resist them, often to my disgust, and I would refuse to go along—which is now too bad."[129]

It was near the end of the G.P.O. period that Grierson coined his famous phrase "the finest eyes in cinema," which easily superseded "escapism" in his lasting evaluation of Flaherty's significance. "Vertov talks of the kino eye," wrote Grierson, "but Flaherty, who never talks of it, has it. Those who like myself have known him for a long time remain in this sense his students. We can whack him in theory and out-distance him in economics but the maestro has caught the eye of the gods."[130]

## Departure

Grierson left the G.P.O. after ten years of government service, on June 30, 1937, to develop his interest in education and public relations over a wider field. At the G.P.O. unit, J. B. Holmes replaced Grierson, as director of productions, with Cavalcanti as chief producer and Watt as principal director. In a valedictory statement Grierson made clear his reasons for leaving: "To-day the inspiration is strong at the Post Office, but much less strong where it could be nationally more useful: in Agriculture, Health, Transport and Labour. The flame lit at the Empire Marketing Board has dimmed, and the documentary film looks more and more outside the Government departments—to the vast operations of oil, gas, electricity, steel and chemicals, to the municipal and social organisations, and to the journalistic treatment of public problems on *March of Time* lines."[131] For some time it had been clear, too, that with the expansion of the documentary field some kind of main advisory body was wanted to act as a consultative center to the movement as a whole.[132] Film Centre Ltd., which he founded on his departure, was intended to become that center.

# 5 ❯❯ FILM CENTRE (1937–39)

## Beginnings

In January of 1937 it was announced that Film Centre (Limited) had been registered in Edinburgh "as a private company to carry on   the business of consultants and business advisers on all matters  relating to films." Capital was entered as £100 in £1 shares. Listed as directors were John Grierson, described as director of Cinema Contact (Limited), Mill House, Fairbourne, Kent (evidently one of the many illusory firms founded by Grierson in his career); Arthur Hallam Rice Elton, film director, 27 Percy Street, London; and Francis B. S. Legg, 16 Shooters Hill Road, London. In addition to its Edinburgh office at 135 George Street, Film Centre was understood to intend establishing a London office.[1] In fact, neither Grierson nor Film Centre operated out of Edinburgh. Elton didn't remember why it was registered there in the first place—perhaps only as a sentimental whim on Grierson's part—but they had a "terrible time" trying to meet the requirements of Scottish law, which were different from English law. Finally, the only solution was to go into voluntary liquidation and to reincorporate in London.[2] They weren't really active until autumn, at 34 Soho Square.

J. P. R. Golightly was also among the first Film Centre personnel. Its roster remained notable for its flexibility, as various of its

110

members left or were posted by Grierson to other assignments. Rotha, Wright, and Anstey, in addition to those already named, worked at one time or another on the production side; Thomas Baird and William Farr on distribution. Its purpose was not to produce or distribute films, however, but to advise sponsors, supervise production, make arrangements for distribution, undertake scenario work and research, open up new markets, and in general stimulate and guide the development of the movement as a whole. Working on a fee basis, Film Centre made investigations and prepared reports for any group interested in the use of documentary films. If production was decided upon, a Film Centre officer acted as film adviser to the client, administered the finance from Film Centre, and usually acted as supervisor or producer of the films—a system not unlike that of some of today's advertising agencies, with their account executives. In addition, Film Centre encouraged research and trained people in promotion work. Several of its staff were sent out to develop nontheatrical distribution—for example, Farr went to Petroleum Films Bureau for that purpose and Baird to the British Commercial Gas Association.[3] As Hardy pointed out, Grierson had now succeeded in setting himself up in an ideal position to act as a powerhouse of ideas and initiative for the whole movement.[4]

The functions of Film Centre were, however, almost exactly those the Associated Realist Film Producers had proposed to undertake. The A.R.F.P., therefore, resolved to relinquish its promotional and consultative work to the new group. It was dissolved as a limited company and reconstituted as a free society, with a greatly expanded membership.[5] In 1938 another organization was established, the Association of Short Film Producers, to watch over the interests of all makers of short films. Despite a divergence of interests among some of its members, particularly between the documentary producers and the producers of advertising films, A.S.F.P. succeeded in helping solve some of the problems of the shorts branch of the industry which were then coming to a head.[6]

## Production and Consultation

The Film Centre projects began with a continuation of the gas industry series which had started in 1935 and had included *Enough to Eat?* and *Housing Problems. Children at School* (1937), an analysis of the public education system of England, was Film Centre's first film, produced by Grierson and directed by Wright. It was followed by *Smoke Menace* (1938), produced by Grierson and directed by John Taylor. Both films were made at the Realist Film Unit; both were distributed initially by Film Centre and then by Technique Distributors, one of the newly organized commercial firms. Film Centre clients in addition to the gas (and oil) groups included a number of the larger national sponsors, among them the Times Publishing Company (*The Fourth Estate*, produced by Rotha at Realist in 1939) and the International Wool Secretariat.[7] There was talk, also, of a production in collaboration with the B.B.C.[8] but nothing came of it.

Elton, for Film Centre, became production consultant and supervisor to the Petroleum Films Bureau and the Shell Film Unit. He developed the latter into what was said to be the best technical film production organization in the world.[9] It was at Shell that Elton demonstrated most fully his "unique gift for presenting a logical, lucid and, above all, economical account of scientific phenomena and processes"[10] as evident in such films as *Power Unit* (1936–37), *Transfer of Power* (1939), and *Malaria* (1939). The films carried no advertising and listed Shell's name only in the credit titles. They gained a high reputation, particularly among educators. On Elton's advice, Shell began to distribute its productions nontheatrically through the Petroleum Films Bureau in Britain and through Asiatic Petroleum Company in a number of foreign countries. Special versions were prepared in Dutch, French, Hungarian, Italian, German, Portuguese, and Swedish. In the countries covered, libraries of Shell films were established, and the films were loaned in sets to schools and other similar institutions. Film shows were also arranged for various adult agencies.[11]

The project with which Grierson was most closely associated at Film Centre was the "Films of Scotland" series. The idea for it began in 1937, when the Scots were in the final stages of planning for the Empire Exhibition to be held in Glasgow the following year. Though a fine film theater had been built as a national showcase, suddenly it was realized that there was a dearth of Scottish material on film, apart from what Grierson had done at the E.M.B. and G.P.O. and the romanticisms of English and American feature studios. To compensate for this lack, a Films of Scotland Committee was hurriedly formed by the Scottish Development Council in consultation with the Secretary of State for Scotland, Walter Elliot, which started canvassing for funds. A Glasgow businessman, J. A. MacTaggart, provided a basic £5,000 and then contributions were cajoled out of the British Council and from the Commissioner for the Special Areas in Scotland. Various national industries were also solicited. As the leading Scottish filmmaker, Grierson was approached at Film Centre to head the project. Working closely with Niven MacNicoll, then public relations officer at the Scottish Office, Grierson drew up a program of seven films which were to describe "in vivid summary," as Hardy wrote of them, "the country's character and traditions, its economic planning for industrial development, its agriculture, education and sport."[12]

Film Centre acted as adviser and coordinator, ensuring that a consistent policy and standard were maintained. Because of the size and urgency of the production the films were made at several companies, and in different styles. *Wealth of a Nation* was produced by Stuart Legg and directed by Donald Alexander at Strand Films; *The Face of Scotland* was directed by Basil Wright at Realist; *The Children's Story* was directed by Alexander Shaw at Strand; *Sea Food* was made at Pathé; Mary Field directed *They Made the Land* at Gaumont-British Instructional. And there were also *Scotland for Fitness* (Brian Salt at G.B.I.) and *Sport in Scotland* (Scottish Films Productions).

Following the completion of the films in 1938, Film Centre arranged a very successful theatrical distribution of the series through Metro-Goldwyn-Mayer. Constituting the first attempt in the history of film to give a coherent account of a nation, these "Films of Scotland" remain, as Hardy rightly says, "a unique and remarkably comprehensive record of a country's achievement and outlook."[13] Norman Wilson, Hardy's Edinburgh colleague, suggested that the films were particularly commendable, given official sponsorship and the temptations of the occasion, in that they "did not attempt to present Scotland as a Fitzpatrick [travelogue] paradise." Eschewing the scenic background, Grierson saw to it that these films were based firmly in social reality. The intention was to make Scotland's very problems—which stemmed mainly from the legacy of nineteenth-century industrialism—exciting. The Clydeside was still well to the fore in this substantial tribute to a native land.

Donald Alexander, who directed the first of the series, recalled an amusing sequel:

Once we took Legg on a ceremonial drive round Scotland, with Grierson and Wright acting as official cicerones to the country he had written up but never seen. [The treatment for *Wealth of a Nation* had been written by Legg.] We remember every roaring detail from the preliminary dinner at Rogano's Sea Food Restaurant to the formal visit to the Grierson ancestors in a churchyard beside Bannockburn, and Stuart's gloomy acceptance of the evolutionary plausibility of a hairy Highland Cow, contrasted with Grierson's rapturous and improbable claim never before to have encountered the species. That time we were stationed in Glasgow—at the Central Hotel—because Grierson insisted (probably rightly) that it was the only place to which important contacts could be decently invited. Stuart stuck it for one night; the next day we moved to a quiet pub in Bath Street where our joint social consciences were not offended by 'plain breakfast' (coffee and roll) at 2s. 6d., and where the beer was better. Our contacts still came to the Central; like them, we just called in.[14]

One other of Grierson's projects at Film Centre, though abortive at the time, is of special interest as a basis for his later work at UNESCO. An American journalist in London, Ernestine Evans, first suggested to him a plan for the enlightened use of film by the International Labor Office, a subsidiary organization to the League of Nations. With Basil Wright, Grierson worked out a scheme and strategy for the I.L.O. They asked, and answered, in effect:

> Why do you not create a great international interflow of living documents by which specialized groups will speak to their brethren in the fifty countries that operate within your system? You are anxious to raise the common standard of industrial welfare. Why do you not use the film to do it? If France has the best system of safety in mines, let other countries have the benefit of this example. If New Zealand is a great pioneer of ante-natal care, let other countries see the record of its achievement.[15]

Grierson and Wright journeyed to Geneva in 1938 and, as a result, the I.L.O. commissioned a memorandum from Film Centre on the use of films in its work. This study outlined the various nontheatrical channels which might be used by the I.L.O., and suggested types of films that it might sponsor. Grierson also presented the plan to the Rockefeller Foundation in New York, seeking additional support. "I will say for both the I.L.O. and the Rockefeller Foundation," he concluded later, "that they took our scheme seriously.

Mr. [Nicholas Murray] Butler [president of Columbia University] did, Mr. [Harry Emerson] Fosdick [American religious leader] did; and only recently Mr. [John Gilbert] Winant [U.S. ambassador to Great Britain] was regretting to me the ill fortune which attended it. In all cases the answer was the same—and it had, of necessity, to be: the sands of peace are running out."[16] This first considered plan for the production and distribution of documentaries on an international scale went the way of the League of Nations itself with the outbreak of World War II in 1939. During the war Grierson again stated his case, in an address to the I.L.O. conference in Philadelphia in April 1944, and it remained valuable as an enumeration of the essential factors which went into film planning by the postwar United Nations and UNESCO.[17]

## Distribution and Exhibition

At Film Centre, Grierson stumped even more actively for nontheatrical distribution and exhibition than he had at the G.P.O. By 1937–38 the nontheatrical audience had reached an estimated ten million annually, and he predicted that it would soon run to twenty million. Admittedly theatrical features commanded even bigger audiences and bigger money, but in them educational purpose and social content were necessarily minimized: "every form of circulation has its own particular inhibitions." In nontheatrical distribution/exhibition,

> You can expect your audience to come a bit of the way in the process of understanding and you are not for ever under the obligation of sugaring pills, tempering the wind to the shorn lamb, remembering to give the little old lady in the back row a dollop of mother love and, in general, acting like a fussy and patronising old hen. . . . [T]he main future of documentary is where it is now: financed by sponsors in the name of public education. . . . It is an educational and uplifting business. Like the Y.M.C.A., the Little Brothers of St. Francis, the Ku Klux Klan and the Holy Rollers—only different.[18]

In spite of his passion for the nontheatrical system he wasn't willing to let the theaters go altogether and was concerned about the British film industry as a whole—it was on his conscience, he said. In relation to the approaching Cinematograph Films Act of 1938 that would come into effect on April 1st, he wrote and lectured vigorously. Analyzing the government legislative proposals, in September of 1937, he granted that they (1) canceled out the "quota quickies"—films financed as cheaply as possible by American distributors to meet their quota obligations; (2) encouraged Americans to invest in more ambitious British features; (3) attempted to secure reciprocity by which British films would be shown in the United States; (4) gave official recognition to shorts and documentary producers. But the legislation (1) did not help the independent producer much—there was still a lot of money for him to risk and the Board of Trade would not be a good judge of quality warranting special consideration; (2) the independent exhibitor could complain that discouraging the independent producer reduced the supply and cut the exhibitor's bargaining position; (3) and the shorts producer was not offered enough protection in the face of the American practice of throwing shorts in with features.

The real problem, however, was that the law did not distinguish between foreign films made in Britain and British films made in Britain. The British industry was faced with two alternatives, he felt; it could either (1) accept subsidy and control from Americans, as was the practice with the big firms and quota quickies; or (2) it could produce films for and supported by British audiences. The British industry first had to develop talent and skill on a more modest scale before it tried to compete with Hollywood in a world market. Alexander Korda's *The Private Life of Henry VIII* (1933), which had made unexpectedly high profits, particularly in America, had been followed by a lot of flops which had attempted the same thing—a big investment for an international audience—he reminded his readers.[19]

Charles Davy, in his postscript to *Footnotes to the Film*, which he compiled and edited in 1937, reprinted in part and relied heavily on the arguments Grierson had presented in another piece, for the *Kinematograph Weekly*.[20] And Stuart Legg with F. D. Klingender contributed to the debate in *Money Behind the Screen: A Report Prepared on Behalf of the Film Council* published in the same year. (The Film Council was an independent research body set up in 1936.) The preface was by Grierson. The facts and arguments of this time would confront him more crucially again at a later stage of his career in the production of modest, quite-British features at the government-financed Group 3.

## International Influence

By the mid-thirties British documentary had begun to attract ever-increasing international attention and to reach abroad itself in its own missionary zeal to extend its influence and gospel. "We are supposed, in this country," wrote Grierson in January 1938, "to hold the secret of film propaganda." Documentaries were made in conjunction with the governments of Ceylon (*The Song of Ceylon*, 1934), Switzerland (*Line to Tschierva Hut*, 1937), and Iran (*Dawn of Iran*, 1938). Furthermore, Grierson went on to point out in the article quoted above, "During the past year or two, several foreign governments have been examining the work of the documentary groups, analysing their methods of distribution, cross-examining the people responsible, on how films can be fitted to different national purposes. Japan, Turkey, Egypt, Denmark, Brazil, Portugal, Belgium, among others, have made special efforts to convey the British experience overseas."[21] But the most consequential two-way flow would be between Britain and the United States.

In July 1935, in New York City, a film library was established at the Museum of Modern Art. A young English woman, Iris Barry, was appointed its first director. Having begun her film career as a founder-member of the Film Society, in London, and as motion picture correspondent for the *Daily Mail*, one of her earliest acts in her new position was to send representatives to London. They returned shortly with a selection of British documentaries, which were then distributed in the United States and brought to the attention of the Rockefeller Foundation, partly responsible for financing the Film Library. Under its program in the humanities, the Foundation was supporting studies of mass communication (as the Laura Spellman Rockefeller Memorial had earlier funded Grierson's investigation into the popular press). Now it was concentrating particularly on the audience for film and radio.[22] It was in 1935 also that "The March of Time" series began to appear and that Pare Lorentz began work on *The Plow That Broke the Plains* for the government Resettlement Administration. In 1936 a Rockefeller Foundation fellowship brought over Tom Baird, distribution specialist at the G.P.O. and then Film Centre, to gain direct experience with the American scene and to inform Americans about what Britain had been doing in the documentary field.[23]

The following year the Rockefeller Foundation enabled the Film Library to invite Paul Rotha, who spent September 1937 to March 1938 working along similar lines. Rotha carried with him a representative sample of British documentaries, including *The Smoke Menace, Housing Problems*, and *Night Mail*, and lectured with them. This new group of films (*Drifters* and *Song of Ceylon* were the only British documentaries to have been previously shown publicly in the United States) were presented before large audiences by the Film Library, Columbia University, and the New School for Social Research, obtaining widespread journalistic comment as well. "It was gratifying indeed," Rotha wrote, "to find that not only were our work and ideas known but that people of all professions were anxious to see our films."[24]

As a result of Rotha's visit, the Film Library acquired thirteen of the British documentaries for circulation throughout the United States.[25] These were the beginning of its circulating collection. Rotha had also started plans for a series entitled "The Non-Fiction Film: From Uninterpreted Fact to Documentary," which would be prepared and presented later by the Film Library in collaboration with the Association of Documentary Film Producers. Its twelve programs ranged from Flaherty's *Nanook* (1922) to G.P.O.'s *North Sea* (1938) and the American *The City* (1939), providing a comprehensive survey of the development of British-American documentary. Richard Griffith supplied an authoritative program note.[26] In 1937–38 Edgar Anstey was also in the United States, as foreign editor of "The March of Time," and he too built up many contacts.

When Tom Baird again visited the States in early 1939, final arrangements were completed for the regular dispatch of British documentaries to the United States, but only one batch of negatives was ever sent under that scheme. Instead the documentary exchange worked out by Film Centre and the Museum of Modern Art Film Library laid the basis for official exchange during the war by the Ministry of Information through British Information Services.[27]

An unpublished Film Centre report of October 1939 ("Overseas Distribution of British Documentary Films, with special reference to the United States of America") reviewed the success of British documentaries in America before the war. It pointed out that these films of British life were being seen because Americans wanted to see them, requiring no solicitation from a sponsor. They were chosen on their merits and because of their distinctiveness. "To most

American critics, education authorities and students of the cinema, the documentary film is Britain's main contribution to the motion picture."[28]

By January 1938 Grierson was able to write that "a flow of students [of British documentary], mostly from American Universities and Washington Departments, has come to London to examine the special possibilities of the film in public administration and social education."[29] One of these "students," from the "Washington Departments," enormously talented but undisciplined by Grierson's standards, was Pare Lorentz, who first met Grierson in May 1938. Lorentz already had the documentaries *The Plow That Broke the Plains* (1936) and *The River* (1937) to his credit and had sailed to England with Hollywood director King Vidor to do script work on an adaptation of the Philip Barry play *Holiday*. (The film version released in 1938 was directed by George Cukor.) Grierson was cordial, Lorentz recalled, and introduced him to all the young filmmakers. Lorentz, for his part, was somewhat scornful of Grierson's theories about documentaries, which seemed to him those of a school teacher, precluding beauty. In fact, Lorentz didn't like the term "documentary"—didn't care what the impulse was called but tried to avoid that label. In relation to his own work he applied the term "Films of merit." Flaherty had somewhat the same feelings and spoke of his films as being based in "discovery and revelation." It was on this trip that Flaherty, probably as a result of his less than happy experience with *Elephant Boy*, told Lorentz that he ". . . had had enough of the British Empire" and would like to return to the United States if anything came up that he could do. (When told of that remark Grierson observed, with some asperity, that Flaherty had done all of his major work in the British Empire up to that point.)[30] Whatever was said, the conversation with Lorentz led to Flaherty being invited to make *The Land* (1941) for the U.S. Film Service.[31]

Brightest and biggest symbol of Anglo-American documentary exchange was the extensive, well-attended and well-publicized exhibition of British documentaries at the New York World's Fair of 1939. But the choice of films to be sent, by the Joint Committee of the British Council, was the ground for a particularly bitter campaign in Grierson's long war on established notions of British presentation of itself abroad and at home—a running engagement that Grierson called the "Battle for Authenticity."[32] The conflict was over *the kind of picture*—knee breeches tradition and pageantry or "democracy in its working clothes"—and the battle for authenticity ended in a draw. The Council stood by the films it had chosen to be shown in the "comfortable little theater" of the British Pavilion. After agitation by American documentary people and press, however, the World's Fair requested the Film Centre to send a selection of the more "socially progressive" documentaries, and the Association of Documentary Film Producers was formed in New York to organize a competitive showing, as it were, in the Little Theatre of the Science and Education Building.

Of this second set of screenings, Richard Griffith wrote from New York: "The British documentary movement has sent a selection of films representing its approach to social problems as expressed in such subjects as nutrition *(Enough to Eat?)*, housing *(Housing Problems, Kensal House)*, local government *(The Londoners)*, and education *(Children at School)*." In the British Pavilion, on the other hand, reported Griffith,

> only a small group of documentaries is to be seen, and the selection is random. *Song of Ceylon* is there, and *Shipyard* and *The Londoners* are occasionally shown, but such historically important pictures as *Industrial Britain*, *Coal Face* and *The Saving of Bill Blewitt* are absent. . . . In place of these, the Pavilion offers a heterogeneous collection of travelogues and "interest" films, incompetent enough and dull enough to alienate the most passionately Anglophile group. . . . [T]hese unimaginative and rather pompous films on British landscapes, monuments and sports, project the England of tradition and stability.[33]

Alberto Cavalcanti, who had succeeded Grierson as chief producer at the G.P.O. unit, commented in response to Griffith's account that he did not seem to have been "particularly well informed," and listed fifteen recent G.P.O. films shown in the British Pavilion Cinema. "Many of these were specially made for the Fair," wrote Cavalcanti, "and the reports show that they were exceedingly well received there."[34] In short, as Rotha summarized, "The British Council would no doubt claim the remarkable success of its New York film-shows. So also would the documentary group."[35]

## Other Activities in England, Canada, and the United States

During this "time of crucial and violent activity in the development of documentary" Grierson had gone in for fruit farming on an intensive scale, at Harrietsham in Kent, which "None of his fellow workers are likely to forget," wrote Basil Wright. "It merely doubled his own work, and also the work of those of his colleagues and employees who were bidden to the somewhat inaccessible heart of the countryside to work on film scripts and, almost simultaneously, to assist in the cultivation of acres of strawberries under glass." The only respite was in the evenings; the Harrow was the nearby pub. "Contrary to all expectation," continued Wright, Grierson won second prize in a national soft fruit show, "in competition with growers who had spent their life at the game."[36]

In London Grierson was also seeing Flaherty, who had resumed relations with the documentary people after the strain of *Man of Aran*'s mixed reception had been overshadowed by even more serious difficulties with the commercial industry on *Elephant Boy*. Rotha and Wright recalled that during 1937–38 Flaherty would often join them later in the evening "at a strange little club on the first-floor of an Italian restaurant called Castano's in Greek Street, which led off the south side of Soho Square. Here would foregather the 'senior' documentary people—Golightly, Legg, Elton, Davidson, Donald and John Taylor, occasionally Grierson and ourselves"— plus some criminal types.

> The only time on which we recall that the documentary world and the underworld mixed was when a man named Max the Red was wanted by the police in connection with a murder somewhere on the outskirts of London. Max the Red owned a garage from which a car, involved in the crime, had been hired. He himself, the newspapers told us, had disappeared. He was, in fact, lounging in the Star Club [the bar upstairs] one night when Grierson, disregarding the usual etiquette of discrete silence between the two kinds of members of the Club, nonchalantly went across to him and asked him if he'd really done the job? What could have quickly become an ugly scene was dissolved by the tactful intervention of Mr. Castano.[37]

But from early 1938 on, Grierson was out of England much of the time. In two trips to North America he began his own tour of the international circuit which he had been so instrumental in forming. At first he traveled for the Imperial Relations Trust. This body, set up by the British government in 1937, had some characteristics in common with the earlier Empire Marketing Board. Founded as a testimonial to statesman Stanley Baldwin (and sometimes called the Baldwin Trust), its purpose was to reinforce ties between Britain and the Dominions. Film it regarded as "an eminently suitable medium," and through its advisory film committee chaired by Lord Clarendon, it appointed Grierson as film consultant.[38] In 1938 it began to commission some films of general interest to the Dominions and the empire—*Welsh Plant Breeding Station*, for instance, a subject which Elton had earlier dealt with in *Shadow on the Mountain* for the E.M.B. In the same year, the Canadian government requested of the Trust that it send Grierson over to advise on film activities.

This request from Canada had come about as an outgrowth of a meeting between Ross McLean and Grierson in December 1935, when the G.P.O. unit was recovering from the birth pangs of *Night Mail*. Wright, Cavalcanti, and Evelyn Spice were also present.[39] McLean was private secretary to the Honorable Vincent Massey, who in November had been appointed High Commissioner for Canada in the United Kingdom.

At the time of the meeting with Grierson, McLean was doing a special study of Canadian films in Britain and in 1936 prepared a memorandum on the subject to the Minister of Trade and Commerce, W. L. Euler. His report emphasized that Canadian films, designed mainly to attract tourists, did not answer all the questions or fully arouse the interest of British audiences. What were needed, he argued, were films on industry, community life, natural resources, and indeed, on Canada as a nation.[40] He suggested that the Motion Picture Bureau in Ottawa (which Grierson had visited in 1931) improve the quality of its films, produce more of them, and adapt them to the demands of the British public. "There is no sounder basis for the expansion of trade," wrote McLean, "than a deeper and wider knowledge of differences in tastes and modes of life. These can be conveyed most effectively by interpreting in a wider sense the function of the Motion Picture Bureau."[41]

It was several years and only after the exertion of much pressure by Vincent Massey, Lester Pearson, and others[42] that the Canadian government decided to act on one of McLean's main suggestions: that Grierson be invited to Canada to advise on methods of making Canadian information films more effective for distribution in other countries. The Imperial Relations Trust then commissioned him to travel to Canada—and to Australia and New Zealand as well—to review government film activities there and indicate further possibilities. In May 1938 he set sail.

The commercial film industry in Canada was even less self-sufficient than that of Britain had been when Grierson returned from the States and began work at the E.M.B. There was no feature production to speak of and theatrical distribution and exhibition were both dominated by the United States, especially by the Famous Players Canadian Corporation, controlled by Paramount Pictures. Of the few Canadian shorts and newsreels, most were produced by Associated Screen News, of Montreal, an offshoot of the Paramount combine, and by Vancouver Films (later Shelley Films), with offices in Vancouver and Toronto, which produced some prestige sponsored films for private industry. "All this means," wrote R. S. Lambert, "that Canadian film taste is standardised on the Hollywood pattern. The country has few theatres specialising in the exhibition of any particular type of film; none that makes a point of exhibiting 'unusual' films; and no news theatres."[43] (Theaters showing newsreels and shorts exclusively appeared in many large cities—in the United States anyway—during the 1940s.)

In the face of this situation, and modeled on the British Film Institute, the National Film Society of Canada (Canadian Film Institute since 1950) had been formed in 1935 by Donald W. Buchanan, Secretary-Treasurer. Honorary president of the Society was Lord Tweedsmuir, one-time chairman of the Scottish Film Council and governor of the British Film Institute. Dr. Sydney Smith, head of Manitoba University, was president. It was concerned both with promoting film as an educational medium and with increasing understanding and appreciation of films not ordinarily shown in commercial theaters. At the time Grierson arrived, its efforts had not been welcomed by the provincial governments or the educational institutions, and it was subject to complaints from film distributors and exhibitors. Nonetheless, there were by then eight branches of the society—in Montreal, Ottawa, Kingston, Toronto, Hamilton, Edmonton, Calgary, and Vancouver—which operated as local film societies, showing foreign "classics" that had never been seen in Canada. Their function was much like that of the "art theaters" in New York City or London.[44]

By 1938 the pioneering Government Motion Picture Bureau had lost some of its earlier prestige and effectiveness. This government film work, begun in 1914 in the Exhibits and Publicity Bureau of the Department of Trade and Commerce, had achieved its subsequent name and independence in 1921. In 1922 the National Parks

Branch of the Department of Interior and the National Museum of Canada also began to make films. For about ten years Canada led all other countries of the British Commonwealth in the use of films for government purposes. By the time of Grierson's 1931 visit hundreds of its films had been in circulation internationally. As McLean's memo noted, the Bureau's production put strong emphasis on scenic and travel pictures. Excellent by the standards of the twenties, they were relied upon heavily by the E.M.B. Film Unit and the Empire Film Library. But because of the Depression and the governmental austerity required, the Bureau was even later in getting sound than the E.M.B. had been. By 1934, when the Bureau's films first had sound tracks, it had dropped behind the surging British effort and had never regained its earlier lead.

"Working as always at speed," as Hardy could surmise from the evidence, in June Grierson submitted to the government a report which "resembled other reports about as much as a machine-gun resembled a plastic pistol."[45] His prescription followed McLean's diagnosis of the ills. Grierson advised (1) that all government film work be coordinated by one agency; (2) that a film officer be appointed to advise the government on production and distribution; (3) that more persons with creative ability be added, temporarily, to the staff of the Motion Picture Bureau; and (4) that the scope of the Bureau's production be widened. Returning to England in July, he was called back to Canada in October to "develop a plan for the co-ordination of the film production and distribution activities of . . . the Dominion Government in accordance with the proposals set out . . . and otherwise to assist in the inter-departmental discussions for making the plan effective."[46]

The plan Grierson developed after he arrived in November was approved in toto and the legislation for the National Film Act which he then drafted was introduced into the Canadian Parliament in March 1939. In the same month, Stuart Legg came to Canada to make *Youth Is Tomorrow* and *The Case of Charlie Gordon* at the Motion Picture Bureau for the Dominion Provincial Youth Training Program under the Department of Labour. The second of these was shot in the coal mining town of Glace Bay, Nova Scotia, and centered around a young garage mechanic. Of it Donald Buchanan wrote, "it went right to the core of the hopes and fears of unemployed youth. Such a youngster as the one in this film, who wanted to master the insides of an automobile, was much more a typical Canadian than were most of the characters generally depicted in our recognized literature, certainly more so than the peasants of *Marie Chapedelaine* or the complex middle-class sons of *Jalna*."[47] A mini-invasion had started, and a British re-colonization was about to begin, as it would turn out.

On May 2, 1939, the National Film Act was given the Royal Assent. The National Film Board thus set up consisted of eight members: the Minister of Trade and Commerce, as chairman, one other member of the Privy Council, and six members to be appointed by the Governor in Council, that is, by the Cabinet. Of these latter six, three were to be from outside the Civil Service and three to be members of the permanent Civil Service. Only two of the members of the board could be members of the party in power. All except the chairman and other members of the Privy Council were to hold office for three years.

The board's chief executive officer would be government film commissioner, to be appointed by the Governor in Council, his term of office also three years. He would be responsible to the board for advising on and coordinating all government film activities. The Motion Picture Bureau was to continue all production of government films except when the commissioner decided that they be made by a commercial firm or by a government department itself. Although the commissioner was to be consulted before work began on any film for government, he did not become the chief agent either for production or distribution. Both these duties remained with the director of the Motion Picture Bureau, who was also empowered to hire temporary production staff as required.

The purpose of the production and distribution of films by the Bureau under the direction of the board, was "to help Canadians in all parts of Canada to understand the ways of living and the problems of Canadians in other parts," and to concern itself with "distribution of Canadian Government films in other countries."[48] On this basis Grierson and Stuart Legg began to formulate a production program.

As it would develop, especially after Grierson and the board swallowed the Bureau in 1941, the board could be described as "a body within the framework of Government but free from the routine inhibitions of civil administration." It was administrative, determined policy, and had its own separate budget. In 1942 it was remarked that, "By its constitution, the Film Board has more direct power probably than any other film-propaganda organisation among the United Nations. It is in effect a Government Department with statutory powers."[49] It spoke in parliament through its chairman. The film commissioner reported once a month to the board, and was left completely free in the interval to perform all executive duties. Among the most remarkable of his executive authorities was the provision which enabled him to choose the staff necessary to the board's creative work on a temporary basis and free from many of the rigidities of the civil service.[50]

Writing to the Hon. Brooke Claxton, newly appointed chairman of the board at the time of his own resignation in 1945, Grierson explained that in drafting the National Film Act ("as an outsider with no intention in the whole wide world of operating it") he had been "primarily concerned to draft an administration shape which seemed to solve some of the problems which had come up in our war with the Treasury in the late twenties, and to eliminate the waste of energy and public money represented by Treasury governance of every detail of expenditure and employment. The various provisions represented therefore a deliberate attempt to secure the freedom necessary to creative work and creative people but still within a framework of public responsibility."

He went on to explain the rationale behind some of the unusual aspects of the Act in terms of this freedom. Clauses relative to employment of personnel and expenditures of money "as production requires" he regarded as vital. Inclusion of nongovernmental members on the board was "intended to give creative workers the extra support provided by the width of view of members of the public who can bring to the board's decisions special knowledge of the educational and cultural activities of the nation." And, finally, the inclusion of two ministers on the board "was to prevent the conception of the National Film Board as an instrument of a single department, or as tied to the apron strings of a single minister, and for the good reason that the National Film Board is a national service or it is nothing. I have also the theory, based on a long experience of ministers, that you get them good and not so good, and out of two there is a better chance of adequate representation in both Council and Parliament. I also thought one would watch the other. . . ."

Grierson then summarized these strategic particulars:

The various considerations, you see, represent a system of balance: all designed to protect creative workers on the one hand from administration processes unrelated to the nature of creative work and creative people; and, on the other hand, from the sort of bosses which the democratic system must unavoidably sometimes ease into administrative power. . . .

Note the special powers of the Commissioner, particularly after giving him the powers of the Director of the Motion Picture Bureau as well as the powers of the Commissioner. His powers are considerable and unique in Ottawa, and such as to make a few of the old buzzards of the Civil Service in Ottawa envious. . . .[51]

The astuteness of Grierson's analysis is attested to by the huge organization in Montreal that the board became, and by the brilliant body of work it has to show for the sixty plus years since its birth. The blueprint provided a solidity that would permit it to weather a succession of severe postwar storms and at the same time a flexibility that would enable it to develop in ways that could not have been fully foreseen in 1939. Modified slightly in 1950, the Film Act and the functioning of the board still continue much as Grierson had planned. A remarkable job it certainly was and an enduring tribute to the statesman's judgment and politician's skill that went into it.

During 1939, especially after the National Film Act which he had drafted was safely through the Canadian Parliament, Grierson spent a lot of time in the United States—New York City mainly. Earlier he had visited Washington, D.C., to see Pare Lorentz and study the legislation being drafted for the U.S. Film Service. According to Lorentz, Grierson borrowed from its form and ideas. They were accepted in Canada, but the U.S. Congress rejected the plan as drafted and the U.S. Film Service, with Lorentz at its head, had a precarious and short-lived existence under executive order. Grierson made the following comparison between Lorentz's work and his own:

Pare Lorentz had a first-rate chance to do in Washington what was done in London under the British Government. He concentrated on a few films, made at relatively large cost (but good ones, like *The River*). He did not develop an apprentice system, did not bring all the departments to his door. He did not develop a systematic coverage of all the possible department ground. The controlling factor in the British development was that it undertook documentary jobs for as many departments as it could get at and made hundreds of small one-reel or two-reel items.[52]

Also, Lorentz had associated himself too closely with the Democratic Party and was thus vulnerable to Republican attack. A partisan approach was tempting because it permitted rapid short-term growth but it did not provide insurance against political change. Grierson had never associated himself directly with British party politics while at the E.M.B. or G.P.O., nor would he permit his subordinates to do so. His basic criticism of the American approach was that the filmmakers wanted to indulge themselves in aesthetics at government expense—that there was no proper tradition or sense of responsibility in terms of public "stewardship."

If Lorentz lacked Grierson's capacity for leadership and salesmanship, he was representative in this respect of the U.S. documentary people in general. In New York, in an attempt to follow the British example, there was formed an Association of Documentary Film Producers in 1939. Its secretary was Mary Losey (later Field; Joseph Losey's sister) who, in London in 1938, had been stimulated by Grierson's ideas when she met him. The Association hoped by joint effort to promote documentary films and develop sponsorship among the big industries, as had been done by the Film Centre. Its membership included, Mary Losey noted, "with the conspicuous exception of Pare Lorentz, all the producers of documentary in America today . . . Joris Ivens and his two Dutch colleagues, John Ferno [formerly Fernhout] and Helen Van Dongen, Herbert Kline and his two Czech colleagues, Alexander Hackenschmied [later Hammid] and Hans Burger. Luis Buñuel from Spain is there, and several refugee German producers; and all those who have been diligently ploughing the American soil for a rich crop, Paul Strand, Ralph Steiner, and Willard Van Dyke." The group numbered sixty full members,[53] about the same size as the British Associated Realist Film Producers on which it had been modeled.

In August 1939 the Association held a party for Grierson and Flaherty. The latter had just arrived from London to join the U.S. Film Service and make what would become *The Land* (1941), sponsored by the Agricultural Adjustment Administration. But the Film Service had recently been killed by Congress, on the ground that it had not been authorized in the first place, and Flaherty was gloomy and uncertain about the project. On that occasion, Richard Griffith wrote to Rotha, "Mr. G. told us all where to get off. . . . Everything he said was to the point, of course, and our boys meekly swallowed it."[54] Grierson also spoke during the special week of documentary programs which concluded the showings organized by the A.D.F.P. at the New York World's Fair. In 1942, with its members dispersed by the war, the Association was disbanded, never to be re-formed (just as the comparable British group earlier).

Discussions began during Grierson's United States visits that led to the establishment of the Association of School Film Libraries (which became the Educational Film Library Association) and of the American Film Center (which continued into the late 1940s), both initially financed by the Rockefeller Foundation.[55] But, though Grierson exerted considerable influence on individual American documentary makers, he ultimately failed to impart his zeal for analysis and organization. American documentary remained individualistic to the point of anarchy, the filmmakers divided in their political ideologies, promoting themselves from job to job with gaps between. "What a people, what a people!" Grierson wrote of Americans generally, in a mixture of affection and exasperation.[56] Hardy, also from the British point of view, saw "[t]he main difficulty" as "lack of enlightened sponsorship." He acknowledged that "Public institutions such as the Rockefeller Foundation and the Museum of Modern Art Film Library did what they could to make documentary as practised in Britain more widely understood. But," he concluded, "industry was not convinced that this new form of public relations would sufficiently serve their ends. The U.S. Government was equally reluctant."[57] As a result, Grierson himself sadly acknowledged, "The more or less communal sharing of monies and opportunities which prevailed in England did not develop in the United States."[58]

## Outbreak of War

On September 1, 1939, when Germany marched into Poland and two days later Britain declared war, Grierson was in Hollywood. (Canada declared war on Germany on September 10.) He was on his way to Australia and New Zealand to continue his mission for the Imperial Relations Trust, having completed, as he thought, his work in Canada. In Hollywood he was trying to talk the industry into dealing with Canadian subjects in theatrical features. "I confess," he wrote, "I was greatly interested to hear how seriously these younger producers talked—the men like Walter Wanger. . . . In Wanger's office, we installed a ticker service from the United Press and daily we sat around it, reading the war news, considering how best film might serve mankind in this new situation."[59]

Grierson's first move was to go to Washington for consultations at the British Embassy with Lord Lothian. While there he was asked to go to Ottawa to discuss whether he would accept the position of film commissioner.[60] Though it had seemed reasonable for Grierson to write reports and even to frame legislation, given his expertise, since he was not a Canadian citizen his selection for a high governmental post was as unprecedented as the creation of the Film Board itself. The government had been surveying the field in Canada and everyone polled had recommended Grierson. Finally a Dr. Corvette, the top man in adult education, said: "Look, there's no one in Canada who can handle the job—Grierson's the only man for it."[61]

Grierson initially was reluctant to accept the offer, according to Hardy, "both because of the immediate commitment in Australia and also because he was anxious to return to Britain; but he was even more reluctant to see an organization he had helped to create falter at the outset."[62] So, on October 14, 1939, Grierson was appointed first government film commissioner of Canada. Further evidence of his reluctance was his stipulation that the contract be for only six months, presumably hoping that someone else could be found to take over after that. At any rate, he placed from the outset an eventual termination on his own services in Canada and always insisted that the board should be run by as well as for Canadians as soon as the personnel could be trained.

Appointed as members of the first board were: Hon. W. D. Euler, Minister of Trade and Commerce (chairman); Hon. T. A. Crerar, Minister of Mines and Resources; Col. V. I. Smart, Deputy Minister of Transport; Major J. G. Parmelee, Deputy Minister of Trade and Commerce; R. S. Hamer, Department of Agriculture; Professor W. C. Murray, Ph.D., University of Saskatchewan; Edmond Turcotte, editor of *Le Canada*; and C. G. Cowan, managing director, British American Bank Note Company. The secretary was Finlay Sim, Department of Trade and Commerce.

The Imperial Relations Trust released Grierson, temporarily at first, in order that he might assume his new position. Although he completed his trip to Australia and New Zealand early in 1940, the Trust decided to cancel most of its film activities due to the war. A small grant was made to the Empire Film Library to enable negatives or prints of outstanding prewar documentaries to be sent to the Dominions in exchange for their films. But Grierson would always acknowledge the decisive role the Trust had played in the worldwide development of documentary, during its brief activity, and the Film Board of Canada—and the government film units of Australia and New Zealand—stand as solid testimonial.

## A Look Back at the Thirties

Grierson had left behind in Britain a legacy of three to four hundred films produced by himself and his sixty or more former "apprentices" during the ten years between the release of *Drifters* and his acceptance of the Canadian post. Although only a few of the films possessed lasting greatness, that body of work represented the kind of steady flow, the constant reinforcement of message, which is well understood by present communication theorists and researchers and practiced by television "communicators" and salesmen. Thirty to forty films a year, three or more a month, playing across the countryside and all bearing a common social view, may have exerted a measurable effect on British public opinion, though there is no way to measure it. With their implicit and increasingly explicit emphasis on the importance and dignity of work and workers, on the need for organized social reform led by government, they may even have played some part in the shifting political balance that would lead to a sweeping Labour Party victory in 1945. If, as Basil Wright urged, documentary was "an approach to public information" and its position rightfully "to be in the forefront of policy,"[63] its worth has to be understood and gauged in terms of the social effects achieved by the total body of work rather than by the artistic value of individual creations or the styles of their creators.

Grierson's exciting debates with Flaherty had been along these lines: films used for social engineering rather than for the beauty and insight offered by the aesthetic experience; the timely rather than the timeless; the production program rather than scattered masterpieces; a cohesive group of disciplined filmmakers rather than a few creative geniuses. The argument, obviously, isn't all on Grierson's side. Perhaps, even strictly within his own terms, the contribution of his wave of films to social progress has been outdistanced by the enduring uplift to the human spirit embedded in the loveliness of Flaherty's few works. Surely the two positions are complementary as well as polar, and forever relevant.

Looking back over what he and others had wrought, Grierson put his own view at the end of the thirties most clearly and forcefully in a piece published in August 1939. The British documentary movement was from the beginning, he wrote, "an adventure in public observation."

It might, in principle, have been a movement in documentary writing, or documentary radio, or documentary painting. The basic form behind it was social, not aesthetic. It was a desire to make drama from the ordinary to set against the prevailing drama of the extraordinary; a desire to bring the citizen's eye in from the ends of the earth to the story, his own story, of what was happening under his nose. From this came our insistence on the drama of the doorstep. We were, I confess, sociologists, a little worried about the way the world was going. . . . As it happened, the film had its special advantages. It could command millions; it had the power of simple image; and a few pioneers—though not allied to our specific social purposes—had shown us the descriptive way. . . .

But the documentary film was, in spite of all these aids and instances, an essentially British development. Its characteristic was this idea of social use, and there, I believe, is the only reason why British documentary persisted when other aesthetic or aestheticky movements in the same direction were either fitful or failed. The key to this persistence is that the documentary film was created to fill a need, and it has prospered because that need was not only real but wide. If it came to develop in England there were three good reasons for it. It permitted the national talent for emotional understatement to operate in a medium not given to understatement. It allowed an adventure in the arts to assume the respectability of a public service. The third reason was the Empire Marketing Board and a man called Tallents.[64]

And later, in another article, he explained:

The whole idea was that we should make of this medium an instrument so sensitive to the needs of the public service that we would always be level with the problems of the time as they came along and, if possible, just a little ahead of the time. The idea was that we should so understand the problems of these sponsors of ours that we would be ahead of them in realizing their creative implications so far as the documentary film was concerned. Our freedom was to come, surely, from our demonstration that we were, in the practical issue, a necessary force for public understanding and public order.[65]

During those Film Centre years of 1937 to 1939, a period that Grierson called the "Indian Summer" of prewar documentary, his preoccupations had shifted from the description of jobs and workers at the E.M.B. and G.P.O. to the sociological problems of the thirties that big industry was talked into sponsoring, and on to an ever-increasing concern with the international scene as the meaning of the Munich accord became clear. The outbreak of war and his vantage point in Canada, backed by an imaginative and benevolent sponsorship, would permit him to further develop and communicate his global view on a vastly enlarged scale.

# 6 ➤ NATIONAL FILM BOARD OF CANADA (1939–45)

## The Country and Its Leader

Canada was something of a sleeping giant at the outbreak of World War II. In certain ways it was a geographical and cultural anomaly that no orderly minded nation planner would have permitted. Larger in area than the United States, its sparse population lay stretched in a two-hundred-mile-wide strip along its southern border; physically it represented an extension of the United States into the uninhabitable arctic. Its prodigious breadth of forest and prairie was blocked at the western end by a fierce mountain range that took considerable conquering before the Atlantic was finally linked to the Pacific by steel rails. By 1939, as a result of its railroad building, it was able to make fully available its enormous natural resources—lumber, wheat, minerals, and ores—for a world plunging into war. And with the air age, Canada's former remoteness would become the main line of global air routes, and the newly established Trans-Canada Air Lines, a government monopoly, would reduce some of the unwieldiness of its size.

In addition to the formidable task of creating a nation out of a wilderness, Canadians had always faced a struggle for national identity. At first it was the matter of establishing independence from Great Britain, greatly aided by the Balfour Declaration which emerged from the Imperial Conference of 1926. It had declared the Dominions to be "autonomous communities within the British Empire, equal in status, in no way subordinate one to another in any aspect of their domestic or external affairs, though united by a common allegiance to the Crown, and freely associated as members of the British Commonwealth of Nations."[1] More recently the gravitational pull of its powerful neighbor to the south had been smothering Canada's distinctiveness. Economically and culturally as well as geographically, Canada was something of an extension of the United States, whose citizens had even appropriated the name "American." What did it mean to be a Canadian anyway? What were Canada's arts and traditions; what was its special character? The national image was further blurred by the many ethnic divisions within its population. Almost four million of its twelve million people were French-speaking, and there were many immigrant minorities. Quebec seemed to have as close an affinity with France as with North America; parts of British Columbia were England itself transplanted; and much of the rest of the vast land was a somewhat drab and pale reflection of Iowa or Montana.

Politically, too, Canada represented a fusion of Britain and the United States, with vestiges of old French civil practice persisting among the habitants. There were three major political parties: the Conservative (like the Republican), the Liberal (like the Democratic), and, since 1932, the Co-operative Commonwealth Federation (the C.C.F.—later called the National Democratic Party), which was socialist. The Liberal Party had come into power in 1935 with Mackenzie King as prime minister. The Film Board and the appointment of film commissioner both came about, ultimately, because of King's favorable impression of Grierson's brightness and dedication to public service.[2]

An observation King made about what he sought among his appointees may well account for the opportunities made available to Grierson: "Integrity, of course, is essential. But what I look for is a sign that a man is anxious to do something for his fellow men, that he is interested in public service or in the job of doing a job. If he has not this zeal or enthusiasm the future is not encouraging. You have to be careful, too, that a man's enthusiasm is not for personal advancement. . . . [T]he first question must be 'does he want to work for his fellow men?'"[3]

In relation to the development of the documentary film, Forsyth

Hardy found it worth noting that "at a time when Britain and the British Commonwealth needed the dramatic psychological leadership film could help provide, it was not the Britain of Chamberlain but the Canada of Mackenzie King that had the vision to offer documentary the opportunity of expansion."[4]

## First Months at the N.F.B., and the Trip to Australia and New Zealand

The National Film Board of Canada, which had been "pulled off the sky," to use Grierson's phrase,[5] began in one and then two rooms in the West Block of Parliament Buildings in Ottawa. Besides Grierson there were Legg and two secretaries—Janet Scellen, who would remain Grierson's personal secretarial assistant throughout his years in Canada and at the World Today in New York City, and Jean McEntyre. Legg was serving as liaison to the Motion Picture Bureau, housed in a former sawmill on John Street with Captain Frank C. Badgley as director. In November Ross McLean was hired as assistant to the commissioner and occupied the outer room with the two secretaries while Grierson and Legg inhabited the inner one. Raymond Spottiswoode, who had been in Hollywood, and Evelyn Spice, herself a Canadian, joined the N.F.B.

The work was confined to planning, advising, and coordinating, and would so continue during the first two years of the board's existence. In addition to the National Film Act, which Grierson had drafted before becoming film commissioner, there was another special advantage in the Canadian situation created by the British North American Act of 1867, which had left education in the hands of the provinces. The federal government, in taking up the modern media of education, was thus free from the weighty academic tradition native to central education authorities of some other countries, notably Great Britain. It was free to plan intensive film programs in any fields of public welfare—health, domestic progress, national unity—that required them. It was free to attune its films to the many levels of discourse demanded by the structure of Canadian society. From the start the board's production and distribution plans were closely linked. No film was scheduled to be made by the bureau until its distribution needs and potentials had been studied by the board. Films were to be tailor-made for special purposes and specific audiences. In this way the lack of facilities for central, directive planning which had made itself felt in British documentary was avoided from the beginning.

In those first few months the March of Time, at the invitation of the board, began production for a February 1940 release depicting Canada's economic contribution to the war effort as well as the part to be played by its fighting forces. In it Grierson himself appears applying censorious scissors to a strip of film featuring a British battleship.[6] Already in the theaters was a Canadian epilogue to the British film *The Warning*, on methods of air raid defense, an interview in which the Hon. Norman Rogers, Minister of National Defense, stated Canadian war aims and means of fulfilling them. Legg's two films on the special problems of youth in a world at war were about to be released nontheatrically. Badgley's film of *The Royal Tour* was enjoying success in theaters across the country. And Grierson was discussing plans with commercial producers—Associated Screen News of Montreal, Audio Pictures of Toronto, and others in the west. The first films of the board's new scheme of national projection were scheduled to appear in March.[7] And by the time March arrived the board had hired ten persons in addition to the bureau's full-time staff of twenty-nine.

But at the end of January 1940, Grierson had left Canada to resume his trip to Australia and New Zealand that had been interrupted by the outbreak of war. He was on leave from the Film Board and again acting on behalf of the Imperial Relations Trust. Margaret had gone on ahead but Grierson stopped off in Hollywood as he had done on his earlier trip. This time, with Donald Slesinger, he made the rounds of the studios and "begged producer after producer to use his control of the most persuasive of all means of communication to inform, to warn the American public; to tell the world that the democratic way of life was in danger."[8] Because of the war, transportation was difficult to obtain, but Grierson "set out about January 31 to get somehow across the Pacific Ocean,"[9] sailing first to New Zealand.

Grierson's work had arrived before him. By the mid-thirties there had been established an Australian-New Zealand British Film League, and it was reported that in New Zealand "British documentary and educational films [had] a greater chance of distribution than anywhere in the Empire."[10] New Zealand had its own Government Film Studios, too, in Wellington, and the Publicity Division of the

Tourist and Publicity Department made the same kind of tourist films as Canada had done. But now the war had cut the overseas tourist trade to the bone, and the government film staff was being whittled down to an unarticulated skeleton.[11] Grierson's visit produced a shift in emphasis and, on the basis of a report he submitted at government request, a National Film Unit was created in 1941.

Its first job was to publicize New Zealand's war efforts and to build up national self confidence. A former journalist, E. Stanhope Andrews, came in as producer, and he brought with him university men with experience in radio and journalism as well as filmmaking. The unit started almost immediately, in the face of considerable technical difficulties, to produce "New Zealand Weekly Review," a one-reel screen magazine distributed free to the theaters. They also published the N. Z. *Film Letter*, which Andrews edited. (In 1940 Grierson said that nobody had ever seen the New Zealander's face on the screen.)[12] Grierson continued to regard New Zealanders with bemused fondness as "polynesian romantics," however, and their efforts never matched, even proportionately, the size or strength of the Canadian ones.

By March of 1940 Grierson was in Sydney. (Writing to Elton from there he was already concerned about postwar plans and economic rearrangement across national lines.)[13] Production by the Australian government had been very modest indeed: two or three films a year at most, made under the administration of the Department of Commerce, chiefly to advertise agricultural products overseas. With the advent of war, the Films Division went over to the newly formed Department of Information, which, consisting largely of newspaper men, was apathetic about the use of film, concentrating instead on still photography and journalism.[14] As the result of Grierson's discussions with various federal and state ministers, documentary film committees were set up in Canberra, Sydney, Melbourne, Adelaide, and Brisbane. Initially they were financed by the Imperial Relations Trust; later they were supported by their respective state education departments.[15] The New South Wales Documentary Film Council was also formed, with Professor A. K. Stout, once an active member of the Edinburgh Film Guild, and John Heyer, a young film director, providing the initiative.[16]

In April 1940 Grierson set sail from Australia to return to Canada. It had been a whirlwind tour involving enormous distances. He had more than fulfilled his obligations to the Imperial Relations

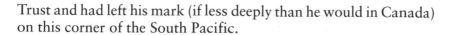

Trust and had left his mark (if less deeply than he would in Canada) on this corner of the South Pacific.

## Recruiting Staff

Back in Ottawa, Grierson resumed the hiring of a staff that would assume huge proportions. By December 1940 there were still under 12 full-time employees at the board with a number of others, such as script writers, working on a special-assignment basis; the bureau maintained its separate staff of from 30 to 35. By October 1941, largely as a result of the merger of the Bureau with the Film Board, there were 55. But then the phenomenal expansion began: by December 1942 there were 293 employees, and the number continued to increase until in April 1945, near the end of Grierson's administration, there were 739.[17]

He looked for the same educated lads, and increasingly lasses, of parts he had in Britain. "So far as my own operation is concerned," he wrote, "the surest way to apprenticeship in documentary is a good degree in political science or economics."[18] And the interview method and capacity for spotting talent remained much the same. James Beveridge, one of the earliest of the young Canadian hirelings, stressed Grierson's "fantastic ability to size people up—to judge their worth—quickly and accurately. A remarkably acute intuitive psychologist."[19] He was right about the people he picked, sometimes on the basis of that single interview, about 85 percent of the time, Marjorie McKay estimated.

Interviews with job applicants usually consisted of discussing what books they had read or what they thought about paintings. If they said all they really wanted to do was to make movies they weren't hired.[20] To the young and inexperienced who passed the scrutiny Grierson might say: "You want to be a director? You've got lots of imagination. Report for work Monday."[21] Another applicant, however, Nicholas Read, an American who joined the board at its beginning in search of training, recalled his first meeting with Grierson as a very down-to-earth affair. "He fixed me with those sea-blue eyes under his bushy eyebrows and his first question went right to the point . . . 'How many films have you made?' He then went on with a whole list of embarrassing inquiries such as, 'You can operate a camera? You know how to operate a hot splicer?'" When Read, and many others who were hired, failed to measure up fully to Grierson's standards, they were ushered off to the sawmill, where Legg was busy training and organizing young hopefuls into filmmakers.[22]

Though very conscious of waste, Grierson was resolute in getting a staff that could do the job. If he never overspent, he did have trouble matching salary, travel, and other expenditures to government categories. This was a particularly pressing problem because, starting almost from scratch, he had to form a unit that could expand into an industry. There was, consequently, a tremendous turnover of personnel at the board, which Grierson justified as the positive value of change.[23] Given the size and urgency of wartime requirements he needed to have his own producer-teacher function supplemented by other experienced filmmakers on a scale which a single Flaherty or Cavalcanti could no longer handle.

From England there was first of all Stuart Legg, who would be a tower of strength throughout Grierson's tenure. Much of Legg's wartime experience at the N.F.B. could be described by a Grierson remark at one early point: "Legg is looking after his own films and fifty or sixty more on the stocks while I am away. . . ."[24] He was especially skillful as an editor and script writer, and the people who worked closely with him greatly profited from and were very fond of him. Others, however, found his intellectualism formidable. A cool type he was said to be, unable to establish relationships with others.[25]

If Legg was "cynical" and "sardonic," as was alleged by some, Raymond Spottiswoode was "prickly." A trained technician and director, he was assigned to work with a commercial firm, Audio Pictures of Toronto, on a Film Board production about the Commonwealth Air Training Plan entitled *Wings of Youth*. He would become supervisor of technical services for the board.

Grierson had also invited over Stanley Hawes, who arrived in Ottawa in February of 1940 while Grierson was in New Zealand. Hawes was a veteran of about ten years' experience in British documentary. In 1941, after the board had taken over the bureau, he became Senior Producer of Non-Theatrical Productions, while Legg was Senior Producer of Theatrical Productions. Hawes was a film craftsman, interested especially in labor and sociological matters. Once described as "a stocky, stubborn midlander,"[26] Grierson referred to him as a "clerk," a "greengrocer," on occasion, but respected his working-class English doggedness.[27] Hawes remained with the Canadian board until 1946, when he resigned to join the newly established Australian board.

J. D. Davidson, the cameraman who had joined the E.M.B. unit in 1930, arrived in Canada in mid-November of 1940 to serve as director-editor. Norman McLaren was in New York City, having left the G.P.O. unit in 1939, when Grierson phoned him just before Christmas of 1940. Working for Caravel, a producer of sponsored films, he was torn between the desire to join the N.F.B. and his dislike of unpleasantness with Caravel, for he was mid-picture. (Grierson once called him "one of the film world's gentlest people.") When he hedged, Grierson simply passed word to the Canadian ambassador to the United States. Within a week McLaren was hard at work in Ottawa.[28] In 1942 he set up the board's animation unit and—using his technique of drawing directly on film, which was at once cheap, practical, and extremely painstaking—produced brief trailers like *Mail Early*, *Five for Four*, *V for Victory*, *Hen Hop*, and *Dollar Dance* to promote early mailing for Christmas, war savings, and anti-inflation curbs.[29] In 1945–46 he continued with a series on Canadian folk songs that began the rich creative experimentation for which he and the board became internationally known and admired. Another of the old boys, J. P. R. Golightly, was seconded from the British Army at Grierson's request to become the London representative of the N.F.B.; and Basil Wright made two extended trips to Canada during the war.

From the United States Grierson drew another contingent. New Yorker Irving Jacoby was the first to arrive early in 1940. He had had considerable experience in making Hollywood shorts and industrial films and had spent a year in England. Working under Legg, and in collaboration with the novelist Morley Callaghan, he "snowshoed all over Canada" to make *Hot Ice*, on the national sport of ice hockey. He followed that with *High Over the Borders* (1941), a beautifully made film on the facts and mysteries of bird migration in the Western Hemisphere,[30] the cost of which Grierson, in an impressive feat of persuasiveness, managed to charge to the Royal Canadian Air Force.[31] After Pearl Harbor Jacoby returned to the United States to join the Office of War Information. Roger Barlow, the fine documentary cinematographer of *The City* and *Valley Town*, arrived in 1940 to work on half a dozen films. The first, *Women in War*, was directed by Hawes. After that Barlow became associate director with Spottiswoode and cameraman on *Wings of Youth*, the sixth in the "Canada Carries On" monthly series. Among other U.S. filmmakers who worked at the board were Nicholas Read (later of Potomac Films in Washington, D.C.), Gordon Weisenborn (who said he was abducted by Grierson from the University of Chicago at the age of nineteen), Leo Seltzer, Leroy Robbins, John Lenauer, Milton Shiffman (an editor), Harold Rawson, Harry Alpert (an excellent cameraman), Fred Lasey, and Harry Randall (later film officer for the Heart Association in New York). Flaherty did some shooting and the novelist Richard Wright also worked for the board for some time. The Americans, of course, carried Grierson's influence back into the States as well as helping to build a Canadian film movement.

The Hollanders Joris Ivens and John Ferno, who had been working in the United States, began their wartime filmmaking in Canada. *Action Stations!* about the struggle of the Canadian Merchant Marine against German submarines, was Ivens's first film at the board, and Ferno edited *High Over the Borders*. From occupied France came Boris Kaufman (Jean Vigo's, and later Elia Kazan's, great cameraman, and brother of Soviet documentarian Dziga Vertov). His was the principal teaching influence on the board's camera work. Alexander Alexeieff, extraordinary animator of the pinboard technique (e.g., *Night on Bald Mountain*), also arrived from France to work at the board.

Canadians who had gained filmmaking experience elsewhere were invited back to assist the new national effort. Evelyn Spice, Grierson's longtime associate in England, was one of these. Julian Roffman was another. He came to Ottawa in September 1941 and remained there until he left with Grierson in 1945 to work at the World Today. He had been something of a child prodigy in New York (e.g., *And So They Live* [1940] with John Ferno) and at the board made the admirable *13 Platoon*, about a young lieutenant and his understanding of and relationship with his men. It was, along with British films of the time, an early use of synchronous sound recording with nonactors. In setting up the production, Grierson told the generals, "This small, young man [he was tinier than Grierson] is a great filmmaker. Let him do whatever he wants." Roffman regarded Grierson as his "film father." (He had two photographs on his office wall, one of his father and one of Grierson.) Grierson gave him the feeling he could do anything and he reveled in the free creative atmosphere at the board.[32]

Ross McLean, who had no previous filmmaking experience, produced and directed some films during the board's early days. His talents were chiefly administrative, however. Though never exactly a film man (Grierson ungenerously if amusingly was said to have said of him that he was "all right as a scribbler, a clerk, but not much imagination")[33] McLean was extremely knowledgeable and well-connected in the Liberal Party. He in part made it possible for Grierson to operate as effectively as he did.[34] McLean became assistant film commissioner in September of 1941 and deputy commissioner in February 1943. With Grierson traveling and in conference much of the time it was McLean who made many of the daily decisions that kept the organization functioning properly. While away on one of his trips, with McLean "in general charge" at Ottawa, Grierson wrote of him: "McLean represents as well as anyone what Canada is about nowadays and keeps it marching into a dream of the Canadian future which in these parts excites almost everyone under forty. I support him in this, with a special affection for the French Canadian viewpoint."[35] When Grierson resigned, McLean became acting film commissioner, and then commissioner in January 1946. Later his nephew Grant McLean became acting film commissioner while Ross served as executive secretary to the Board of Broadcasting Governors of the Canadian Broadcasting Corporation.

Donald Fraser, the first of the young Canadian apprentices who would form around the core of foreign veterans, was hired late in 1939. He had met Grierson in England in 1938 and, during the year prior to commencing his Film Board career, had been executive secretary of the Canadian Film Committee (subsequently called the National Film Society), which received sponsorship from the Imperial Relations Trust. At the N.F.B. he started as a cameraman. James Beveridge was another of the early recruits who would become senior members of the production staff. He first became a director and cutter on nontheatrical films. F. Radford ("Budge") Crawley had had some amateur experience before working for the board, and he and his wife Judith became professional 16 mm producers and color specialists, with their own firm, which would continue to undertake much work for the board. Tom Daly, who has his name as producer on a disproportionately high number of the finest of postwar N.F.B. films, graduated from the University of Toronto in English language and literature in June 1940. In September he was interviewed and subsequently hired by Grierson, home ill and sitting up in bed in an old grey sweater with people flowing in and out of his bedroom. Daly waited through lunch for his turn and Margaret Grierson took him in hand. Since there was as yet no stock footage library Daly was assigned to start one, with the outtakes lying around the rooms at the Motion Picture Bureau. He became Legg's assistant, researching the stock footage and editing.[36] Michael Spencer met Grierson in 1940, too, and was hired to work with Crawley, already on his second film for the board, as cameraman and editor. He would later move into distribution at the N.F.B., and subsequently became first head of the Canadian Film Development Corporation.

Guy Glover joined the board through his friendship with Norman McLaren. He had been trained as a biologist and then went into the theater—his first film work was at the board, under Legg and Spottiswoode. When Grierson was impressed by an animated film he had worked on, *Marching the Colours*, he was placed in a supervisory position. Glover conceded that he found the English intolerable at times and that he fought with Grierson to give the Canadians more responsibility—they were not really on their own until 1945–46. Instead of disciplining the rebel, Grierson promoted him: Glover headed the French unit during the second half of the war. He followed Grierson to New York and worked as a producer at World Today during its short life, and then returned to the Film Board where he remained for the remainder of his career.[37]

Dallas Jones, who would later work in the United States, was one of the most talented of the young Canadian directors, and his *A Man and His Job* one of the good early films. Graham McInnes, with Budge Crawley, began a Canadian artists series for the board; one of the best of them was *Canadian Landscape*, centering around the work of the painter A. Y. Jackson. Sydney Newman (who would much later work in British television contemporaneously with Grierson and subsequently become head of the N.F.B.) came on. Other early recruits include Stanley Jackson (who had been a teacher and would become a specialist in agricultural films), Sol Dworkin (later in charge of film production at Bell Telephone Laboratories), and Ralph Foster (who subsequently formed a partnership with Julian Roffman in commercial production in Toronto).

A group of young female filmmakers and assistants were hired as well. Aside from Evelyn Spice (to become Spice Cherry), there was Gudrun Bjerring (later Parker, a former newspaper woman), Margaret Ann Bjornson (then Adamson, then Lady Elton), and

Daphne Lilly (Anstey), among others. When suitably provoked, Grierson would maintain that "The National Film Board was a matriarchy."[38]

In 1941 a young Canadian musician, Louis Applebaum of Toronto, began a distinguished career as a film composer at the board during the war; at the end of it he was loaned out to do scores for two Hollywood features, *Tomorrow the World* and *The Story of G.I. Joe* (both 1945). Maurice Blackburn was hired as an N.F.B. staff composer at the same time.

## The Board and the Bureau

With the expansion of personnel and production, the Motion Picture Bureau had to use its meagre equipment at John Street to the best advantage of everyone. The day shifts would bustle around the cutting rooms and laboratories concerned with their own projects, to be followed at night by other workers intent on different productions altogether. The difficulties of the board and the bureau were characterized as similar to those of someone trying to pour a quart of milk into a pint bottle. Raymond Spottiswoode recalled how

> Back in 1941, a four-reel review of the second year of the war was produced in little over a week by the entire staff splitting up the cutting processes between them—editing, music, effects, negative, and so on—and putting themselves on twenty-hour shifts to do it. A year before that, our chief engineer would often find himself awakened in the middle of the night to come down to the Board and fix a broken printer working on a late shift. Arriving, he would go out into the back yard, clip off a piece of barbed wire fence, file a cotter pin out of it, and set the printer going again.[39]

Problems of equipment, time, and personnel were overcome in part by assigning productions to the few existing outside firms such as Associated Screen News of Montreal, where Gordon Sparling made the highly popular *Peoples of Canada* for the board in 1940, and the newly formed Crawley Films.[40]

But Grierson was beginning to see that the real impedance to the board's development was the administrative anomaly by which it set policy but did not itself produce. Inevitably friction had grown between the enterprising, ambitious new people and the members of the original Motion Picture Bureau who wanted to retain the status quo and who resented the ways films were now being made.

Standing in Grierson's path most prominently was the bureau's director, Captain Frank Badgley.

Grierson had tried to maintain an amiable relationship with Badgley and was reluctant to take the step he now felt necessary. Badgley had been an "intimate, if only an alcoholic one,"[41] who claimed to have loaned equipment for *Drifters* and was under an exaggerated impression that he had been responsible for Grierson's being invited to Canada in the first place[42]—assistance which, if rendered, he clearly had come to regret. Apparently he was disappointed that he had not been appointed film commissioner, and he did not like Grierson's kind of film.[43] By October 1940, Badgley had become a "mule and a nuisance," and Grierson had decided he would have to take action.[44]

The action was dramatic to say the least. At the December meeting of the board, Grierson tendered his resignation. He stated his grounds as the unmet need for: (1) more money and flexibility in hiring filmmakers to remove them further from the strict civil service categories, and (2) full supervision by the film commissioner of the Motion Picture Bureau. He was resigning, he said, so that he could speak on these two matters crucial to the future of creative government filmmaking without it being charged that he was simply trying to increase his personal power in government.

A year before this contretemps, Grierson had written of W. D. Euler, chairman of the Film Board and Minister of Trade and Commerce, "I have served with many distinguished British Ministers in the development of the film as an instrument of National Information but I have known none who more handsomely took the big view."[45] Now, in an exchange of letters with Euler immediately after the December board meeting, Grierson reaffirmed his intention of resigning—pointing out that he had taken the job for only a short time and that there was good reason for a Canadian to be film commissioner—and re-emphasized that those two central problems would face the new incumbent. Euler replied that Grierson was trying to get altogether out from under regular control by the Treasury, "contrary to the established principles of democratic government." Grierson was furious and went "to see a lot of very high officials indeed."[46] During this crisis the French were most loyal in their support of him; with his "special affection for the French Canadian viewpoint" he had seen to it that more French films were produced than had been the case previously.

At first his intention was to depart around the end of January. Badgley was to be given back the film work—at least his own. In February the resignation still stood but no replacement was available or qualified, and the Griersons planned to be in Ottawa another six months, wrote Margaret, "but nothing definite has been decided."[47] In March the resignation still had not been accepted. There had been a prompt and continuous press response urging that Grierson be retained and, it was reported, "In view of the Prime Minister's announcements of his special interest in the retention of Mr. Grierson in Canada for further development of the National Film Board, it is indicated that he will stay on for at least some months."[48] During those same months Grierson held his ground, and the government eventually capitulated under the mounting pressure.

On June 11, 1941, by Order in Council P.C. 4215, the Film Board absorbed the Motion Picture Bureau and the film commissioner established himself in the John Street premises in July, instructing the guards not to admit its former director.[49] (Badgley's checks were mailed to his home; he was paid for a year after he stopped work.) It was thus that the N.F.B. became responsible not only for planning and advising on all government films but also for making them or having them made by outside producers. On June 11, also, the powers and duties of the Minister of Trade and Commerce as defined by the National Film Act were transferred to the Minister of National War Services, Maj. Gen. L. R. La Fleche. Two months later the Stills Division of the Motion Picture Bureau was also transferred by another Order in Council from the Department of Trade and Commerce to the N.F.B.[50] The way was now clear for total coordinated effort.

## Up to Speed

Of the board's new home Grierson wrote:

> Standing fairly high up on the banks of the Ottawa River and thereby considerably open to the sun, sky, and a pretty good hunk of Quebec scenery opposite, the National Film Board is a largeish ugly building. Across the road, with sublime inappropriateness, lies the best piece of architecture in Ottawa—the Embassy of Vichy France. There are a lot of swallows, the tugs tow huge lumber rafts downstream, and the Film Board building never closes, or at any rate not till very late at night.

... it has been enlarged and re-equipped. There are two projection theatres, one of which is also a recording and dubbing studio as well as being large enough for minor sets. The labs have just been overhauled and new machinery installed. There is a big stills department. And rows of cutting rooms, camera rooms, stock rooms; and lots of offices full of people writing scripts and commentaries, wrestling with financial schedules and location accounts. A busy joint, in fact; for it houses virtually the whole Canadian production set-up, and of the 250 men and women employed by the Board some 190 work at these headquarters.[51]

Spottiswoode's description of the converted lumber mill was much less glowing. While it had been "roomy enough for the 30 or 40 members of the former Motion Picture Bureau, it [was] hopelessly over-crowded by its present staff," he said. "The flimsy wooden partitions which were hastily built . . . and the unvented interior cutting rooms, formed a very serious fire hazard. The conversion of this old building into a fairly safe structure was a difficult business, and involved rebuilding the whole of the inside while the 200 people continued to work."[52] Daphne Anstey, who was a negative cutter, remembered one night in 1943 when the building caught fire and the staff passed strips of negative for Legg's *The War for Men's Minds* by hand and spread them on the lawn of the Vichy Embassy (!) across the street to keep them in order.

As for the staff, Grierson wrote that "Most of them are Canadians, learning their job in very much the same tough way as the British documentary people did in the 'thirties,"[53] and Spottiswoode detailed the training:

Two principles have guided the development of film skills from the start: maximum interchange of information between everyone, and maximum individual responsibility for everyone. There is a constant transfer of staff between departments. Our present personnel manager has been successively head of the negative cutting department, the film library, and the laboratory. The laboratory staff has frequently exchanged members with the camera department, and directors and script writers have often handled cameras. Shifts of this kind mean constant training and retraining, and are sometimes disconcerting to those who have to plan continuity of production. But they have supplied an invaluable versatility of skill and have certainly helped to prevent the Film Board from getting stale and falling into a rut. . . .

The experience . . . of having to learn everything from the bottom, and of having to use resourcefulness when there was no proper equipment to do the job—all this has been of inestimable value to the staff. It has led to a give-and-take which has prevented individuals from getting overspecialized, and has speeded up the development of unexpected skills.[54]

Collectively and anonymously (there were no personal credits on the N.F.B. wartime pictures), the production personnel set out to make hundreds of films. The first year closed in October 1940 with some forty pictures either in distribution, in production, or in script preparation; by fiscal year 1943–44 the annual rate of release had increased to two hundred. Films were to become weapons of war, helping to weld together home-front efforts and also telling the story of Canada's contribution to her partners in the world struggle. From the outset, films were needed for a great variety of special purposes. National Defense used them to help recruiting (Canada never adopted a draft) and training. Munitions and Supply wanted Canadians to see on their screens the urgency and importance of the industrial front. The Wartime Prices and Trade Board wished to explain controls and the rationing system to consumers. Films became a powerful aid in the sale of bonds and war savings certificates by the War Finance Committee. The Wartime Information Board showed Canada's share in the total effort to the audiences of its allies.[55]

But under the pressure of wartime urgencies, Grierson never lost sight of the ongoing requirements of peacetime. His social conscience and vision led him to accentuate the positive and to avoid the negative propaganda of hate so easily available. In his conception, the board was using films as they had never been used before, "in a planned and scientific way to provide what might be described as a supplementary system of national education."[56] "All our Canadian war films were also peace films: there was nothing we founded but was not founded to stay on for peacetime purposes."[57] "The main thing is to see this National Film Board plan as a service to the Canadian public, as an attempt to create a better understanding of Canada's present, and as an aid to the people in mobilizing their imagination and energy in the creating of Canada's future." He firmly believed that "A country is only as vital as its processes of self-education are vital."[58]

Of the vast communication empire the N.F.B. would become, Marjorie McKay wrote: "At the top, and no one was in any doubt, was John Grierson—a fiery, aggressive, brilliant Scot, sometimes domineering, sometimes hard and cynical, sometimes sentimental—with one object, to build an organisation as fast as possible to carry the government's message as effectively as possible to every Canadian and to people of other countries."[59] By late in the war there were eight principal administrators working under Grierson: Marjorie McKay, supervisor of business management; Jack Ralph, production secretary; D. P. Wallace, coordinator of production and distribution; Wesley Greene, coordinator of distribution; Ralph Foster, coordinator of graphics; Graham McInnes, information editor; R. J. Spottiswoode, supervisor of technical services; Percy Newman, chief of liaison staff. The work of the board was divided into three main sections: Production, including technical services; Distribution; and Photo Service and Display. The Production staff consisted of twelve producers—each responsible for the actual production and charged with a specific program—who worked in the field with their own teams. Senior producers were Stuart Legg ("The World in Action"), Alan Field ("Canada Carries On"), Stanley Hawes (Industrial Relations), Evelyn Spice Cherry (Agricultural and Consumer films), Guy Glover (French Language Unit), and Norman McLaren (Art and Animation Unit).[60]

The allocation of production funds followed the double view which war had necessitated: Civil Estimates and War Estimates. Most of the N.F.B.'s War Information Programme was on behalf of the war departments of government already mentioned; by fiscal year 1944–45 a million and a quarter dollars were budgeted for such production. From its own budget, the board produced the National Film Programme, designed to promote unity and understanding among the various segments that made up the nation, and to interpret Canada to the world at large. The latter budget was small, however—most of it required to maintain staff and facilities—and a good deal of ingenuity and argument were constantly employed to encourage sponsoring departments to subsidize Grierson's broader view. What he accomplished was "through the initiative of the government and with the support of all the political parties," to be sure. "But," he pointed out,

> that support has not been given out of any special interest in education, or films, or art. If I asked baldly for money to film "the work of Canadian artists" I doubt that, in time of war, I would easily get it. On the other hand "national unity" is a matter of great concern to every party in Parliament.

This alliance with political necessity has a great deal to do with the vitality and the future of education and of art. The film on Tom Thompson's paintings [*West Wind*, 1943] is none the worse for having a job to do in creating national unity and giving homesick soldiers a glimpse of their native land. A film, like any other work, discovers new energies when it knows it is going places.[61]

The day-to-day supervision of his own operation and liaison with other government departments were reported at the monthly board meetings. The board allowed Grierson a great deal of latitude, however, and it was he who set the course as well as remained at the tiller. An extraordinarily busy and important job it was, with a sense of satisfaction resulting from the hard work. "Taking it by and large," he wrote, "you could say, to those who remember Blackheath, that the National Film Board is like Blackheath multiplied by five, fully equipped and working one hundred per cent to schedule on an enormous production programme. The place feels good. The people are purposeful and not arty, and they know how to work. And they are not only making the documentary idea an integral part of Canadian life but also helping to push it forward towards new and lively international perspectives."[62]

## Production

At first Grierson involved himself closely with production. He continued to mastermind "The World in Action" series which Legg, with a small unit, actually produced. Legg's experience with Grierson in creation, he said, was always that of a collaborator: because of Grierson's dominant personality the films he supervised were really his films made through other people.[63] But as the huge operation began to take shape under him, much time was required for general administration and leadership. More and more responsibility devolved onto the production units themselves—there were seven of them by the end of 1941, twelve by the end of the war. Spottiswoode explained their functioning:

The production unit, through a liaison officer, often makes its own initial contact with a government department for the making of a film, acting under general guidance in policy from the Commissioner and Deputy Commissioner. The unit budgets its new picture, and is solely responsible for holding to this budget with the aid of weekly reports from the accounts department. From the beginning, the producer steers his film himself, negotiating the script, choosing director, cameraman, and composer, and supervising the editing and sound recording. Only at this final stage does he call in the Commissioner or his Deputy for approval, and if any changes have to be made, they are invariably made by the unit itself. This kind of self-determination has had excellent results. It has developed individual styles. It has trained people in the rough school of "sink or swim." It has given producers a fine sense of how to discharge a public service.[64]

With the N.F.B. practice of picking "only the keenest and most intelligent men and women" and then giving them their heads as quickly as possible, "the skills of the better workers" developed with a speed which "proved astonishing."[65]

In those critiques of films near their completion, Grierson went directly to the central problems, never dealing with details but invariably hitting a principal weakness to be corrected or a virtue to be strengthened. He was very concerned that the people about whom the films were made should like them as well as the filmmakers and audiences—was very strong for honesty and decency in relation to the subject people.[66]

As early as Grierson's tour of Australia and New Zealand, Legg had already begun work on the first of the two major wartime series, "Canada Carries On." Intended to depict Canada's part in the war to its own people and others, it was designed for theatrical and subsequent nontheatrical distribution. Grierson had planned the series with G. Herbert Lash, then director of the Public Information Division (later called Wartime Information Board), of the Department of National War Services, which sponsored. One and two reels in length, it was released monthly, by Columbia Pictures, throughout the war and afterwards.

The first production, *Atlantic Patrol* (April 1940), dealt with the part played by Canadian escort vessels in the convoy system. It was made up mainly of stock footage from England and elsewhere. *Churchill's Island* (June 1941) received a Certificate of Merit from the Hollywood Academy of Motion Picture Arts and Sciences as the outstanding documentary short of that year. It cost a modest $4,990.15. *Warclouds in the Pacific* (November 1941) achieved a remarkable scoop by appearing only ten days before Pearl Harbor with a compact survey of the smoldering situation which exploded when the Japanese attacked the United States base. It contained some March of Time footage, and that organization tried unsuccessfully to hold up its U.S. release through the courts until its own film on the subject could be distributed.[67] It was with *Warclouds in the Pacific* that regular distribution of N.F.B. productions in U.S. theaters began.[68] In Canada, by March of 1942, approximately nine hundred of a thousand-odd theaters were showing the "Canada Carries On" series and paying better prices for them than for any other short subjects.[69] *Zero Hour* (June 1944) scored another scoop with the first account of the invasion of Normandy. It was made possible by the use of footage on D-Day preparations and the provision of more than a dozen different endings covering possible invasion points from Norway to the Mediterranean.[70] By the end of the war, "Canada Carries On" was being distributed to theaters in the United Kingdom, Australia, India, and the West Indies, as well as North America.[71]

The American Richard Griffith wrote of "Canada Carries On" that

> *Churchill's Island* (1941) and *This is Blitz* (1942) easily illustrated the novelty of the series. . . . Whatever their official subject, they focused on the interplay of historic forces which linked the individual action to the total picture. They gave a sense of competence, of foresight, of ability to anticipate emergencies. They had an intellectual toughness and realism that stood out from the welter of patriotic or moralistic indignation at Nazi horrors. They met the Nazis on their own grounds. They were the first films to tell of Total War.[72]

Clearly, "Canada Carries On," with its edited stock footage and dramatization of issues and events, was closely modeled on "The March of Time." But Grierson and Legg went beyond de Rochemont in the eyes of some and, especially in the companion series, "The World in Action," began to compete heavily with "March of Time" in the world market.

This second monthly series, of two reelers, made its appearance in June 1942. Sponsored by the Wartime Information Board, it was distributed by United Artists. Stanley Hawes took over "Canada Carries On" and Legg produced "The World in Action" throughout the war. The latter series adopted an even broader international point of view, offering concise analyses of the war and of the probable postwar world[73]—a kind of analysis at which both Grierson and Legg were adept. "This isn't a documentary war, it's a newsreel war," Grierson maintained. In order to keep pace with events, it was necessary to use more and more newsreel footage shot by anonymous cameramen scattered around the globe; less and less of the material could be specially shot. The director, or director-cameraman, hitherto dominant in documentary, gave way to the writer and editor as controlling figures.[74] In addition to the work of Canadian combat cameramen, footage was drawn from Britain and the other Commonwealth countries, from the United States, the Soviet Union, and China. The style was hard-hitting, the diverse images briskly edited to a preconceived commentary. Edgar Anstey said of Legg's technique that it "had some links with the *March of Time* manner, but with more literary grace. . . . maximum commentary impact depended on a very precise relationship between picture and, not only word, but sometimes even syllable."[75] And Margaret Ann Elton fondly recalled Legg's artful "rodomontades" (boastings).[76]

*Inside Fighting Russia* (April 1942), the first release, set the position of that war ally within historical and geographical context. It established precedent by running two weeks in the Washington, D.C., newsreel theater, the Trans-Lux. About *Food—Weapon of Conquest* (June 1942), *Time* magazine exclaimed: "This cinematic editorial is almost a blueprint of how to make an involved, dull, major aspect of World War II understandable and acceptable to moviegoers."[77] *The War for Men's Minds* (June 1943) marked Grierson's and Legg's first attempt to predict and discuss the world beyond war. It fully embodied Grierson's ideas about propaganda and his internationalism. Richard Griffith noted, however, that though it "bore all the earmarks of a consciously intended masterpiece," it "was one of those spectacular failures which are often impossible to analyze or explain."[78]

Emphasis on postwar matters—that is to say persistent social-economic-political concerns—became one of the special distinctions of "World in Action." For example, *Labour Front* (October 1943), according to the *New York Times*, asked: "Could not the same cooperation and consideration for the working man be used to build a peace-time economy as strong as that in war . . . ?"[79] *Global Air Routes* (April 1944) explained the revolutionary changes war had made in earlier conceptions of geography and communication from the point of view of German general and geographer Karl Haushofer (1860–1946)—an awareness of geopolitics and strategy pervaded the series. (Grierson claimed he had been introduced to Haushofer's theories by a young Scottish teacher while still in secondary school—

that he knew about geopolitics before Hitler did.)[80] *When Asia Speaks* (June 1944) was a review of the new situations developing in the Far East, and of the problems and potentialities there which closely concerned the United Nations. It was pitched so correctly that it was in active nontheatrical distribution years after the end of war. *Inside France* (December 1944) surveyed that country's recent past and future—internal dissension, conquest and occupation, defiance and the Maquis resistance against Vichy, and new unity and hopes for victory. *Now—The Peace* (May 1945) explained the organization of the United Nations, and *Food—Secret of the Peace* (July 1945) returned to the subject of *Food—Weapon of Conquest* with an analysis of nutrition as the chief problem facing the peacetime world.

It was noteworthy, as Grierson himself remarked, that the two series were not "hand-outs by the government as [were] the government films in other countries. They go out commercially and that is a good test of their standing in the theatre world. . . . *World in Action* has had especial success in the United States where it plays every month to some 6,500 theatres. . . . Like many other Canadian films, it is translated into several languages and goes all over the world."[81] At the same time "World in Action" was being shown in about eight hundred theaters in Canada—reaching a combined United States–Canadian monthly audience of 30 to 40 million— another thousand theaters in the United Kingdom, and was distributed in South Africa, Australia, New Zealand, India, and Latin American republics.

Grierson's contribution to the two theatrical series rested first of all on his capacity for working months in advance toward what were going to become big issues. (*Salute to Victory*, marking the end of the war, was rushed through in the amazing time of forty-eight hours and was on Canadian screens from Halifax to Vancouver the day Germany capitulated. *Guilty Men* [December 1945] came out a month before the verdict on war criminals—the commentary written so that it would retain its relevance no matter what the outcome.)[82] Grierson had, James Beveridge said, an "ability to sense and anticipate public needs and values, ways of apprehending." He "had his antennae out all the time to the popular climate"—was "very sensitive to change and incredibly right about predicting what would be the public mood and need shortly."[83] The global view was, too, a distinguishing mark at a time when nationalism and patriotism easily offered the more obvious approach. Finally, the looking ahead to peace, while other wartime propagandists confined themselves to the pressing urgencies of survival, was his own special slant.

Not that there weren't grounds for criticism of this massive output—the mere production of the two series for alternate release every fortnight was a prodigious technical accomplishment that added a burden. They were quickly and often roughly made, with the commentary too frequently carrying more than a justifiable share of the communication load. Richard Griffith made an admirable summary of the strengths of Grierson's newly adopted approach.

> For what they had to say, the *World in Action* series stands among the most remarkable films made at any time. In striking contrast to other forms of news-interpretation, they rarely over-simplified. Instead, they assumed more knowledge, intelligence and interest in world affairs than anyone else had been willing to grant the community. The mature, tough-minded realism which they continually featured would have caused consternation in other centres of Government propaganda. But Grierson had the faith to find decent goals in the midst of the grim business of war, and it is of the essence of the man that he could assume people generally wanted that same faith and only waited for it to be kindled to act upon it. . . .
>
> In terms of policy and content Grierson's experiment still stands unsurpassed, and does not seem likely to be surpassed in a world where "information" increasingly does as it is told, means what it is told to mean.

Griffith also had an acute eye for the limitations of these hastily produced films.

> Brilliantly organised as were such outstanding films as *Now—The Peace* and *Inside France*, there were others in the series—many others—which achieved a dull monotony. Visuals were slapped to the portentous, stentorian commentary in a fashion so meaningless as to leave the spectator neither knowing nor caring what he was looking at; he might as well have been home listening to a broadcast. Technical criticism of the series rose not alone from the petulance of those who were not equipped to understand Grierson's aims; not alone from the anguish of other film-makers who saw their loved footage cut up and strewn about with no regard to its original purpose. Criticism was justified because too many of the films ignored those fundamental principles of film creation and audience-manipulation which Grierson himself so painstakingly preached in the early 'thirties.[84]

The criticism that nettled Grierson most, however, came from his former British colleagues and pupils. Grierson would not take it lying down.

> The style comes out of the job. Since it is a question of giving people a pattern of thought and feeling about highly complex and urgent events, we give it as well as we know, with a minimum of dawdling over how some poor darling happens to react to something or other. . . . If our stuff pretends to be certain, it's because people need certainty. If our maps look upside down, it's because it's time people saw things in relativity. If we bang them out one a fortnight and no misses, instead of sitting on our fannies cuddling them to sweet smotheroo, it's because a lot of bravos in Russia and Japan and Germany are banging things out too, and we'd better learn how in time. If the manner is objective and hard it's because we believe the next phase of human development needs that kind of mental approach. . . . So the long, windy openings are out and the cathartic finishes in which a good, brave, tearful self-congratulatory and useless time has been had by all.[85]

A running argument about the kinds and contents of film proper to the wartime situation was part of a strain in relationships between Grierson and his British opposites which will be dealt with later.

In addition to the two units producing the "editorial" series, a Newsreel Coordination Unit was set up in September 1942 for the purpose of coordinating the newsreel releases more directly with the Canadian war effort, to stimulate Canadian production, and to increase the Canadian content in newsreels distributed in Canada and abroad. Newsreel items made up by the N.F.B. were distributed by the Hamilton Wright Organization, New York, to six newsreel companies in the United States and four in Canada; and of course news stories went out to other parts of the world as well.

The Animation Department and the French Language Unit were both established in January 1943. The Animation Department had within it a service section, for animated maps and diagrams, titles and special art effects required in live-action films, and a production section engaged in making entirely animated films. Head chef was Norman McLaren and the specialties of the house were various kinds of cel-less techniques: animated flat paper cutouts, paint on glass, chalk and pastel drawings on paper. Each month a pictorialized, animated sing-along called "Let's All Sing Together" was produced, a one reeler made up of four or five well-known songs. Several of the French series, "Chants Populaires," were made every year, each reel containing two French-Canadian folk songs, sung by the well-known Quatuor Alouette or the Trio Lyrique.[86]

From the beginning the policy of the board had been to make some films particularly suited to the needs of French Canada. The French Language Unit, headed by Guy Glover, produced original films in French and French-language versions of the two main theatrical series and of the nontheatrical 16 mm films. During 1944 "Les Reportages," the weekly newsreel produced by the French Unit, was distributed by France-Film through seventy-two Canadian theaters with a total audience of 720,000. As the war came to an end, the board was able to increase its distribution of French-language films in a liberated France and Belgium.[87]

In addition to the theatrical production, the burgeoning nontheatrical production dealt with a variety of subjects. These included intimate regional studies (e.g., on the life of a Quebec priest or on Grand Manan Island), the building of the Alaska Highway, a pictorial analysis of the workings of credit unions, animated charts on the meaning of unemployment insurance. There were also cultural shorts like the *Flight of the Dragon*, about the collection of Chinese art in the Royal Ontario Museum. Gudrun Bjerring made a 15-minute film called *Before They Are Six*, intended particularly for mothers who ran a home and worked at a lathe or a workbench in a wartime plant.[88]

## Distribution

Altogether, theatrical and nontheatrical, between January 1943 and June 1945 the Film Board produced 432 films. Most of the 16 mm films were designed for Canada's comprehensive system of nontheatrical distribution and exhibition, unequalled anywhere in the world, which was reported to have an annual audience larger than the national population. The films, in fact, grew out of the needs of the audiences to an unprecedented degree; "feedback" was the key term, uniquely important to the growth of the N.F.B.

In January 1942 the rural circuits began to take shape. Projectionists were hired by the Film Board, with the help of local educational and other authorities, to tour rural communities every month showing carefully arranged programs in libraries, church halls, schools, and other community buildings. The shows were free and by the end of the year more than thirty circuits, each with a score of screening points, had been established. By the end of 1945, the number of rural circuits had grown to ninety-two; of these sixty-one were financed by the N.F.B. and thirty-one paid for by the N.F.B. in cooperation with agricultural and educational groups in the provinces. At that time, about 1,700 community and school shows were held every month and were attended by some 250,000 persons. One typical programs was: *Food as It Might Be*, on the postwar future of farming and food marketing; *Getting Out the Coal*, on coal mining; *Trees for Tomorrow*, on forest conservation; *Mites and Monsters*, a natural history topic; and *News Roundup*, a report on the latest war developments.

Complementary to the rural circuits were the National Trade Union film circuits organized by the Industrial Division of the N.F.B.'s Distribution Branch for special showings of carefully planned educational films to labor unions. Started in May 1942, the project was sponsored by the Canadian Congress of Labour, the Trades and Labour Congress, and the Workers' Educational Association. Monthly programs on one topic each month were screened for unions in communities across Canada by field representatives of the N.F.B.'s Industrial Division. By 1945, members of three hundred union locals in eighty-four districts were attending the screenings, which were held from September to May each year. Topics included postwar employment, rehabilitation, labor-management committees, recreational programs, and international relations. The board prepared discussion trailers to accompany each film and also distributed reviews of each program in English and French.

In January 1943, N.F.B. fieldmen, both full-time representatives and others, began to open up industrial circuits in addition to the trade union circuits. These were financed by the four government agencies especially concerned with workers in war plants and factories: Munitions and Supply, Labour, National War Services, and Wartime Prices and Trade Board. Screenings were held during working hours and with the fullest cooperation of the trade unions. The programs, which lasted about twenty-five minutes, contained not only war information and educational films but also travel subjects and comedy. By 1944 sixty-six representatives were showing films on these circuits, and in the month of October, a Victory Loan period, there were 2,856 showings and an attendance across the country of 385,615.

In addition to the three circuits, the N.F.B. found other means to spread the influence of its films. By the end of 1943, Regional Film Libraries had been opened in every province. Usually attached to university extension departments, departments of education, public libraries, chambers of commerce, and other community institutions, by June 1945 they totaled forty-eight collections of N.F.B. 16 mm films in English and five in French. At that time it was estimated that six thousand prints were in library circulation, which reached an audience of three million annually.

The distribution-exhibition work of the N.F.B. during those war years was greatly assisted by a system of Volunteer Projection Services. Service clubs, boards of trade, and other groups concerned with public service provided projectors and projectionists. The Film Board agreed to keep the equipment in good working order and to lend projectors from time to time. It also provided help in training projectionists, and the Film Libraries gave advice on the choice of pictures. The service, which was available not only to community organizations but to individuals, brought 16 mm documentaries to areas near towns and cities not covered by the other circuits.

As the tide of war turned and the board's growing distribution framework took on substance, becoming a part of the nation's culture, communities themselves responded with energy. Many of them began to set up their own Film Councils. These included members from active and representative organizations in the community and acted as sponsors for the Volunteer Projection Service. They encouraged the development of film libraries and film societies, arranged previews, and did much to arouse and stimulate interest in documentary films in Canada. Through the N.F.B., Grierson had, in fact, planted an idea across Canada; some of the means by which films were distributed in wartime were to change afterwards, but documentary films had, in a manner envied by other countries, become an integral part of Canadian life. They were to continue to be so. This was indeed Blackheath and the G.P.O. more than fivefold, unfettered by departmental restrictions and serving a whole nation.

In other countries, nontheatrical distribution of N.F.B. films was also growing quickly. During the year ending March 1944, 592 prints were sent to 11 countries, and, during the following year, the figures were 1,948 prints sent to 31 countries. This record does not cover the United States where, during the fiscal year 1944–45, 207 prints of 51 new titles were in circulation through 20 film libraries which rented National Film Board documentaries to users. By March

1945, 4,184 prints of 446 different titles had been distributed by N.F.B. in the United States since January 1942. Canadian diplomatic and trade posts in other countries, as well as the N.F.B.'s own offices in London, Washington, New York, Chicago, Mexico City, and Sydney were the staging areas in a spreading international campaign.

## Wartime Information Board

As if running this huge concern were not enough, Grierson took on a second, even bigger job. In January 1943 he accepted for one year an appointment as general manager of the Wartime Information Board, the overall coordinator of war propaganda (press, radio, film, graphics, etc.), equivalent to the British Ministry of Information or the United States Office of War Information. He continued as film commissioner as well.

Along with its size, the new job was uncertain and tricky in many respects. Since the outbreak of war there had been three directors of information, all subjected to considerable criticism of one sort and another. First was Walter Thompson, public relations director of the Canadian National Railways, who retired due to poor health after a few months, and turned the job over to his assistant, G. Herbert Lash, in 1940. Lash continued in office for approximately three years, operating as Director of Public Information responsible to the Minister of National War Services. Under Lash's direction, Public Information gradually became a producing department with its own staff of writers, photographers, and artists. Lacking the authority, it did little propaganda work outside Canada.

In September 1942, when the prime minister decided that propaganda could properly be conducted in the United States, Charles Vining of the Newsprint Association was named chairman of a new Wartime Information Board. It took over the Department of Public Information and added to it an external branch with offices in New York and Washington. Domestic propaganda at that point became of secondary importance, and the main attention was directed to the U.S. offices.[89] Since the United States had by now entered the war, one "mordant wit" on Parliament Hill suggested that Vining was "getting his team on the field when the spectators are deserting the stands."[90] He meant that the United States, engrossed in its own war, would no longer give much attention to the Canadian effort.

Five months later, in January 1943, Vining resigned and Dr.

Norman Mackenzie, president of the University of New Brunswick, became the new chairman of the board, responsible to the War Committee of the cabinet. The other members of the board were senior departmental officers representing the needs and problems of the government services. Grierson, whom the prime minister had been advised was the best man for the job, was named general manager.[91] As did the film commissioner in relation to the National Film Board, the general manager of the W.I.B. appeared once a month "to give an account of his stewardship, but for the rest of the time exercise[d] the right and privilege of running the show."[92]

About Grierson at the W.I.B. it was written that

> Five years ago he was an unknown in Canada. Now he is the most talked about personage in Ottawa, a city where one doesn't remain talked about long, because the procession of notables is too rapid, and too many of great consequence have to have their share of the passing hour.
>
> Grierson has held the spotlight a long time now. He has aroused more fierce pro and con discussion than any of the figures thrown into bold relief by the exigencies of war. He has provoked a lot of it on his own, set the stage for a lot of it by deft showmanship which while it never fails to attract attention to his policies, also manages to keep his personality to the fore.
>
> When he took over the Wartime Information Board his detractors said he would soon find he was over his head, would be engulfed in the swirling eddies of political intrigue that were supposed to infest the area.
>
> Nothing like that happened. The Board gained momentum. Direction, added to its output, has achieved a stature unexpected some months ago. He has turned the trend towards film propaganda, has heard actual praise for the department which earned nothing but censure in its early period of functioning. . . .
>
> Grierson has the spectators among United Nations not only back in the stands, but cheering his efforts. There are also some loud huzzas on the home front, no mean feat considering the almost outright hostility that greeted his acceptance of the onerous post of information distributor.[93]

Some of the outright hostility remained, however, and there were brickbats as well as huzzas. One of the detractors, Leonard L. Knott, complained in *Canadian Business* in October 1943 of "a plethora of information offices," and assessed the changes that Grierson, "one of the capitol's most unusual characters," had wrought in the shifting policy of "one of those strange wartime creations, the Wartime Information Board."

> Immediately interest was reconstructed upon domestic propaganda. The American offices continued to function but the real emphasis was once more placed upon information at home. The department, however, has never, since the Lash regime, been a production department. Photographers and some of the old D.P.I. writers were transferred to the National Film Board, where they were soon joined by the members of the art department. Newspapermen, some of whom have remained in the organization during the Vining episode, departed as they found themselves outnumbered by professors, film makers and social scientists, and adult education replaced news, or information, as the apparent function of the board.

It was about Grierson's long-term and social-planning emphases and his future ambitions that Knott was most uneasy. Since the Order in Council creating the W.I.B. gave "no acceptable outline of functions," Knott observed, "It is occupied, apparently by its own choosing . . . with such things as 'national morale,' 'the background of the home front war,' 'adult education,' 'cultural relations' and 'external affairs.'" He concluded that while "Other publicity sections will close as the work of their wartime departments end . . . the Wartime Information Board, or at least its general manager, has different plans. Whether he operates from the National Film Board, W.I.B. or some other occupation, Mr. Grierson is in the social, adult education business for keeps. And adult education, like information, may be just another name for old-time propaganda."[94]

Both Knott and the pseudonymous ZAB of the *Montrealer*, whom Grierson may have encouraged into the field to help answer Knott's allegations, hinted at an even bigger postwar design. ZAB, granting that Grierson had plans for the W.I.B. "extending into after war years," stated that "they are only in the making. In good time they will hit with the usual Grierson impact." More concretely, he suggested that Grierson might head a merger of the W.I.B. and the N.F.B., but that "At the moment he is also being mentioned as a future manager of the Canadian Broadcasting Corporation."[95] Without conceding that Grierson was "being mentioned," Knott admitted that ". . . he is said to be showing extreme interest in radio broadcasting as a medium of adult education, and that interest is causing some worry in C.B.C." But Knott was on the right track, as it would turn out, with another conjecture.

During recent weeks at Ottawa there have been consistent rumours that Mr. Grierson, having lopped off from W.I.B. the departments he likes, and having attached them to his own National Film Board, where they will become more or less permanent fixtures, is now anxious to retire as W.I.B. general manager and go back to the Film Board. These rumours have neither been admitted nor denied but the willingness with which Mr. Grierson permitted his assistant to handle the Quebec Conference would indicate that there might be some truth in them.[96]

Grierson himself entered the argument with the title observation "Wartime Information Board: It Is Not Done with Mirrors." He addressed himself particularly to attacks about "secrecy" surrounding the organization and about high expense accounts and salaries, especially in the U.S. offices. (ZAB had referred to his phone bills for long-distance calls to Hollywood, which would later plague Grierson, but coupled them with the impressive showing of "World in Action" in the United States.) In his defense, Grierson repeated an earlier statement that, "as Film Commissioner no political pressure had ever been put upon me, nor was there ever a hint of it. . . . My experience justifies the opinion that the Prime Minister allows organizations like mine, founded after public demand, the full freedom of their own natural path."[97]

Knott interpreted Mackenzie King's behavior in another way: the W.I.B., "because it operates without benefit of any official Government policy, is responsible to the Prime Minister, who offers it neither hope, comfort nor guidance, and is consistently denied the confidence of even the humblest cabinet minister." Further, "There can be no question of the Liberal Government attempting, in the name of information, to establish either a national or political propaganda bureau, for the Prime Minister, by word and deed, has demonstrated that he has no faith in, or use for, propaganda as such. There are, however, individuals other than those elected to office who have more confidence in the utility of propaganda, under whatever name it may be operated, now or in the future [e.g., Grierson]." Taking off on another tack, Knott made a passing reference to the ideology of the personnel: "nor is the fact generally known that the information services referred to are dominated by C.C.F.ers [Cooperative Commonwealth Federation—i.e., socialists] or 'others.'" Grierson would hear of this again, particularly of the "others."

Grierson's plans obviously depended on Mackenzie King's plans;

and Knott, whatever the partisan motivation for his charges, may have accurately foreseen postwar developments. In closing he referred to remarks made by Brooke Claxton, MP, parliamentary assistant to the prime minister in the House of Commons, stating that Canada's information services "would not go on after the war in their present form."[98] Ultimately this proved to be a more correct assessment than Grierson's, who, in an address in Montreal in June, had stated that the Wartime Information Board hoped and expected to be in operation long after the war.[99]

Evidently there was some sort of showdown between King and Grierson, and whatever plans the latter may have been conceiving for a postwar career in Canada were altered at this point. Grierson resigned quietly as general manager of the W.I.B. at the end of his year's appointment and was succeeded by the assistant general manager, A. David Dunton, thirty-one-year-old former managing editor of the Montreal *Standard*. Grierson remained Special Adviser to the government on questions of information generally—a kind of knighthood for service performed, it would seem: prestige without authority, though naturally his advice would be as valuable as anyone's in the country and one would suppose respected.

Grierson returned to the Film Board with the departments he had "lopped off": an Order in Council of June 15 had transferred to the N.F.B. the Poster and Bulletin Division and the Graphics Division of the W.I.B.—that is, all of its production of still pictures and other graphic material. If his resignation from the W.I.B. represented some sort of large battle lost, Grierson was readily enough reconciled and in many ways glad to be relieved of the responsibility. He later conceded that the W.I.B. was a "rather rough neck of the woods." Also, by definition, the Wartime Information Board was limited to wartime, and the National Film Board, founded in peace and for peacetime purposes, would go on. The general managership had been fierce hard work, too much really even for Grierson, along with his film commissionership, and the N.F.B. had been neglected. In a speech in Vancouver he said, "I have had myself and my sins with the Wartime Information Board to worry about . . . this has kept me very much 'on deck.'"[100] He had been away from the Film Board much of the past year and there had been some deteriorations: rivalry and uncertainty among the producers and resentment at what was viewed as a kind of desertion.[101]

## Administrative Style, Personality, and Relationships

According to Gordon Weisenborn, one day during his W.I.B. job Grierson came striding through the Film Board as if he hadn't been away for several months. Peering over Legg's shoulder at the Movie-ola he growled, "For chrissake, have you forgotten everything I've ever taught you about editing?" Without taking his eye off the flickering image, Legg muttered, "I'm running the sonofabitch backwards." Whereupon Grierson stalked out of the room without a further word. Weisenborn's point, and presumably Legg's, was that Grierson should not have talked as a filmmaker if he wasn't going to be one.[102] Some place along the line Grierson *had* become hooked on the film medium. In spite of his protests that it might have been documentary radio or documentary writing, he never worked happily completely removed from film production (as in the UNESCO job later) and was, Legg insisted, "a damn good film maker."[103]

Even his office routine at the N.F.B. was imbued with the formative, frenetic impulses of creation. Of his own first impressions of Grierson at work, Michael Spencer wrote:

> being hired by Grierson was an experience which few will forget. The prospective employee hardly ever opened his mouth. He simply sat in the office for an hour or two while Film Board satellites continued to orbit round the Film Commissioner. Several conferences took place simultaneously—long distance phone calls one after another. Quick decisions were reached: people in Washington and more distant points might be hired (or fired), and then finally you were sent out and told to report to someone or other, and the next day you found yourself on a train, familiarizing yourself with a camera—or the techniques of scriptwriting. If Grierson thought you could do a job for the Film Board, it never occurred to you to question his belief.[104]

"Grierson is the sworn foe of red tape," wrote ZAB of the *Montrealer* at the time of Grierson's resignation from the W.I.B. and full-time return to the N.F.B.: "[He is] a man of many opinions. He gives them freely. He loves to talk and he loves to talk shop. There is nothing formal about him. He is as liable to talk to you in shirtsleeves in his office, or with his feet high up on his polished desk. He has collected around him some of the most vocal and forthright people you will meet in Ottawa, a city where subtlety and subterfuge are so often the refuge of the great and near great."[105]

Marjorie McKay, one of the vocal and forthright people, supervisor of business management at the Film Board, recalled that Grierson worked all the time. He might conduct business at home, or in a coffee shop, or when meeting people in the halls at the board. He was also likely to phone at 8:00 P.M. and ask a staff member to come to his house for work. Rarely in his office before 10:00 A.M., he was usually there in the afternoons. Marjorie would then go in with a list of problems she wanted decisions on. As she explained each situation briefly, Grierson would grasp it, say "Yes" or "No," and move on to the next. If memos were necessary they had to be kept to a paragraph—Grierson would ask if he wanted to know more. He was right 90 percent of the time in these fast decisions, she estimated.

As far as the complicated matter of allocating the various government monies available to him, Grierson's attitude was "To hell with Treasury and their account categories. I have $500,000 and if I don't over-draw, I'll spend it any way that's necessary to bring in films—more for travel, less for salary, whatever."[106] During his last year at the board his own salary was $10,000, and he spent an additional $6,694 on his travel,[107] a figure that would be noted critically later.

Stuart Legg spoke of the great strain, the intense concentration of Grierson in solving creative and practical problems—trying to work around difficulties and getting solutions exactly right—and pantomimed him gnawing his fingers. At other times he would have flashes of insight—would see exactly how a thing ought to be done and who should do it, and would cut through with strong force to achieve the desired end.[108]

The *Montrealer* further characterized him:

> Grierson isn't an impressive person physically speaking but otherwise he is a dynamo. He gets by upraised guards by the deft use of a disarming approach, a most pleasing Scottish accent. He can be brusque, very decisive too even in ordinary speech but he can also be suave and charming, and his tact and diplomacy are notable.
>
> Grierson is an idea man always on the make. He likes people with ideas and he gives them full rein, but usually they wind up in agreement with him. . . .
>
> . . . Already a celebrity he is being eyed in other countries as a man who gets things done. . . . He is a sort of Empire crusader.[109]

Grierson liked the freedom of Canada, away from and somewhat antipathetic towards the English establishment. "It offered the possibility of becoming a big fish," as Legg put it, and corrected himself, "a *very big* fish, in a small pond."[110] He was a privileged adviser to Mackenzie King and active in Canadian government and politics at an influential level. Perhaps he wanted to become "the Bernard Baruch [American businessman and statesman] of Canada, the counselor," as Gordon Weisenborn put it. His associates at the Film Board were split on the desirability of political astuteness, and the anti-Grierson faction hated that aspect of his administration.[111]

But Grierson's relationship with Mackenzie King, the key to his position in Canada since the drafting of the National Film Act and his appointment as film commissioner, became complex and equivocal. King once said "Patience comes with experience. It is one of the fruits—you learn patience. I have always sympathized with younger men's desires for quick reforms. As a young man I was impulsive."[112] King was no longer young, of course, and by no means impulsive; in respect of patience Grierson may have remained one of the "younger men" in King's eyes. Like Grierson, King was one to get on with the job. He also remained disinterested and objective, working through an analysis of what could be done to how to do it; but Grierson was flashier. King did not capitalize on his position for personal publicity or advancement, and this could be said of Grierson, too, up to a point. Though King didn't mind catching the headlines if it would advance the cause, he was neither the phrase-maker nor the publicist that Grierson intuitively was.

Yet King, who was Grierson's hero in a way, never really liked him, though he obviously respected Grierson's ability. In May 1940, the prime minister had the film commissioner to dinner. King was much impressed by Grierson's "knowledge of the whole work of propaganda, publicity, etc., but not particularly taken with his personality." He further recorded in his diary that he felt Grierson "the best man available to carry out a really effective programme for films of our war effort, and so have asserted my authority in seeking to get action in the matter." (This is the only mention of Grierson in the four-volume biography of King written by his longtime secretary J. W. Pickersgill.)[113] A month less a day after the dinner the Motion Picture Bureau was absorbed by the National Film Board.

When King appointed Grierson to the Wartime Information Board in January 1943, Legg observed, he did so in spite of what he regarded as Grierson's "unprepossessing" personality. Legg felt that Grierson tried to insinuate himself with the prime minister by matching his own anti-English establishment and pro-Canadian feelings with King's. But the latter may have thought he was trying too hard. King, after all, was a wily old politician who may not have liked a Johnny-come-lately trying to climb onto a bandwagon he had pretty much constructed. Perhaps King thought Grierson too clever, too ambitious. He was hungry for power over people, Legg conceded—to get them to follow his will; he was never interested in personal financial gain. Grierson even admired Hitler in a curious way, as King simply loathed him, because Hitler had frankly and openly gone after power to knock down the German ruling classes. Grierson would quote a Hitler saying, "All it takes is six per cent of the populace," with admiration. In essence, Grierson thought Hitler honest in setting forth, in word and deed from *Mein Kampf* on, precisely what he was trying to do, and had a respect, grudging of course, for Hitler's extraordinary success in achieving his ends.[114]

Let James Beveridge's impressions round out this somewhat harsh aspect of the portrait. He felt that Grierson had as his goal the Renaissance man who knows everything; that his ambition was to be the most brilliant person in the world—top in an aristocracy of intellect. This led him to an arrogance towards those less bright. It also made the few officials who had or could respond to his intelligence respect and value him enormously. It led to a distrust of him among lesser minds, those Grierson called "the little men." He was not afraid of making enemies, Beveridge conceded, and made a number of them.[115] "He stepped on a lot of toes" was a phrase used by several Canadians.

Grierson insisted, however, that, as a veteran in public information systems, "I can actually say that I have never been associated with a partisan political play and cannot imagine a situation in which a responsible minister would ask it of me."[116] He made this kind of remark more than once but, though it may have been true, or he may have been protesting too much, there were certainly differences in liberal and conservative points of view among the responsible ministers which grew out of and were supported by partisan politics. Marjorie McKay recalled one instance of Grierson checkmating an attempted political play. J. F. Macdonald, a senior Conservative statesman in the House of Commons, had been given the job by his party to go after the Film Board. At the time, Macdonald's daughter was working for the board. When Grierson surmised what was afoot he promoted her, over Janet Scellen, who was entitled to the job, thus successfully tying Macdonald's hands. Scellen was rewarded by being put in charge of the N.F.B. office in London.[117]

Just after his resignation from the Film Board, Grierson wrote to Brooke Claxton, who had become chairman of the board (and would later be Defense Minister). The letter is unusual in its informal candor and in the incisiveness with which Grierson expresses his opinions about the men in power with whom he dealt.

> . . . your own appointment to the Board is the first evidence of the Prime Minister's interest since he backed me against McKinnon's foolish attempt to set aside the provisions of the Act in 1940, and thereby reduce the Film Board into an abject section of his mausoleum in the West Block. . . . It places upon you a responsibility for the creative development of a Film Board and for the securing of the relative freedom necessary for its creative development. Only two of your predecessors understood anything of this. They were, curiously enough, Joe Thorson, whose native ardour for Canada and for the long term view combined to make him a most satisfactory chairman; and, of course, Crerar, who has a native instinct for the arts which often outweighs his caution. A Highlander must sometime have crept into his family bed.

McKinnon is presumably James A. MacKinnon, Minister of Trade and Commerce and National Film Board chairman at the time of Grierson's threatened resignation in 1940. J. T. Thorson was Minister of National War Services, and chairman of the board beginning in June 1941. T. A. Crerar, Minister of Mines and Resources, was a member of the original board. Grierson apparently regarded MacKinnon and La Fleche as the least imaginative and most reactionary of the ministers concerned with the N.F.B. (Maj. Gen. L. R. La Fleche became Minister of National War Services and also chairman of the National Film Board.) To Claxton he exclaimed, "Think of Jimmy McKinnon or McCann passing on the adequacy of a film!"[118] Dr. J. J. McCann, Revenue Minister, succeeded Claxton as Film Board chairman; reason for a *double* exclamation mark Grierson no doubt would have thought!!

Within the N.F.B., it was said, by Michael Spencer, and others, that Grierson "carried on a one-man operation"—that he "didn't build an administrative system. He ran the whole show—made all the decisions." Admittedly he "got it going in a powerful way but this lack of organization would make the N.F.B. vulnerable to later attacks." After Grierson left, those remaining had "to work out administrative procedures so they could account for all actions and expenditures." Grierson "didn't permit very strong leadership to grow up under him," concluded Spencer—he was, in short, a "dictator."[119] Of this dictatorial tendency, Marjorie McKay gave an example that occurred at the board during a period when A. G. McLean (brother of Ross and father of Grant, both subsequent film commissioners) was in charge of administration. The treasurer and assistant treasurer had been discovered dipping into N.F.B. funds, with phoney checks and the like. Grierson summarily asked for A. G. McLean's resignation at a board meeting which both A. G. and Ross were attending.[120]

Julian Roffman recalled that Grierson disliked committees forming at the N.F.B., that he used a divide-and-conquer principle with people. He would call in whomever he assumed was the leader in a particular situation and say, "Why do you want to go along with that nonsense?" thus undoing the group decision. He was often ungenerous with his subordinates, too, according to Roffman. One time Grierson peremptorily removed veteran Stanley Hawes and put the young Roffman in charge of a unit—Hawes had been Roffman's boss. Shortly thereafter Grierson remarked to Roffman, "They're calling your outfit the Palestine Unit. Too many Jews." When Roffman answered "There's only me and one other," Grierson replied, "That's too many." He tried to control absolutely, Roffman felt, but decisions had to be reached while he was away. Invariably on his return he would be impatient with the changes that had been made.[121]

Still, the Film Board workers seem to have been devoted to Grierson—some of them all of the time, all of them some of the time. An official N.F.B. statement late in the war assessed the operation, not inaccurately it would seem, as being "carried on with the least amount of formality, results and efficiency . . . the keynote, and the board is noted for its corporate spirit, enthusiasm and loyalty to the Commissioner."[122] Of the production staff, Marjorie McKay wrote, "The world was their oyster and Grierson was going to help them open it. There was going to be a brave new world after the war, and they would have a part in it. . . . Here was hope and opportunity. Here was excitement and probably most of all, a sense of doing something which mattered."[123] They were at the very center of things Canadian. Raymond Spottiswoode observed that "Ottawa is a small and friendly capital. At half an hour's notice you may find a Minister or his Deputy dropping into the screening room to see and discuss the rough-cut of a film you are making for his department. And to present your unfinished, soundless film in a true light, you must have a very clear sense of the 'why' and the 'how' of what government is trying to do."[124]

Daphne Anstey also stressed the devotion to Grierson of the young people at the N.F.B. He made everybody feel important, she said, including the negative cutters, one of which she was. They all thought they were winning the war single-handedly. Everyone worked into the night and on Saturdays and Sundays—Grierson didn't make them; they did it out of loyalty and inspiration. He would wander in and out, prop his feet on a chair in a cutting room and hold forth. All felt that he cared and was sympathetic about each part of the job, but they were also in awe of him, owing to the high standards he set.

Anstey as well as others told of Grierson not permitting them to screen the English documentaries, like *Night Mail*. One night a group sneaked into a projection room by flashlight, all breathless to see it. *Listen to Britain* was also considered too heady. An amusing crotchet, especially since Grierson was himself screening all the best stuff from Britain and the States, but his anti-aestheticky fever was particularly virulent at the board, and evidently he didn't want his fledglings to be corrupted by beauty in the face of wartime's rigors. Also, and possibly more importantly, he wanted the young Canadians to make their own way, to develop their own national style.

Grierson's continuing sensitivity to artistic form was attested to inversely: by the repetition and increasing intensity of his arguments in favor of utilitarian function. An inference could be made of a Calvinistic uneasiness with the sensuous pleasures of art on the part of one all too susceptible to them. Edgar Anstey, on the other hand, said that Grierson took aesthetics for granted, and perhaps he did. In the earlier analyses of rushes, often uncomfortably recalled by the learners, Grierson had always and almost exclusively been concerned with camera angle, light, and so on.[125] Some of this concern would move below the surface now, as a result of the number of films being produced under him as well as of the new requirements of Canada and of the war. His theoretical and pedagogical approach to film in large part followed the changing shape of his own job.

Nonetheless, Julian Roffman recalled, Grierson encouraged

people to try anything. Though no longer closely involved in production, he would see the completed films. "It stinks," he might say. Or, "Great camera movement. You move the camera like the Russians. You're the only one here who has it. You must light a torch for these other young men—and stick it under their asses." The door to Grierson's office was always open and the personnel would stream in to see him when they became sufficiently excited. It was like a Renaissance court, Roffman said, and, changing his analogy, Grierson was "a freebooter, really, a great pirate."[126]

Norman McLaren, for his part, said that though he had had ideas about art in public service, Grierson offered a fresh and fuller way of looking at this matter. At the board, McLaren's contacts with Grierson were somewhat infrequent and brief, but he always found them stimulating. He felt that Grierson's greatest contribution, one that applied particularly to McLaren's own work, was in protecting the artist from outside pressures and encouraging him to grow and experiment freely.[127] Guy Glover, on the other hand, observed that a sense of vocation to public service carried a lot of weight with Grierson—perhaps more than one's qualities as a filmmaker. Glover admitted some feelings as a Canadian and an artist against "the British boys" and what he regarded as their didacticism and lack of creativity. Of Grierson personally he conceded, as did others, that he never stood on formality—even after hours he was apt to drop in at their homes for a drink and a chat.[128]

Donald Fraser connected Grierson's relationships with his young people at the board to the Griersons' childlessness: he viewed his young men, especially, as his "children." (Roffman thought of Grierson as his "film father.") There was a certain strain, in England and Canada, after the young men grew up and away from him, but even when the feelings turned negative they always had a family intensity, Fraser judged. There is something to this, but a single concept scarcely accounts for a personality as divergently many-sided as Grierson's. In fact, the attempts by his friends and associates to "account for" Grierson often tend to cancel each other out.

Gerald Noxon, one-time member of the G.P.O. Film Unit, suggested that the key to Grierson was that he was a Scot forever—and to the extent that there is a Scottish view and a Scottish way, there is something there, too. On the other hand, George Stoney, American documentary filmmaker, was under the impression that Grierson hated the Scots, and pointed out, quite rightly, that he had taken some pains not to live in his homeland. Even when he worked for Scottish Television, as he did for over ten years, he commuted to Glasgow from southern England. Donald Fraser said that the only time he discomfited Grierson was when—attempting to explain and defend Joris Ivens's difficulties with the Dutch government over Indonesia—he started an analogy: "Supposing you went back to Scotland. . . ." During this sally Fraser could see Grierson's temper silently mounting, until he left the room. In a little while he came back, less red in the face, and said "That was a low blow. . . ."[129]

The eye of the beholder figures strongly in assessments of Grierson's attitudes toward women, too. Fritzie Weisenborn, who felt he "used" people, said that he interfered with their lives and marriages. (Others gave specific instances.) "Sleeping around was fine," she said, "but none of that love stuff": his young men were permitted to love and be married only to film, if he could help it. Mrs. Weisenborn also felt that he didn't like women in business except as sexy ornaments.[130] This latter assertion is scarcely borne out by the number and quality of the women hired at the board, however, or by the responsibilities given to them. Donald Fraser said that along with the gruff, masculine exterior Grierson was a "softie inside, particularly with women."[131] It *is* true that in his writings women are excluded from the tougher concerns of the man's world, and femininity is associated with softness and sentimentality, though it is hard to say where he got this view—not from his mother, surely—or how firmly it was held. During his career he worked well with a lot of bright and resolute women.

Fritzie Weisenborn also implied that Grierson was promiscuous, though one might wonder where he would have found the time and energy for sexual dalliance. He once told Forsyth Hardy that he wouldn't write his autobiography because it would involve the woman (or women, Hardy thought he might have said) in his life.[132] Mrs. Weisenborn suspected that the Griersons had some serious marital difficulties at the time of the W.I.B. job. When the N.F.B. was small, Margaret had served as a "mother" to the staff. When it became large, there was nothing for her to do and she became merely a housewife. Grierson was harsh in his demands on her, according to Mrs. Weisenborn—he ordered her around, and she was quietly compliant.[133]

Margaret had taught editing mechanics to the Canadians and liked to comfort the people Grierson was abusing, Tom Daly recalled. In return, "All the Canadian film makers were passionately in love with Margaret Taylor Grierson," he added with gallant hyperbole. Stuart Legg remembered that back in the E.M.B. days Margaret at first had acted superior to the young men as the boss's wife—and that she was very beautiful. (She had always had a crippled hip, however, which caused a limp and considerable pain. The hip could have been repaired by surgery and re-set with a metal pin, Edgar Anstey said. But, though this would have relieved the pain it would have made the hip stiffer.)[134] Legg subsequently came to regard Mrs. Grierson as "an angel among women," and to wonder how she managed "to put up with" her husband.[135] "Whatever the things were they said to each other," though, Tom Daly observed, "you got the feeling they couldn't live without one another."[136] Edgar Anstey said simply that she understood Grierson better than anyone.[137] When with them you were aware of a strong bond, stronger than either his harshness or her sweetness.

If Mrs. Grierson didn't have enough to do at the Film Board, Grierson had too much. The hard work from childhood onward finally caught up with him. With more hard work there came a tiredness that may have led to some bad decisions, to being "off" one day and "on" the next. Usually he constantly pushed ahead with more work,[138] but he was stopped, briefly at least, early in 1941. Margaret Grierson, writing to Basil Wright in February of that year, said that John had not been feeling well. He had gone to a doctor who told him that he had ". . . just about worn his heart out and if he wants to be around much longer he has to alter his way of life completely—no more dashing around in aeroplanes, no cigarettes, no liquor, no late hours, a month's holiday."[139]

Evidently he became quite ill that late winter and early spring. Wright thought it was in the nature of a "crack-up," a nervous breakdown. At any rate, in a letter to Wright at the end of April, Grierson confessed to having followed some of the doctor's advice—had stopped drinking, mostly—and whereas he had been "pretty well dead" he was now "pretty well alive again."[140] In the early fall of 1942 he was in Florida on vacation, once more recovering from what had been diagnosed as heart trouble. Grierson himself thought the problem was "too much liquor and bothering, particularly bothering,"[141] and spent at least part of his time writing about propaganda while relaxing on the sands.[142]

In addition to official busyness, Grierson's gregariousness continued, with acquaintanceships that ranged over social classes, among the vocations, and across Canada. To Donald Fraser he seemed a man full of emotion, with strong feelings for particular people.[143] One of his best friends in Canada was George Ferguson,[144] then editor of the *Winnipeg Free Press* and later of the *Montreal Star*. Apart from its personal basis, this friendship was in keeping with Grierson's lasting interest in newspapermen and was also part of his desire to keep channels of communication open. Ferguson served not only as a supporter but as a kind of pipeline. Quiet, high-principled, he helped educate Grierson in Canadian politics. Other newspapermen were often at his house—drinking and discussing international affairs. Or Grierson might go fishing with an editor.[145] Lawrence Freeman, of the Freeman department store in Ottawa, was another good friend.[146] The Griersons rarely entertained at home formally: Margaret Ann Elton could not recall their having people over for dinner.[147]

Grierson also liked boxers, dancers, actors, and low-life types, and had them around him often. The mystique of the star personality fascinated him. (He claimed to have made a personal discovery of Gary Cooper, as well as of Thelma Todd.)[148] He enjoyed the contrast of hobnobbing with Mackenzie King and Arthur Gottlieb—the two ends of the social scheme. Stuart Legg described Gottlieb as "a lovable gangster," whom Grierson nicknamed "The Butcher." Born on the Lower East Side of Manhattan, son of Jewish immigrants, he had been a New York City cop, a prize fighter, and had carried a gun for mobster Dutch Schultz. During the time Grierson knew Gottlieb, among multiple enterprises he ran a film laboratory called DuArt, in New York City, and the N.F.B. did a lot of processing there, mailing the film back and forth from Ottawa. Gottlieb also had some sort of "in" with United Artists, and it was he who arranged for distribution of "The World in Action."[149]

The earlier traveling in Canada was accelerated and key acquaintances across the nation and abroad became even more a part of Grierson's operating than they had in Britain. Of the W.I.B. under his tenure he wrote: "Personal contacts are so easy in a small country with a small population the Canadian information service did not need to rely on printed material. It sent people from one end of the country to the other to talk to editors regularly. It employed a large number of newspapermen for various jobs, gave them special trips to the United States or England, brought people over from

England to go through the Canadian newspaper offices, and so forth."[150] Hardy added, "in his ceaseless and restless travels across the country he soon knew more of its feelings and moods than most Canadians. He talked with university people in every province, with the editors of newspapers and magazines, with writers and broadcasters, with teachers and adult education workers, with people engaged in every activity. He had an insatiable curiosity about, and interest in, people—what they did, how and why they did it, and what they thought about it and everything else."[151]

A story about Grierson dropping in on a dour Scottish bank manager in China, Saskatchewan, may illustrate this point. After a stiff and dull conversation the manager eventually asked, by way of terminating the interview, "Is there anything I can do for you, Mr. Grierson?" "Yes," Grierson replied, "you can tell me if there's any place a man can get a drink before noon in this damned town." "Nothing simpler," answered the manager, and pulled out a bottle of whiskey from his desk drawer. At about 3:00 P.M. Grierson, getting ready to leave the office, said "There's one other thing you can do for me—show me the horticulture in this area." "That's easy enough, John," was the reply, and a car and driver were summoned. After a ride of about thirty miles they arrived at "one skimpy little tree which some lunatic had preserved against the hostile environment." It was the only "horticulture" in the whole area.[152]

# 7 ✒ REACHING OUT FROM CANADA (1939–45)

## Speaking and Writing

Of course Grierson was speaking formally to even more and larger audiences than he had in Britain and at a high level of statesman-like rhetoric. A sampling of occasions and titles will give some sense of this activity.

Just after his appointment as film commissioner he made a broadcast entitled "The Film at War" from Ottawa, in November 1939; a slightly abridged version appeared as "Broadcast to Canada" in *Documentary News Letter*, April 1940. "The Eyes of Canada" was the title of a speech made in January 1940. An address entitled "The Nature of Propaganda" was delivered to the Canadian Club in Montreal, February 1941. "Education and Total Effort" was a speech in Winnipeg during the early fall of 1941; it is included in *Grierson on Documentary*. He spoke in New York before the National Board of Review (of motion pictures) in November 1941 and before the Institute of Inter-American Affairs, at the Museum of Modern Art, in October 1942. "Propaganda and Education," another speech in Winnipeg, was made to its Canadian Club in October 1943.

A talk to the Rotary Club of Ottawa at its St. Andrew's Day luncheon meeting, November 1943, was a fine and wonderfully amusing tribute to Scotland and the Scots, full of literary quotations (damning the Scots), native jokes, and historical allusions. Grierson pointed to the leaders Scotland had given the world and the way they had moved into all corners of the earth, particularly Canada. That the Scots didn't insist on making a better Scotland but a better world was his major thesis. "Films and the I.L.O." was addressed to the International Labor Organization in Philadelphia, April 1944. "Films as an International Influence" was presented to the Vancouver Advertising and Sales Bureau in December 1944. The National Conference on Adult Education, meeting in Winnipeg, heard him on "Education in a Technological Society" in May 1945. (While there he also broadcast over radio station CKRC.) The Winnipeg talk proved to be essentially a rehearsal for his June 1945 address to the Conference of the Arts, Sciences, and Professions in the Post-War World at the Waldorf Astoria Hotel in New York City. The title for the latter version became "The Future of the Films"; it appears in *Grierson on Documentary* as "The Challenge of Peace." Finally, sometime in 1945, before his resignation from the Film Board, he spoke to the Ontario School Inspectors' Association on "Education and Political Reality."

As has been noted, many of the talks were published; in addition, Grierson wrote some pieces solely for publication. (*Education and the New Order* is perhaps the fullest statement of Grierson's educational theory, as "First Principles of Documentary" had been of his aesthetic. The two statements were arrived at not quite ten years apart; both appear in *Grierson on Documentary*.) These essays spoken and written during the Film Board years constitute the fullest expression of the ideas by which he then lived and worked. Two things distinguish this outpouring from his earlier writing: the scope is global, with broad political-economic-educational considerations predominant, and the creative process is always at the core. Much of the writing seems to be directed at readers in the United States as well as to the people of Canada and Great Britain. Hardy makes this latter point emphatically:

> His exposition is largely addressed to opinion in the United States, the last considerable community which holds fast to the old theory of education which bans, or tries to ban (and succeeds in having only the illusion of banning), the deliberate influencing of men's beliefs. Nearly every American can find within himself some trace of the propaganda-phobia, but as Grierson notes we turned to propaganda with eager

acceptance when it was used in pursuit of goals we really meant to attain. The wholeheartedness with which we mobilized for total effort in the war, psychologically as well as materially, indicates that we are already unconsciously prepared to liquidate our fear of propaganda so long as its creative root and nature are assured.[1]

Nonetheless, an early aspect of Grierson's propagandizing earned him some resentment and distrust in the United States. Before the United States was in the war, Britain had agreed to refrain from pushing for American entry through its own U.S.–based information services, but Grierson apparently felt this restriction need not apply to Canada. The British point of view seems to have been effectively presented in Canadian packages. In discussing that activity years later he referred cryptically to the N.F.B.'s development of "subliminal" techniques and stated that Stuart Legg was "an expert at this sort of thing." Jokingly he likened himself to Josef Goebbels, Nazi Minister of Propaganda, and said that other people referred to him by that name. He also remembered that in a piece in *Esquire* magazine, author and playwright Laurence Stallings had described him as the "dirtiest operator in the war."[2]

But, Grierson argued at length and with persuasive eloquence, propaganda *is* (or should be) education—and vice versa. That was one of the main themes sounded throughout the talking and writing, and motivated the production of the films. "A government's use of educational films is not 'propaganda' in the ordinary sense. Certainly we cannot impose on a government the duty of planning the national effort without giving it the means of informing the people what it is doing and of obtaining their support. This is generally admitted today in every country except the United States, where, or so it appears to the outsider, the fear of the partisan political use of information services looms very large in the public argument."[3] Speaking in New York six months later he explained, however, that

> Nothing can be expected from governments beyond what I shall call the degree of general sanction. If the degree of general sanction is accurately gauged maximum support is forthcoming for creative work. Where, however, advantage is taken and the degree of sanction is estimated on partisan lines, ineffectiveness and frustration result.
>
> This imposes a clear limit on the creative artist working within the public service for, obviously, the degree of general sanction does not allow for forthright discussions of such highly controversial problems

as say, America's record with the Negroes in the South, or England's record with the Indians in the East. The creative worker must not, however, simply denounce this limitation and dissociate himself from government service. If he is a practical operator and a practical reformer he will take the situation for what it is and do his utmost within the limitations set, and this is one of the disciplines which the creative artist must learn in this particular period of society.[4]

Earlier he had written that "What we are trying to arrive at is the point where we abandon that purely mystical concept of Democracy which encourages the illusion that ten million amateur thinkers talking themselves incompetently to death sound like the music of the spheres. We want to arrive at the point where the democratic ideal can be brought down to the realm of practical consideration and achievement." He came, therefore, to certain conclusions. "The first is that the State is bound to take a more direct hand in the terms and shapes of education. The second is that much of what we now know as education will become what we now know as propaganda. The third is that a dramatic approach, as distinct from an intellectualist approach, to education must increasingly develop. The fourth is that the machinery of what is called public information must inevitably be extended far beyond its present state and purpose."[5]

He believed, he wrote, that "propaganda is the part of democratic education which the educators forgot." Traditionally education stressed facts and skills but had not offered "that fourth R which is Rooted Belief." He felt that "education in this essential has left men out in the bush without an emotional map to guide them; and when men are starved of belief they are only too prone to believe anything."

If you recall the origin of the word propaganda, you will remember that it was first associated with the defence of a faith and a concept of civilization. Propaganda first appeared in the description of the Catholic office—Congregatio de Propaganda Fide—which was to preach and maintain the faith. It may be just as easily today the means by which we preach and maintain our own democratic faith. Man does not live by bread alone, nor the citizen by mind alone. He is a man with vanities to be appealed to, a native pride to be encouraged. He has a gambler's heart to be allowed a flutter and a fighting instinct which can be associated with fighting for the right. One part of him at least asks to live not safely but adventurously.[6]

And finally:

> Talk as you will of pursuing the highest ends of man and the service of God, the base of the pyramid is in deeds done and in results achieved. In that sense, education is surely never anything other than the process by which men are fitted to serve their generation and bring it into the terms of order. It is the process by which the minds of men are keyed to the tasks of good citizenship, by which they are geared to the privilege of making a constructive contribution, however humble, to the highest purposes of the community.
>
> Grant that in so doing education does, in man's high fancy, tune the human spirit to the music of the spheres, none the less its function is the immediate and practical one of being a deliberate social instrument—not dreaming in an ivory tower, but outside on the barricades of social construction, holding citizens to the common purpose their generation has set for them.
>
> Education is activist or it is nothing.[7]

Another striking characteristic of Grierson's writing at this time (as of the Film Board's films) was his insistence on thinking in the more permanent terms of peace rather than the temporary ones of war. His disdain of hatred and repugnance for destruction are constant and unwavering throughout the period.

In the uncertain days of late autumn 1939 he wrote:

> I remember coming away from the last war with the very simple notion in my head that somehow we had to make peace exciting, if we were to prevent wars. Simple notion as it is, that has been my propaganda ever since—to make peace exciting. In one form or another I have produced or initiated hundreds of films; yet I think behind every one of them has been that one idea, that the ordinary affairs of people's lives are more dramatic and more vital than all the false excitements you can muster. That has seemed to me something worth spending one's life over. . . .
>
> But—so it seemed in these early months—one way, too, in which we could maintain our defenses and keep our spirit for the struggle ahead was to remember that the aims of our society lie beyond war and in the love of peace. It would be a poor information service, it seemed, which kept harping on war to the exclusion of everything, making our minds narrow and anaemic. It would be a poor propaganda which taught hatred, till it violated the sense of decency which ten thousand years of civilization have established. . . . In war as in peace, strength lies in hope, and it is the wisest propaganda which keeps men rich in hope.[8]

In 1942 he elaborated the same point: "It will be apparent that I do not regard wartime information as different in kind from public information in days of peace. The only difference is in degree."

> In fact, the test of a good information is not to be found in the slickness with which it drums up public attention, but rather it is in the wide reaches of education which lie behind the immediate news. It is in the creation of national unity and the promotion of concord between one part of a country and another. It is in the promotion of better industrial relations, better knowledge of food and nutrition, better preparation of youth for a life of good citizenship, and is the mobilization of national forces which, like local and voluntary activities, are now only partially used in the national effort.[9]

A year later Grierson was combining his ideas of propaganda, education, and peacetime national purpose more intricately:

> A horror program followed by an appeal from the Minister of Finance may increase the sale of war savings stamps or contributions to a Victory Loan Campaign. But the effects of such propaganda seldom go beyond creating a general disposition to follow the lead of the government more willingly. It fails to impart to people a positive desire to expand the scope of their activities; it does little to heighten their own initiative; it fails to inspire their total psychological participation. Such propaganda, as a result, is failing to achieve total mobilization for total war. . . .
>
> A basic problem of war information and administration in Canada today is therefore the psychological one: that of creating the kind of atmosphere in which men and women will put forth their best efforts at their various tasks not as a result of legalistic compulsion but of their own recognition of what is at stake in this conflict and their faith in the promise of the future.[10]

Finally, in January 1945, towards the close of the war:

> [T]he day of din and terror in our war information is well over. . . . I think we shall not be taking the war less intensively, if we take it more quietly. One bursting shell is so much like another bursting shell, and I, who have had to see miles on miles of film with death and destruction on every inch of it, understand perfectly when people say they are bored. They are not being disrespectful of the fighting front or the fighting effort. They are merely indicating that death and destruction, the onward roll of guns and tanks and armies do not, in themselves, create a pattern of war sufficiently significant to them, and I heartily agree. . . .

It is the prospect to come that we must somehow find in the smoke and storm of battle, and articulate as best we can for all to realize.[11]

One of Grierson's own attempts to articulate the prospect to come can be seen in the following:

As I see it, the really hard and disagreeable task of education to-morrow is that it will have, willy-nilly, to re-examine its attitude to such fundamental concepts as Property and Wealth, Natural Rights and Freedom of Contract. It will have to think more cautiously when it comes to the word Opportunity and the phrase Free Enterprise. The concepts themselves will not be obliterated. They are simply due for a sea change which will leave them somewhat different from what they were before.

On the positive side, we shall find new concepts coming more powerfully into our lives; and we shall find ourselves dramatizing them so that they become loyalties and take leadership of the Will. We shall talk less of the world as everyone's oyster and more about Work and Jobs. We shall talk less about free enterprise and competition and more about the State as a partner in initiative. There will be less about Liberty and more about Duties: less about the past and more about the future. Already you hear the new words in the air: Discipline, Unity, Co-ordination, Total Effort, Planning. They are the first swallows over the horizon; and there are going to be more of them. . . .

I am not going to pretend that I do not realize how "totalitarian" some of my conclusions seem. . . . You can be "totalitarian" for evil and you can also be "totalitarian" for good. Some of us came out of a highly disciplined religion and see no reason to fear discipline and self-denial. Some of us learned in a school of philosophy which taught that all was for the common good and nothing for oneself and have never, in any case, regarded the pursuit of happiness as anything other than an aberration of the human spirit. We were taught, for example, that he who would gain his life must lose it. Even Rousseau talked of transporting *le moi dans l'unité commune*, and Calvin of establishing the holy communion of the citizens. So, the kind of "totalitarianism" I am thinking of, while it may apply to the new conditions of society, has as deep a root as any in human tradition. I would call the philosophy of individualism Romantic and say we have been on a spectacular romantic spree for four hundred years. I would maintain this other, "totalitarian," viewpoint is classical.[12]

With all the charity that should accompany hindsight, it still must be recognized that Grierson was at best only half right in his prophecies. The big new words he favored over the big old ones surely were no more strongly operative generally postwar than they had been prewar and in some ways less so. His brand of "totalitarianism," classical or no, existed perhaps only in the totalitarian countries of Eastern Europe and some Third World nations, unless a "welfare state" in Britain could be thought to have qualified. Surely Grierson would have guessed that the end of a second World War would bring the same lapse of vigor and discipline as had the end of the First; prosperity, isolationism, and political reaction were repeated, in North America at least. It seems likely that he was describing what he wanted to have happen in the hope that he could thereby help it happen, which is rather unlike him. The "totalitarian" note was a new one, at least in the clarity and force with which it was sounded, and it would not always be easy for him to obtain complete sympathy for (or was it understanding of?) his position.

## The U.S. Connection

If indeed many of Grierson's arguments were directed towards the United States, informed people in the United States were aware of the vigor of Grierson's thinking and respectful of the work of the National Film Board. Bosley Crowther, film reviewer of the *New York Times*, praised Grierson's speech before the Conference of the Arts, Sciences, and Professions in the Post-War World and quoted from it at length.[13] In reference to the success of "The World in Action" series in the United States, Grierson had earlier acknowledged: "We have helpful spectators on papers like *Time*, the *New York Times*, and the *New Yorker*, and one gathers the impression from *Variety*'s reviews that it has at last found in the war something tougher and bloodier than itself."[14]

Before the United States's entry into the war, Grierson's observations about Americans' distrust of government information services and warnings against the dangers of filmmaking too close to partisan lines had been borne out. In March 1940 the Senate Appropriations Committee of a Republican-dominated Congress refused for the last time to grant a budget to the U.S. Film Service,[15] and in June it was officially terminated.[16] This act on the part of Congress and Pare Lorentz's lack of success in defending his program had an especially bitter irony since with the imminent entry of the

United States into war, government filmmaking would have to be reinstituted from scratch and on a vast scale.

In New York City, attempts were made to follow other Grierson advice, with somewhat better results. In the same year the U.S. Film Service ended, a Joint Committee on Educational Films was set up, including representatives of the American Library Association and four other organizations. Grierson and Mary Losey drafted a mimeographed "Brief for an American Library Association Grant." A response from the Rockefeller Foundation enabled the committee to conduct a study of the use and circulation of educational films in libraries of all types. Gerald D. McDonald, of the New York Public Library, was appointed to gather information for the study and to write a report, which was published by the American Library Association in 1942 under the title *Educational Motion Pictures and Libraries*. In 1943 the Educational Film Library Association was organized as a professional association of film librarians and of representatives from all kinds of educational institutions and agencies. The American Film Center gave E.F.L.A. office space at first.[17]

The American Film Center was paralleled by an Association of Documentary Film Producers; both organizations were formed in 1939 and Mary Losey was a key figure in both. She had become interested in the ideas and films that Grierson, Baird, Rotha, and Anstey had brought over with them on their prewar trips. Visiting England herself, on her return she "set to work after the Grierson pattern," as Rotha put it, "to organize the jangling sects of American documentary into a purposeful group geared to attack the citadels of sponsorship and distribution."[18] Along with Renée Gathman, Losey edited *Documentary Film News* for the association, the first issue of which appeared in August 1940. In that year also the A.D.F.P. set up the Institute of Film Techniques at City College of New York, and Grierson seems to have had a hand in its formation. Irving Jacoby, one of the American filmmakers who had worked at the Film Board, wrote in connection with the establishment of the Institute:

> In only one film centre in North America was there any sign of an organised, directed movement for training youth. And the National Film Board in Ottawa obviously had enough to do. To train the Canadians needed for carrying out a national film programme would be a heroic task in itself. We had long hoped to have Grierson, or at least

part of Grierson, in the States, but with the increasing importance of the Film Board to Canada's war effort such hope gradually faded. Here we had to be content with his advice, criticism and too infrequent visits. But his name cannot be kept off the Institute of Film Techniques' credit cards. He scorned us into action, filed down our vanities, unmuddled our political thinking, and most important, through his work in Canada, gave us vistas of a hopeful future.[19]

Grierson and Legg both spoke to Institute classes during the 1941–42 academic year.[20]

But with the U.S. entry into war and its members scattered about the globe, the Association of Documentary Film Producers was disbanded in 1942 never to be re-formed. *Documentary Film News*, its last issue April 1942, was reincarnated in October 1945 as *Film News*, published by the American Film Center. Though the publication continued an independent if precarious existence, the American Film Center itself ended a few years later owing to lack of financial support and differences in points of view among cooperating producers and its personnel.[21]

At the end of the war Grierson acknowledged the creative work done in the United States by documentarians like Lorentz, Willard Van Dyke, Irving Jacoby, Ralph Steiner, Paul Strand, Joris Ivens, John Ferno, John Huston, Herbert Kline, Alexander Hammid, Helen Van Dongen, Henwar Rodakiewicz, and of course Flaherty, and by "sponsors of great enlightenment like Arthur Mayer and Osgood Field."[22] In fact, he said, "In the United States you enjoy in the matter of documentary films the very finest record of individual achievement." But, he once more sadly noted, "There is little continuity in the documentary development here and little sign of a large-scale plan which envisages the progressive coverage by the documentary film of the main aspects and problems of the fast moving society in which you live. You will have to organize far better than you have ever done before if you are going to enjoy the very rich opportunities for creative careers which exist today and must increasingly appear in the future."[23]

During his junkets to New York, Grierson saw much of his old friend Flaherty. Among other things he recalled of this time was Flaherty's "quite personal discovery" that the machine could "do away with poverty. He told me so himself on a famous occasion," continued Grierson.

We had as usual dined rather well. Perhaps I was slower in sympathy than I should have been; perhaps I had heard it before somewhere; perhaps I had lived through some of the disillusionment of the original Industrial Revolution on my own Clydeside. I did no more than grin, but the old boy caught, as ever, the red light of a world to be thought out as he natively hated to think it out. Here he was in his big rich liberal moment, and still I seemed to be telling him that things did not happen thataway. He was on his feet with anger, his fists in the air—and with those big shoulders of his he could in his earlier days look as big and wide as a sort of handsome blond gorilla—"My God, John, you don't realise it but some people starve in this world." I rose to it but did not compete with the Man against the Sky. "That's what I've been trying to tell you, you old baron, for twenty years."

I forget how long this particular silence lasted, but it was happily not as long as the one after *Man of Aran.* . . .[24]

Stuart Legg observed that Grierson's baiting scarcely bothered Flaherty—"a big bear who didn't really give a damn," Legg fondly said of him. Frances Flaherty took a sterner view, however, and felt that Grierson, with the drink and disputation, was a bad influence on her husband. Legg told about one time when Grierson, getting ready to return to Ottawa from New York, received a phone call from Flaherty at the farm in Vermont. He complained that Frances had him stranded there without a drink in the house and would John please stop off with a supply on the way. When the Flahertys met Grierson at the train he was carrying two large suitcases. Trying to help with one Frances expressed surprise that she couldn't lift it off the ground. "Some equipment I'm transporting from New York," explained Grierson, and the men carefully put the bags to rest on the back seat. That evening after Frances had gone to bed the two of them had a good talk into the morning. When they retired, Grierson heard a considerable altercation coming from the Flahertys' bedroom. Shortly Bob reappeared, leaned against the doorjamb, and said: "The trouble with you, John, is you drink too much." Grierson once observed, said Legg, that it was Frances who put the Minnehaha in Bob's films.[25]

It may be true that those discussions interlaced with profanity, as Guy Glover described them, usually ended with the two men at each other's throats, yet he exaggerated the hate surely when he applied the term love-hate to their relationship.[26] There were, evidently, intermittent strains. Richard Griffith recalled Flaherty's speaking of his resentment of Grierson's offering him a job as a cameraman at the Film Board.[27] But there can be no doubt that Grierson loved Flaherty deeply if in his own fashion.

One final link with the United States needs to be examined rather closely—for its own importance and as it relates to Grierson's views about government information, which were most fully articulated during this period. He again became involved with the University of Chicago, now under the leadership of the dynamic Robert Maynard Hutchins. In 1944 E.R.P.I. (Electrical Research Products Inc., a subsidiary of Western Electric and one of the largest and most important producers of classroom films anywhere in the world) was purchased by Encyclopaedia Britannica, which in turn belonged to the University of Chicago. (E.R.P.I. Classroom Films became Encyclopaedia Britannica Films, which later became Encyclopaedia Britannica Educational Corporation.) Grierson served as board member of Encyclopaedia Britannica Films, along with Hutchins, Henry Luce, Marshall Field, Paul Hoffman, and others.

More important, perhaps, Grierson also became a foreign adviser to the Commission on the Freedom of the Press, which operated out of the University of Chicago and included old associates from the twenties, Charles Merriam and Harold Lasswell, among its distinguished membership. Characteristically, Grierson became an extremely active adviser, drafting a memorandum which startled the commission and became the focal point of a significant debate. Zechariah Chafee Jr., a member of the commission, quotes at length from this memo in his *Government and Mass Communications*, and gives the counterarguments raised by the commission. In the course of the controversy, basic and mutually contradictory positions were outlined, as well as differences between wartime and peacetime situations and between the political systems of Britain and Canada on the one hand and the United States on the other. Clearly Grierson had gone one step further in his insistence that once government assumes initiative it must educate and persuade in order to implement policy. "The main point," he now said, "is that you pass from a state of facilitation, which is a simple thing, to the direct initiation of what opinion you want. That, of course, is never an easy matter."[28]

Nor was it an easy matter to convince others to take this next step: "his position was not at all shared by the Commission on the Freedom of the Press," noted Chafee. Getting close to the matter of Grierson as "dirty operator" mentioned earlier, Chafee went on to explain that

This impressive picture of energy and skill in Canada left many members of the Commission disquieted by the way the government had taken the newspapers into camp and was manipulating public opinion. Suppose a less friendly neighbor were injecting what it wished into our own channels of communication in the manner just described. Only the exigencies of war against the deadliest of enemies could, I believe, justify the full extent of the Canadian government's participation in the distribution of news and ideas.[29]

Grierson, of course, reiterated his point that information services should never be the instruments of the party in power but should be run only for the national enterprise and the citizens as a whole. The distinction suggested was between government as the community's business and government as persons in power. When he was asked, Chafee reported, "How does your group of officials distinguish what is in the general interest of Canada and the Canadian government and the people from what is in the interest of, let's say, Mr. William Lyon Mackenzie King, the Prime Minister?" Grierson replied:

We claim certain rights in carrying out a plan of government or national management which has been in general agreed to by Parliament. We try to make that national plan successful. We claim the right to give information that is news, and also information that is pre-news, in order to prepare people for a situation so that they are not caught. We also claim the right to motivate actions. All these rights we claim are relative to our duty of informing the public so as to make the national plan succeed. We would be very foolish if we confused that large educational duty with the party in power. The distinction has to be drawn by rule of thumb, by finding the point of compromise—that is, by seeing that we operate within the limits of general consent. For example, we avoid using films, etc., on issues where the opposition is critical of the Administration. If we feel that we are secure on general consent, then we go ahead.[30]

The final extension of the sort of information service Grierson urged and in part had achieved thus became a kind of government within government. The Wartime Information Board had its intelligence service which kept it abreast of public opinion through numerous informants and polls. It was better informed about the national mood than either press or Parliament and could use this information in the initiatory way that made Chafee and the

Commission on the Freedom of the Press uneasy. Grierson provided an example:

> on one occasion when many members of Parliament were quite sure that the public was against the whole system of wartime price and wage ceilings and complained strongly about it themselves, some of the Information Board believed that Parliament and also the general opinion of officials in Ottawa were not reflecting the true will of the people in this matter. So the Board did a Gallup poll and proved there was a 75 per cent vote in the country for the existing system of controls, however harsh. The Board advised the government to turn down Parliament in the matter and take a chance on the Board's advice. The government took that chance with enormous success. Here was a case where the intelligence service came to a correct conclusion about public opinion which was just opposite to the reactions among editors and members of Parliament. The inference is that the legislature may be a complex of self-regarding interests rather than a true mirror of public opinion.[31]

By creating this sort of "direct relationship between public and government (in the sense of bureaucracy)," Chafee noted, the W.I.B. "by-passed Parliament and indeed made the authority of the officials more solid as against Parliament. As Mr. Grierson put it . . . 'Because you cannot rely on the intelligent backing of the legislature—here I exaggerate a little—you create a definite body of criticism over and beyond through the media with the public, which will secure you vis-à-vis the legislature.'"[32]

This is government by public opinion indeed, and something quite different from showing one part of the empire to the other or the workings of one government service to the population at large. No wonder Grierson's ambitions in Canada were viewed darkly by some. The issue of "totalitarianism" which he himself raised earlier in another context, only to discharge it honorably, seems central to an evaluation of Grierson during the Canadian period. Somehow, in his desire to achieve the power to do good the balance between *power* and *good* becomes equivocal. The means to his ends clearly called for an alteration of the democratic system as he found it operating. It wasn't the Commission on the Freedom of the Press alone which was not ready to accept his grand design. In the United States at the end of the war the Office of War Information metamorphosed into the United States Information Agency; in Canada the Wartime Information Board became the Canadian Information Services; both agencies were restricted to activity abroad. Only in Britain did the Ministry of Information become a Central Office of Information, but it was greatly reduced and limited to assignments from particular government departments—scarcely the powerful, monolithic, and independent entity Grierson envisioned. Though he would become head of the Films Division of that organization, one might well suspect that his consent to its weakened responsibility came from bleak necessity rather than a change of mind.

## The U.K. Connection

In addition to straddling the North American continent, Grierson kept a close eye on the work of his former colleagues across the Atlantic. They were, of course, very active. As elsewhere, with entry into war British documentary production increased to unprecedented proportions. Rotha estimated that "Between 1941 and 1945, well over 500 films must have been made for the Ministry of Information alone by a handful of independent documentary companies. That figure does not include the output of the Ministry's own Crown Film Unit or films for the Services."[33] The people trained by and associated with Grierson in the thirties moved into key positions and were responsible for much of the high quality as well as the vast quantity of this production.

At the Film Centre during Grierson's absence in Canada, Wright, Elton, and Anstey were at different periods in control.[34] *Documentary News Letter*, which succeeded *World Film News* in January 1940, continued to be published throughout the war under the auspices of the Film Centre in association with the American Film Center. Though Grierson continued to write for it, less and less frequently, his name was dropped from its editorial board after 1941.

Perhaps of all Grierson's former colleagues in England, Wright remained in closest contact during the war. In 1942 he spent four weeks in Canada being indoctrinated in the reason and method of "Canada Carries On" and "The World in Action" as preparation for pushing these films into British distribution—he became "English editor" of the two series. Under the sponsorship of the Canadian government, Wright was again in Canada from August 1943 to January 1944. The purpose of the second visit was to help him interpret Canada, not just its films, to Britain on his return.[35] In 1942 documentary pioneer J. P. R. Golightly was seconded from the Army to become Grierson's personal representative in London.[36]

The Ministry of Information, created immediately after Britain's declaration of war, took over the General Post Office Film Unit (and the G.P.O. and Empire film libraries and distribution services as well) and renamed it Crown Film Unit early in 1940.[37] In retrospect, the most brilliant and certainly the most lasting of the wartime work seems to have come out of Crown. Its two most vigorous and poetic documentary talents in ascendance during the war were indisputably G.P.O. veterans Harry Watt and Humphrey Jennings. Watt wrote and directed *Squadron 992, Britain at Bay, Dover—Front Line,* and *Target for Tonight,* prototype for the wartime semi-documentary form. Jennings's most notable successes were *London Can Take It* (codirected with Watt), *Listen to Britain, Fires Were Started,* and *A Diary for Timothy.* It was Jennings who became the film laureate of England at war. Though Grierson appreciated the aesthetic qualities of Jennings's achievement after it had come into existence, he still felt that, in the case of *Listen to Britain* at least, it was marked by certain *longueurs.*[38]

Ruby Grierson, after codirecting with John Taylor the simple and affecting *They Also Serve,* accepted an assignment from her brother John to work on a film about evacuated British children being transported to Canada. It was on this production that she lost her life when the refugee ship *City of Benares* was torpedoed by a German submarine in September 1940. According to a survivor, she was one of a number of people hanging onto the side of a life raft following the sinking. It was terribly cold and completely dark. After a short while she said "Oh, to hell with it," and let herself go from the raft. Arthur Elton thought it characteristic of her to sum up a situation, make a decision, and act upon it. The others on the raft were rescued within half an hour.[39]

Ruby was one of John's younger sisters and his favorite. Her death was a cruel blow, no less painful, one can imagine, because it occurred on an assignment from him. She was much mourned by other documentary people as well. Obituaries in both *Documentary News Letter* and *Sight and Sound* extolled her charm as a person and achievement and promise as a filmmaker.[40] The refugee-children film, put aside for a time after her death, was eventually completed (with footage from John Taylor in England, and Roy Tash and Evelyn Spice in Canada) as *Children From Overseas.* It was designed largely for the parents of British children shipped to Canada for safekeeping.[41]

The relationship between Grierson and his former colleagues during the war, conversely, bore some resemblance to that of a father who had left home. Though he hovered over his "children" with affection, he seemed to feel increasing puzzlement and some dismay at the directions they were taking (or not taking). They, for their part, at first may have felt his absence keenly and seemed uncertain in their movements. Then they gained new strength and assurance, reaching a peak of accomplishment during wartime. But those same years saw the remarkable coherence that had existed in the British documentary group begin to diminish. Grierson never completely regained his leadership in the postwar years.

Writing in 1941 to Elton about the changes required of British documentary by the war, Grierson looked back at their efforts in the thirties. "It was fine in that brave decade of ours," he wrote. "We were a liberal force wearing away the props of complacency. We hadn't a chance of winning, or winning in time, without a political movement to use us: and that failed, for us, when the Labour movement lost its internal steam after the general strike [of 1926]."[42] On the other hand, he thought that "Without *Housing Problems* and the whole movement of social understanding such films helped articulate . . . history would have found another bloodier solution when the bombs first rained on the cities of Britain."[43] Cryptic though this statement is, by "bloodier solution" he may have meant revolution and defeat.

One might not regard the British documentaries of the 1930s as preparing a country to accept and persist in a war. In fact, one might be inclined to fault the Griersonian system of "general consent" as not allowing for the sort of anti-fascist films the Americans somehow managed to produce in the 1930s without governmental or industrial sponsorship. Yet, though not dealing directly with politics or war, the British documentaries quietly and steadily pushed attitudes that would be most helpful in wartime: getting the job done, social cooperation, the obligation to be informed, the value of government service. Perhaps Grierson was right, to one degree or another.

However, despite (maybe in part because of) his hovering attention over the movement he had founded, there developed during the war the first evident strain in the loyalties of the British group towards Grierson—some fierce arguments and some defections. Part of this was brought on by his steady criticism of the propaganda approach of the British documentaries—and, in fact, of Britain's wartime stance—offered in private and public correspondence. In a letter from Australia to Elton in March 1940, Grierson conceded that the war may have been doing some good in making the English think about what other people thought of them. At the same time he felt that England insisted on seeing every event in political—national—terms and missed the "boundary-crossings in economic terms of world events." He complained that England looked forward to a postwar world in which things would be back to normal, rather than seeing the "need for new economic integrations."[44]

During the war Grierson returned briefly to Britain at least twice. Michael Spencer, one of the early National Film Board recruits, remembered him as a passenger on a troop ship in August of 1941.[45] Perhaps it was this visit that English documentary veteran Edgar Anstey told a story about.

Anstey had been trying to get Grierson, who was staying with him, to go see the people of London bedding down in the subways in preparation for the night's raids by the Luftwaffe. Grierson resisted, on the grounds that Anstey's interest and pride in their ability to endure was merely another evidence of the British defensive position (as in *London Can Take It*), whereas Grierson favored a more positive, aggressive approach. He said, according to Anstey, "Oh, you people sentimentalize all that. I know about it from reading about it." When Anstey finally did succeed in getting him down into the subway shelters, he was tremendously impressed and moved—like Henry Moore of the marvelous series of shelter sketches. In a characteristic about-face, Grierson talked about it for a week to everybody he saw and demanded to know why the British filmmakers weren't putting that great story on the screen.[46] By October 8 he was in Lisbon, on his way back to Canada.[47] Another of Grierson's former lieutenants, Basil Wright, surmised that he had visited England mainly to talk with Jack Beddington, head of the Films Division of the Ministry of Information, regarding Canadian films in Britain and British films in Canada.[48]

Much better documented is a trip in 1944. Grierson arrived in London in mid-July and returned to Ottawa in mid-August.[49] During that stay, not long after D-Day, he also visited France. In a talk over C.B.C. radio, on August 20, he noted that "Two Sundays ago at this hour I was driving in a jeep from Brittany to a Canadian encampment near Caen. This was the day before the great Canadian breakthrough from Caen to Falaise." His own special mission, he said, was "to see and talk to the film and still photographers who were up there in the front line, sending back the pictures of action." Incidentally, that broadcast was a superb bit of war correspondence, in the Ernie Pyle manner, with vivid details of the French countryside, of soldiers, and operations.[50]

In the September 1940 *Documentary News Letter*, there appeared a communique from "a correspondent in America" dated August 10. On the basis of internal stylistic evidence, the "correspondent" seems pretty clearly to have been Grierson, anonymous possibly so as not to offend former colleagues or put his personal weight behind this criticism, mild and constructive as it was. The American correspondent was critical of the British documentary and semi-documentary productions reaching Canada and the United States as being "too little and too late." He felt it was the job of the British documentarians to make the "American spirit feel at one with the English spirit," and complained about the "inept resuscitation of the snob message" in the film *King's People*, which was about Canada. "Ironically," he offered, "the people who are trying hardest—and perhaps do best—are not the English but the Americans. Walter Wanger's *Foreign Correspondent* and *Long Voyage Home* are typical of that effort."[51] Another "American Correspondent," in the following issue, gently and partially disengaged himself or herself from Grierson (it seems likely the writer was Mary Losey, a prime mover in efforts to organize documentary in the United States) before going on to attack *Foreign Correspondent*. "With the general criticism in the article I am in entire agreement; but there are some statements of fact which make it obvious that the writer knows intimately about films in Canada and not so completely about films in the United States."[52]

In the January 1941 letter to Elton already mentioned, Grierson had much to say about the parochial, selfish, class-ridden view of England, which still expected the world to look to her and had lost the real picture of the world—that it was increasingly a small country prepared to go down with its own bravery, savoring courage in defeat, as it were. In the same letter, he also argued at length that rather than completed documentaries, British footage should be sent over to be made into films for Americans by people, for example himself and Stuart Legg, who knew the mentality.[53] In general he thought reportage better for American audiences than documentary: the Americans thought fast and in a straight line, while the English were slower but more complex and devious.[54] Admitting the quality of *London Can Take It*, he wanted instead films of people "doing something about the war, doing something, not feeling something sadly and wearily à la Quentin Reynolds" (American war correspondent who wrote and read the commentary for *London Can Take It*).[55]

To Wright in October 1941, Grierson expressed the view that the British filmmakers didn't have as much freedom within the government as the Canadians did—that they had to make only what the government wanted. He also repeated the theme that England was not looking to the future (or present), and re-emphasized the geopolitical advantages of Canada and global concerns in an air age. The British view was too parochial, he once more charged, too rooted in tradition: it was a tight little island. Some of this complaint seemed to stem from his acknowledgement that Beddington, of the M.O.I., had felt the Canadian films were too removed from—ahead of—the British position and were not suitable for showing in the United Kingdom.[56] Grierson was trying to instill in his "old boys" his own viewpoint and get them to push it. Wright observed that the documentary people had earlier wanted Grierson to return to the United Kingdom as Minister of Information, but that there had been no offers from the government.[57]

Regarding Grierson's views of Canadian merits and British shortcomings, Anstey amusedly recalled that on the 1944 visit Grierson had some young Canadian filmmakers with him, whom he put in an awkward position by praising them and pointing out the old fuddy-duddies of British documentary.[58] After that visit, however, he wrote for *Documentary News Letter* in a conciliatory, if somewhat contradictory, vein: "It has been a wonderful thing to see, in spite of the war and the special difficulties of film making in Britain, the documentary people there have remembered the essentials of social reference. They have not been fooled into the fallacy that fighting films give anything more than one layer of the present reality." Still, he had a "but," which foreshadowed some of the difficulty documentary would encounter in postwar Britain: "I keep on feeling that the documentary group as a whole is not at the centre where political and social planning is being thought out and legislated, or not close enough to the centre. It is not good enough to be on the outside looking in, waiting on someone else's pleasure for an opportunity to serve social progress."[59]

There was also the brouhaha over *Foreign Correspondent*, the 1940 release produced by Walter Wanger and directed by Alfred Hitchcock. Grierson, as "a correspondent in America," had praised the film. Mary Losey, if she was the "American Correspondent," disagreed with him and took strong exception to the film: "Not only to me, but to many others who have complained bitterly, it is incredible that Wanger and Hitchcock would have devised a noble and heroic death for their fifth-column politician, followed by a justification of his way of life from his daughter. Is this what we are to expect when 'Hollywood tries hard'"?

But the furor in Britain centered on another scene. At the end of the film, Joel McCrea, playing a correspondent modeled on Quentin Reynolds and/or Edward R. Murrow, who actually broadcast from the roof of the B.B.C. during the German raids,[60] broadcasts to America from a London radio studio. The crucial monologue is as follows:

> I can't read the rest of the speech I had because all the lights have gone out—so I'll have just to talk off the cuff. All that noise you hear isn't static. It's death coming to London. Yes, they're coming here now. You can hear the bombs falling on the streets and the homes. Don't tune me out. Hang on a while. This is a big story—and you're a part of it. It's too late to do anything here now except stand in the dark and let them come. It's as if the lights are out everywhere—except in America. Keep those lights burning there. Cover them with steel; ring them with guns. Build a canopy of battleships and bombing planes around them— Hello, America! Hang onto your lights. They're the only lights left in the world![61]

Although it reviewed *Foreign Correspondent* quite favorably as the "Film of the Month," *Documentary News Letter* nevertheless felt it necessary to address itself quite specifically to the McCrea speech. "The importance of the sequence is that it is a message to the States—and not to us—sent out by an American journalist and, in fact, conceived at script conferences at which Walter Wanger had the last word." The latter part of this statement was a veiled allusion to a rumor starting to circulate that it was Grierson who had written the final speech for his friend Wanger. *DNL* went on: "It is neither a warlike nor a political piece of propaganda; it stimulates thought, and its message should strike home on the other side of the Atlantic; to us over here it does at least bring evidence of a good will backed by clear thinking."[62]

The *DNL* reviewer's opinion was not, however, held unanimously among the British documentary people; Paul Rotha started a public debate with a letter published in the succeeding issue. Of the speech, Rotha wrote, "I describe it as an insult to the 'only army which,' claims *DNL* itself in an editorial in the same issue, 'will win the war'; an army of civilians, I maintain, in whom the lights have never burned more brightly and more proudly than they do now." Further, "I can assure these leaders of the British documentary film that the people who are really suffering as well as fighting this war do not share this view that the lights are even dimmed in Britain. If they did, the Fascist propagandists might well claim to have already won the war."[63]

As for Grierson's role in the indignity, Rotha wrote:

> The tale has gone the rounds that the words spoken by Macrea [*sic*] were either written or inspired by Mr. John Grierson when he was in Hollywood. If this is true (though to me they sound more like Mr. Kennedy [presumably Joseph Kennedy, United States Ambassador to the Court of St. James] than Mr. Grierson) they reveal a grave lack of knowledge of public opinion in Britain, a lack one does not usually associate with a propagandist so sensitive to the public pulse as Mr. Grierson. . . .
>
> . . . My own belief is that if the Editors of *DNL* had not been under the impression that the words in question had been written or inspired by Mr. John Grierson, they might not have been so quick to agree that their own, as well as other people's beliefs in democratic Britain had vanished. Assuming he is responsible, Mr. Grierson's 4,000 odd miles remove from Britain may explain his rare misjudgment of public opinion, but Film Centre Ltd. [which published *Documentary News Letter*] is, after all, quite close to the Front Line.

Others who wished "to associate their names with this letter" were Michael Balcon, Ealing Studios; Ritchie Calder, *Daily Herald* and *New Statesman*; Alberto Cavalcanti, Ealing Studios; A. J. Cummings, *News Chronicle*; Aubrey Flanagan, *Motion Picture Herald*; Michael Foot, *Evening Standard*; Dilys Powell, *Sunday Times*; and Grierson's old friend from Glasgow University days, Alexander Werth, *Manchester Guardian*.[64] It is interesting that Cavalcanti was the only documentary filmmaker among this group.

In the next issue of *Documentary News Letter*, Brian Smith wrote:

> The speech at the end of *Foreign Correspondent* has aroused such distinguished controversy that someone should record the simple probability: it has not the same meaning on the screen as in print. . . .
>
> Maybe James Hilton, Charles Bennett, Joan Harrison, John Grierson and other stray advisers from Hollywood's British colony failed to see the tactlessness of the words, but I guess Hitch directed for the effect, and it's the screen effect which matters: argument ignoring this is academic.[65]

With this, the allegations and arguments were allowed to drop from view.

Publicly Grierson remained silent, but in a letter to Basil Wright in December 1940 he said he did not write the *Foreign Correspondent* speech, and it did not represent his view. If he didn't quite echo Rotha's assertion that the lights weren't even dimmed in Britain, he did feel that they were just beginning to come up. In terms of North America and relating it to Europe, he approved the ending and deplored Rotha's having written his letter.

Even before the *Foreign Correspondent* controversy, another divisive argument had started that would last longer and prove much more basic and damaging. It revolved around the relative contributions and different views of Grierson (propaganda) and Cavalcanti (aesthetics) in British documentary. It would finally center on a feature-length anthology made up of excerpts from famous documentaries compiled by Cavalcanti and Ernest Lindgren, of the British Film Institute. Its title was *Film and Reality*.

The rivalry started, publicly at least, in a curious, indirect manner. In the April–May 1940 issue of *Cine-Technician*, published by the Association of Cine-Technicians (A.C.T.), Kenneth Gordon, who regularly wrote the column "Cinema Log," told a story about Cavalcanti being hauled off to a police station while shooting *Squadron 992* in Scotland because of his foreign accent. Gordon concluded: "I dare say that the local cops are still rather puzzled as to why British film technicians should have foreign accents."

Basil Wright, in a letter in the June–July issue, reproached Gordon for his ungrateful chauvinism and testified to Cavalcanti's great contribution to British documentary. Gordon, replying to Wright in the same issue, wrote that wages and conditions at Cavalcanti's unit (the General Post Office Film Unit) were bad and that the A.C.T. had experienced difficulties in negotiating with him. Also, somewhat gratuitously, Gordon added: "I would say that the documentary movement owes more to John Grierson than anyone else"—which put Wright's good will and fairness towards Cavalcanti in a strange light of contest.

In the August–September issue R. McNaughton, who had come to the G.P.O. in 1934 and worked as editor and director, jumped into the fray "on behalf of some of the older members." "Any technician worth his salt will admit that the genius and guidance of Cavalcanti is behind by far the majority of worthwhile British documentary films." He went on to say that Cavalcanti was not responsible for the bad conditions at the G.P.O. unit, that he had displayed generosity, and so forth. "Finally," McNaughton wrote, "we consider that the influence of Cavalcanti is at least equal to that of John Grierson. British documentaries have obtained a high following both at home and overseas and Cavalcanti has undoubtedly been largely responsible for this."[66]

During this time Cavalcanti and Lindgren had begun production of *Film and Reality*, with its survey of the international development of documentary films up to 1940. When it was released early in 1942 it was reviewed by Basil Wright in the March issue of *Documentary News Letter*. Wright identified and, to an extent, rekindled the running controversy when he wrote that *Film and Reality* was, to himself at least, "in many places controversial as regards its choice of material, and its attitude towards the social, as opposed to the academic or aesthetic development of the realist film."[67]

What Cavalcanti had done (the selection and interpretation of the examples were his) was to treat documentary films as an evolving artistic discipline, the impetus for which had been to render the raw fact of the material world into aesthetic form ("the creative treatment of actuality," after all, Grierson had first written). Cavalcanti's selections comprised the most dramatic and loveliest sequences from a large number of films, going back to pre-documentary origins. No mention was made of the educational-social preoccupations of the British (or for that matter of the Soviet) school. Significantly, following the intertitle "The Realistic Documentary of Life at Home," British documentaries were lumped with various continental efforts, including the city symphony films and highly stylized sports films. The final section was devoted to "Realism in the Story Film." Clearly *Film and Reality* represented a dereliction to Griersonian eyes.

It was Lindgren, not Cavalcanti, who responded in the following issue of *DNL* to Wright's criticisms. In his defense, Lindgren quoted from a letter by veteran documentary director Harry Watt to the *New Statesman*. "It was Grierson's drive and initiative that obtained the formation of the Empire Marketing Board Film Unit ... it was the introduction of Cavalcanti's professional skill and incredible film sense that raised the standard and reputation of British documentary," Watt had written.

A letter from Wright was printed alongside the one from Lindgren:

> Grierson, like all great men, is well able to ignore attacks made on him from whatever motives. But in the interests of accuracy, and also because I am sure that I am expressing the feeling of documentary workers as a whole, I must point out that Grierson has always been and still is a remarkable technician, a magnificent teacher, and, in short, a great producer. . . .
>
> Grierson is not merely the founder of the documentary movement. Since its inception it has been his own understanding of film technique, his encouragement of experimentation and (to meet Lindgren on his own ground) his uncanny grasp and knowledge of aesthetics as regards art in general and film art in particular, which have been the driving force and inspiration of the progress of documentary.
>
> These qualities, out of deference to Lindgren, I have put first, but I must now add Grierson's political grasp and foresight, his incredible energy and organizational drive, and, above all, his unswerving loyalty not merely to the idea of documentary but to all those working for him.[68]

Wright's response is quite unprecedented in the polemics that accompanied documentary film from its birth. There is no earlier public instance of this degree of personal praise of Grierson from a member of his group; any hint of a "cult of personality" was studiously avoided in Grierson's own writings and those of his associates. Lindgren did not "attack" Grierson, as Wright alleged; the closest he came to it was the quote from Watt, whose contribution to the "disloyalty" is pointedly unacknowledged by Wright. It would seem that only in the face of growing defection—Cavalcanti and

Watt were the targets; Lindgren in a sense had merely stepped into the fight—could Wright be goaded into such a furious defense.

Wright's position was supported by an editorial in that same issue of *DNL*: "The documentary film movement as it was created and developed under John Grierson was and still is directed to one purpose and to one purpose only—the formation of a body of skilled propagandists trained to express their propaganda ideas by means of film."[69]

The earlier-mentioned letter from Grierson which had grown into "The Documentary Idea 1942" stemmed from this same controversy. Prefaced with an explanation that it was a letter "to a member of the Editorial Board of *DNL*," readers were advised, "Its content is so important that it can be regarded as a considered and categorical article on propaganda policy." Grierson wrote:

> In our world, it is specially necessary these days to guard against the aesthetic argument. . . . Documentary was from the beginning— when we first separated our public purpose theories from those of Flaherty—an anti-aesthetic movement.
>
> What confuses history is that we had always the good sense to use the aesthetes. We did so because we liked them and because we needed them. It was, paradoxically, with the first-rate aesthetic help of people like Flaherty and Cavalcanti that we mastered the techniques necessary for our quite unaesthetic purposes.[70]

The article, in its entirety, is indeed a marvelous statement of Grierson's purposes.

Though he never wrote directly of *Film and Reality*, Grierson was said to have hated it.[71] Some five years later Cavalcanti ruefully recalled the events surrounding its production. The problem of "'who' did 'what' in film history and film aesthetics is a problem both involved and perilous," he wrote. "After working two solid years on a film essay about film criticism—*Film and Reality*—I burnt my fingers so painfully I ought to know." But, still not content to let the argument rest, he continued: "I know, too, that the use of Cinema as a social weapon is an urgent necessity. Nevertheless the exaggerated utilitarian approach to the film medium which it entails could become a reactionary influence as dangerous as the aesthetic one. The utilitarians claim that film-making ought to be reduced to the task of collecting a series of shots and accompanying them by a rousing election speech. They forget that by doing so they are blunting the edge of their weapon."[72]

Going beyond mere arguing, some of the veterans were leaving documentaries in the direction of the fiction film. The same year that *Film and Reality* was released, 1942, Cavalcanti completed his first British feature, as associate producer: *The Foreman Went to France* (produced by Michael Balcon, directed by Charles Frend). Having some semi-documentary elements, the film did not represent as big a jump as one might suppose: in Britain "the bridge between feature and documentary is shorter than anywhere else," Cavalcanti later wrote.[73] It was, after all, Harry Watt who had established the prototype for the subspecies of wartime semi-documentary with *Target for Tonight* out of Crown. The studios were merely following the documentarians' lead, and Watt shortly followed Cavalcanti to Ealing to help.

If in some ways the semi-documentary represented a reaction against Grierson's first principles, it nonetheless stemmed from the movement he had founded and the people he had trained. As Grierson's editor and biographer Forsyth Hardy wrote, "It was during the war that the first unmistakable signs of documentary's impact on the studio film became apparent." If several of the documentary directors, including Cavalcanti and Watt, were making features, "the realistic approach was also adopted by other directors whose work had previously shown little tendency in that direction," Hardy continued. *One of Our Aircraft Is Missing* (1942), *Next of Kin* (1942), *Millions Like Us* (1943), *San Demetrio, London* (1943), *The Way Ahead* (1944), and *Waterloo Road* (1945) "were a few of the films which applied to feature production the principles hammered out in the documentary movement."[74]

At the same time, this output was being matched by the official documentary units with an increasing tendency towards feature length, narrative construction, characterization, and synchronously recorded dialogue—all standard attributes of the fiction film. The semi-documentary form, which would carry over into the post-war era, earned for documentary a much wider and more enthusiastic audience than the more austere shorts of exposition and persuasion had ever achieved. Grierson, though he may have resisted the impulse during the war years on grounds of too much aestheticism and artistic self-indulgence, would be closely associated with the semi-documentary form and even the fiction film in postwar

Britain. By that time, however, the British documentary movement as movement, as a Griersonian movement at least, had ended or become diffused.

When asked whether British documentary would have come through the war in stronger array if Grierson had remained in England, Stuart Legg, the British veteran who had worked most closely with Grierson in Canada, said simply: "Possibly so, but then we would be without the Film Board."[75]

## Departure

On August 9, 1945, there appeared in the *Ottawa Journal* a story headed "Grierson Confirms Resignation from Film Board." It was followed by similar announcements in the New York (August 10) and London (August 11) *Times*. The *Journal* account began by quoting Grierson's statement to the board confirming his intimation of the month before that he would at the August meeting formally present his resignation as government film commissioner, "to take effect, if it please the Board, three months from now."

In some respects Grierson's decision to leave Canada remains puzzling and must have been arrived at only after the careful weighing of a number of complex considerations. True, he had said when he accepted the commissionership that it would be for a limited period, and that as soon as feasible a Canadian should occupy the post. This statement was often repeated, especially at the time of his earlier threatened resignation which ended in the absorption of the Motion Picture Bureau by the Film Board. Tom Daly even recalled Grierson's expressed feeling that it would take about five years (it was now six) to train the Canadians so that they could take over for themselves, the understanding being that he would depart when the job was finished.[76]

As he was leaving Canada, Grierson spelled out another side of his feelings about the situation—strangely harsh on government work in general and that in Canada in particular, with a note of hope pinned on the young:

> I pretend very much to like the ways of the civil service and to endure its inhabitants; and I do, to get my work done. But the truth is their mediocrity of spirit—so often—makes me physically sick; and I sometimes wonder if I shouldn't have contented myself making a few films of my own like Flaherty, taking my time and be damned to organising

national instruments of information and enlightenment, and such.
. . . Canada certainly doesn't reach into the sky when it comes to supporting its art and its artists, far less the living and moving things in its public service. In the circumstances it is not we who have done well, but that younger generation which still, thank God, believes in the impossible. The funny thing is that they are going to be right, and whatever happens, in poverty of spirit around them, they will take Canada to places it has never so far dreamt of.

The above was written on a ship sailing to Europe; presumably he was to consult with the Ministry of Information. Earlier in the same letter he had mentioned that the Minister of Information had asked him to be a guest of the British government.[77]

On the other hand, the kind of facility Grierson had been able to construct at the National Film Board was unique—the largest and best coordinated government film operation in the world. By 1945 it was producing three hundred films a year with an audience of four million for most releases. The total annual budget of $4 million kept seven hundred persons busy in production, distribution, and graphic arts. That all this organized activity was supported by a nation of twelve million people made it all the more remarkable.[78] As noted earlier, there were signs, particularly during the W.I.B. days, that Grierson hoped to extend information–adult education activity more widely during the postwar years. He was even said to have an estate picked out along the Ottawa River.[79] One comes back to the suspicion that the attitudes of Mackenzie King or the general political situation indicated to Grierson that his ambitions, spelled out so grandly before the Commission on the Freedom of the Press, would not be fully realized in Canada. There is no suggestion that he could not have stayed on as film commissioner—he may in fact have been sincerely urged to do so—but his eyes now turned to the wider world.

In resigning from the board, while conceding that "It is not the easiest thing in the world to give up what is probably the best and happiest job of its kind anywhere," Grierson went on to say: "There are, however, new things I ought to do in the field of documentary films. In particular, the production of films on international themes and the international exchange of films of common social interest ought now to be strengthened. This is now, and I hope properly, my principal interest."[80]

Grierson's feelings were consistent with the times. At the end of the war and with the establishment of the United Nations, there began a euphoric if short-lived period of internationalism. The notion of one world seemed possible, and Grierson, who had contributed substantially to a global view through his work at the board, would have wanted a more direct and freewheeling role in addressing the world audience. By now his friends and colleagues were established in many nations, and the models of the use of film in public service he had provided in Britain and especially in Canada were being copied widely. These resources might be available to him if he could create a documentary network directed toward international ends, he must have thought.

There was the Film Board itself to draw upon, which, in addition to the consistently international outlook of its films, had worked specifically to promote film activities in connection with the United Nations Relief and Rehabilitation Administration. (Former Grierson lieutenant and loyal supporter Basil Wright had been approached to serve as U.N.R.R.A.'s first Film Officer.)[81] Film Board veterans Ralph Foster and then Stanley Hawes became the first and second commissioners of the Australian Film Board, modeled after the Canadian one. Donald Fraser, another of the N.F.B. staff, was sent over by Grierson to work with the Australian Board and to assist comrade-in-arms Joris Ivens in Australia as the newly appointed film commissioner of the Dutch East Indies. Old Griersonian Harry Watt had arrived in Australia, too, to begin his semi-documentary feature *The Overlanders* for Ealing Studios.[82]

Back in Britain, the alumni and friends of the E.M.B. and G.P.O. units now occupied key positions at the Ministry of Information, which would become a peacetime Central Office of Information, and at Crown Film Unit. In an appointment which involved consultation with Grierson, the French had named Jean Painlevé their national film commissioner;[83] and old friend Flaherty was in the States beginning research for Standard Oil of New Jersey on what would become *Louisiana Story*. It perhaps seemed the right time to tackle on an international scale the kinds of jobs Grierson had begun in Britain and continued in Canada; that is, showing one part of the world to the rest, explaining and supporting the work of the various United Nations agencies, and attacking particular social-economic problems.

In any case, when Grierson did leave the board (Legg left at the same time) his successor had not yet definitely been fixed, though Ross McLean, deputy commissioner, immediately became acting commissioner. Rumors going around that Grierson had recommended someone else as commissioner[84] seem to have had some basis in fact. Marjorie McKay recalled that Grierson had favored James Beveridge rather than McLean, feeling that Beveridge, though somewhat lacking in experience, could grow into the job.[85] Beveridge remembered Grierson telling him that he had chosen him as successor, that he thought he could handle it. Unlike McLean, and by his own admission, Beveridge would have been quite young and without sufficient government contacts. Grierson didn't seem to think that mattered so much; the board evidently did.[86] As for Grierson himself, he wrote to the Hon. Brooke Claxton, chairman of the board, in November 1945: "Please do your utmost to secure the succession for the youth. You will never regret it and I will put up a plaque for you in the not un-notable history of the documentary. If it is not to be Ross, let it be Jim Beveridge."[87] As it turned out, Ross McLean became film commissioner and James Beveridge production secretary (i.e., in charge of production).

Looking back over the hundreds of films produced under Grierson at the N.F.B., it must be admitted that artistically they had little staying power—not one of them remains in active circulation, unlike a number of the British wartime and even a few of the 1930s documentaries. If the films were not valuable aesthetically, it would not have mattered to Grierson at the time since the need for direct and rapid communication and education was so great. They were seen by their audiences as well as by their producers for what they were—almost a television-like flow and coverage before television was available. The "five-and-a-half films a week" were often skillful, usually timely rather than timeless, always quickly produced, and designed to reach as wide an audience as the subject and purpose permitted. Aside from notable exceptions such as Norman McLaren, Tom Daly, and Guy Glover, there were few really creative filmmakers among the board's veterans; Grierson was devastatingly effective in the anti-aestheticky discipline he imposed.

His chief contributions were undoubtedly the part he (and the N.F.B.) played in helping give Canada a sense of national identity and pride that had never existed before—the look to the North and to the future—and in building the Film Board foundations so firmly that the N.F.B. not only endured but achieved a unique excellence (including aesthetic) in later and less demanding times. Grierson's forte as producer-teacher-politician was most fully employed at the N.F.B. and on the largest scale.

Grierson was never really a filmmaker as Flaherty was—there is something in what Fritzie Weisenborn had observed about an ultimate lack of artistic creativity, at a very high level of course. His saying that what he knew he learned from Flaherty and the Russians was not merely an expression of modesty and a tribute to his predecessors. *Drifters*, brilliant and effective in its time and in its way, was essentially synthetic: an analytical mind coming to understand how films are made and being able to repeat the process short of the personal and the intuitive which mark *Nanook of the North* and *Battleship Potemkin*. (Soviet montage imposed upon Flaherty's man against nature is its chief stylistic originality, and even that distinction now seems a bit incongruous: Flaherty's slow pace and unbroken shots being perhaps better suited to the material than Eisenstein's rapid and complex cutting.) Grierson could not have been, as he wondered in the letter to Basil Wright earlier quoted if he might not better have been, a maker of a few personal films and achieved the kinds of results his own high standards would have demanded. He did what he had to do—by reason of character and ability—as the hero of the western says.

Even before *Drifters*, at Glasgow University, Charles Dand had caught him out in a total digestion and regurgitation of a socialist writer. It was not, as Dand rightly insisted, a lack of originality, but rather an extraordinary ability to use fully another's contribution—more fully than the contributor could have done—and with a force of application that changed and increased its quality. This is what Grierson did with *Nanook* and made out of documentary—something which Flaherty could not have foreseen nor achieved—a new film mode and a coordinated movement.

Grierson had taken over Lippmann intact, too, but had transformed him positively with his own special genius for activist education, coming as close as anyone has to introducing the kind and scale of education for citizenship that Lippmann thought necessary but despaired of achieving. Never again would Grierson be able to exercise his special function on quite the magnitude or with quite the assurance of success he had at the Film Board. His retirement in October 1945 represents a watershed in the contours of his career.

# 8 ✦ INTERNATIONAL FILM ASSOCIATES (1945–47) AND WORLD TODAY (1946–47)

## International Film Associates

In his resignation from the board, Grierson proposed in the future "to produce for international theatre circulation two monthly series of [short] films: one dealing with international affairs, the other with scientific and technological developments in various parts of the world." He also proposed "the extension of documentary production in Canada for non-theatrical circulation at home and abroad,"[1] though the nontheatrical activity would not be primarily in Canada. Instead, as headquarters for his new operation he chose New York City because, as he wrote to J. P. R. Golightly, in July 1945, he felt that "from any internationalist viewpoint," "the really weak sister" was the United States. Grierson went on to explain that "the international outlook of the American people has to become greatly strengthened if we are to avoid the danger of a major clash between the American idea and the Soviet one." He intended to keep his residence in Ottawa, however, as he had "no personal liking whatever for absorption in the States. If a half, or even three-quarters of my time is to be spent there, it is, I assure you, only because of the destiny of the documentary movement, as an international movement, seems to me at this stage to demand it."[2]

So, International Film Associates was organized as a nonprofit foundation aimed at promoting production and distribution on an international scale of motion pictures dealing with economic, social, and educational subjects. Repeating the Film Centre pattern, I.F.A. was not intended to engage in production but to provide research and planning assistance on a consultative basis for international agencies, government bodies, and all associations or individuals interested in organizations of this kind. Associated with Grierson on the new project from the outset were Stuart Legg and Raymond Spottiswoode representing Great Britain; Margaret Ann Adamson (later Elton) from Canada; Robert Flaherty and Mary Losey, the United States; Jean Benoit-Lévy (soon to become first head of the United Nations Film Board), France; and John Fernhout (who subsequently changed his name to Ferno), the Netherlands. The organization was chartered in Washington, D.C., and in addition to New York expected to maintain offices in Ottawa and London, with an extension to the European continent planned.[3]

## Trip to Britain

Before descending on New York, however, Grierson made a trip of several months to Britain and Europe, keeping in mind the establishment of International Film Associates on a viable basis but undertaking other obligations as well. Writing from London in November 1945 to Legg (still in Canada), Grierson observed that the British documentary men in the immediate postwar days had lost access to "the higher levels" of government. "They talk about people not things; trivial immediacies not plans." The Conservatives, who had just lost decisively a first postwar general election, were "out of favour and full of advances." He said he could lunch every day at the Conservative Club if he chose. As for the new government, "everywhere civil servants sit over the creative poll like watchful crocodiles. It is not going to be easy to free the creative people, especially from themselves, and I have my doubts whether the Labour Government will be of any special service in the matter. If you remember, they never did understand information except on the most parochial basis."[4]

Of his own activities he wrote in considerable detail. He had prepared "a big memorandum on the future of information" in

Britain which he thought "o.k. as a government document"; "even SGT [Stephen Tallents] says so." He had gotten it to four ministers— Herbert Morrison, Sir Stafford Cripps, Hillary Marquand, and Ellen Wilkinson—and might "even get it to [Ernest] Bevin and the P.M. [Clement Attlee] (but it is late in the day)."[5] Noting that his efforts were not universally applauded, he elsewhere wrote that Legg would appreciate that "we are not exactly regarded as Englanders first and last and only the other day I found myself denounced in Whitehall as an internationalist whose fidelity to the English cause could not be assured."[6]

With Tallents he also gave an address to the British Council about the requirements of an information service: international viewpoint, knowledge combined with creative skill, etc. He saw David Owens, of United Nations, who talked of bringing Grierson on a Technical Committee that would plan the United Nations Information Service. "I can have the film thing if I want it," wrote Grierson, "but some are talking of the Directorate of Information itself, which again takes me away from my principal point of focus." He also became involved in talks with Marquand and Cripps on the future of the British film industry. These talks would be heading toward what, in 1949, was to become the National Film Finance Corporation, to support British theatrical films, and Grierson had an idea in advance of the subsequent Group 3 for the production of features out of government funds.

International Film Associates had received "a big play in the Trade Press" and Alexander Korda had agreed to back him with all the money he could need if only Grierson would "get the hell out of this government business." Specifically Korda was interested in the two projected series of theatrical shorts and would not, "like Selznick 'want his name on it' either." Grierson told him he would consider it but to Legg he thought "no." "This is one thing we want for ourselves and especially for you in trust for the rest of us, with as little let or hindrance as possible." Finally, he said that he had had an invitation from the Dutch government and expected to receive one from the Belgians; he now wanted an official invitation from Czechoslovakia.[7]

In writing to Mary Losey, in New York presumably, in December, he explained that he had felt it important to do the brief on the shape the information services ought to take because he thought the British documentary people had let the civil servants get the better of them and before they know where they are they will be making pictures for committees and the way they are told. . . . The key, of course, was to know as much about health and reconstruction and nutrition and education etc. as the experts and read and speak about them with an air of both insight and authority. They have not done so, or at least less than they should. I am ashamed of them. Rotha is an exception because he has lined up very positively with the Labour Party and occupies a place in the higher councils which the others have lost. It is, however, in the long run dangerously partisan. Elton has also been good, obliquely so by making the first rate show of his scientific film association.[8]

Apart from "trying to tell the Cabinet what to do about information," and discussions with United Nations personnel, Grierson had set himself "the weary task of belatedly muscling in on the higher discussions of what to do with the existing British Council, the B.F.I. [British Film Institute] and all and it is a big task that needs half a dozen people going hard for the next two or three months. I wish I had them." Instead he was going to Holland and Belgium in January with old friend and former head of the Ministry of Information Films Division, Jack Beddington. He hoped to return to America by the end of January.[9]

## The World Today

By the time Grierson did return, International Film Associates was operating in the old Fox Studios above News of the Day and De Luxe Laboratories on West 54th Street. Shortly thereafter, in May 1946, Grierson announced a second firm and phase of the ambitious plan he had in mind: The World Today, Inc. (Incidentally, this name had been used ten years earlier for a short-lived newsreel made by a left-wing group to counter the conservative and dominant "March of Time" series.) Whereas I.F.A. was to make nontheatrical films for sponsors, World Today was conceived as producing not two but now three series of shorts for theatrical release, one per month for each series. "Worldwise" would explain and interpret the great events upon the international scene. "Wonderfact" was to relate "the marvels of scientific discovery and technological development to the welfare of the man-in-the-street in every land." "Venture" would highlight "the perfection of human skills in the realms of sport and outdoor achievement. . . ."[10] Grierson hoped to distribute these series through United Artists, using contacts established during

N.F.B. days and following the precedent of the now-defunct "World in Action."

Of the two phases of the overall plan, the nontheatrical one limped along for a while, even after Grierson had left the firm, but the theatrical shorts never got off the ground. The principal and immediate problems were that United Artists decided to abandon the short-subject field and World Today's operating margin of capital was too small to sustain it.[11] Though Grierson had gotten a guarantee of distribution from United Artists, after several months of negotiation he couldn't raise the necessary production money.[12] Arthur Mayer, one of the investors, recalled that World Today was capitalized at about $50,000; in a letter from Grierson to Legg the even more modest sum of $35,000 was mentioned.[13] Maynard Gertler, whose father-in-law was a wealthy businessman associated with Macy's department store, seems to have been the chief investor. He had been in the State Department and was attracted by the international outlook of I.F.A. and World Today. Gertler remained with the firm, as did Legg and Spottiswoode, after the theatrical series idea had been abandoned. (Legg left mid-1948 and Spottiswoode a little later; Gertler carried on for a year or two after that.)[14]

People involved to one degree or another with the operation besides those already mentioned (Grierson, Legg, and Spottiswoode being the main architects), were Guy Glover, Nicholas Read, Helen Grayson, Harry Alpert, Werner Schott, and Carlton Beals. The last was an authority on South America and a CBS correspondent who was later blacklisted. His wife was secretary for I.F.A.–World Today.[15] Across the hall from the World Today studios, at the end of the company's history, Robert Flaherty and Helen Van Dongen were editing *Louisiana Story*.

*Magic Eye*, the first of the planned theatrical shorts, was never completed.[16] The only one that was, in fact, was *Gun Dogs* (made in England by Basil Wright at of his International Realist firm), which would have fitted into the sports series presumably. Of the nontheatrical shorts released by the firm (which came to be called World Today rather than International Film Associates), the most successful by far was *Round Trip: U.S.A. in World Trade* (1947). Produced by Spottiswoode and directed by Roger Barlow, it was sponsored by the Twentieth-Century Fund, a foundation which sought to promote liberal economic policy including the lowering or total removal of tariff barriers. Three films were made for the U.S. Children's

Bureau on childhood diseases, premature babies, and infant mortality,[17] and a film was edited for the Polish government through the United Nations.[18] UNESCO and the World Student Service Fund sponsored *Letter from a Student* (1948), portraying student life and reconstruction in war-devastated universities of Europe and Asia.[19] Another film, called *Seeds for Tomorrow*, financed by Elliott Pratt, was shelved, according to one source.[20] According to another source, *Seeds for Tomorrow* (1946) was produced by Thomas J. Brandon for Public Affairs Films, Inc., directed by Julian Roffman, from a scenario and dialogue written anonymously by Stuart Legg and John Grierson, edited by Sidney Meyers, and sponsored by the National Farmers Union.[21]

If Grierson had been right to an uncanny degree in his major decisions up to this point in his career (though Film Centre, his other venture into private enterprise, needed propping up from time to time), he clearly was wrong about World Today. There were several reasons why it didn't work. The inadequacy of financing and distribution has already been mentioned in relation to the theatrical series. Hardy suggested that what Grierson was trying to do would really have worked better for television (if it had been available), "with its immediacy and mass audience," rather than having to depend on the "slow and cumbersome distribution methods" of the theaters.[22] On the nontheatrical side, the Film Centre advisory lines along which International Film Associates had been conceived had to be abandoned in favor of actual production for sponsors. The international bias which affected all of the projects had seemed natural and of preeminent importance in 1945. It became less popular and hence less viable economically in a country heading toward a Cold War with the Soviet Union and political reaction which came to be known as McCarthyism. The "defeat" may have been, as Hardy suggested, "in method only," adding that "Grierson, who once said that 'good films are international and good film-makers are internationalist,' was still concerned to resist and fight the recession of international understanding."[23] Later Grierson himself conceded that he had "thought too much in the immediate post-war period of the analogy of the 1919 post-war period."

> I thought there would be a lull before the new storm, of some ten years or thereabouts. I thought that the war-time discovery of social fronts and the conjoining of the Roosevelt liberal force with that of British Conservative-Socialism would, for a period, command the political

scene in the Western world and its related territories: that in the home field it would bring new reforms to the Southern States as to the East End of London; and, in the foreign field, to the sovereign poverties of Latin America as to the unsovereign poverties of Africa and the East. It was, of course, not on the cards, whether in the name of Chisholm of W.H.O. [Dr. Brock Chisholm, director-general, World Health Organization], Orr of F.A.O. [Sir John Boyd Orr, head, Food and Agricultural Organization], Huxley [Sir Julian Huxley, director-general] of Unesco, or myself. As the *Chicago Tribune*, the State Department, Edgar Hoover and Senator Bill Benton with his World Radio Network [Assistant Secretary of State, 1945–47, who organized this program, which created the "Voice of America"] announced, the war was on before the peace was started.[24]

Finally, Grierson's own hurtful involvement in the breakdown of international understanding—the strange episode of the Canadian "spy trials," to be dealt with shortly—meant that he was not in New York directing the operation much of the time and eventually could not be. Whether he would in any case have left World Today after only a year to accept the directorship of Mass Communication and Public Information at UNESCO cannot be said. (Earlier he had conjectured that it would take three or four years before the "international exchange instruments of the new international body" would have any "reality" and that during that period it was the American people who needed his attention.)[25] He did not have the option of remaining at work in the United States. He never got a working visa.[26]

## Other Activities, Writing, and Speaking

When Grierson resigned from the Film Board, some possibilities other than The World Today may also have been open to him in the U.S. On a trip to Washington he seems to have been approached by Eric Johnston, president of the Motion Picture Association of America, to accept a position promoting Hollywood films abroad. Both Mary Losey and Archibald MacLeish knew about this.[27] Another recollection was that Frank Stanton, president of the Columbia Broadcasting System (CBS), offered Grierson a job as head of television public affairs, partly because Stanton was interested in the title The World Today for an Edward R. Murrow series.[28] (At the same time, in 1946, Nicholas Murray Butler, president of Columbia University, published a book entitled *The World Today*.) Grierson advised on the setting up of the important if short-lived Southern Educational Film Production Service, with the vigorous aid of Mary Losey and under the direction of Nicholas Read, a Film Board graduate.[29] Located in Athens, Georgia, it served agencies of nine Southern states.[30] Grierson continued his work with the Commission on the Freedom of the Press, and in a 1947 volume, *Freedom of the Movies*, its author, Ruth Inglis, acknowledged that Grierson had been of "invaluable assistance" in its preparation.[31]

During the World Today period he also continued to write and speak. In January 1946 an article entitled "Postwar Patterns" appeared in the *Hollywood Quarterly*.[32] In February he spoke before the New York Film Council, reviewing the situations for documentary films in Britain and Canada, and urging a much greater organization of documentary production and means of distribution in the U.S. in order to meet the many postwar needs of the country and of the world.[33] In May he addressed the International Conference of the Junior League, at Quebec, on "The Political, Economic, and Educational Implications of the Atomic Bomb." Consisting of observation and theory on a statesmanship level, it contained no reference to films. Instead it was a sharply intelligent, well-informed antiwar plea. Grierson's heaviest weight of criticism fell on U.S. saber rattling, but he granted that Britain and the Soviet Union didn't look much better. The main thrust of his argument was the avoidance of total human suicide through nuclear warfare.[34] In June he spoke to the American Library Association, in Buffalo, New York, on "The Library in an International World." There he did urge the use of the new media but also called upon librarians to engage in an educational crusade the end of which was to be the "internationalization of men's minds."[35]

In December 1946 Grierson's "Film Horizons" appeared in *Theatre Arts*,[36] and in January 1947 he contributed to "Notes on 'The Tasks of an International Film Institute'" in the *Hollywood Quarterly*.[37] *Grierson on Documentary*, Forsyth Hardy's splendid collection, was published in 1946 by Collins in London and in December 1947 by Harcourt, Brace in New York. The American edition contained additional notes and editing by Mary Losey and Richard Griffith. Both versions were reviewed widely and enthusiastically.

Grierson's social life continued on its usual gregarious course during this period. Though he had written that he didn't intend to be absorbed in the United States, he seems to have had a genuine fondness for the excitement of Manhattan. He once observed that if the greatest cooks in the world were the Chinese and then the French, both cuisines were available in New York City. A cook of some expertise himself, he was said to be especially good with the preparation of fish which he felt must always begin with lots of garlic and butter.[38] Did he remember Montaigne having said that "Great men pride themselves on knowing how to prepare a fish for table," or Lao-tse, "Govern the Empire as you would cook a little fish"?[39] At any rate, the Weisenborns remembered evenings in New York with the Griersons that began with John taking over the preparation of fish from Margaret, commenting on her lack of skill, and then, after vast quantities of bourbon, the whole party leaving the fish on the stove to go out for hamburgers or a Chinese dinner.[40] Margaret Ann Elton observed simply that Grierson liked good food but liked drink better.[41] During the brief World Today interim the Griersons were living in a big duplex apartment, first floor and basement, on 57th Street, as the Weisenborns recalled.[42]

## Spy Trials

On the evening of September 5, 1945, before Grierson had left the Film Board, a chain of events began that would coincide with his World Today activity and finally put an end to it. On that evening Igor Gouzenko, a young Russian code clerk on the staff of the military attaché in Ottawa, left the Soviet Embassy with a sheaf of documents. They contained evidence of an extensive espionage network directed from the Embassy but involving a number of Canadians, some in important posts in the Canadian government and including a member of Parliament. The information being fed to Moscow ranged widely over technical, scientific, economic, and political subjects; atomic energy and radar were of particular interest. After considerable difficulty, Gouzenko succeeded in getting his documents into the hands of the Royal Canadian Mounted Police.

Prime Minister Mackenzie King was apprised of the situation. Since the Canadian network was evidently linked with similar espionage activities in both the United States and Great Britain, a potentially violent strain in the relations between the Soviet Union and its allies was now in the making. King consulted leaders of his own government and the opposition, took up the matter with President Harry Truman in November, and then proceeded overseas to see Prime Minister Clement Attlee.[43] After further deliberation, the Canadian prime minister announced to Parliament on February 5, 1946, that "secret and confidential information" had been communicated "directly or indirectly by public officials and other persons in positions of trust to the agents of a Foreign Power to the prejudice of the safety and interests of Canada."

As a result, a Royal Commission was established to investigate the espionage activity. It heard evidence from February 13 until June 27, when it published its report.[44] One of the espionage agents exposed during the hearings was Freda Linton, a former employee of the International Labor Office and the National Film Board—secretary to the film commissioner in the latter organization. Among the witnesses summoned was John Grierson.

Gouzenko's evidence made it "reasonably plain" that Linton "was not communicating information herself, but was a *'contact'* or medium through whom information was received from various agents and funnelled through Fred Rose or otherwise to the [Soviet] Embassy."[45] Rose, later convicted as an agent, was a Labour Progressive MP for Cartier, Quebec; Freda Linton was his mistress. Diaries and notebooks in Gouzenko's possession contained an entry reading "Freda to the Professor through Grierson," in Soviet Assistant Military Attaché Lieutenant Colonel Motinov's handwriting. "Fritzie Linden, Greerson's Secrta [*sic*]." appeared in a diary found in the possession of M. S. Nightingale, another suspected agent, former R.C.A.F. Squadron Leader and Bell Telephone Company engineer.

Gouzenko explained in regard to the first entry that since the work Linton was doing at the Film Board "was not satisfactory to Moscow," she was, therefore, to be placed "in some more important department." "The Professor" was the cover name for Professor Raymond Boyer of McGill University, another agent and a highly respected scientist with an international reputation who worked for the National Research Council during the war. The suggestion was one of "using Grierson's influence to get her into the position."[46]

When Grierson was questioned about Linton, at first he said she was his secretary for a year (later he corrected this to no more than six months) and that he thought she had gone with him to the War Information Board. She "belonged to about the 1942 period. . . . Or 1943 at the latest," he said. As far as the Gouzenko exhibit, Grierson stated: "I must say it is the most sterile document in this sense, that the Linton girl asked for no offices and no services in that matter. I merely think of her now as an ambitious girl who certainly wanted to get on in terms of the Film Board." She was, in fact, "promoted to a job in our Distribution Branch," as Grierson remembered, "not a high job, a junior distribution job connected with American circulation." For all he knew she was still holding that position.[47]

But the real issue, as both the examiners and Grierson recognized, was the implication that the Soviet Embassy or somebody there thought he would be of service to them. Grierson dryly observed, "The basis of the presumption, I say, is not very considerable." Asked if he knew Colonel Zabotin, Soviet military attaché and director of the espionage network, he replied that he had met him once. He did not know Motinov, Zabotin's assistant whose handwriting the note had been in, nor Major Sokolov of the Commercial Section of the Soviet Embassy, another important figure in the network. Asked if he knew "any of the officials of the Russian Embassy at all" he answered: "Yes; of course I knew the Ambassadors. I am only talking of meeting people in the usual diplomatic level." Grierson went on to say that he knew Zheveinov, the TASS correspondent, and that he "liked Pavlov," that the latter was the only person he "had any kind of personal interest in. That is the boy who is still here. . . ." (Vitali Pavlov, second secretary and consul of the Embassy, was also head of the N.K.V.D. [Soviet secret police] in Canada, which ran another espionage network parallel to the military one. It was Pavlov who led the frantic effort to try to stop Gouzenko from contacting the Canadian authorities.) "The only person I knew really was Pavlov," Grierson reiterated. The questioner attempted to conclude that line with "Just casting your mind back, can you recall any of those men even intimating to you that they would like to have somebody—" but Grierson cut in with, "All I can say is that the Russians, as far as I am concerned, were correct." He had "no reason to associate them with anything like that."[48]

Grierson seems to have given a great deal more testimony than appears in the published report, and much of it, like the later U.S. House Un-American Activities Committee and the Senate McCarthy hearings, must have centered on the identification of persons' political beliefs—whether they were communists or communist sympathizers. The justification for this line of inquiry advanced by the Royal Commission was that espionage agents were recruited through a kind of political escalation conducted under careful guidance. Someone might begin as a liberal, become a socialist, a Marxist, a communist sympathizer, a communist, and finally an agent working for Moscow if he/she were picked up at some point in the chain by someone already totally committed to the cause of world communism. Evidently Grierson refused to blur distinctions among political beliefs and reasserted the generally held democratic notion that one is entitled to whatever political convictions she or he finds congenial; that is, to be left of center does not make one automatically suspect as being disloyal or a subversive agent for a foreign power. What can be pieced together outside the public record is (unavoidably) largely distant recall of hearsay—often contradictory. It is being offered so that the effect of this event on Grierson's career (and on the Film Board) and his strong feelings about it can be better understood.

On the matter of Freda Linton's working relationship with Grierson, some of the recollections reduce her role from secretary for six months, as Grierson conceded, to assistant secretary for only two weeks. It was further recalled that she was an inefficient worker, that Grierson didn't like her, and that as well as espionage she was guilty of strikeovers in the commissioner's letters. It may have been Grierson who decided to have her transferred to international distribution.[49] Another contemporary thought of her as an innocent-enough person in a way—not malicious—rather like the more widely notorious Rosemarie of Germany, who slept around and passed along information. Freda Linton would have been unhappy to have implicated Grierson, it was said.[50]

At any rate, the officer who endeavored to serve her a subpoena in Montreal on May 12, 1946, was informed by her sister that Freda had left for an unknown destination about two weeks previously and had not been heard from.[51] A warrant for her arrest was issued and she became a fugitive from justice. Later, a member of the R.C.M.P. conceded to Stuart Legg that they knew where she was and were keeping an eye on her but that there wasn't enough to her case and that she wasn't very important.[52] When she finally turned herself in (in Montreal in 1949) charges against her were withdrawn.[53]

Though, as Legg pointed out, anyone who talked with Grierson for five minutes would know he wasn't a Marxist, some people were willing to suspect his loyalty—or pretend to suspect it. As part of a general tendency to poke at the establishment whenever he had the chance, he enjoyed especially teasing and puncturing pomposity. In Canada he had offended a number of the Rideau Club conservatives (Colonel Rideau was a famous figure in the War of 1812), sometimes baiting them by pretending to be a communist. Of course he was shocked when he was actually taken to be one.[54] He loved to dramatize and may have talked about things loosely that he shouldn't have discussed.[55] It may also have happened, as both Richard Griffith and Donald Taylor suggested, that the Russians flattered Grierson as the world's greatest mass communicator and that he flirted with them in regard to approaching international developments and positions.[56] It certainly does seem, as a number of others besides Griffith observed, that Grierson did not take seriously enough what were in reality charges of espionage and treason, and tended to approach the Royal Commission as if they were merely a band of witch hunters.[57]

Apparently Grierson was unwilling or unable to name communists he knew, and when asked about various persons under question he would say, "No, he's a Social Democrat," or make other distinctions along the political spectrum. His testimony took the form of lecturing on the kinds of communism and socialism to what he apparently regarded as pompous and not very bright Tories.[58] (Richard Griffith had the impression that Grierson's testimony included a reading from John Stuart Mill's essay "On Liberty.")[59] Of the two commissioners, one was of French (Justice Robert Taschereau) and the other of Anglo-Saxon extraction (Justice R. L. Kellock). The Quebec man, Legg thought, enjoyed Grierson putting down the English-Canadians, who felt he was laughing at them and were furious.[60]

Grierson also tried to make a distinction between an elected official (MP Fred Rose), whose politics were subject to the voters' approval, and a civil servant (like himself), who simply could not, would not have outside allegiances.[61] (He remembered pulling himself up at one point to say, "I am from Whitehall, sir." Whitehall, in London, was headquarters of and symbol of the British civil service. This observation would have seemed more impressive then than after the defection and flight to the Soviet Union of high-ranking British public servants Burgess and McLean some years later, he ruefully admitted.)[62] At any rate, the distinction was felt by his sympathizers to be too subtle for the politically unsophisticated Canadians (and Americans).[63] At the time, however, James Beveridge recalled that

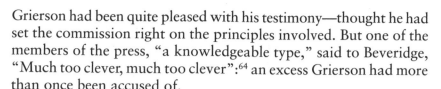

Grierson had been quite pleased with his testimony—thought he had set the commission right on the principles involved. But one of the members of the press, "a knowledgeable type," said to Beveridge, "Much too clever, much too clever":[64] an excess Grierson had more than once been accused of.

## Attacks on the Board

The innuendoes and implications surrounding the spy trials were attached to Grierson not only personally but became ammunition for ongoing political assaults on his legacy, the National Film Board. There was in Canada as well as in the United States, it became clear, a native suspicion of government information services, particularly in peacetime. The usual concerns about propaganda being designed to keep the incumbent party in power by promoting its policies and programs appeared; and, more generally, critics worried that cherished individualities would be smothered under the weight of monolithic bureaucracy. On this occasion the charges of subversion and, later, extravagance and unfair competition with private enterprise were added.

Critics of the board tried to alter history by making the institution seem a wartime creation for wartime purposes. Before he left, Grierson had foreseen that line of attack and had made certain that the scale of budget allotments continued over into peacetime, at least into the first year of peace. He had rallied national organizations—from agriculture, adult education, labor, and elsewhere—so that, at the time the budget came up for approval, the Cabinet was being swamped by briefs in support of the board. As a result, the 1946 budget was only a little less than that for 1945.[65]

During the period of the trials, Brooke Claxton, Minister of National Health and Welfare, was chairman of the Film Board; Ross McLean was acting film commissioner, and James Beveridge production secretary. The latter said that of the 750 some members of the N.F.B. staff, 90 percent, never doubted Grierson's motives, but that perhaps 10 percent, who didn't like him because he had stepped on their toes, gave credence to the suspicions.[66] The attacks came mainly from conservative opposition politicians and press, and were supported and sometimes instigated by segments of the commercial film industry which felt it could gain from the removal of the main competitive force.

In April 1946 a question was raised in the House of Commons about an N.F.B. film, *Our Northern Neighbor* (1942), which had shown the Soviets favorably.[67] In July, Gordon K. Fraser (Progressive Conservative, Peterboro) asserted that funds were collected from board staff for the benefit of those accused of espionage, and he implied that there were known communists within the N.F.B. He further argued that the board was a waste of taxpayers' money and its production "all for the Liberal party, because practically everything they put out has a political twist to it."[68] Other charges, by Norman Jacques (Social Credit, Wetaskiwin), that the board was particularly responsible for the spawning of a Red spy network in Canada and that the board itself was a communistic propaganda medium, were emphatically denied by Claxton, who termed them "ridiculous."[69]

In August the accusations shifted to financial matters, and it was revealed that Grierson's taxi bills totaled $2,460.54 for a five-year period ending October 31, 1945. (Legg's totaled $1,019.74.)[70] These announcements foreshadowed a sustained effort to, if not eliminate, at least whittle down the board's appropriations at every budget renewal. Fraser and Jacques continued to lead the fight on the new grounds, with the former comparing the board to a "hungry 'white elephant.'"[71] Grierson figured again in July 1947 in relation to approximately $340 advanced to him early in 1946 for a flight from Prestwick, Scotland, to Montreal—apparently at the end of his first postwar (and post–N.F.B., of course) trip abroad. On November 8, 1946, the federal treasury board had ordered the expenditure "unwarranted" and Grierson had refunded the money. It was believed by the auditor general, Watson Sellar, that Grierson "had acted 'in good faith' because he had agreed with the Film Board to return for consultation at any time, provided his expenses were paid. It had been 'intimated' to him that he was wanted in Ottawa for this purpose," said Sellar.[72]

Accusations and defenses went on during the late 1940s, with Fraser expanding his earlier metaphor into "a herd of white elephants," as well as describing the N.F.B. as "socialization of the worst kind."[73] Commercial still photographers started echoing the criticisms—e.g., Everett Rosborough, president of the Ontario Society of Professional Photographers[74]—and it was suspected, but always denied by Budge Crawley, that Crawley Films had subsidized an article in the Toronto *Financial Post* criticizing N.F.B. business methods.[75] If true, Crawley's actions could be viewed as particularly ungrateful since he was a Film Board veteran whose firm had virtually been established through substantial board contracts in the early days.

The charges of communist infiltration, never totally silenced, returned in more virulent and current form at the end of 1949, along with the supporting theme that board personnel were not completely and firmly under Civil Service (as Grierson, to guard creativity, had taken care to see that they would not be). In November Brooke Claxton, now Defense Minister and no longer connected with the Film Board, informed the House of Commons that the N.F.B. was not being permitted to film confidential military subjects.[76] A police security check of all N.F.B. staff and then an investigation by a private firm into its business administration were both ordered.

On December 16, 1949, the Film Board "declined to continue" Ross McLean's tenure as film commissioner and appointed in his place W. A. Irwin, a prominent and respected editor of *Maclean's* magazine.[77] Lack of "public confidence" in the N.F.B. was given as the reason for the shift by Robert H. Winters, then chairman of the board: "Criticism has involved allegations of wasteful expenditure, of unfair competition with private enterprise, and the loyalty of certain members of its staff." McLean, who had received no prior official word of his ouster, first learned of it from a news story in the *Ottawa Journal*.[78]

This unhappy epilogue to Grierson's career in Canada was not the end of the story by any means, as all who know the prolific and brilliant production of the Film Board since 1950 are aware. It survived the storm and went on to even greater achievements, partly because of the firmness of the foundations built by Grierson but also partly because, in the face of all of the opposition, his former assistant and successor, Ross McLean, fought the battle of attrition resolutely and skillfully. McLean was described approvingly by James Beveridge, rival candidate for the commissionership and then head of production under McLean, as a "nineteenth-century liberal";[79] and Marjorie McKay, business manager at the board, conceded that he was "more scrupulous" than Grierson, that the latter was "operating all the time."[80] Beveridge felt that McLean did a superb job during those difficult years and held the board together through his quiet expertise in government functioning——that Grierson could not have managed this.[81]

As for Irwin, he did well what he was hired to do: rehabilitate the reputation of the board. Trusted as a journalist, he simply told the press that the house was in good order, and they turned off the pressure.[82] There were no firings and, though the act drafted by Grierson under which it had operated was amended slightly in 1950 to clarify and somewhat restrict the nature of its independence, the board moved ahead firmly on its own feet. With a younger generation of Canadians coming to work, the post-Grierson years really started.

## Postscript

The immediate and main repercussion of the spy trials, as far as Grierson personally was concerned, was the threat that his visas would be withdrawn for both the United States and Canada. Legg and the World Today lawyer tried with no success to talk a State Department official into an immigration visa for Grierson. His visitor's visa was extended briefly, but he couldn't work with that and it was clear it would not be renewed when terminated.[83] It was rumored that a man in the American Embassy in Canada who hated Grierson and regarded him as "dangerous" was able to influence the U.S. attitude towards Grierson, and that the F.B.I. was going through his mail.[84] "Unreliable" was a softer term suggested by Donald Taylor for the American attitude towards him.[85] Grierson complained that Legg hated the States and was welcomed, while he loved the U.S. and wasn't permitted to stay.[86] It was at about this time that, as Pare Lorentz recalled it, Grierson cordially denounced America and Americans and launched into a long and witty attack on the United States Constitution.[87]

The question of what Grierson felt about the suspicions growing out of the spy trials received a different answer depending on whom one asked (and obviously on how Grierson talked to that person). Donald Taylor, for example, doubted that Grierson was deeply affected. On the contrary, Taylor thought he rather enjoyed the drama of it all. He recalled Grierson telling with relish of passing one of the Royal Commission justices and overhearing him remark, "There goes the biggest spy of them all and him unhung."[88] John Taylor thought Grierson, being a tough customer and a realist who would expect to encounter that sort of attack in public life, took it in stride.[89] Edgar Anstey, while not placing as great an importance on the incidents as some others, acknowledged that Grierson was unable to understand how anyone could have conceived that he would have loyalties outside his own group.[90] Among those most closely associated with him at the time, however, both Stuart Legg and Margaret Ann Elton felt he was deeply hurt by the events, especially as they hit at his high sense of public service. He simply could not imagine being suspected as a traitor.[91] Twenty years later Grierson himself remembered having been terribly angry and still could not understand why not one of the ministers he had worked with rose to his defense.[92]

Two of Grierson's public statements at the time are particularly interesting in the way they bear obliquely on the spy trials and their sequel. (He never wrote or spoke publicly of this matter, nor did any of his friends or associates.) The first is from an address given in May 1946, during the hearings of the Royal Commission.

> I have no brief for the Soviet Union and indeed there is much in its international manners that I do not like. I dislike their secrecy and their suspicion and their silence and I particularly deplore the melodramatic atmosphere of conspiracy with which they seem to invest their simplest acts. But I ask you to remember that for 20 years we put them to the wall and gave them the deepest reason to be secretive, suspicious, silent and conspiratorial. We have Russia not a little on our conscience and are reaping a harvest we ourselves have done something to sow. . . .
>
> Strangely enough, at a time when statesmen, churchmen and political philosophers are calling for an understanding of Russia by us and of us by the Russians, any attempt to do so becomes the badge of subversive activity.[93]

The second comment occurred in a March 1948 piece in which Grierson was defending and praising some N.F.B. films that had been criticized. "I love Canada dearly," he wrote, "but in some respects, it is not good at all." He then presented a detailed and balanced accounting.

> I have the impression . . . that Canada is not very knowledgeable about political philosophy or the law, especially in the higher branches of those disciplines, though on the other hand it is enormously good at economics. It is somewhat crude in parliamentary debate and there are more cockerels crowing on local editorial dunghills than you could conceive outside Lilliput, but on the other hand, it has a remarkable Institute of International Affairs and solid groups of political study in every town in the country.

Its public life lacks courage and Canada is the village that voted the earth was flat, in the denial of its size and destiny. Yet, its carelessness of distance is fantastic and its individual adventures into the Arctic, epic. Its educational standards are in many quarters grotesque and, in some quarters, subject to a species of provincial fascism which is both ignorant and vicious. Yet, the library work, the adult education developments and the extension services of the voluntary associations are heartening and good.

Canada, especially, can be a great bore when it tries to match its sophistication with the larger and deeper versions thereof. 'Sunset, and evening star and one clear call for Bill the lone fisherman.' But over and under these variations and anomalies, there is a profound element of common sense and good taste about Canada and Canadian life which is a precious thing to know.[94]

Grierson would have to wait some years, however—until the twenty-fifth anniversary of the Film Board—before there would be any general and public appreciation expressed by the Canadian government for the great contribution he had made to that national life.

# 9 ⇸ UNESCO (1947–48)

## Founding

In the spy-trial affair, Grierson felt, the British government was the only one that had acted with either honor or effectiveness as far as he was concerned.[1] No doubt furious at the demeaning treatment afforded a respected civil servant (by two former colonies at that!), the British evidently offered Grierson a position with the Ministry of Information as it was being converted into the Central Office of Information.[2] Then, as further evidence of faith, he seems to have been considered for the director generalship of the United Nations Educational, Scientific, and Cultural Organization (UNESCO). Because his recently acquired reputation might have represented a liability for the newly formed agency, he thought it better not to accept the top job. Instead he was chosen to serve under Julian Huxley, where his political astuteness could still be put at the service of an old friend.[3] Huxley intervened with the United States and Canada, saying he must have Grierson for UNESCO,[4] and on February 21, 1947, an announcement was made that Grierson had been appointed adviser to the UNESCO director general on mass media and public information matters.[5] (Ross McLean would take the same route when he left the Film Board under fire in 1950: rather than serve the new film commissioner in a subordinate capacity he became head of UNESCO's Film Section.)[6]

The idea for UNESCO had begun during a meeting of the Conference of Allied Ministers of Education in London in 1942. One of the main functions of the conference was to consider what help could be given to the rebuilding of the educational systems of Europe after the war. Out of this consideration came the original draft proposals for an educational and cultural organization. On behalf of the Allied Ministers, the British government called another assembly which would actually form UNESCO.[7]

The Conference for the Establishment of the United Nations Educational, Scientific, and Cultural Organization was held at the Institute of Civil Engineers, London, in November 1945. (As noted earlier, Grierson was in Britain at the time, after leaving the Film Board and before returning to World Today.) Forty-three nations were represented. Among the members of the delegations who would have been known to Grierson were Vincent Massey, High Commissioner for Canada, and Archibald MacLeish and Senator William Benton of the United States. Ellen Wilkinson, British Minister of Education, was elected president of the Conference; she was nominated by Léon Blum (France) and seconded by MacLeish. Prime Minister Clement Attlee had addressed and extended welcome to the group on the afternoon of November 1;[8] on November 16, by the end of the day, the representatives of the forty-three states had signed the Final Act establishing UNESCO.[9]

Three main fields of activity were prescribed by its Constitution. The first was directly related to peace, and to the mass media "to collaborate in the work of advancing the mutual knowledge and understanding of peoples, through all means of mass communication." In this connection the organization was given the special duty of recommending "such international agreements as may be necessary to promote the free flow of ideas by word and image." The second field was to "give fresh impulse to popular education and to the spread of culture." The third to "maintain, increase and diffuse knowledge."[10]

After the conference a Preparatory Commission was established in London. (The move to Paris didn't begin until September of 1946.) Julian Huxley was appointed executive secretary and among the personnel, which numbered around one hundred fifty,[11] was William

Farr, one of the British documentary group, who had the title Counselor of the Mass Communications Section.[12]

It wasn't until the first annual conference of UNESCO, held in Paris in November 1946, that a program was articulated. One of the main steps taken was the establishment of Commissions on Immediate Technical Needs, including those of press, radio, and film. Twelve countries hit hard by the war—France, Belgium, Luxemburg, Holland, Norway, Denmark, Poland, Czechoslovakia, Yugoslavia, Greece, China, and the Philippines—were selected for initial survey.[13] Film was emphasized by the British delegation while the Americans and the French stressed press and radio.[14]

## Operation

By the time Grierson reported to UNESCO House in Paris, the disused Hotel Majestic at 19 Avenue Kleber, the Secretariat staff was being shaped up. Huxley was director general; Walter C. Laves (U.S.A.), deputy director general; Jean Thomas (France), assistant director general. Grierson's official title was director of Mass Communications and Public Information, one of four major divisions. Under him were René Maheu (France), head of the Press Section; Philippe Desjardins (France), head of the Radio Section; and William Farr (U.K.), head of the Film Section. Other members of the Film Section were Ernest Borneman (Canada, an N.F.B. alumnus), Henny de Jong (Netherlands), Lusia Krakowska (Poland), Roger Shattuck (U.S.A.), and Alena Bykova (Czechoslovakia). Also in Paris, at the United Nations proper, Jean Benoit-Lévy (France) was director of Films and Visual Information, and Mogens Scot-Hansen (Denmark) was representative of the Film Section of the Department of Public Information for Europe.[15] Scot-Hansen, who had been head of the Danish government documentary production unit, joined the UNESCO Film Section shortly after Grierson's arrival.[16]

During Grierson's first few months, UNESCO was mainly employed in reformulating projects approved by the November General Conference so as to produce a working program with a detailed budget. This activity included planning and putting into operation a satisfactory organizational structure, working out the best means of cooperation between the Executive Board and its committees on the one hand and the Secretariat on the other, and completing the recruitment of staff. It was not until the April meeting of the Executive Board that the revised program and itemized budget were ready for approval. Only then could UNESCO really begin active operations in regard to its program.[17]

By the end of August, reports were ready summarizing the technical press, radio, and film needs of the first twelve countries under investigation. Recommendations made by the Commission on Technical Needs were to be approved at the second General Conference, to take place in Mexico City in November. It would there be decided whether the lines of actions proposed for re-equipping the communications industries of Europe and the Far East were to be implemented.[18]

Scarcely one to be content with surveys, in September, in preparation for the Conference, Grierson appointed Basil Wright to draft a "plan for the production of a series of films on UNESCO subjects by national film-producing groups, and to set up a plan for their distribution internationally."[19] The proposal which Wright developed paralleled the abortive prewar one he and Grierson had conceived for the International Labor Office of the League of Nations. It included a list of forty-eight films to be produced by member countries about their own "specialities"; e.g., French cooking, English landscape painting. Production costs of individual films were to be amortized and the producing nations reimbursed out of the distribution income for the entire series—an international film production cooperative, as it were.[20]

The second General Conference, in Mexico City, November 6 through December 3, 1947, was suitably festive as well as important to the future of UNESCO. The Mexican authorities had allotted as a site the remarkable modern building, newly completed, which was later to house the immense Normal School for Teachers. In addition, a special UNESCO month was organized, including exhibitions of Mexican art, colonial and modern, and of pre-Columbian art of the entire region from Mexico to Peru, concerts and folk dances, and a series of lectures on aspects of Latin American culture. Visits by delegates to beautiful and interesting locales and activities away from the capital were also arranged.[21]

Members of the working party on Mass Communications included Louis Joxe (France, chairman), Henry French (U.K., vice-chairman), Luther Evans (U.S.A., rapporteur), William Farr (UNESCO, secretary),[22] J. B. Priestly, and Ritchie Calder (U.K.).[23]

Three principal decisions were reached. First, it was decided to continue the survey already begun of the technical needs of various countries in regard to equipment, facilities, and trained personnel required for the dissemination of information through the media of press, radio, and film. The second was to support efforts to increase the freedom of the flow of information across national boundaries. And third, to create a Bureau of Ideas within UNESCO which would (1) seize hold and take appropriate action respecting important instances of nations cooperating with each other for mutual benefit and the good of the world, and (2) provide stimulation to all member states to put out for distribution to other countries information concerning examples of what was described as "human excellence,"[24] a favorite Grierson phrase. It was under the latter subcategory that Wright's scheme for international film production and distribution was approved.[25]

Though Grierson was very active at the Conference, perhaps mainly assisting Julian Huxley, his name does not appear in the official records. One can infer that his proposals, if not entire budget, passed according to plan. The only discernible irritation would have been the question of whether the State Department would permit him to re-enter the United States on his way back to Paris. He was allowed to pass through but not to stop over.[26]

After the November conference in Mexico City, Grierson had only three months of work left at UNESCO. The year in total consisted of extraordinarily wide-ranging and also detailed planning. Some of the main activities contemplated or underway at the time of his departure are worth noting. There was the International Ideas Bureau, which was to employ artists and writers to prepare stories of world cooperation and achievement. This material was to be used to promote the production by member countries of articles, books, broadcasts, documentary and feature films. In the field of radio, UNESCO was to prepare special program material and to set up "flying squads" of radio experts to maintain contact between UNESCO and the national systems. A World University of the Air recorded leading personalities in education, science, and the arts. The survey of press, radio, and film needs was extended, and included seventeen more countries in Europe, Latin America, and the Far East when it was published in September 1948.[27] Loans, barter schemes, and exchange of technicians were among the remedies proposed to meet the needs of countries found to be lacking essential facilities. The main emphasis in 1948, however, was to be on production. The Film Section hoped that its proposed forty-eight films would be undertaken in the current production of nineteen member countries, and additional budget allocations were earmarked for the stimulation of further production in all fields of mass communication.[28]

If the nonprint production emphasis clearly marked Grierson's presence, it may also have been true that every publication of UNESCO some twenty years later had been started during his year there.[29] He had much less interest in the free flow of information, however, than some of the others active in UNESCO; Americans Archibald MacLeish and William Benton backed this strongly. (MacLeish, poet and statesman, had been Librarian of Congress, 1939–44, and in 1944–45, Assistant Secretary of State who helped plan UNESCO. Benton, businessman, educator, and political figure, was Assistant Secretary of State concerned with UNESCO in 1945–47. In collaboration with the bartender at UNESCO House Grierson concocted a cocktail which he irreverently named a "Free Flow.")[30] "Being brought up in another school of thought," he later said, he "was always sort of disinterested in the free flow of information because [he] knew it wouldn't happen. There would be many hazards. . . . The Catholics wouldn't want too much free flowing of Protestant information and vice versa. Little countries might be very cagey about big countries having free flow. It would depend on who was controlling material and who was controlling the flow."[31] If a country had something to give that another country wanted—his notion of national "specialities" and human "excellence"—then let there be no hindrance. But every country had the right to keep out the information it didn't want, Grierson felt.[32]

## Other Activities

In efforts related to his main job, Grierson assisted in establishing the United Nations Film Board through administrative arrangements amongst the UN, UNESCO, FAO, and ILO, to promote cooperative action where appropriate and prevent duplication of activities where required. Joint projects on behalf of all UN member nations, such as film catalogues and an information service, were being carried out by the staffs of UNESCO in Paris and of the United Nations at Lake Success, New York.[33] Also, Grierson may have accompanied UNESCO director general Huxley on an extensive tour of Latin America in June of 1947.[34]

It is certain that in that summer, Grierson attended the International Film Festival held at the Palais des Beaux Arts in Brussels. While there he participated in a conference in which representatives from nine nations exchanged views and information on the documentary and educational film situation in their respective countries and in additional countries which had recently been visited. Others attending the meeting included some of the major international figures in documentary film: Joris Ivens (Holland); Jean Painlevé, Jean Gremillon, and Henri Langlois (France); Paul Rotha, Basil Wright, Edgar Anstey, and Ralph Bond (United Kingdom); Henri Storck (Belgium); Iris Barry (U.S.A.); Theodore Balk (Yugoslavia); Georges Lehovec (Czechoslovakia); Jerzy Toeplitz (Poland); and Geoffrey Smith (South Africa). After two days the sessions concluded with those present passing a resolution forming a World Union of Documentary. A Preparatory Commission was appointed to meet before the first Congress, planned for Prague in 1948. A resolution was also passed reaffirming the traditional values of documentary films as a powerfully effective means of social interpretation.[35]

An even more significant event of 1947 was the First International Festival of Documentary Films at Edinburgh (which would subsequently become the Edinburgh International Film Festival), August 31–September 7, held concurrently with the three-week Festival of Music and Drama. Organized by the Edinburgh Film Guild, with the assistance of a widely representative Selection Committee (Wright and Rotha being advisers) and the cooperation of the Central Office of Information, the festival was designed: "(1) To present for the first time a world view of documentary achievement by showing examples of the best realistic production from many countries, and (2) To create an opportunity for the reconsideration and reassessment of the principles and methods of the documentary movement." The festival opened with speeches of welcome by Sir John I. Falconer, lord provost of Edinburgh, Norman Wilson, chairman of the Edinburgh Film Guild, and Grierson.[36] Grierson was reported to have spoken "vigorously and inspiringly."[37] He concisely restated his central and enduring conception of documentary as an art, a public service, and an educational instrument. "It is one of the few arts that has these three elements," he said. "It is a mirror held up to nature, but also it is a hammer shaping the future."[38] Earlier he had written one of his important articles, "A Time for Enquiry," for the special publication, *Documentary '47*, issued by the Guild to coincide with the festival.[39] During the week seventy films from seventeen countries were shown to an audience totaling over five thousand, with many more turned away.[40]

In October, in Paris, Grierson played an indirect hand (Arthur Elton was a main force) in a congress to establish an International Scientific Film Association. In January 1948 he journeyed to London for the first meeting of British Documentary, an organization which had grown out of the Brussels conference and was intended to serve as a national constituent of the World Union of Documentary. The meeting of about 150 people was introduced by Sir Stephen Tallents and addressed by Grierson.[41]

Two days later, on January 16, he attended a conference on the Film in Colonial Development sponsored by the British Film Institute and held at the Royal Empire Society Hall. Creech Jones, Secretary of State for the Colonies, opened the conference, which was then chaired by Adrian Crowley, Undersecretary of State for the Colonies.[42] Addresses were given by Tallents, George Pearson, of the Colonial Film Unit, Grierson, and many others. The proceedings were published by the B.F.I., and Grierson's remarks received even wider dissemination by being reprinted in its international quarterly, *Sight and Sound*. In his talk he described some of the related work at UNESCO and then applied to the British Colonial Film Unit his main proposition: "that it is not a question of films coming from outside but of films being created from the inside by and for the Colonial peoples themselves." His sights were set firmly on Africa, foreseeing the needs of what would become the new nations rising out of the "Colonial peoples."[43]

Finally, after he had left UNESCO, Grierson seems to have been represented at a United Nations Conference on Freedom of Information and of the Press (held in Geneva from March 21 to April 22, 1948) through a speech delivered by Julian Huxley. Grierson said that he and "a Frenchman" wrote it. He recalled the title as being "The Philosophy of Need,"[44] and it was probably this speech that Grierson referred to when he told Forsyth Hardy it was the best thing he had ever written.[45] An anecdote which Mary Losey Field cherished may have stemmed from this time, too. While she was working as film officer for the World Health Organization, Grierson visited her in Geneva. After a morning spent screening films being used by WHO, he turned to her and said, "Losey, do you know what you're doing?" "I hope so," she replied. "You're boring the world to death," growled Grierson, as his considered judgment on her and WHO's contribution to world health.[46]

## Personal Concerns and Frustrations

At UNESCO the salaries were "fancy," as Grierson conceded and others bore out,[47] probably because with budgetary and other uncertainties in the new organization, personnel were hired on the basis of one-year contracts. The Griersons had a large apartment at 4 Avenue Emille Pouvillion,[48] complete with Chinese cook, and Grierson was said to have lived like a lord.[49] It was not a happy time, however. His concern and indirect responsibility for the events affecting the Film Board in Canada continued. In a letter to Basil Wright, at the end of June 1947, he wrote of

> a full dress debate in the Canadian Parliament this month when a bunch of reactionaries, still I suppose bothered over the progressive thing the Film Board has rooted for keeps in Canada, wanted to declare me persona non grata and take my passport away. There were, happily, stout denunciations of the characters by Caldwell of the CCF and the old friend Phileas Coté. Nonetheless, ugly reading it is and the poor darlings cannot articulate a single reason for their bother and can only use the freedom of the House of Commons to throw out innuendoes of the kind you know about that silly spy business. They dont say it and they can't say it but the doubt is built up laboriously till the politicals of all kinds are afraid may be.

Characteristically he went on to analyze the situation, dispassionately but not without spirit, along broader lines: "Yet the real root is simply this business of serving a larger purpose beyond the immediately apparent purpose which is the essence of your own story: the fact that two and two with us have made not four but somehow five. The four they voted and authorised, so to speak, but not the five. The magic that goes with a sense of plan and purpose becomes of course mystery to the yokels and the mystery becomes witchcraft, not least in circumstances when they are afeard of the devil." Finally, in response to those, including Wright, who felt that there was personal vindictiveness involved, he wrote: "So I do not agree with your analysis of enemies. It will sound silly to you but I was never conscious of any at the time. I have always assumed the old liberal position that you could disagree with people and even push them round without there being need to take difference to the point of doing harm other than the usual operational kick in the teeth."[50]

In addition to the Canadian reverberations, there was the frustration of trying to make UNESCO "real." Hardy said that during this period, Grierson was at a "lower ebb" than he had ever seen him; that once, in despair, he asked "What shall I do? What shall I do?"[51] The drinking became bad, too, and to some he seemed to be nearly out of control emotionally.[52]

The inertia and "unreality" of UNESCO, which Grierson had predicted for the first three or four years of the new international organizations, was made up on the one hand of the enormous needs and potentials for its work and on the other by its inability, because of political divisiveness and lack of budget, to get on with that work, "The great trick," he had written, just before joining UNESCO, "is to relate one's high intentions to political realities." "[A] United Nations film service will have to accommodate itself to . . . patent needs and to the political support which can be guaranteed for them."[53]

Though forty member nations readily offered the kind of political friction Grierson referred to, UNESCO was perhaps even more handicapped by not including all of the members of the United Nations—most importantly by the absence of the U.S.S.R. and the Soviet block (except for Czechoslovakia and Poland). Grierson felt this limitation was so serious that he suggested the United Nations proper, rather than UNESCO, might have been the "politically correct body" within which to start his kind of information service.[54] Similarly, the director general, in September 1947, conceded that UNESCO could not "adequately fulfill its responsibilities as a United Nations Specialized Agency unless it succeed[ed] in associating with its work all members of the United Nations."[55] And of course any UNESCO efforts were dependent upon and refracted through the member governments rather than having direct contact with and support of their peoples.

The other horn of the dilemma, UNESCO's inadequate budget, limited even more strictly what could be accomplished, constructively and creatively. In practice there was money for surveys, which continued and expanded somewhat uselessly with no money to implement what they revealed as advisable or even crucial. The director general himself was forced to emphasize that the basic method of operation was, "of necessity, the stimulation of production by others and not the production of articles, films and broadcast scripts by the members of the Secretariat."[56] J. B. Priestly, for his part, pointed out that member nations were prepared to spend very much more on their own propaganda overseas than they subscribed to UNESCO. Great Britain, for example, spent far more on the Foreign Office's overseas information services and the British Council. By comparison, UNESCO's total budget for a worldwide program was a mere two million pounds, of which seventy-five percent was subscribed by the United States. Or, to put the financial disparity in another way, the total cost of UNESCO's program for world education was equivalent to the price of one light cruiser or ten bombers.[57]

Because of its limitations, UNESCO was confined to a kind of paper exchange of surveys and publications, with appeals to member nations and commercial interests to do something actually to help the needy countries. This situation was an unhappy one for Huxley, too,[58] and he left within a few years after Grierson's departure. Once more Grierson had articulated his misgivings in advance, in words aimed at a proposed International Film Institute but equally applicable to UNESCO: "I am scared of another big international bureaucratic establishment, lost in the mists of cultural detachment, recording and cataloguing and evaluating us all to death. I am scared, too, that we might people it with the boys and girls who, having failed to get anything done on the national home fronts, might find in this international business only a self-important asylum for their own impotence and frustrations."[59] It was to his national home front that Grierson returned at the end of his twelve-month contract. English colleague William Farr, who had been head of the Film Section, succeeded him as acting head of the Department of Mass Communications[60] on "the cloud cuckoo barricades of the Avenue Kleber," as Grierson put it.[61]

# 10 ✈ CENTRAL OFFICE OF INFORMATION (1948–50)

## Conversion of M.O.I. to C.O.I.

What Grierson returned to in 1948 was the Films Division of the Central Office of Information, which had been constructed at least partly along lines he had laid down during his visit to England in the fall and winter of 1945–46, just after resigning from the Film Board. His intention at that time was to convert the Ministry of Information, with its Films Division and Crown Film Unit, into an ongoing postwar operation that would undertake new peacetime purposes without loss of continuity and with as much of the sizable structure kept intact as possible. Key government personnel during the war had been solidly documentary in persuasion. Jack Beddington, with a background in oil public relations and film, had been head of the M.O.I. Films Division. Producers in charge of Crown following Cavalcanti were Ian Dalrymple (up to 1943), J. B. Holmes, and, from January 1945 through Grierson's visit, Basil Wright. Grierson then arranged for Wright to resign from Crown to become part of a Films Committee that, from February through April 1946, made plans for the Central Office of Information. Chairman of the committee was Bernard C. Sendall, principal private secretary to the Minister of Information from 1941 to 1945, who had just succeeded Beddington as head of the M.O.I. Films Division. (Sir Eric Bamford had recently replaced Brendan Bracken as director-general of the M.O.I.) Other members were screen writer Montagu Slater, a Mr. Watson (representing the Principal Finance Officer), and a Mr. Fletcher (secretary of the committee and a Treasury official going back to 1929 in Grierson's dealings with him).[1]

On April 1, 1946, the Central Office of Information officially took over the film-sponsoring activities of the M.O.I. In the transition the basic problem, as *Documentary News Letter* identified it, was that of liaison "between the necessary administration of national monies on the one hand, and the equally necessary creative work of the film-makers on the other."[2] In spite of Grierson's scheme and Wright's efforts, that problem was not solved satisfactorily from a Griersonian point of view. Unlike its predecessor, the C.O.I. Films Division was not provided in its terms of reference with any power of initiation, nor did it have ministerial status as had the M.O.I. Instead it was controlled by a committee composed of the public relations officers of the ministries of the British government. An annual sum was set aside to cover its expenses, but even that money it did not administer itself. Each item of expenditure had to be submitted to and authorized by the Treasury.[3] To Grierson this would have represented a much longer backward step in postwar adjustment than any forced on the Canadian Film Board, and, as it would prove, a loss of ground that was never regained.

Much of M.O.I.'s administrative personnel, whom Grierson regarded with less than enthusiasm, carried over into the C.O.I., including Bernard Sendall as chief film controlling officer.[4] At Crown, the largest documentary unit in Britain, housed in a requisitioned feature studio at Pinewood, Alexander Shaw succeeded Basil Wright as producer in charge from January through December 1946, and was followed by John Taylor in January 1947.[5]

## Transition of Documentary from Wartime to Peacetime

The move of documentary films in general from war to peace was understandably difficult considering the nature and size of the problems faced. Though Crown had made the finest of the wartime documentaries, 90 percent of M.O.I. Films Division output of almost eight hundred films had been produced on contract by the independent units.[6] In fact, during the war all units were working totally on government contract—there was no other sponsorship available[7]—and many small new units, like Rotha's, were formed on the basis of the vast government demand. The continuation of government-commissioned production under the C.O.I. was therefore crucial not to Crown alone but to the entire field. As Irmgard Schemke observed, at the time Grierson joined the C.O.I., government sponsorship had not merely become a tradition or habit, it was now a necessity.[8] In addition, other economic underpinnings had to be found if the greatly expanded production apparatus and output of war weren't to deflate suddenly and entirely with peace.

One of the directions in which documentary filmmakers increasingly looked was to the theaters. Though Grierson had been at pains to develop a nontheatrical distribution-exhibition system in the thirties, which had continued and grown during the forties, the wartime appeal of documentary authenticity and semi-documentary form had carried it back into the theaters with new force. In 1946 the C.O.I. renewed the M.O.I. wartime agreement whereby official documentaries were released free to the theaters. Even more important, a number of government-sponsored documentaries far in excess of that before the war were shown commercially according to ordinary trade practice. Some proved to be box office successes: war films like *Target for Tonight*, *The True Glory*, *Journey Together*; and also *World of Plenty*, on the problems of international food distribution, *Today and Tomorrow*, on the work of the Middle East Supply Center, and a number of others of feature length.[9] Strong documentary influences were soon evident in the postwar Italian neorealist films, in the semi-documentaries and "problem pictures" from Hollywood, and finally in the delightful series of comedies from Ealing Studios which mixed whimsy with social comment and realistic settings.

To some it must have looked as if documentary films might simply walk across the street to the box office but Paul Rotha, with the aid of hindsight, was able to evaluate the actual situation more accurately.

> In Britain, the possibilities of the so-called feature documentary after the war were grossly over-rated, largely because of a more or less overt desire to escape from the system of sponsorship. Ostensibly, the call was for more humour, more liveliness, more personal dramatisation. In fact there was often little evidence, among the protagonists of this solution, of any drive to find humour, liveliness and a dramatic quality in the subjects they had to deal with. They wanted somehow to hang

those missing attributes on the outside like Christmas tree decorations. Moreover, as a number of them were to discover, the creative and economic opportunities available in the feature film industry, though undoubtedly different, could also be vastly more inhibiting.[10]

Grierson, who had taken pride in the theatrical success of the Canadian "World in Action" series and would himself work in features after the C.O.I. period, never regarded the theatrical route as the main one. Once more he tried to warn against its seductions: "the illusion rears again its ugly head that the odd spot among the theatre millions is worth more in public information than the persistent influence of the community groups that in every known way lead the opinion of the community." What disturbed him was "the limiting and rotting effect of a theatre distribution policy for documentary as a whole; and it was ever so from the beginning." ". . . in times of urgency, yes, documentary is a national asset which even the theatres will recognize, but in lesser times, no; it belongs to where the serious purpose is continuous; and that is where the community leadership of all kinds quietly and continuously lies."[11]

Supporting Grierson was Roger Manvell, who observed,

There are many people who do not like him and who feel that his influence has been too academic, and that documentary films, if they are to stir the wider public, must be prepared to stir them through the emotions. But this does not alter the fact that the large nontheatrical audience in Britain for films made largely according to Grierson's pattern has survived the war with its loyalty unimpaired, and that the regular roadshows of the wartime Ministry of Information are being maintained by the peacetime Central Office of Information. Grierson's later essays and articles persist in emphasizing the need for the state-sponsored film for the nontheatrical audience, to bring alive the problems of the world to the citizen, or, to use his words, "to make peace exciting."[12]

Rotha echoed the theme but added a reservation: "To make peace exciting—that has been the problem since the war. It can be done by the artist of faith and vision, but only if the sponsor will go along with him. The will to peace, the will to general betterment, the will to more happiness, security and warm relationships must be there in the sponsor before the artist can create. And evidence of that kind of goodwill has been hard to find in a world intent on rearming."[13] In fact, as Hardy noted, "The most imaginative films emerged not from the Government but from the large industrial concerns like

Shell which had taken up with fresh vigour their film-making experiments interrupted by the war."[14]

As it happened, under governmental and industrial sponsorship, soon even more films were being made each year than had been during the war.[15] Documentary filmmaking had shifted from a minority to a majority movement[16] with a considerable increase in personnel over the prewar days. There was a difference though. The older workers were tired after the war. Some of the leaders had defected to the studios. Grierson was abroad during the first critical years—1947 was marked as *the* crucial one by Rotha.[17] The "R.A.F. types," as Stuart Legg called them, who moved into documentary after the war, were lacking in indoctrination and dedication. The cohesion of the earlier days had vanished. There was no longer unity of purpose, no longer a closely knit group.[18] Films were simply made to a sponsor's specifications, whereas the earlier documentary filmmakers had decided what they wanted to make films about and then found sponsors who could be persuaded to pay for them.[19] "The technician who does what he is told," complained Rotha, "becomes the whore of the P.R.O. [public relations officer] and the sponsor. The artist with a mind and will of his own is feared by the tyro P.R.O. and the petit-bureaucrat. He is something unpredictable, undefinable and without label. Yet it is the artists, not the technicians, who have made documentary a living thing in twenty years of cinema and in world social advance."[20]

Be that as it may, there was one special irony in the social advance that documentary films had helped to make. In 1945, startlingly soon after war's end, Labour won a general election in a "resounding victory at the polls" over the "Tories who mismanaged the nation's affairs for 18 of the 21 years between the two wars," crowed *The Cine Technician*.[21] Socially progressive and therefore implicitly pro-Labour, the documentarians of the thirties and forties had done more than a little to prepare for that victory and for the kind of governmental program it heralded. "After years of revelling in opposition," observed Charles Oakley, "they now had their own Labour Government."[22]

On the other hand, the documentary people had been resolutely nonpartisan in their stated positions, being above party, or at least aside from it. This stance led to some confusion. Rotha presented the matter this way:

One of documentary's greatest strengths over the years has been that we in Britain never allied ourselves to any political party. As Grierson put it: "Our job specifically was to wake the heart and will; it was for the political parties to make before the people their own case for leadership."[23] This refusal to be henchmen or mercenaries—at any rate among the old guard—is an attitude towards social progress and reform that has been difficult for our sponsors, our critics, our politicians and even for some of our younger colleagues to understand. I believe it to be fundamental to the documentary idea and purpose. Without it, documentary as a movement in Britain would never have survived for twenty odd years. And in these dim days of misgiving and mistrust, I wish that some of our more intelligent politicians, publicists and educators could be induced to read and re-read those sections of Grierson's essays on propaganda, education and democracy. Both they, and the nation they serve, would profit.[24]

Grierson had often complained about Labour's lack of imagination or interest in public information, as he conceived it, and now the new government was further shackled by postwar austerity and more pressing priorities. Rotha sadly conceded: "none of us foresaw that during the next six years the Labour Government was to shirk its responsibility to the film people who had served social democracy so loyally during the struggle of the thirties and in the strain of war."[25] Even Sir Stafford Cripps, one of documentary filmmakings's earliest and staunchest supporters, could do little. Just before Grierson came on at the C.O.I., Cripps publicly granted that "films for educational and propaganda purposes" were "the most powerful means of spreading essential knowledge" that Britain possessed. But "Now that the expenditure upon all Government propaganda has had to be cut down," the only way to support their production that he could see was to have documentary shorts substituted for inferior second features in the theaters. This would require programs of single features and shorts rather than double features, and he confessed that he was stumped to know how to bring that about since, "as a Minister and as responsible to Parliament," he must "try to give a fair deal to all the conflicting interests."[26]

## Uncertainties and Loss of Direction

The emptiness of the Labour victory, as far as documentary was concerned, was not the fault of the government alone, as Grierson saw it. After he had been at C.O.I. for a few months he repeated the kind of criticism *cum* exhortation he had been leveling at the British documentarians since the early war years.

> I have suggested that documentary may have been remiss in not keeping up with the advancing armies of Whitehall as they reached into ever-widening territories of Government interest and an ever more central position in regard to the reality of the time. We may have fallen into the old and fundamental aesthetic fallacy of believing that these immediate matters of State lie outside the higher considerations of art. . . .
>
> . . . our place is where the creative operations of the State and the nation can be taken hold of, and this carries the conclusion that while our primary intention may lie in education and art, we have of necessity to be leaders, in our own fashion, in public thinking and public service, and specialists in one or other of the principal public concerns of the day.[27]

Underlying and partly causing the problems of support and effectiveness of documentary film was the difficulty the filmmakers experienced in finding their way to themes and forms that would be relevant, let alone vital, to their postwar audience. "British documentary's pioneering sociological themes," wrote Anstey, "deriving as they did from unemployment and poverty, are not only less appropriate in Britain today, they long ago became cliché-ridden."[28] Part of what had happened, wrote fellow-veteran Stuart Legg, was that the things documentary had been for had come about: ". . . social sanctions, exciting enough to chase as screen dreams in the '30s, became tedious when seen in the light of legal and administrative actuality in the late '40s."[29] In other words, by acting on them, the "welfare state" had usurped those topics of more inclusive planning, greater collectivization, and increased material well-being. What it had not inspired and had perhaps reduced was pride, liveliness, a sense of beauty and humor, energy, and faith—in short, spiritual sustenance in a changing and uncertain postwar Britain to substitute for the loss of prestige and power and the old values.

Nor had the high levels of epic poetry and drama which documentary had achieved during the war years provided a solid basis on which to build in the inevitable emotional slump of peace. Acknowledging the wartime success, Grierson wrote in 1948: "one feels today that in the very urgency of the event there was no time to consider where the roots would very differently lie at the war's end;

and the M.O.I. did not prepare for it. Nor did the film-makers." In the same article, with italicized emphasis, he added that in some respects *"the war period was an unmitigated disaster for documentary in Britain. It enabled the documentary people to avoid the real problem of their medium and escape the duty of founding an aesthetic practice on the actual materials of the public service. It enabled them to beg the whole question and escape into the normal— but, as I think, ever-weakening—paths of dramatic fashion."*[30]

Most of the documentary leaders recognized that something new in subjects and styles was being demanded, but the question was what. Some twenty years later, Grierson spoke of those new horizons opening up after the war. Making a distinction between "depth values" and "junk values," he said that to be able to re-evaluate the British as a nonmaterial people was what they were attempting. This had special importance as well as difficulty because "England has more depth to it than any other country."[31] In the postwar years themselves, however, he wasn't sounding so nonmaterialistic. For example, he wondered sometimes, he wrote in the summer of 1948, "if we who did so well once with the social reform perspectives of the 'thirties—slum clearance, the problems of nutrition, etc., etc.— have sufficiently bothered our heads to take documentary excitingly into those other perspectives of economic reorientation and reorganization, of scientific development and technological revolution, which are as much the reality of today, and therefore as much the deepest concern of government, as the problems we helped the government to illuminate in previous times."[32]

Other spokesmen, too, seemed to be speaking the language they knew; it became clear that their goals hadn't changed even if the people's needs may have. Thus Rotha:

> I cannot see that the social motives which underlay so much of our work in the 'thirties have changed. . . . There is more need than ever before for a clear interpretation of issues, for explaining governments and organizations one to another and to the peoples they represent. There are still many, many social problems to be solved, many miseries to be exposed for action, many inequalities to be spotlighted and many constructive causes to be made widely known. In all the countless fields open to it, on the international as well as the national level, the documentary ideology can be carried forward in these next years provided that its creative workers maintain that integrity of purpose which has distinguished their contribution up till now.[33]

247

Anstey, a little later and a bit less certain, conceded that "Today the issues are less clear, the arguments and images less obvious." But his prescription, if different from Rotha's was so in degree rather than kind: "Today the documentary producer should be busy with films on industrial incentives, the moral structure of the welfare state, the sanctions which may justly exist between society and the individual. . . ."[34]

Still later Stuart Legg, also invoking that favorite Grierson term "sanctions," wrote of postwar documentary filmmaking: "Perhaps it now has to contribute to the creation of a more important and more difficult set of sanctions; for the themes of change which it ought now to grasp are inevitably those that descend to the deepest roots of national living and thinking." It is not altogether clear what Legg meant by "deepest roots," though he did urge "the building of a new ship rather than the vain caulking of the old." In any case, the stance was still positivist, collectivist, and materialist—to make the system work better rather than question it.[35] From the old guard there was nothing resembling the New Left or the Angry Young Men, who would perhaps reflect and speak more clearly to the postwar mood, nor of their filmic equivalent, Free Cinema, shortly to constitute the first fundamental break from the Griersonian tradition.

## Attacks on the C.O.I.

If doing little for the uncertainties, some of the frustrations of documentary in the immediate postwar years were released through increasingly bitter attacks on the Central Office of Information Films Division. Because of its pivotal position in the British film situation, and because of its size, it was an obvious target. The criticism and controversy began within six months after the C.O.I. came into existence.

In August 1946, the Federation of Documentary Film Units, with Rotha as chairman, expressed to the C.O.I. concern over the delays and confusion surrounding the production of many of its films. Promising improvements, the C.O.I. suggested regular consultations between representatives of the producers and itself. No such meetings were ever called, according to Rotha, and in November the Documentary Federation wrote again to the director-general, now Robert Fraser, requesting action. "As satisfaction was still not forthcoming, a meeting was held of over fifty senior creative technicians," who adopted a resolution highly critical of C.O.I.'s lack of smoothness and efficiency. The resolution was supported by a damning statistical analysis of man-hours lost by eight film companies producing for the C.O.I. due to delays and cancellations.[36] In December the resolution and analysis were sent to Herbert Morrison, then lord president of the Council and responsible for the C.O.I. in the House of Commons.[37]

"It was about that time," as Rotha remembered it, "when, questioned in the House about the C.O.I. films output, the Financial Secretary of the Treasury (who answered, when it was embarrassing for Mr. Morrison) stated: 'I can assure my Hon. Friend that the relationships of the Films Division of the C.O.I. with the Trade are happy, intimate, cordial and continuous.' The only continuity," added Rotha, "was that of frustration," and the only result of the whole exchange was "promises, most of which failed to materialize."[38] Relations between the documentary companies and the C.O.I. were felt to have deteriorated still further during 1947.[39]

In August and September of that year, in connection with the first Edinburgh Film Festival, Grierson commented on the British scene in both his article for *Documentary 47* and in his festival address. In the former, acknowledging that "[a] great deal of gloom surrounds the British documentary operation in this summer of 1947," he continued: "I think the situation is urgent and warrants an immediate official enquiry if a great national asset is to be saved from damage. . . ." Then he gave his own assessment.

> There is criticism on both sides. The units charge the sponsors, and particularly the Government sponsors, with a lack of decisiveness and a lack of imagination. They say they have lost the conception of a total driving plan for the use of the documentary film in the urgent service of the nation. The sponsors, on the other hand, say the film makers are too independent by half and cannot be relied on to deliver efficiently or even to deliver what they have undertaken to deliver, and finally that the boys are so full of small politics these days that nary a one of them has time to throw his cap over a steeple.

He had heard (from his colleagues) that "the great art of sponsorship" was now "progressively usurped by the little people playing for departmental exactitudes and personal safeties; and that we, on the other hand, have only created directors capable of making competent pictures which, for all their technical adequacy, are dead in the eyes." After once again outlining the principles upon which the sponsorship of documentary had been founded, he concluded by returning to the present need for a commission of inquiry and by listing thirteen questions it should consider.[40]

In the address to the Edinburgh Film Festival, Grierson dealt with some of the same issues in a broader context and again mentioned the need for an inquiry.

> Perhaps the documentary people are not at the moment so vigorous in new ideas as they might be, but who, pray, is? The gap created is a spiritual one which is evident everywhere. The documentary people are part of a larger picture, and there is no great difference between the frustrations of the COI and the frustrations of the units who think they are afflicted by it. Neither are yet at the stage of seeing where the positive way of the public will flies, and who can blame them when the leaders themselves flounder in equal uncertainty? . . .
>
> I do not want to push the point too far in this difficult situation, but I do not like the loss of direct and confident relationship between the artist and the Government official; and I am bound to think that if something is going out of documentary, it is because something has gone from its essential underpinnings. Ground has to be made up. A notable understanding of the needs of the nation is the first condition of a positive, fresh and imaginative contribution toward their fulfilment.
>
> The second condition may be in recognizing the need to reorganize the documentary business, and radically, from an administrative point of view. . . .
>
> . . . now is not the time for complacency. I do not think the documentary people can afford the independent luxury of so many units. I do not think they can afford the present high cost of films. I do not think they can afford the present laboriousness in which film is conceived, or the present tempo in which it is made. We cannot afford it for the simple reason that we are shooing our sponsors away.
>
> Short of a proper enquiry, I have myself no conclusions to offer. . . . Above all, I do not want the documentary group to wait around for things to happen to it from the outside, when now, as it has always done, it can write its own brave ticket. It requires, however, a special effort; and I think now, and not later, is the time for it.[41]

Two aspects of this address are particularly worth noting. Grierson saw the job to be done with documentary in Britain as one he was peculiarly well suited for—he was setting up the requirements in his own terms. Second, though this was an *international* festival he chose to talk about the United Kingdom, rather than UNESCO, and especially the British government and documentary.

Rotha, in an eight-page privately circulated memo in August 1947, continued his more combative approach, concluding with an italicized charge: "*As the major sponsor of documentary films, the C.O.I. must be held responsible for the lack of drama and vitality that regrettably characterizes its current product. British documentary is in danger of resting on its past achievements and is failing to maintain its lead in this branch of the medium.*"[42]

In the same month, the "Financial Notes" department of *Penguin Film Review* repeated charges of "delays, indecision, and mismanagement" which had first been leveled by the Federation of Documentary Film Units a year earlier. The *Penguin* writer, however, went on to say that the fault lay with the system itself: the Public Relations Officers' Committee, Treasury control of expenditure, piecemeal production attached solely to department needs. "The new directorate may be timid in adopting a critical attitude so early in its career," explained *Penguin Review*, "but its feelings cannot be spared at the expense of the product or of the producers—or indeed of the taxpayer, for public money will be wasted in trying to make the unworkable work. It would be more to the credit of those responsible to take a strong line at an early stage. . . ."[43] It was to adopt this strong line that Grierson would be brought back.

Finally, with its November-December 1947 issue, *Documentary News Letter* began a steady pot-shotting at the C.O.I. A devastating article by Philip Mackie entitled "Production History of a COI Film"[44] touched off a series of editorials and pseudonymous correspondence (e.g., from "Nero Nonflam"). The tone was frequently heavily satiric, with ironic exaggeration of the waste, red tape, and questionable relevance to purpose and audience of the C.O.I. production.[45] With the February 1948 issue, the month Grierson came on board, the stream of criticism ended.

## Grierson's Administration: Structure, Personnel, Policy

When Grierson arrived, the C.O.I. Films Division, if not altogether healthy, was still whopping in size. Regardless of the alleged difficulties, it was the largest source of sponsorship in Britain, supervising the production of about 107 films in 1947.[46] During that calendar year fifteen films were sold to theatrical distributors, the highest such figure achieved in any one year by the government information services.[47] More importantly, the C.O.I. organization included the Central Film Library in London and twelve regional offices. In all, over eighty thousand prints had been mailed in 1947. One hundred forty-four projection vans provided shows in factories, institutes, and clubs which had no projectors of their own.[48] It was estimated that during 1947 the mobile units played to an audience of nearly five million, who attended some forty-five thousand showings.[49]

The Crown Film Unit, which had been under the M.O.I., had achieved considerable postwar autonomy through a charter drawn up by Alexander Shaw, putting it on an equal level with the C.O.I. Both organizations reported to the controller of the Treasury; the producer in charge at Crown was classified as a sub-accounting officer and could be called to report to Parliament.[50]

Crown had become something of a headache, however, in terms of size and "creative personalities," according to Basil Wright.[51] With many of the key personnel having left for the feature industry, booming at the time, Crown writers and directors were mostly inexperienced. The unit's morale was particularly low right after the war during a period when they hadn't made a film for six months. In 1947 they moved from Pinewood, which became production center for the Rank Organization, to Beaconsfield, one of the oldest studios in the country, which had been converted to an aircraft factory during the war. When they arrived there was nothing there, recalled John Taylor, the producer in charge, not even heat. The two hundred people on the staff were scattered in cutting rooms and labs at other places. At Beaconsfield, two kerosene stoves had to heat the whole studio, with the winter of 1947–48 one of the worst in a hundred years. A Niessen hut was put up outside the main building and army barracks were used to supply adequate work space for the studio. Most of the staff simply stayed home. It took two years to rebuild, owing to postwar shortages of materials.[52]

When Grierson took over the job as "controller of Government film activities," as the *Times* announced on February 20, 1948,[53] part of his responsibility was to coordinate the work of the Crown Film Unit and the C.O.I. Films Division.[54] As Crown was in direct succession from the E.M.B. and G.P.O. units, it was in a sense, as Hardy observed, a return to the work Grierson had begun some twenty years before. In fact, the documentary people had petitioned the government to bring him back[55] and, when he returned, he was still at the height of his prestige because of the enormous achievement the Canadian Film Board represented.[56] Going far beyond C.O.I–Crown coordination, Grierson was to take overall charge of the planning, production, and distribution of government films.[57] Curiously, Bernard Sendall, who had been chief films controlling officer at the C.O.I., was not removed from that position. Sendall remained titular head while Grierson was advisor in charge, as it were. A job had been created for Grierson in which he had all the authority, though nominally it appeared to be Sendall's, and he ran the show while Sendall soon went to work on the approaching Festival of Britain.[58]

Under Grierson, C.O.I. Films Division production continued to be undertaken by the two official units, Crown and the Colonial Film Unit, and by commercial producers. (The only other government production organizations were those of the armed services—Army, Air Force, and Navy.)[59] Distribution was via both theatrical and nontheatrical avenues. The film activities could be further broken into home and overseas services, with the output fairly evenly divided between the two.[60]

One of Grierson's early moves was to reduce Crown's autonomy and put it under C.O.I. administration. Redundancy and confusion had resulted from three separate systems of accounting (Crown, C.O.I., Treasury) and, in addition, Grierson felt Crown to be insufficiently responsible in its financial control.[61] John Taylor had reorganized it into four sub-units: one to make feature-length documentaries (which Donald Taylor took charge of); the second made informational shorts aimed at the theaters, which were still showing one free government reel a month (and was headed by Stuart Legg); the third, educational (classroom) films; and lastly, instructional titles (aimed at specialized groups like farmers, doctors, housewives, and so on). This scheme was accepted by Grierson at first, but then he decided to break Crown down into three departmental heads: finance, studio management, and production.[62] The aim may have been to establish clearer and more comprehensive administrative and fiscal control.

At any rate, Grierson evidently intended to increase Crown's production, reducing the number of films contracted to outside producers. The change in proportions was substantial enough to indicate a new policy, wrote Irmgard Schemke in the spring of 1948. "The government film unit will expand while the independent makers of documentaries, which at the moment consist of nine-tenths of the movement as a whole, will contract."[63] Legg, back from America, was to start another "World in Action."[64] Together with other projected series—"Wonderfact," "Venture," and "Britain '49"[65]—this aspect of Crown's production seems more than a little like the abortive World Today. Donald Taylor, yielding to Grierson's persuasion, had reluctantly left theatrical features to assist at Crown, and was later made producer in charge when John Taylor left to go to the Colonial Film Unit.[66] Among the directors, Humphrey Jennings was the only notable veteran on the staff.[67]

The Colonial Film Unit, founded in October 1939, just after the outbreak of war, had as its director W. Sellers; executive director was George Pearson,[68] and its staff numbered thirty-seven.[69] During Grierson's first year, it produced sixty films for and about the colonies and also contributed items to newsreels circulating in the colonies. In addition to the staff in London, local units were set up, as Grierson had urged they be in his speech to the conference on Film in Colonial Development. In East Africa, workers were attached to the public relations departments of the Kenya, Tanganyika, and Uganda governments, while another unit worked on a regional basis. Under a separate scheme, cameras and film stock were supplied to local cinematographers in nine different territories, who returned the film to London for processing. Thirty-two films of local interest were made in this way during the year. In September 1948, a school of instruction for colonial film workers was set up in Accra.[70]

Altogether, as Grierson liked to point out, the Central Office of Information was the biggest producer of short films in the world.[71] Among the commercial units most active in contract production for C.O.I. during Grierson's regime were Basic Films, Citizen Films, Data Film Unit, Verity Films, Greenpark Productions, Technique Film Productions, Horizon Film Unit, Paul Rotha Productions, International Realist, Realist Film Unit, and World Wide Pictures.[72] In the first budget year under Grierson's direction, Crown and the private contractors produced 155 reels (88 films) and the Colonial Film Unit 102—a total 46 reels above the preceding year and even farther above the wartime peak of 1944–45.[73] In its *Annual Report*, the C.O.I. disclaimed "any merit in sheer weight of numbers," however. "If these figures have significance," it was explained, "it is because they reveal a broadening discovery by Departments that films can give them help, both direct and indirect, in discharging their public duties."[74] This statement does not prevent one from guessing that Grierson was doing everything he could to speed the discovery.

Film production lay within the outlines of C.O.I. work as a whole, which in turn was based on the four main fields of government activity: defense, economic affairs, social welfare, and international affairs. As far as defense was concerned, the main C.O.I. job was the simple and single one of assisting recruitment; the armed forces met their other information needs through their own public relations. In economic affairs, the tasks were much more intricate and varied, dictated by Britain's straitened and altered economic situation resulting from the war and new government policies. The messages could be subdivided further into information about production and consumption. In production, the nation needed more miners, more men on the land, more textile workers, more in the export industries as a whole. Publicity was employed not only to redistribute the labor force but also to help bring home the need for higher output per worker through improved methods and greater pride in work well done. As for consumption, less of it, or making the most of what was consumed, was the main thrust. In social welfare the C.O.I. had the task of explaining the substantial volume of postwar social legislation and new government schemes for social security and national health—to enlist the support of the public and professional workers in those matters.

The fourth field of C.O.I. activity, international affairs, was so complex and pervasive that it defied departmental allocation. Instead, the C.O.I. forged a path for itself. One topic involved was promotion of a wider understanding of the significant overseas relationships which the people of Britain had either inherited or into which they had entered—especially of the changing Commonwealth relationships and the defense of the West.[75]

## Production

Out of these diverse departmental interests, there emerged a pattern of films which reflected many aspects of the national life, the progress and achievements of the nation, and its difficulties and needs. In the period under review, emphasis fell on the nation's efforts in the economic and industrial fields. Films such as *Inside U.S. Aid* and

*Robinson Charley* were made to promote a clearer understanding of Britain's situation in the world's changing economy. The purpose of others—for example, *Queen of the Border*, *Once Upon a Time*, *Furnival and Son*, and *Gates of Power*—was primarily to make known to Britons and to others the qualities of skill, research, and invention which lay behind the production of British export goods (as had *Industrial Britain* some fifteen years earlier). Another group—*Report on Steel*, *Cotton's New Look*, and the "This Is Britain" series—dealt with progress made in industrial reconstruction. Others—*One Man's Story* and *Man Alive*, produced for the Foreign Office—told the world of the human relationships and humanizing influences developed through the work of the Medical Officers of Health and the Factory Inspectorate. Still other films primarily for overseas audiences included *Steps of the Ballet*, made for the British Council as a sign of British cultural vitality, and *Waverly Steps* and *Voice of Ulster*, whose purpose was the attraction of visitors from abroad, both tourist and commercial.[76]

"Grierson hoped he could give fire and conviction to the Government's filmmaking effort," wrote Hardy, adding: "There was no doubt about the impact he made and the change in mood under his leadership."[77] The impact and nature of the leadership perhaps had more to do with the quantity of production and range of purposes just discussed than with a change in artistic quality. One can't be sure which films Grierson actually had a hand in (though, as in the later years in Canada, the proportion would have had to have been small) or even which were begun during his incumbency (given the slowness of production and his relatively brief tenure). In general, though, the best of the C.O.I. films, *circa* 1948–50, seemed to follow a new dictum he uttered at the time, which sounded strangely unlike him and suggested some desperate flailing in the postwar backwash.

Since the subjects available lacked the drama of war, he was said to have declared in an interview that they had to be handled with the maximum amount of entertainment compatible with their purposes. The goal seemed to be, to one observer, "information films plus showmanship."[78] Entertainment and showmanship looked like a continuation of the narrative/dramatic characteristics of the semidocumentary developed during the war, of which Grierson hadn't altogether approved. In fact, the best and certainly the biggest of the C.O.I. films were precisely those which leaned most strongly in that direction.

256

Take *Waverly Steps* (1948), for example, which was made by Greenpark Productions for the Scottish Home Department and directed by John Eldridge, who had started at Strand during the war. A "city symphony" in the tradition founded by Cavalcanti and Ruttmann in the twenties (and one can't help but recall Grierson's suspicions of the aestheticism inherent in the form), it attempted to give the "feel" of Edinburgh by tracing a dozen minor human incidents through a period of twenty-four hours. Lovely and moody, it even contained some of the ambiguity thought proper to works of art and rarely consciously permitted by orthodox documentarians.

At the time, *Daybreak in Udi* (1949) was generally considered the most successful of the C.O.I. releases. Made for the British Colonial Office by Crown, with the cooperation of the Nigerian government, it was produced by John Taylor and Max Anderson and directed by Terry Bishop, who had just joined the unit. William Alwyn composed the score, which was performed by the London Philharmonic. The script, by Montagu Slater, recounted the building of a maternity hospital by native Nigerians and a British district officer. Short-feature in length and form, using indigenous nonactors, it won a number of international prizes, including an Oscar. Of it Grierson wrote a year after leaving the C.O.I.:

> If indeed I were facing the issue of sponsorship as a young man, content with the earlier dream of documentary, I would draw a conclusion from the appearance of *Daybreak in Udi*, and its kind. Politics is the art of the possible, and the great possible for liberal documentary sponsorship today must, I say, lie where nations have progressively to face world opinion, progressively have to give an account of their stewardship, progressively have to consider, through Colombo Pacts and Fourth Points, the relationship of social progress to political and economic events.[79]

[The Colombo Plan for Cooperative Economic Development in South and South-East Asia was established in 1951 by India, Pakistan, Ceylon (now Sri Lanka), Australia, New Zealand, and Great Britain. The Point Four Program was the U.S. policy of technical assistance and economic aid to underdeveloped countries begun in 1950.]

Today, alas, *Daybreak in Udi* looks strangely patronizing and naive. It's almost hard to believe the British made it in their own self interest, but in 1949 the course of African national aspirations had yet to be run.

*The Undefeated* (1950), from World Wide Pictures, was produced by James Carr and directed by a young Paul Dickson for the Ministry of Pensions. It chronicled the bravery and endurance of a former glider pilot who had lost both legs and the power of speech in the battle of Arnhem as he struggled to become a useful and active member of society once again. Somewhat sentimental, perhaps, it was nonetheless regarded as highly effective when released, the performance of the amputee being singled out for special praise. The British Film Academy named it Best Documentary of the Year.

Pushing the narrative-dramatic tendencies even further were a group of three feature-length documentaries (Grierson had originally announced six)[80] produced under Donald Taylor at Crown. All were completed in 1950 and cost about £25,000 each. Though these substantial productions meant fewer films, counter to usual Grierson tactics, Donald Taylor pointed out that they did make full use of the large facilities which Crown had acquired and followed the inclinations of the creative personnel towards features. *Life in Her Hands*, on nursing, and *Out of True*, on mental hospitals, were both directed by Philip Leacock, who had earlier started work for Donald Taylor at Strand and would follow Grierson to Group 3. They were distributed by United Artists. "Essentially studio pictures," wrote Rotha, "the main roles were played by known professionals and there was a striving for technical gloss which, despite good direction, tended to weaken authenticity." The third film, *Four Men in Prison*, directed by Max Anderson, "disappeared under a ban of official disapproval."[81] It was as a result of *Life in Her Hands* and *Out of True* that Grierson first became interested in the possibility of feature production for himself, Donald Taylor thought: the experience of those two films made Group 3 seem possible.[82]

## Distribution and Exhibition

As far as the audience for its films, C.O.I. statistics swelled during Grierson's first year on the job. The *Annual Report* for 1948–49 (April 1 through March 31) provides the following information. On the nontheatrical side, the mobile units which operated from the regional offices and the Scottish Information Office provided 54,172 shows to audiences numbering 4,928,000. Grierson transferred the Central Film Library, which had been administered by the Imperial Institute, to the C.O.I., and it, along with the Scottish Council Film

Library and the sub-libraries at Bristol and Cardiff, issued to borrowers 132,142 prints, which were seen by audiences totaling 5,962,000. The entire audience which saw official films outside the ordinary cinemas was, therefore, just under eleven million—an increase of nearly 700,000 over the preceding fiscal year. Through most of the winter months, the staff and accommodation at the Central Film Library were quite insufficient to cope with the demands, and many borrowers had to be informed that their requests could not be met. "Such figures and facts seem to afford proof of a growing public demand for films of fact and explanation, and go far to explain and justify the use made by Departments of the medium," observed the *Report* with editorial flourish.

Further, twenty-six films were placed with commercial distributors and shown in cinemas on the usual commercial terms. This was an increase of five films over the previous year's record figure. The agreement with the Cinematograph Exhibitors' Association continued, under which, in addition to the above twenty-six, a one-reel film was shown each month and about thirty "trailers" each year in approximately 3,500 cinemas.[83]

For the second year of Grierson's tenure, however, though the number of films distributed in theaters repeated its record high, nontheatrical distribution and exhibition fell off, most heavily with the mobile units. This fact was explained in the 1949–50 *Report* as due to the suspension of almost all shows during the general election campaign and to some reduction in the number of mobile units. More prints were mailed by the libraries and reached a larger audience, but still the total estimated nontheatrical attendance, using both means of distribution and exhibition, dropped from 10,890,000 of 1948–49 to 10,074,000 for 1949–50,[84] which couldn't have been cheering.

## Reduction of C.O.I. and the Effects on Documentary

The faltering of film distribution and exhibition gives only faint indication of a general cutting down that occurred during Grierson's administration of Films Division and continued after he left. The reduction was general in the sense that it was aimed at C.O.I. as a whole: overall expenditures were cut almost 25 percent in two years; total staff fell from 1,738 in April 1949 to 1,564 in April 1950.[85]

In fact Grierson had been hired "to let blood."[86] Apparently he didn't dread the role of surgeon-physician as much as one would have expected, since he seemed to feel that the government film operation had become unhealthily bloated in size of staff and expenditure. Though he was relatively gentle with the personnel at Crown (it still had 191 people when he left),[87] he "decimated" the Films Division, according to John Taylor, cutting especially the new people who had come in after the war. Grierson liked to boast that of thirty-six persons in key positions he forced thirty-five to resign and sacked the thirty-sixth.[88]

As of April 1949 the total C.O.I. film staff (production, including Crown and Colonial units, and distribution in home and overseas services) was 761; as of April 1950 it was 646 1/2 (half units were used to account for part-time workers.)[89] As for the budget, while the *percentage* of film expenditures in the C.O.I. total *increased* from 30.3 percent in 1948–49 to 32.2 percent in 1949–50, Grierson actually spent £1,186,454 in 1948–49 and only £1,030,830 in 1949–50—a reduction of over £155,000.[90]

In summary, then, though Grierson was keeping his forces and funds comparatively intact, the whole C.O.I. was being cut in the name of economy and the usual and general lack of enthusiasm for information services. Government film production, which had increased from the 211 reels of the year prior to Grierson's arrival to 257 during his first year, fell to 167 during his second—the lowest figure recorded in the history of the Ministry of Information and the Central Office of Information up to that time.[91]

Given the proud tradition of British government documentary filmmaking, it was small comfort to know that it was suffering as part of a general attrition. Given the centrality of the E.M.B.–G.P.O.–Crown succession to the development of documentary theory and practice, its weakening could hardly be compensated for by the postwar burgeoning of independent commercial units. Affected by prevailing conditions as it was, there were special things wrong with the central government operation which Grierson wasn't able to remedy, and a decline set in which he wasn't able to arrest. Two months after he left C.O.I., the Colonial Film Unit was transferred to the Colonial Office. Exactly one year after his departure, Crown Film Unit was disbanded under a newly elected Conservative government. The baby whom he could claim to have sired had progressed through maturity to decrepitude and, in spite of all efforts, was finally put to death.

## Afterthoughts

Most of the defects of the government film service were there when Grierson took the job: lack of an imaginative information policy on the part of government; filmmakers' failures to make the issues of peace exciting; confinement to specifications and budgets of separate administrative departments; inefficiency and waste at Crown. Though Grierson may have made temporary progress with these problems, he failed to solve them, and together they constituted a sinking weight. He may also have added or at least exacerbated a fifth difficulty with his handling of money and relations with the Treasury. In any case, Rotha felt that Grierson had arrived too late "to restore confidence and inspire fresh initiative"; that "[e]ven Grierson's ruthless methods could not blow fire into the sterility of the C.O.I. and documentary."[92]

Writing from an acknowledged filmmaker's bias, Rotha also said that government sponsorship, which accounted for some 80 percent of the total documentary work, was "unreliable, supine and without direction in the national sense." "No longer did the Labour people want films to expose bad housing conditions; *Land of Promise* was uncomfortable to the Labour Ministry of Health! They wanted films to instruct local authorities how to build pre-fabs. The emphasis had passed from attack to construction; it was too early to praise. What could and should have happened under Government guidance was for the larger documentary themes to have taken Britain's place in the world community of nations." Instead, "Between 1946–51 the Labour people threw away one of their strongest aids to interpret and make acceptable the aims and ideals of social democracy, not just to Britain but to the world."[93]

Compounding the ideological and political uncertainties of the government was the bureaucratic structure of the C.O.I. Lacking ministerial status or funds of its own, dependent upon the specifications and budgets of individual departments, it was a weak vessel from the start. For all practical purposes, as again Rotha observed, the arbiter of policy became the Treasury and the criterion one of finance alone.[94] The films "became more and more *little* films cautiously required by departments"[95] and "chiefly concerned with short-term objectives."[96] Though the departments may have been "commanding as best they could," conceded Grierson, "it was as dreary a business of the halt leading the blind" as he had ever encountered. The "privilege of making imaginative films for Britain was removed and the staid particulars of departmental interest took over." In support of his view he quoted Goebbels on the subject, as he was wont to do: "'In the day to day pedestrian pursuit of departmental interests, the national interest is forgotten.'"[97]

When looking back to Grierson's sweeping vision of a national information service which so startled the Commission on the Freedom of the Press, it is clear what a downward spiral he and his ideas had taken, not least in postwar Britain after he was on hand to help determine the course. If, contrary to his own understanding of the necessities, departmental commissioning had succeeded a truly national information policy, the civil service structure free of party considerations (which he had equally insisted upon) also had had to bow before the winds of political change—paradoxically by the postwar victory of Labour over the Tories. The "terms of reference of the C.O.I.," as Grierson ruefully reminded his readers, were "laid down not by a Conservative government but by a Socialist one."[98]

So what could be done to try to overcome the limitations of a faulty structure, the short-sighted if not misguided economies, and lack of imagination of the party in power? How could one ensure that some public money was devoted every year to "making film poetry about Britain"? "The only—and traditionally English—guarantee of this," said Grierson, "is to put the policy job . . . the sponsorship—in the hands of two or three imaginatively generous people who have the wit to know what that means."[99] Curiously, in those difficult times he had circled around to a reliance on good men, whereas earlier he had insisted that a succession of able ministers was one thing that could not be relied upon. He felt himself tied to always looking for sponsors: that his kind and use of film required an aristocracy.[100] Though Labour ministers Stafford Cripps and Herbert Morrison both had an understanding of the function of the documentary, especially Cripps, they weren't in a position to help at the time. Grierson was even more impressed with the potentials of Aneurin Bevan, then Minister of Health, whom he felt truly understood the "creative push" and would have made an even greater Minister of Culture than André Malraux in France. If he had met Bevan two years earlier, Grierson felt, the C.O.I. might have stood a chance.[101] As it was, all he could do was go round the departments, hat in hand, trying to get them to make films, or better films. This was no role for a person of Grierson's calibre and experience by this time, insisted Basil Wright, who thought it Grierson's gravest mistake to have come to the C.O.I. at all.[102]

At the time austerity was closing in, C.O.I.'s production arm, the formerly much respected Crown Film Unit, had swelled with what would prove a fatal elephantiasis. After Pinewood, rather than trimming its wartime size, it had moved again and begun to rebuild another large feature-type studio operation at Beaconsfield. It had become a big and cumbersome organization—ten plasterers, electricians, and so on—with featherbedding and the unions very powerful.[103] There were, in fact, more facilities than could be used, especially with the money being cut back. This was the situation that Grierson sent Donald Taylor in to try to correct. He relieved John Taylor, who, though a good filmmaker, was charged with being less than a good organizer or administrator. The "mess at Crown," Donald Taylor said, had been "caused, or at least not helped, by John Taylor."[104] Later, at the time of Crown's demise, Grierson granted, without naming individuals, that "There have been mistakes. Beaconsfield was one. The building up of large vested interests in the technical departments was another. The bureaucratic overhead came, like a tail the size of a kangaroo's, to wag the poor benighted hound. It represented a shocker in civil service misconception of duties and limitations. We committed the traditional sin in film making: 'pinched the money off the screen.' The illusion that techniques, vital as they are, provide the secret of creative work was a deeper error still."[105] Many years later, Grierson said much the same thing more simply: "Crown went down because it was costing too much. Techniques of this sort of operation get very good but the tendency then is to pursue technique for its own sake."[106]

On the latter occasion, Grierson also said in regard to Crown, several times, that he just "couldn't get it under the wire," meaning financially. A Public Affairs Committee investigated Crown's bookkeeping and—although, according to Grierson, they knew he would not tell a lie, that he was a totally responsible public servant—"found it to be false."[107] Edgar Anstey, however, suggested that Grierson had lost patience with the bureaucratic necessities—that he felt he had been through it all before—and simply wasn't able or willing to operate totally within the tedious requirements of the system. He didn't realize, said Anstey, that everyone he was dealing with hadn't been through it all before.[108]

Basil Wright, for his part, saw the pressures being brought to bear as the Treasury getting back at Grierson. They had always looked askance, noted Wright, at the kind of freewheeling the film people had been capable of[109] (a recurrent issue in Canada as well), but then Wright tended to see personal vindictiveness where Grierson saw none. Forsyth Hardy felt that it was Sir Robert Fraser, director-general of the C.O.I., and other civil servants who took advantage of Grierson's "recklessness, caught him out as it were." Cautious and careful, they never did anything and so never made mistakes, whereas Grierson probably was careless about finances and may have been extravagant, acknowledged Hardy. He considered Grierson to be "foolish about money—certainly in terms of personal income and expenditure—[he] would plunge ahead without it." Nonetheless, Hardy read Fraser as the villain of the piece and felt that there was a deep conflict between the two men.[110] John Taylor, in turn, spoke of Grierson's commissioning films without having the funds and said that during the C.O.I. period he got into a "terrible mess." This was atypical of Grierson, who prided himself on being a civil servant's civil servant, Taylor added, but he gave as an example of what he meant the following instance. Grierson had commissioned Wright to do a series of scripts on exceptional British personalities and public figures. When the project came under question, having had no authority for the films in the first place, Grierson "kind of denied that they had his backing." That hurt Wright particularly, said Taylor.[111]

There was a widespread suspicion that Grierson was willing to sacrifice the government operation because of the things he didn't like about it—e.g., the extravagance, the doctrinaire leftists among the personnel—while others urged that the C.O.I. and especially Crown must be preserved in spite of their flaws for the strength and continuity they could still provide to the movement. Many felt that it would be regrettable to cut anything that wasn't absolutely forced; that at least part of the baby would inevitably go with the bath water. Grierson, however, if he had a choice in the matter (and he may not have had), was thought to regard the cutting as a necessary cauterizing. Whatever the possibilities and reasons for the decisions, it is true that as a result of these trying days, enemies were made, considerable unhappiness was caused, and British documentary finally collapsed as an organized movement and social force.[112]

If Grierson's failure to solve the C.O.I.'s problems constituted a costly defeat for documentary films, the effects it had on individual loyalties of members of "the group" seem even sadder and perhaps ultimately more damaging, if one recalls the effective power generated by their earlier solidarity. John Taylor, who had been head of Crown when Grierson came on, simply could not understand why Grierson had permitted Crown to be brought back under the C.O.I. when Taylor had been at pains to establish its autonomy (in conformance with Grierson's usual policy, as with the Film Board). Not that Taylor objected to working under Grierson, he insisted, but Grierson wouldn't always be there and could very easily be followed by a politician who had little sympathy or experience with film. Maybe the Crown productions were dull and out of touch, Taylor conceded, but Grierson had no alternative plan. He was in a sort of frenzy—his actions unaccountable, Taylor felt.

It could well be, of course, that Grierson thought he could protect Crown only by having full authority over it in order to correct the generally admitted malfunctioning (for which Taylor would have been in no small part responsible) before others brought it to the ground. At any rate, Crown's change of status was the reason Taylor gave for resigning. He felt that Grierson was quite decent to him personally in moving him to the Colonial Film Unit rather than firing him (accepting his resignation), but their relations remained strained for several years. Though he spent 1949 at the latter unit, on assignment to reorganize it, Taylor felt completely at a loss in that highly specialized kind of filmmaking. How could he advise staff who had been working in Africa for twenty years? After a year, he was "paid to retire gracefully," he said.[113]

Apparently Legg, too, felt some bitterness from actions during this period. Grierson's cryptic explanation was that although Legg had an English arrogance, at the time it was needed he couldn't do something required that would have hurt people.[114] Legg resigned from Crown in 1950 to return to private production.[115] Of all the old boys, Wright was especially unhappy at this time, according to John Taylor, because his relations with Grierson had been closest: Grierson had become "like his other self."[116]

All things considered, then, it came as no great surprise when Grierson resigned from the C.O.I. in January 1951. Recent staff cuts at Crown had meant that the Beaconsfield sound stages would not be used again, and the general tightening up on cost and restriction on the number of films to be made did not leave much scope for a man of Grierson's ability, as one observer put it.[117] His post was not to be filled. Director-General Fraser explained that the position was created specially for Grierson and that it "disappears with him."[118]

## Extramural Activities

Grierson's outside activity during his three years at the Central Office of Information seems to have been less than in earlier periods, as one might expect given the manifold difficulties at the C.O.I. Shortly after coming on the job, he spoke to the general meeting of the Association of Cinematograph and Allied Technicians (A.C.T.) about the government information service and trade unions. The other "distinguished visitor" who addressed that April 1948 meeting was Harold Wilson, then president of the Board of Trade.[119] In June Grierson received an honorary LL.D. from his alma mater, Glasgow University, an award which seemed to please him very much. As a result of this honor, he was frequently referred to as *Dr. Grierson*. (During the same month he was mentioned in the espionage trial of Judith Coplon in the United States, along with "writers, actors and other prominent personalities being linked to the Communist Party.")[120]

In August he attended the second Edinburgh Film Festival and reported on it for *Documentary Film News*. While there he saw his great good friend Robert Flaherty, whose *Louisiana Story* received its world premiere. "Yet another evocation of the damn fool sense of innocence this wonderful old character pursues," wrote Grierson, "his eye keener than ever, sensibility ever softer and so on, and Frances still around."[121] (This seems to be his only published comment on Flaherty's last film.)

At the second meeting of the International Scientific Film Congress in London in October, he introduced Jean Painlevé, the pioneer French scientific filmmaker, and Otto Storch, an Austrian scientist who used the camera as "an indispensable instrument of fundamental research."[122] That same autumn Grierson became a vice-president of the New London Film Society, along with Dilys Powell and Iris Barry; Paul Rotha was president.[123] Grierson also joined Rotha, Ivor Montagu, Marie Seton, and Herbert Marshall in a published tribute to Sergei Eisenstein, who had died that year.[124]

In 1949 Grierson visited South Africa at the invitation of its government and advised on the setting up of a National Film Board along Canadian and Australian lines.[125] He was again active at the

Edinburgh Film Festival, and wrote an important statement for *Documentary 49*, published in conjunction with the festival.[126]

During 1950 his extramural activity seems almost to have ceased, but just before leaving the C.O.I., he did assist the British Film Institute in presenting a series of film programs on the evolution and anatomy of screen comedy, a favorite subject with him.[127] In introducing the New London Film Society program during his last days at the C.O.I., he gave a hint of what would preoccupy him in his next undertaking by stressing the need for finding fresh film talent in Britain.[128]

Throughout the C.O.I. period, Grierson was active on the film committee of the Brussels Treaty Organization. Concerned with cultural relations, this organization had representatives from Belgium, the Netherlands, Luxemburg, France, and Great Britain. The film committee not only aided the exchange of films but undertook some coproduction (e.g., *The Open Window*). With the addition of West Germany and Italy, the body became the Western European Union and later the Council of Europe. Grierson's connection with it ended, however, once he had left the C.O.I.[129]

## The Ending of British Documentary Film as the Grierson Movement

To return to the Central Office of Information's Films Division and its problems, it must be added that the criticism of it and of British documentary generally, which had in part helped to bring Grierson back to Britain, did not cease when he became films controller. If anything, it gradually increased in volume and virulence until the death and burial of the Crown Film Unit in 1952, a year after Grierson had left the C.O.I.

As the Griersonians had been the attackers from the outside before Grierson took charge, so now those in power were attacked by a new set of voices. Leading off were a group of young Oxonians—Lindsay Anderson, Penelope Houston, Gavin Lambert, and Peter Ericsson—who began the quarterly *Sequence* in the fall of 1947. In its third issue, spring 1948, Anderson aimed directly at Grierson and fired. Few of a newer generation, he wrote, "are any longer able to summon up that ardent, proselytizing enthusiasm for social-democracy which was the inspiration of the documentary movement." He then quoted Grierson re British documentary, beginning "not so much in affection for film *per se* as in affection for national education," its origins were "in sociological rather than aesthetic aims." Anderson continued his exegesis of Grierson's long-standing tenets: "Again, rather gruesomely (he approves the attitude he is describing), '. . . you may not be so interested in the individual. You may think that the individual life is no longer capable of cross-sectioning reality. You may believe that its particular belly-aches are of no consequence in a world which complex and impersonal forces command, and conclude that the individual as a self-sufficient dramatic figure is outmoded.'" Regarding that familiar Grierson position, Anderson observed:

> Against this attitude most (though not all) of us have reacted, and have come to realise more and more that the particular belly-aches of the individual life remain of the extremest importance, that they affect society as much as society influences them. Add to this the disillusion which it is impossible not to feel when we look back on many of those films made so earnestly, with such high hopes (*World of Plenty? Land of Promise?*), and the lessened enthusiasm for documentary becomes understandable enough. Also, of course, documentarians are now civil servants: as a result good scripts are pigeon-holed for years before they are made, and films are held up for years before they are seen. The urgency as well as the enthusiasm has gone out of things.[130]

In the same issue of *Sequence*, Irmgard Schemke offered some general observations on the subject: "Nobody who has worked in a Documentary film unit during the past twelve months can have emerged from the year's work with a feeling of confidence and satisfaction that all's well with Documentary"; or, "The story of the C.O.I. films division has been a sad and difficult one for the Documentary movement as a whole." He then supported these observations with an itemized description of real and practical difficulties at the C.O.I.[131]

But it wasn't just the young bloods in pursuit of their elders. Winifred Holmes, one of the G.P.O.–Crown veterans in her own right and wife of J. B. Holmes, who had succeeded Grierson as head of the G.P.O. Film Unit, appeared that same spring in the British Film Institute's *Sight and Sound*. In a cogent analysis, she repeated many of the criticisms of the C.O.I. specifically and documentary film generally that have already been noted, and contrasted the then-present restrictive conditions and lack of vigor with the fresh experimentation of the thirties and, especially, the solid achievements of the war years. She did, however, allow that "[t]he return of John

Grierson will also have an effect. No one can predict exactly what, but the atmosphere is sure to be charged once more with excitement, enthusiasm and controversy; it will be alive."[132]

Grierson replied to Mrs. Holmes in the next issue, first dealing with the present:

> while there may be incidental weaknesses, documentary today is as big as a house and bigger than anyone had, at the beginning, any reason to expect. It represents on its Government side alone by far the biggest single operation in short film production in the world. Like any other founded house, it has had, and may be now having, its pedestrian stretches, but there is nothing that cannot be cured by (a) a few first-rate films, (b) two or three first fine careless raptures by new talents, and (c) a certain reorientation of documentary policy in the light of its present-day circumstance.

Then about the past:

> There can of course be a great deal of argument about that 'fulfilment' of the war years. I find myself one of the scurvy people who doubt if there is ever any real 'fulfilment' in war-time: in films or anything else. One might as well talk of 'fulfilment' in a lunatic asylum. . . .
>
> The ultimate limitation of war as an inspirer of documentary is that the themes were to a large extent 'found' from a dramatic point of view. They were physical, with most patent death and disaster for a violence-loving medium to play with; and, in the nature of things, the world wore its humours and its sorrows on its sleeve. The achievements of documentary were not, therefore, inconsiderable, but they were, shall we say, relatively easy achievements, involving less of that hard discipline, mental and creative, which in other times than war finds the drama under the less garish stone of peace.

As Grierson drew to a close, his analysis and suggested solution were characteristic.

> This is what Mrs. Holmes's argument finally amounts to. Some people are going from documentary to the studios. There is a sense of frustration among documentary film-makers in spite of the actual scale of the operation. There is a widespread view, right or wrong, that documentary pictures are not as exciting as they once were. I say to this that the failure lies in not organising the sponsor relationship in such a manner as to make all of these phenomena unnecessary. . . .
>
> I hate the prospect of so much labour as much as anyone, but we have, after all, got what we wanted; and we may not escape from it now, simply because it has become big and complex and cumbersome

269

and difficult to handle. We may not escape it, and not only because we willed it ourselves but because we willed it once in a cause that is as great to-day as ever it was.[133]

By July, Jack Beddington, oil PR man, head of the Ministry of Information's Films Division during the war, and Grierson's old friend, had leaped into the growing fray and added considerably to its fury. His title, "Off with Their Heads," was bloody enough, and the article lived up to its promise. "The trouble with the documentary film world today," he stated simply, "is that the old gang is still in charge. It was, therefore, a great delight . . . to hear considerable criticism of them by younger people at a private debate the other day." Further on: "The old gang twelve or fifteen years ago were pioneers with new ideas, great enthusiasms, courage and honesty. They are now middle-aged, much fatter or thinner than they were, and no longer potential geniuses. I cannot see that they have made any advance in the last five years. Humour they do not understand; criticism they resent. This is no state of mind with which to startle, tickle or impress the world."

After a bit more whacking and thumping, Beddington arrived at the "cardinal weakness of the old gang." There could be little doubt about whom he was thinking.

> They are constantly pressing a political point of view. . . . the moment a piece of propaganda in a film is considered of more importance than the film itself, the film is bound to fail and to preach to none except the converted. If only the old gang would realize this and even that their political points of view are both well-known and old-fashioned, they might be induced to give up intrigue and wire-pulling and come back to film-making.
>
> In their early days they freely announced that they were only using films for propaganda purposes, but in those days they were young and enthusiastic and deceived themselves in a more agreeable fashion than they do now. In fact, they loved making films and it was for this reason that beauty and humour crept in despite their *professed* attitude of abhorring the aesthetic. This is one of their silliest and most self-conscious tricks.

Beddington concluded with the hope that the newcomers would "retain their enthusiasms and their energy and vigorously chase out the old gang as soon as possible."[134]

After Grierson left the C.O.I. and as the dismantling of Crown approached, the squabbling erupted again at a still higher level of vituperation. Over the qualified anonym "Government PRO (name and address supplied)" there appeared in *World's Press News* the following blast: "It is time somebody said something to (and about) John Grierson. In the Edinburgh Film Festival magazine 'Documentary 51' he has made another attack on his former colleagues in the COI and the Government Information Service. The cause of his spleen is that the Government is making so little use of the medium which he founded—and of Grierson himself—in tackling the big information and propaganda needs and opportunities of the present time." Then on to more *ad hominem* attacks with extraordinary relish:

> Grierson's sermons are couched in a jargon-language of an emotive and allusive kind which may have a meaning to himself and the initiates of his cult but becomes frustrating and annoying to others who would like to be able to understand him. They reiterate ideas which sound impressive and exciting the first time they are heard but which descend into the wild and woolly when one finds them being monotonously repeated without any clear indication of how they can be given practical shape and content and how Grierson would like us to go about helping him to have them translated into tangible results.
>
> The trouble about Grierson is that he is writing and talking himself out of any useful contact with the Government Information Services machine from which he is demanding so much.

Finally: "It goes against the grain a bit to write this article. I like John Grierson and used to have a profound respect for him. . . . But it is Grierson at his best that we want and deserve, Grierson employing his abilities in a truly constructive way, and not just playing the peevish prophet—hurling filth at us one moment and repeating his oracular and unhelpful cries in the next."[135]

Some months later, in the wake of Crown's demise, Denis Forman defended the unit against "Charges of extravagance . . . made, by Grierson among others,"[136] and B. Charles-Dean wrote a nastily disparaging letter in regard to Grierson's arguments and suggestions about government information after Crown. Containing phrases like "burst of ego," "anxious nonsense," "ambiguous suggestion," "seemingly losing all sense of proportion in reading his own wordage," Charles-Dean's piece is virtually unique in publicly dismissing Grierson's grasp of the situation with such scorn.[137] Either Grierson now seemed less acute than formerly, or his position as leader of British documentary no longer carried the weight it once did, or both.

Peter Price terminated the debate on much the same note as Lindsay Anderson had begun it some five years earlier:

> So it is hard to wonder if the leaders of an avant-garde don't subconsciously hope to stay young and in the swim, tending to cling to the ideas that excited them in their youth and quick to repulse any suggestion that their arteries might be hardening. They don't appear to recognise that in the course of a minor social revolution (which they helped to bring about) people have found that being "progressive" isn't quite enough and that the old phrases about collective subjects don't mean a thing. . . . There are some old habits of thinking which one can only hope are not too deeply ingrained. The chief of these is, 'We are social servants first and film makers second.' This dogma would do for the factual film, the string of images linked with left-wing statistics, for the film which set out to teach. But the consumer resistance to being taught has killed this sort of film, and must kill the dogma.

Price concluded by saying, "So down with how they do it, and up with an imaginative understanding of how they are and how it *feels* to do it. Wouldn't it be rather exciting to try to get ahead of the feature film again, and have something worth stealing the next time it loses touch with *its* audience?"[138]

After this there was little published argument about documentary, and in the purest Griersonian sense there were few documentary films to argue about. The leader himself had by this time followed other old boys into feature fiction film production, carrying with him some of the trappings of actuality and social observation, to be sure. It was twenty-five years, a quarter of a century, from Grierson's hiring at the Empire Marketing Board until Crown and documentary production by a British government unit came to an end. Not a bad record perhaps, but it is a question if it did have to come to an end, never to be resurrected; if the idea had a limited life—in Britain at least—which could be lived only at a certain time.

Another aspect of the C.O.I. period which warrants conjecture is Grierson's apparent misunderstanding of the situation, as he did with World Today, but also acting in contradiction to his own analysis, as he had begun to do at UNESCO. Earlier and often he had explained how the Canadian Film Board had been constructed to last, and how a system like that of the C.O.I. could not function in the best interests of the nation. Yet he accepted the C.O.I. terms and, according to some, even exacerbated their restrictiveness. For decades he had stoutly maintained that the fiction film did not offer opportunities for the civic education and inspiration he was interested in and criticized those who defected to features, only to follow them.

Perhaps there was no other way to go, and to some extent he regarded Group 3 as a "saving" of Crown;[139] that is, salvaging what was salvageable of the people and of the spirit of films in the national interest. Maybe Grierson privately had come to feel that the diffused documentary qualities that did adhere to the modestly budgeted postwar Italian neorealist films, the semi-documentaries and "problem pictures" of Hollywood, and the delightful series of Ealing comedies in Britain were the only viable solution, for the time being at least.

Rotha seemed to see the situation in that light: "The fact that Grierson—preacher, prophet and pontiff—now operates as a kind of Zanuck second-feature producer indicates that documentary may have to find new paths to follow."[140] Hardy, too, felt that "Grierson's experience at this time . . . made him more and more conscious of the limited opportunities there were in Britain for documentary film-makers to extend the range of their work—to do in Britain what the younger film directors in Italy and France apparently found it so easy to do."[141]

In any case, it was to the studios he went in January 1951.

# 11 ❖ GROUP 3 (1951–55)

## The Setting Up

British feature film production had a long history of instability; prior to 1951, government efforts to prop it up in the face of foreign (that is to say American) competition had taken several forms. One was the quota system, first established in 1927 and subsequently modified in various Cinematographic Films Acts, whereby a certain percentage of screen time had to be allocated to British films—the 1948 act set this at 30 percent of the features and 25 percent of the other films shown excluding newsreels. The acts were administered by the Board of Trade, which was advised by a Cinematographic Films Council made up of representatives of the film industry and independent members.

In 1948, in addition, as part of the planned economy of the Labour government and at the urging of Harold Wilson, then president of the Board of Trade, there was set up what would become the National Film Finance Corporation (N.F.F.C.). It was granted £6 million of Treasury money for loan directly to British producers and distributors to subsidize production in cases where finance could not be obtained "on reasonable terms from an appropriate source." The loans bore interest and had to be repaid within five years. In September 1950, the government introduced a broader scheme to subsidize film production by a levy which the industry itself collected from exhibitors (the so-called Eady Plan)—initially a farthing (0.3 U.S. cents) per ticket sold.[1] By early 1951, about one hundred productions had been thus assisted.[2]

Finally, and the most radical measure of assistance, was the establishment of a studio to undertake actual filmmaking with government (i.e., N.F.F.C.) money. "A Wilson invention" as well,[3] Group 3 got its name as it followed in inception the two N.F.F.C. groups which dealt with subsidies to the existing industry. The notion behind the third group was that with modestly budgeted features, it would serve as a training ground for young filmmakers, to strengthen the British industry in its competitive stance. Since Grierson had had no fiction-feature experience, some of his friends were horrified when they learned he was entering that commercial arena. Margaret Ann Elton mentioned particularly the American exhibitor-distributor Arthur Mayer, who had put some of his own money into Grierson's The World Today, as one of those.[4] It seems likely that the training aspects of the Group 3 idea would have made Grierson, the greatest of film teachers, a likely candidate. Arthur Elton and Edgar Anstey both remembered (albeit vaguely) a dinner at which the recommendation of someone to head Group 3 was to be finalized. The two of them, along with Basil Wright, pushed for Grierson. Michael Balcon and James H. Lawrie appeared doubtful.[5] Balcon, head of Ealing Studios, was also chairman of the N.F.F.C.; Lawrie was a banker. It was a rare occasion which gave the old boys an opportunity to "promote" the master as he had them early and long.[6]

In what may have been a hedging of bets (though Grierson remembered it as having been done at his urging),[7] he was paired with a veteran feature film producer-director, John Baxter. Grierson's title was to be executive producer and Baxter's production controller.[8] Once selected, they established themselves at Southall, Middlesex, in a small studio with one sound stage owned by Alliance Film Studios, Ltd., and leased to the N.F.F.C.

## End of Crown

A little more than a year after Grierson's start at Group 3, a development occurred which he surely could have foreseen before he left the C.O.I.: the illness of the Crown Film Unit proved to be terminal. The Conservative government, which had been returned to power, announced in January 1952 the closing down of Crown and the C.O.I.'s nontheatrical distribution and exhibition services.[9] "It was thrown away overnight," wrote Rotha, "while Parliament was not even sitting to raise a voice in protest. Even Tory high-ups, such as Lord Waverly and Lord Woolton, privately admitted the folly of the act—after it had been committed. No face-saver could be found."[10]

Despite subsequent wide protest in Parliament and the press, the action took effect at the end of March. Thus ended the main instrument of government filmmaking and distribution as a public service in the United Kingdom[11] with a lineage that could be traced back through the Ministry of Information, the General Post Office, and the Empire Marketing Board to almost a quarter century of more or less steadily expanding size and scope. The Colonial Film Unit had earlier been removed from the C.O.I. to the Colonial Office and was closed down a year or two after Crown.[12]

Though the need for governmental economy was certainly a prime factor, and Grierson himself had acknowledged wasteful extravagance at Crown, some inferences were also drawn that the Conservatives were less than pleased by the tendency toward the political left of documentary people in general[13] and perhaps of Crown in particular. (Grierson was said to have expressed his impatience with the more doctrinaire Marxists at Crown as being "parlor pinks.")[14] The documentary movement had proclaimed its radicalism from the beginning, and even if Grierson insisted it remain free of party, it had certainly made some contribution to the defeat of the Churchill government in 1945.[15] Whatever the reasons, once the Conservatives were returned to power, their action was both prompt and decisive.

Grierson's reaction to the death of the offspring (and Tallents's, too, for that matter) remains equivocal in retrospection, and downplays what a disaster the closing of Crown would prove to be. It marked not just the termination of the government main line but the end of British documentary as a movement. Either Grierson didn't see this, or chose not publicly to consider it that way at the time. He wrote, "I think it would be sensible not to blame the present Government overmuch for the decision about Crown. . . . Crown, as Sir Stephen Tallents pointed out in the *Times*, is no longer the single and privileged centre of an experimental development, but merely one unit—and a good one—among others." Continuing in the same vein, he said: "In particular, I do not like to see the present Government blamed because to do so is to miss the point. Crown has been coming unstuck for a long time. Its work has always been fine and it is right that we should honour its good taste to the last. But, as we all know, its singular uniqueness as a unit has gone. For me, Crown—the best of Crown—is more or less everywhere."[16]

Never inclined towards self-commiseration, and perhaps attempting to put as good a face on the present as he could since there was nothing much else he could do, what Grierson said was nonetheless wrong. The loss of its leadership and training would never be compensated for.

In 1953, Group 3 moved to Beaconsfield Studios, which had housed the Crown Film Unit. Later Beaconsfield would become the site of the National Film and Television School.

## Documentary and Feature

The forces that had started pushing documentaries toward the feature form and theatrical distribution, which Grierson had tried to avoid, proved, temporarily at least, to be stronger than his own system of production in the national interest, and had in fact carried him along in the tide. "There's always the movement away from documentary," he later said in relation to the semi-documentary short features which had come to dominate the attention at Crown. Further, he regarded Group 3 as a "saving" of Crown, one of the best "rescue" operations he had managed in similar straits.[17]

Curiously, and according to Rotha even before the end of the war but when its end was foreseen, a move had been made by the documentary people to establish some sort of viable connection between the documentary and feature personnel and industries, not unlike what Grierson was now attempting to achieve at Group 3. "[T]here was an offer made to the Rank Organisation at Pinewood by some of the major directors and writers of the Crown Film Unit, plus a number of independents in documentary," Rotha later revealed. "They offered a complete programme of people and pictures, small budget pictures, to the Rank Organisation. . . . But the offer was never taken up."[18] As Lindsay Anderson pointed out, by the spring of 1949, when Grierson had been at the C.O.I. for a year, there were a number of directors at work on features who had sprung from the documentary tradition or who testified their allegiance to it: "Ian Dalrymple, Harry Watt, Jack Lee [who had] all produced or directed for the Crown Film Unit; Charles Frend and Charles Crichton, although not raised in documentary, [had] made their sympathies clear in the films which they [had] so far directed for Ealing Studios. From such men," Anderson predicted, "we may expect films realistic in style, shot to a large extent on location, and with that awareness of social issues—the social-democratic bias—which has always been the inspiration of the documentary movement."[19]

Perhaps it was Sir Michael Balcon, production head at Ealing and chairman of the board at Group 3, who best summed up the evolving thinking vis à vis the fiction and documentary traditions in England. His feeling, in 1951, was that the feature film had "largely taken over from the documentary"; that "the beliefs of the few of the '30's" were now widely held, their aims generally accepted, their approach vindicated.

> [T]he feature film today is carrying on the documentary tradition. More and more it is using for its backgrounds parts of the contemporary scene such as made the subject matter of the past documentary: farm, slum, factory. More and more it makes use of characters and action arising out of contemporary problems, such as were handled by the documentarists: labour problems, class problems, problems of psychology. More and more it is prepared to break away from the studio and its hothouse plots, to use real places and real people.[20]

Much earlier Grierson had written about his efforts as attempts to find "drama on the doorstep."

## Personnel and Functioning of Group 3

Balcon's background qualified him uniquely for his role in forming and guiding the beginning Group 3. Throughout some twenty years of experience in English films, he had demonstrated a rare taste and integrity and a flare for realistic and national subjects within modest budgets. Before Ealing he had been production head of Gains-borough Pictures, which he founded, and later of Gaumont-British, which had distributed the E.M.B.'s "Imperial Six" package of documentaries. Among his many productions were *Man of Aran* (1934), *The 39 Steps* (1935), *Dead of Night* (1945), *It Always Rains on Sunday* (1947), *Kind Hearts and Coronets* (1949), and *The Blue Lamp* (1950).

In addition to Balcon and Grierson, the other directors of the

Group 3 board were John Baxter, Grierson's partner in the actual operation of Group 3, and J. H. Lawrie of the N.F.F.C.[21] Baxter was a producer-director of no great distinction but of robust staying power. Two years older than Grierson, he had been a theater manager before entering production as a casting director in 1932. Confined to second features (that is, the lesser film on a double-bill), his substantial output was punctuated by "more or less sentimental studies of the hardships of the poor." His one notable success, *Love on the Dole* (1941), though said to be indifferent technically, was thought even in a long view to be remarkable for the "truth and generosity of its feeling for the industrial North."[22] These latter qualities Grierson certainly would have valued.

The directors selected for the pictures were mostly young; a number of them were making their first features, which was in keeping both with the relative inexpensiveness of the production and with the training school mandate. Many of them came out of documentary units, including Crown. The impression one gets of their work overall is that of good sense and taste. The attention to regional and social themes and comment had not been common in British fiction films—at least before the series of Ealing comedies beginning with *Hue and Cry* (1947), *Whiskey Galore!/Tight Little Island* (1949), and *Passport to Pimlico* (1949), which Group 3 films tended to resemble and perhaps imitate.

If some of the directors, producers, and writers given first or early chances on Group 3 features had stable and modestly successful subsequent careers, it must be granted that high creative potential did not emerge. Grierson admitted to disappointment in not developing more and better writers.[23] On the other hand, Group 3's record of performers "discovered" at the beginning of notable screen careers was considerably better. Peter Finch made his first appearance in Wolf Mankowitz's *Make Me an Offer* (1954). *Orders Are Orders* (1954) launched both Peter Sellers and Tony Hancock.[24] The group can also claim credit for giving Kenneth More and Joan Collins their first chances.

## Group 3 Films

If the "training school" function was a qualified success at best, what of the nature and quality of the films produced? Initially it was felt necessary to inspire commercial confidence, and Group 3's first effort, *Judgement Deferred* (1951), was directed by veteran John Baxter. A melodrama with a London setting and introducing Joan Collins (who was quickly taken over by Ealing), it was felt by one reviewer to be "sadly conventional and old fashioned."[25] The next feature, however, *Brandy for the Parson* (1951)—personally supervised by Grierson, produced by Alfred Shaughnessy, and directed by John Eldridge—was generally liked. A comedy about smuggling, much of it was shot on location in Cornwall. The crew and cast were all young; cameraman Martin Curtis had photographed Eldridge's *Waverly Steps* and *Three Dawns to Sidney*, and Kenneth More was featured for the first time.[26] More was contracted by Alexander Korda after a viewing of the uncompleted film.[27]

*Time Gentlemen Please!* (*Nothing to Lose* in the United States, 1952) was a comedy centered around the figure of an agreeable old Irish tramp in an English village. Thematically it was based, in Grierson's words, "on the simple but I hope civilised idea, that maybe someone somewhere shouldn't work as hard as they keep on telling us to do"[28]—a sentiment that doesn't sound much like the Grierson of documentary. Though Edgar Anstey found its manner "at the opposite extreme from documentary naturalism," he noted that in it, as well as in the third release, *You're Only Young Twice* (1952), there was "social criticism wrapped up in the fantasy."

The latter was treated harshly by many critics, Anstey acknowledged, though he himself found it the most interesting of the first Group 3 films.[29] Produced by Baxter, it appears nonetheless to have been thoroughly Griersonian. It was from a little-known comedy by Grierson's friend and favorite, James Bridie, *What Say They*, with a Glasgow University setting which both had shared and some apparently disrespectful academic satire. (The film was defended in the *Times* by fellow Glasgow alumnus and another old friend, Walter Elliot, who described it as "a documentary of the spirit.")[30] It was directed by documentarian Terry Bishop. The four films were completed in not much over six months.

Of these and the subsequent Group 3 productions (some twenty-two in all,[31] of which Grierson personally supervised about nine),[32] the fifth most clearly bore Grierson's mark. It has also generally been regarded as the best of the lot—one of the few with enduring value, and the second most successful commercially.[33] Among the first five films it was the only one fully to "develop the realist principle," as Rotha observed somewhat complainingly.[34] Even the title, *The Brave*

*Don't Cry* (1952)—adversely commented upon as "curiously arrogant" by Anstey (*Sight and Sound*), and "appalling" by Richard Rowland (*The Quarterly of Film, Radio, and Television*)—could be seen as reflecting a Grierson stance. The script was constructed by Montagu Slater from records of the then-recent Knockshinnock Colliery disaster, in which more than a hundred miners had been trapped in a Scottish mine when sodden ground subsided. Grierson himself produced the film; Philip Leacock directed. The performances were mostly by members of the Glasgow Citizens' Theatre. It was shown at the 1952 Venice International Film Festival, though it won no prizes, and it opened the Edinburgh festival to high praise. From there it went immediately into London theaters. Associated British Film Distributors (A.B.F.D.) distributed. (The other principal distributor for Group 3 films was British-Lion.)

Another early production, *Laxdale Hall* (*Scotch on the Rocks* in the United States, 1952), was also quite successful and endured long after its initial release.[35] This was the third Group 3 film to be set and shot in Scotland. It was by the same producer-director team who had made *Brandy for the Parson*. Taken from an Erik Linklater novel, it was a simple tale of remote Scottish Highlanders trying to get a new road. During the same time (late summer 1952), two other films were in production at Group 3: *Miss Robin Hood* and *The Oracle* (*The Horse's Mouth* in the United States). Both were comedies; the former starred Margaret Rutherford; the latter was filmed in Northern Ireland.

A bit later were: *Background* (1953), detailing the various reactions that the news that their parents are getting a divorce provokes in the three children of the marriage, and starring Valerie Hobson; *Devil on Horseback* (1954), vaguely based on a true story about a boy jockey, with Googie Withers; and *Conflict of Wings* (1954), relating the struggle between villagers and the Air Ministry for possession of a local nature preserve which the R.A.F. wants to use as a rocket firing range.

*Man of Africa* (1953), which Grierson personally produced, must have been one of his biggest disappointments. Made in color and featuring an all-black-African cast, it dealt with ethnic tensions between settled Africans and aboriginal Pygmies in Uganda. It was shown at the 1954 Cannes Film Festival, but "was not greeted with much acclamation," as Lindsay Anderson put it,[36] and was never released commercially. The most financially successful undertaking was a Group 3 film in name only. For the production of *The Conquest of Everest* (1954), N.F.F.C. money was routed through Group 3. It was in no other way a Group 3 film[37] and, as Group 3 received most of the profits, the actual production firm, Countryman Films (which included John Taylor), came to regard the arrangement with something less than enthusiasm.

Taken as a whole, certain tendencies of Group 3 production were early evident: the use of real backgrounds for indigenous stories (the documentary bias), and alternative efforts to develop unconventional narrative material (*You're Only Young Twice* and *Time Gentlemen Please!*), or to reanimate popular genres of comedy and melodrama.[38] Forsyth Hardy, granting the variety of forms, felt that in general the films were "vigorous and lively, unpolished and anti-establishment," a location outside London also being a common characteristic.[39] In gravitating towards satiric comedy, Grierson and Baxter ran into resistance from Michael Balcon, however, who allegedly wanted to shield this area from competition.[40] "Comparisons with the Ealing comedies immediately come to mind," wrote Anstey. He felt, though, that Group 3 had "faced up to the need cheaply to provide British entertainment which would stimulate and amuse the regular cinemagoer" and that "something characteristically British [was] emerging."[41]

From the reviews, and then lack of them, one can gather that the early Group 3 films were considerably more interesting than the later ones. Donald Taylor, who was among the Group 3 producers, placed the beginning of the change at a period when Grierson was ill and away from the studio. During that time he lost his power to control, said Taylor, and silly and cheap comedies and chases appeared among the last of the Group 3 releases.[42]

## Grierson's Additional Activities

Extra job undertakings were reduced while Grierson was at Group 3 in comparison with earlier periods when he had been promoting the idea of film in the public interest, but they by no means slacked off altogether. Out of loyalty to the documentary idea and perhaps to Scotland, or at least Scottish friends, he continued to be active at the annual Edinburgh film festivals. During the first year of Group 3, 1951, Grierson, Basil Wright, Forsyth Hardy, Norman Wilson (one of the organizers of the festival) and others convened a special luncheon to discuss the hiatus in documentary production.[43] In 1952 he lectured at the British Film Institute's summer school, held in conjunction with the festival, along with Max Ophuls (director), Dilys Powell (critic), Compton MacKenzie (writer), and Duncan Macrae (actor). He also appeared on a panel, and chaired another on which Wright and Rotha sat and which, not surprisingly given the company and the times, devoted itself to the relationship between the documentary filmmaker and the sponsor.[44]

The eighth Edinburgh festival, in 1954, coincided with the twenty-fifth anniversary of the first showing of *Drifters*, and Grierson was feted handsomely. A dinner in his honor held at the George Hotel was attended by some 150 distinguished film persons. They came from Australia and New Zealand, from Canada and the United States, from India and Malaya, from Yugoslavia, Scandinavia, and other parts of Europe. Sir Stephen Tallents was there, as were Basil Wright, Paul Rotha, Alberto Cavalcanti (who had come from Brazil for the occasion), Arthur Elton, J. P. R. Golightly, James Beveridge, Walter Elliot, Harry Watt, and Edgar Anstey. Presiding was Norman Wilson, chairman of the festival, and Tallents proposed a toast to Grierson's health.[45] Among those who spoke of the documentary movement and of Grierson's work were Dilys Powell, Paul Dehn (screen writer), Denis Forman (director of the British Film Institute), C. A. Oakley (chairman of the Scottish Film Council), John Maddison (Central Office of Information), and Forsyth Hardy. Some were unavoidably absent. From Ottawa, Norman McLaren cabled regrets and a remittance of two guineas to pay for the dinner he couldn't be there to eat. This noble gesture from a brother Scot across the Atlantic was greeted with cheers and laughter. From London, Michael Balcon wired his regret that production commitments kept him from Edinburgh. He added, "Warmest greetings to my old friend Grierson—and long may he flourish!" There were many similar messages from near and far.[46]

The twenty-fifth anniversary of British documentary also provided the occasion for a B.B.C.–TV retrospective which took Tallents's phrase as its title: "The Projection of Britain." Elton wrote it; Rotha, then head of B.B.C. Television documentaries, introduced the program. Tallents, Elton, and Grierson appeared, but the bulk of it was made up of excerpts from the 1930s, extending from *Drifters* through *North Sea*—twelve films represented in all.

Grierson's response to these tributes was (characteristically) complex, mixed, and equivocal: "instead of feeling grateful and gay," he wrote, "as of course I should, I have felt unnaturally depressed and not a little sceptical of the whole affair."

> Asking myself, as I must, why I feel so scurvy on a complimentary occasion, I can answer quickly, of course, that I don't like being old. When it is the case of an exploratory branch of the art like Documentary, I do not, in especial particular, like to have it dwelling on the past.
>
> I have thought so not just often, but always. It has been a matter of principle never to see any film I was associated with after it was made and presented. *Drifters* I have never seen yet. I was too scared to see it at the Tivoli [i.e., at its premiere]—which is another and younger matter—and all I know of it now, except of original recollection, is the excerpt that was dug up for me for the television broadcast.

After further analysis of his feeling on the one hand and of documentary in 1954 on the other, he concluded: "I know now why I am depressed. I am not depressed because of the record, which will serve very well and the better for being thought of as one contribution among others to a larger affair. I am not really depressed because, abstractly, a young art is looking on its past. I am depressed because this exploratory art has lost the particular impetus which makes for exploration."[47]

Grierson's writing about film while at Group 3 was less than at other periods, though of course there was the occasional piece, for example, a statement in an industry journal,[48] an essay for the Edinburgh festival magazine,[49] a review of the new edition of Rotha's *Documentary Film*,[50] a comment on the Australian Film Board,[51] and a rambling four-part series in *Sight and Sound* on the state of contemporary film criticism.[52] Curiously, though his film writing was down, throughout the early fifties he wrote what Margaret Ann Elton described as "incidental thirty-shillings-a-week literary criticism" for the magazine *Scotland*,[53] perhaps as a diversion. He appeared in almost every issue (it was a monthly) and his name was frequently featured on the cover as a regular reviewer of "*Scotland*'s book of the month," with no connection made to his film career. One particularly lively review was of a book about Scotch whiskey, a subject tackled with gusto, authority, and references to himself and his family.[54] Another book, entitled *Fresh Woods*, evoked the following observation: ". . . I grew up by the Gillies Hill, which was a wood and a half . . . [but] Born and bred in the country, I was one of the natural-born city spivs. . . ."[55] Nonetheless, reading this review, one would think Grierson had never done anything but read and write about and ponder nature.

Finally, at the end of the Group 3 period, Grierson did his first writing about television. Under the title "The B.B.C. and All That," he came down in a careful way on the side of private broadcasting, though at the same time granting that "[f]rom some original prejudice," he hated commercialism with every sense he had. In three years he would begin broadcasting for the commercial Scottish Television.[56]

## The Documentary Veterans

In spite of the brave show of reunion at Edinburgh festivals, Grierson's former colleagues were scattered and, like himself, many of them not working in documentary proper. Those who were, were now producers rather than directors, for the most part. Cavalcanti and Watt, who early had deserted to features, were followed by members of the younger generation: John Eldridge at Group 3, as already noted; Jack Lee (*South of Algiers*, 1952; *Turn the Key Softly*, 1953) and Pat Jackson (*White Corridors* and *Encore*, both 1951; *Something Money Can Buy*, 1952) at other studios. Even Rotha made a fiction feature the year before Grierson left the C.O.I. for Group 3. Elton, Legg, Anstey, Stewart McAllister, and Ralph Keene remained in documentary as producers; Wright was the only one still directing. Jennings had been killed in an accident in 1950.

In that year, Cavalcanti had returned to his native Brazil to supervise, with government cooperation, feature film production at the São Paulo studios. After a year, because of disagreement with the financiers, the unit was disbanded. Later he was commissioned to set up a National Institute of Cinema—"Many British technicians took part in this adventure"—and in the next several years, he directed a couple of features and produced a documentary. Taken altogether—with a Brazilian quota system and quota quickies, government subsidies, and an "aim, for the first time in this country, at a strictly regional production, with local actors and much exterior shooting"[57]—his efforts appear to have been not unlike those of Grierson at Group 3, including the ultimate lack of success.

Watt in 1951 made the semi-documentary feature *Where No Vultures Fly* (*Ivory Hunter* in the United States), shot on location in Africa, and *West of Zanzibar* in 1954. He joined Granada TV as a producer in 1955 but resigned the following year to return to Ealing as a director.[58]

Rotha's feature, *No Resting Place* (1950), was a story about Irish tinkers, made completely on location in Ireland with some Abbey players but many nonprofessionals. It was presented at the 1951 Edinburgh festival.[59] Rotha's and Wright's *World Without End* (1953), produced under a special grant from UNESCO, was the last big brave representation of internationalism from the old Griersonians.[60] In May 1953, Rotha became head of documentary at B.B.C. Television.[61] Despite what was said to have been "rapidly improving product,"[62] the B.B.C. disbanded its Documentary Department at the end of April 1955.[63]

Elton continued to head the Film Centre and to produce and advise for the Petroleum Film Board and Shell Film Unit. Legg also produced for Shell. Anstey headed British Transport Films and maintained a steady output of extremely well-made shorts.[64]

In July 1951, Robert Flaherty died. Grierson led in the quantity and most especially in the quality of eulogy for his old friend and source of inspiration. In three remarkable pieces published in rapid succession—in the *New York Times*,[65] the *Reporter*,[66] and *Sight and Sound*[67]—Grierson made eloquently clear his continuing sense of indebtedness and affection. The *Reporter* article was the most complete assessment of Flaherty's special qualities as man and filmmaker, but the *New York Times* appreciation, written within a few days after the news of his death, was the loveliest and most moving. In it Grierson seemed to concede that in the long view, Flaherty's concern with the timeless and universal verities might have contributed as much to man's progress as Grierson's own more immediate and particular efforts. He admitted that it had often "suited" him to protest—"as we tried to keep our documentary people close to the pressing social problems of our times"—that the "rarity of vision was too rare, that Flaherty went too far afield from the ordinary and everyday life to find his satisfactions, that he was altogether too romantic and—hardest word of all—that he was escapist." On the other hand, Grierson remembered how hard Flaherty had taken it when he was "criticized for not making clear the social burden of Aran Islanders" and "how plaintively he tried to explain that perhaps the 'burden of the horizon' could be as heavy as any. Who will deny that it is?" asked a saddened and noncontentious Grierson.

In conclusion he quoted from a favorite poet. "One feels like saying shortly, with e. e. cummings: 'Buffalo Bill's/defunct . . . Jesus/ he was a handsome man/and what I want to know is/how do you like your/blueyed boy/Mister Death.'"[68]

In September the following year, there was broadcast on B.B.C. Radio's Third Program an hour-long "Portrait of Robert Flaherty." Its participants, all warm in affectionate praise and fond recollection, comprised a distinguished international cast. Among them were John Huston, Orson Welles, Lillian Gish, Jean and Dido Renoir, Ernestine Evans, Sir Edward Peacock, Peter Freuchen, Sir Alexander Korda, Sir Michael Balcon, Henri Matisse, Oliver St. John Gogarty, Sabu (Flaherty's Elephant Boy), Denis Johnston, Pat Mullen (cicerone on Aran), and Michael Bell. Speaking for the British documentary camp were Sir Stephen Tallents, Paul Rotha, and John Grierson.[69]

As for Grierson, there can be no doubt that Flaherty's death was a deeply felt personal loss which left a vacant place that could never be filled. The two men, in their arguments, in their films, and even in their temperaments, occupied polar positions that all subsequent documentarians have had to range between. Explaining the implications of the seminal Grierson-Flaherty contributions in his survey of *Documentary in American Television*, A. William Bluem, though fundamentally Griersonian, concluded by advising, "If the documentary in television is to attain its maximum potential as an agent for intelligent change in our civilization, it must continue to recognize and express the diverse philosophies and attitudes revealed in both the Flaherty and Grierson approaches to reality."[70] Theirs was an extraordinary relationship, amalgam of friendship and dialectic, from which we have all since profited.

## The End of Group 3

In the spring of 1955, Group 3 became subject to what was officially described as a "considerable modification" in output. Henceforth it was "to engage in only very occasional production, without the continuity essential to a positive overall policy," as *Sight and Sound* put it. Its functioning was virtually terminated in July,[71] by which time Grierson had already left. "The true reasons behind the failure of Group Three are probably known only to a limited number of people," concluded the *Sight and Sound* writer.[72]

If the failure was hardly "ignominious," as Rotha averred,[73] Group 3 was undoubtedly "an unhappy experience," as Elton more gently put it.[74] Grierson conceded that he "would hate that anyone should live through" it.[75] Penelope Houston thought it a "sad case," and it must finally be evaluated largely in terms of her charges: that it failed "to establish itself, to make films of sufficient individuality, or to uncover the kind of talent needed to sustain a vigorous production programme."[76] Curiously, establishing itself, in a financial sense, was ultimately what it may have done best. According to Grierson, anyway, the films did eventually recover their costs,[77] making a case for the low-budget feature, but long after this could be of any help. Admittedly they were not of memorable quality and it is not clear that the use of British themes, characters, and locations was much of a contribution to the public interest. Finally, the discovery and development of creative personnel, the primary training-ground mandate, was only a qualified success. It seems likely that most of the talented actors would have found their way into commercial cinema in any case and that the majority of writers and directors given their first chance at features by Group 3 could have remained undiscovered without great loss to the industry. By 1955 several factors were present finally to end whatever usefulness Group 3 may have had.

In 1946 the British Broadcasting Corporation had begun regular telecasting. In Britain, as everywhere, television would become a powerful force in changing the shape of the motion picture industry. In many ways, it took over the functions Group 3 had been set up to perform. Rather than the small picture of domestic appeal made by new talent, what was needed to compete with TV was the big picture in CinemaScope and Eastman Color. Grierson saw this as clearly as anybody. Just before leaving Group 3, he wrote sadly of the conversion to spectacle and the forcing out of directors like Alexander Mackendrick (of *Tight Little Island* and *The Man in the White Suit*) and Philip Leacock (of *The Brave Don't Cry* and *The Little Kidnappers*), who had worked so ably within a realist fiction tradition that could claim to be distinctive and influenced by the earlier documentary impulses.[78] When the Independent Television Authority, in September 1955, took its commercial place alongside quasi-governmental B.B.C.–TV, the threat was complete. It seems more than coincidental, then, that 1955 was the year Group 3 discontinued functioning.

On the other hand, television may merely have accelerated the inevitable, for Group 3 bore within it from the outset some of the seeds of its own destruction. First of all, its leadership was strangely divided. Though Grierson denied any personal tension between himself and Baxter,[79] some felt their incompatibility to be one of the principal causes of Group 3's demise. Donald Taylor, for example, thought Baxter "very ambitious" and anxious to get rid of Grierson. According to this version, when Grierson became ill, Baxter was able to edge him out and keep him from regaining control.[80] John Taylor, on the other hand, described Baxter as an "amiable old-time feature director" who was merely "not very competent."[81] Others, including Grierson, saw the relationship with Balcon as a major difficulty.[82] Certainly the latter had what would seem a rather extraordinary conflict of interest, holding simultaneously positions as head of Ealing Studios, chairman of the N.F.F.C., and chairman of the board of Group 3. Balcon's feelings must have been further complicated by the fact that Ealing, which had been purchased by Rank, was going under at the time. Specifically, Grierson charged that Balcon tried to reserve for Ealing the kind of whimsical comedy for which it had become famous; that he attempted to thwart Group 3's encroachments in that field.[83]

Another problem was the pressure on Group 3 to pay its way as it went. This requirement was not necessarily compatible with the obligations to develop new talent and express native themes. Though taken together, the films were said to have shown an eventual profit on re-release, the only picture to recover its costs by the time continuous Group 3 production ceased was *The Conquest of Everest*.[84] This lack of commitment on the part of the N.F.F.C. to the risks involved—trying to have it both ways—must have exerted a restrictive pressure throughout the group's operation.

Because of the documentary background of many of its people and because it represented government entry into rather than just subsidy of production, the Group 3 experiment was not welcomed by the trade. Hence Group 3 films never received the kind of distribution-exhibition deals required for success. Again, this was particularly true on a short-term basis, which demanded the films play one of the big circuits. British Lion, Korda's company, which had shut down its own production arm during this period, did not or could not arrange circuit release, and the films had to get revenue by slower and more uncertain methods of distribution.[85] Looking back on the experience, Grierson would say, "As independent producers must testify, it is foolish to be asking the exhibitors for favours where a matter that touches the *élan vital* of the nation is concerned."[86]

With hindsight one can wonder, too, if the operation of a studio was necessary or even desirable; certainly it contributed a high fixed expense while the slow returns were awaited. The goals of using regional subjects and location shooting conflicted with the impulse to keep the studio floor space in use to justify the overhead.

Finally, there was Grierson's lack of commercial feature background plus Baxter's inexperience in administering a whole program of films. Even when the strategy looked interesting and imaginative, as Grierson's planning invariably did, the actual implementation of the ideas may have been riddled with errors. There are indications in the production and distribution of the films that suggest this. Whatever the case, if Grierson could be convincing about what might be done with a Group 3, eventually he failed to prove it through demonstration.

In the summer of 1953 he became ill with tuberculosis. It was not a serious bout—no surgery was performed—but he did spend two or three weeks in the hospital.[87] Perhaps there was a lingering recuperation or a recurrence of the illness. At any rate, late in 1954[88] or early in 1955,[89] he left Group 3. During the first months of 1956, Balcon closed the Ealing studio and sold it to B.B.C. Television. Baxter subsequently became head of Wales Television.[90] Eventually Grierson would make his own way to the new medium.

# 12 ✈ INTERIM (1955–57)

The years between Grierson's departure from Group 3 and the beginning of *This Wonderful World* on Scottish Television were the only ones since 1927, when he started at the Empire Marketing Board, in which Grierson did not hold a position that occupied him centrally and in which he was not at the center of some ongoing project to advance the cause of film and media in the public interest. Though much too young at the age of fifty-seven to be contemplating retirement, without a central focus he seemed to engage aimlessly in various desultory activities. The first alternative—in many ways opposition—to the Griersonian tradition of documentary shorts emerged during these years in a movement known as Free Cinema. Its origins go back to a shift in the British film criticism scene that began shortly before Grierson came on at the Central Office of Information.

## Critical Spokesmanship

The short-lived Free Cinema production of the late fifties originated with a group of young Oxonians who first attacked the films of the now middle-aged Grierson men (the majority of whom had come down from Cambridge, some twenty years earlier). In 1947 they founded the magazine *Sequence*, to which Grierson, curiously, wrote a welcome—though belated, guarded, and brief. Here it is in its entirety: "'Sequence' is brave, irreverent and new, and I have a strong suspicion it looks like a new generation coming up. Speaking as an old-time operator in this field—with wounds to show—I give its editors my blessing, for what it is worth. I leave the salute proper to someone younger." Evidently the younger someone was Philip Mackie, who seemed to be glancing over his shoulder at his elder as he wrote: "And now, fresh and unscarred, into the ring step these brash young men from Oxford—Peter Ericsson, Gavin Lambert, Lindsay Anderson [and later Karel Reisz] to state anew what the fight is all about. Their function is painful but necessary. Critical principles ossify in the hands of pundits, the experienced backward-lookers; for the good of its soul, creative art needs to be looked at with an eye ever-new and ever-young."[1] Whatever his age, Mackie clearly pointed ahead to a critical schism and intellectual jousting that would reach a climax in the mid-fifties.

In 1949 the traditional documentary house organ, *Documentary News Letter*, died. *Sequence* lasted until 1952, although Gavin Lambert left it in 1949 to become editor of *Sight and Sound*, published by the British Film Institute. Penelope Houston, another of the *Sequence* group, joined him there in 1953. Naturally they brought to *Sight and Sound* many of their earlier enthusiasms and prejudices. The new films coming out of Europe, insufficiently admired film "poets" (John Ford and Humphrey Jennings), and Free Cinema, when it became available, were celebrated. What was regarded as the bland politeness of the British feature and the dull didacticism of the documentary were watched over with distrustful attention. Regarding documentary films, Lindsay Anderson (later) wrote:

> Energetic and radical in their youth, the surviving members of Grierson's band of pioneers (many of them now established in positions of influence) have abandoned the treatment of contemporary life in their films. This retreat they are apt to rationalize: there are no problems today—or the problems are different—things are more complex—we must think dialectically, internationally, intellectually. . . . Yet people still exist, and housing problems, and night mails—as well as Teddy Boys, new schools, automation, strikes and sex crimes. All these are subjects for documentary, and of the right kind: the human kind.[2]

Since the first showing of a full Free Cinema program didn't occur until 1956, after Grierson had left Group 3 and that organization had expired, the warfare was initially largely polemical. What Free Cinema was for and against, however, was clearly outlined in Anderson's first films and fleshed out in his writings. Politically somewhere in the area of the New Left, it was also part of what would be called the Angry Young Men of the arts—it antedated, in fact, those in theater and literature.

It was *against* the dull gray conformity that accompanied the welfare state—the loss of individuality, of eccentricity, of beauty. It resented the continuance of class distinctions which limited opportunities in education and employment to the few. It was anti the establishment that controlled the state, the church, the communication media, and which it felt had reduced the populace to a vegetable-like mass conditioned not to think and feel but merely to produce and consume. In short, it didn't much like the collective life, however comfortable materially, that the Grierson films had urged and may have helped bring about. Free Cinema was not for everyone working together to make the system function better.

It was *for* asking some basic questions about the system, and most likely altering that system in radical ways. It was for the working class but not so much as workers as individuals, for lively and vigorous expression of feeling—in the popular arts, in styles of dress, in love-making, in beery conversation, and in any other way one might declare one's particular humanity and thumb one's nose at decency, duty, and authority once in a while. As can perhaps be inferred, the position, as it would develop in manifestoes and films, bore resemblances to the preceding ideas of D. H. Lawrence.

The Free Cinema stance shortly provoked debate, which was carried on most spiritedly by Anderson and Grierson themselves, with others pot-shotting from time to time. It concerned first of all the proper functioning of criticism, and then the value of Free Cinema as theory and force. (Grierson never wrote about the Free Cinema films specifically, possibly out of a kind of courtesy, or indifference, but one can doubt that he liked them much.) In the April–June 1954 issue of *Sight and Sound*, a piece appeared by Grierson, who was then still cohead of Group 3, which was introduced by an editorial comment explaining that he had been invited to contribute a regular independent column over the next year. He had chosen to write a series of commentaries on the state of contemporary film criticism, to be entitled "A Review of Reviews." Deputy editor Penelope Houston (if it was she; Gavin Lambert was not listed on the masthead) continued: "Having, as it were, invited a knife in the back, the editors would stress the usual proviso—the opinions expressed here are not necessarily their own."

The disclaimer was hardly necessary. Rather than a knife Grierson took up immediately what proved to be more nearly a broadsword. Writing as a producer he began, "For my part I accuse the critics of standing on the side lines waiting for the producers to stir up the new phases of film. I say let them help stir, as of course they can. . . . The big thing around the corner is never the criticism but always the discovery." In case the reader wasn't quite clear who all was included in his accusation Grierson offered this guidance:

> One great sinner in this respect has been *Sight and Sound* itself. Anderson recently has been telling us how wonderful Stroheim was and how weak our present-day stuff is in comparison. Well, some of us knew how good Stroheim was when he first came along, and we said so, and we fought his battles for him at the right time. Now, when these younger people come along to tell us, not only what we already knew, but what we actually discovered for them, I have the odd thought that they would be doing better to discover something for themselves in the here and now.[3]

In the July–September issue Grierson continued in much the same vein, establishing firmly that he was aiming at the former *Sequence* and present *Sight and Sound* group. For that issue Anderson reported on Cannes and the lack of success of Group 3's *Man of Africa* there, and wrote a full and sensitive reappraisal of Humphrey Jennings's major work, which was far from being in the main line of Grierson documentary and which, in some ways, would serve as models for Free Cinema films. In that issue, too, Richard Griffith, Grierson's long-time supporter, now curator of the Museum of Modern Art Film Library in New York City, had praised his first "Review of Reviews" and complimented him for bouncing lumps of hard Glasgow rock off heads that needed it.

By the October–December *Sight and Sound* Anderson had readied his reply to the "Review of Reviews" in the form of a long letter to the editor. Quotes from it may serve to suggest Grierson's main lines of attack as well as the somewhat patronizing tone which clearly infuriated Anderson.

Dr. Grierson talks a lot about "the Sight and Sound critics." But what does he take their values to be; what are the theories, or the fallacies, on which the critical writing in *Sequence* and *Sight and Sound* is based? I am charmed to have stimulated Lady Elton [she had written a letter which Grierson included in his July–September column; it criticized, among other aspects of *Sight and Sound*'s treatment of documentary, a piece by Anderson: it was, in her view, "a slight to the several real poets in documentary to contend that Jennings was 'the only real poet.'"]: but what does *Dr. Grierson* think of my estimate of Humphrey Jennings? . . . What are the distinguished or emerging talents that the critics have wrongfully neglected? What of the directors first made known in this country through the pages of *Sight and Sound* and *Sequence*? Bresson, Becker, Visconti, Sucksdorff, Gremillon, Polonski [*sic*], Antonioni, Castellani, Rouquier, Franju, Broughton. . . . Were these not worth discovering?[4]

For his part, Grierson, in the "Review of Reviews" of that issue, alluded to the rising controversy by remarking that, "Comments on my first column have reminded me that criticism has as many facets as Mr. Baldwin's truth [presumably Stanley Baldwin, former Prime Minister] and the elephant of the Seven Blind Men of Benares. I blew in as a producer with a blast for a state of criticism which seemed to have given up the, to me, essential process of discovery; but others with other interests equally essential to them insist on a widening of my own range of criticism on first principles."

In the next, and final, column, Grierson returned to the fray, unrepentant and also unresponsive to Anderson's "straight questions." "I watch the bright young fellows who are bright about everything except that they have nothing new to believe in and nothing new to say," he wrote. "They will discover nothing, because they are dedicated to the thought that exploration and discovery in the past only discovered a world which somehow swamped their vanities." Instead there was, he believed, "an order to be grasped and an inspiration to be given," and he thought it was "to be found yes, simply, where the people are and not in the concerns of the orders or individuals who batten on their aspirations, or for that matter are being crushed by their progress."

In more direct response to Anderson, he concluded the column with a "Footnote on Recent Correspondence":

You may have noted a certain amount of brawling in the back alleys of this august quarterly. It was, I am afraid, pitched on too excited and quarrelsome a note for the public exchange. It appears that I started it by talking of the teddy boys of criticism, which shows what a phrase will do. I was, in the result, apparently much righter than ever I expected to be, except that the phrase did invite a smarter and less unhappy answer. Nor am I alone involved. There was a claim to discovery of a lot of important films and people, or at least of having introduced them to this country. I would not for a moment diminish any effort or achievement in that direction, but, on the whole, I think that a balanced judgment and considered statement would have found time to share the honor with, let us say, Miss Olwen Vaughan of the New London Film Society.

A laconic footnote was appended by the editor (Gavin Lambert listed as editor; Houston now listed as associate): "To save correspondence on this subject: three of the twenty-eight films mentioned by Mr. Anderson were first shown in Britain by the New London Film Society ('Los Olvidados,' 'Farrebique,' and 'La Regle du Jeu')."[5] So ended the critical exchange, though Grierson's probable response to the Free Cinema films was anticipated by a passing comment in that last column. He had been screening "a lot of old documentary material," he wrote (no doubt in preparation for the B.B.C. retrospective mentioned earlier), and confessed that it didn't seem to him "that the young fellows [were] shooting any better than their elders shot with Devries twenty years ago."[6]

## Free Cinema

We can wonder if the young fellows' shooting that Grierson was thinking of included Lindsay Anderson's *O Dreamland* (1954), which became the prototype Free Cinema film, and/or Guy Brenton's and Anderson's *Thursday's Children*, made at the same time. In any case, it was Anderson who, though Scottish, followed a practice usually associated with the French by starting to make films in order to demonstrate critical theory. And it was Anderson who became Free Cinema's proud, arrogant, and iconoclastic leader, the acknowledged spokesman for the demi-movement, articulating its aims, arguing and promoting much as Grierson had done a quarter-century earlier. The other principal filmmakers who gathered in loose configuration around, or at least alongside him were Tony Richardson, Karel Reisz, cameraman Walter Lassally, and sound man John Fletcher. Anderson himself saw that "the division between generations that was apparent with *Sequence* [was] equally apparent in its film-making extension through a movement like Free Cinema. There has been no handing on," he continued; "instead, there's a sort of war between the generations. . . ."[7]

After the Free Cinema films had risen above ground, David Robinson, writing about documentary filmmakers generally, observed, "Among them there is often too little regard for one another's aspirations; the Free Cinema people look jealously at Shell, where they are actually *paid* for making films, and where they spend more on a single shot than all the Free Cinema films have cost together; while Sir Arthur Elton calls Free Cinema 'sad and dull' and Grierson finds it 'baby stuff.'"[8] It was in fact the lack of economic base for Free Cinema that puzzled and annoyed Grierson most, because of its illogic.[9] When Anderson later was asked what was "free" about the cinema he tried to create, he replied, "All the films were made without reference to any kind of commercial considerations, without reference to demands of distributors or producers. They were entirely the free expression of the people who made them, which is relatively rare in the cinema, certainly rare in the British cinema."[10] How can the most expensive art form in existence be "free," Grierson would have asked? How can one attack the establishment, which might otherwise sponsor, and ignore the entertainment tastes of the audiences, who might pay to see, and still pay for production?

A temporary answer was that the first Free Cinema films (*O Dreamland* [1954], Lindsay Anderson; *Momma Don't Allow* [1955], Karel Reisz and Tony Richardson; *Together* [1955], Lorenza Mazzetti and Denis Horne) were partly sponsored by the British Film Institute (which also published *Sight and Sound*). The ubiquitous Michael Balcon chaired the B.F.I. Experimental Production Committee which dispensed the grants. The funding source consisted of a small proportion of the money returned to British production from the entertainment tax on theater admissions. Asked if the filmmakers made any money at all out of it, Anderson answered "Oh, no. I mean later some of the films that were shown under that banner were commissioned [e.g., *Every Day Except Christmas* (1957), Anderson; *We Are the Lambeth Boys* (1959), Reisz—by the Ford Motor Company], and one was paid to make them, but it was never an economical operation. The distribution of short films is such that they can't really make money. That's really why it came to an end."[11] Point, set, match for Grierson.

Though at the time Grierson did not write about Free Cinema

297

films specifically, later he did write a perceptive paragraph on the subject in which he concluded with the suggestion that Free Cinema had probably not ended but more likely had metamorphosed.

> Here a note in parenthesis about the group which called itself Free Cinema. It is easy to dismiss it but in my point of view it will turn up again in more powerful form. It was an attempt to fill the gap left by the after-war failure of government sponsorship but in fact it found no alternative source of finance for ambitious documentary films and perished like the French *avant garde* in the late twenties and for the same reasons. Its origins were mixed. It was partly influenced by the neo-realist movement in Italy and by the *Nouvelle Vague* in France. It reflected—oddly in Britain—something of the spiritual pessimism of a defeated France. It was conscious too of the neo-anarchism of the beatnik movement in America. In so far as it was English it was close to the lower middle-class protest against upper-class privilege of the so-called Angry Young Men. In so far as it adopted a working-class motif its affection was a little like the Jewish affection for the Negro in the United States. What was best in it, and most native, turned up in the theatre with two or three very considerable talents—John Osborne, Arnold Wesker, etc.—to give it reality and with an economic root that proved a practical one. I haven't a doubt that you will hear of it again as the group's success in the theatre emerges as a phenomenon of the commercial cinema.[12]

And it was thus that it happened. The first Free Cinema program was shown in February 1956; Osborne's seminal play, *Look Back in Anger*, opened three months later at the Royal Court Theatre (directed by Tony Richardson, incidentally). Because of the lesser costs of live theatrical production, it was true, as Anderson later said and maybe then anticipated, "that the break through the accepted cliché of middle-class drama came before the breakthrough in the cinema."[13] Fused with "angry" theater and literature, Free Cinema turned into the cluster of social-realist features that began with *Room at the Top* (1958, Jack Clayton), continued with the screen version of *Look Back in Anger* (1959, Richardson), *Saturday Night and Sunday Morning* (1960, Reisz), *A Kind of Loving* (1962, John Schlesinger, an Oxford classmate of Richardson's), *The Loneliness of the Long Distance Runner* (1962, Richardson), among others, and ended, or at least became diffused, after Anderson's first feature, *This Sporting Life* (1963).

The transition of Free Cinema into features seems not unlike the earlier move of documentary into the wartime and postwar semi-documentaries, the regional and socially conscious Ealing comedies, and the best of the Group 3 films. If in those instances the original documentary impulses were brought to larger audiences in the cinemas, they were also weakened and ultimately checked. Looking back near the end of his career, Grierson still (or again) felt that in the long view there was more freedom and artistic control within government for filmmakers with a sense of social purpose than within the commercial entertainment industry.[14] By the mid-fifties, B.B.C. Television had arrived and was the only substantial sponsor of films in the public interest. Though Grierson would turn to the new medium, the opportunity opened for him not at the governmental B.B.C. but with its commercial rival, the Independent Television Authority.

## Personal Life and Additional Activities

These interim years between leaving Group 3 and starting his own television show must surely have been the saddest and most uncertain Grierson had ever experienced. The tuberculosis or its effects may have lingered; his drinking seems to have become very heavy. His brilliance took on a perversity, it was said, with his arguments becoming hard to follow as he jumped from one idea to another in speech and in writing.[15] He could—remembered Norman McLaren, who saw quite a bit of him at festivals around this time, especially at the Brussels Festival of 1957—be "brutal" and a "boor."[16] The principal problem may have been that he was unemployed, and broke as well.

"There was never a time," Grierson had once written proudly, "when anyone could say of the documentary people that they took personal advantage from the work they did, or served their own comfort."[17] As for Grierson himself in this regard, Basil Wright would say that during his career he had made less money than one would have thought possible.[18] At this time of desperate finances and morale, a huge income tax bill, accumulated over several years, was presented to him.[19] Evidently he appealed to Arthur Elton, who refused to loan him cash but did give him tax credit notes with which he could pay off the tax. (Legg is said to have remarked that Elton would give Grierson the shirt off his back but not the money to buy one.) Attentive to business matters himself, Elton was always uneasy about Grierson's casualness concerning money; Margaret Ann Elton said that Arthur hovered over Grierson, quizzing his accountant and keeping an eye on his affairs. Margaret Ann also said that, during part of this period at least, Grierson was "living on crumbs" in Scotland.[20] Grierson himself would subsequently put a brave front on this wretched time. (Forsyth Hardy thought he had completely erased it from his memory.)[21] As a television celebrity, he later told an interviewer that he had "decided to get out of the rat race of filmmaking at 55; that's the outside limit." He "found a 17th-century ruin on the Marquis of Lansdowne's estate in Wiltshire—actually a miller's cottage . . . patched it up and retired there—officially."[22]

This was of course the lowest point, not the quiet end of a long career. From this bottom Grierson picked himself up when he sold Lord Roy Thomson, the newspaper and broadcasting tycoon, on his idea for a television series. "Along came ITV" [Independent Television Authority had been renamed Independent Television], was the way he put it, "with the offer of *This Wonderful World*. I agreed to do a few programs to keep my hand in," he said.[23] It was his "sinew," observed Arthur Elton, that made Grierson admirable.[24]

What seemed to occupy Grierson's attention most during this otherwise bleak time was the reconstitution of the Films of Scotland Committee. Fifteen years earlier, he had supervised the series of Scottish films out of Film Centre, his last big project before leaving to become film commissioner of Canada. With the outbreak of war Films of Scotland Committee ceased to function. It lay dormant until early in 1955, when it was re-formed by the Scottish Council (Development and Industry) in consultation with the Secretary of State for Scotland. Its chairman was Sir Alexander B. King, who owned the Caledonian Associated Cinemas; its treasurer was Sir Hugh Fraser, of Glasgow (later Lord Fraser of Allander), who owned Harrod's department store and whose initial gift served to finance the project. Among others on the committee, along with Grierson, was Neil Patterson, the Scottish novelist who had recently become a much-sought-after screen writer. Forsyth Hardy was appointed director and, in the spring of 1955, an office opened in Edinburgh.

The aim of the committee was to facilitate and promote the making of films in and about Scotland. Like Film Centre, it did not itself produce.[25] From the outset and afterwards, Grierson remained active on the committee. Though he did not attend the regular business meetings, at the production sessions his unimpaired ability to analyze a problem until he found the central issue and its solution kept him naturally in a position of informed leadership. Often critical and impatient with particular actions (or inactions), he nonetheless supported wholeheartedly the committee's work.[26] And he continued to serve on it throughout the television years.

# 13 ❧ SCOTTISH TELEVISION (1957–68)

## Background

Even though the British Broadcasting Corporation had been telecasting since 1946, this quasi-governmental monopoly, supported by a tax on television sets (collected by the General Post Office, Grierson's onetime employer), had not attracted anything like the audience that would develop when commercial broadcasting was permitted to operate alongside B.B.C.–TV in 1955. As conscious or unconscious preparation for his own next endeavor, Grierson commenced writing about television in 1954, while still at Group 3.

In regard to the independent service then under discussion, after stating his misgivings he added, "Now that I have demonstrated the difficulty of the commercial case, let me say immediately that I am for it. I am for it in spite of the danger. Perhaps I am for it especially because of the danger. I wish the commercial-television people had not made a case for their eminent respectability. I wish they had made a case for their vulgarity." He felt the question really was whether, "with its orthodox educational and cultural policies, the B.B.C. has put life at a greater distance than it would be if it were, like the movies and the newspapers, closer to the people, commoner about its function, and altogether more exciting in its habit."

He explained that he was involved in the argument about television "as any film man must be." For, "when all is said, it is just another way of presenting films without the cumbersome process of carting them around in cans and projecting them with fuss, expense and danger in theaters all over the country." No doubt smarting from the distribution problems being faced by Group 3, he added that "television provides now, and will more and more provide, an outlet for the creative talent which does not make or want to make, the grade of commercial cinema." And, even more precisely prophetic, he wrote: "Since television represents the alternative basic economy for film-makers, the more certainly must they turn to it."[1]

A bill to create an Independent Television Authority had been introduced into Parliament in March 1954. In July of that year it became law. Scarcely fully commercial in the American manner, the I.T.A. was set up as a corporation something like the British Broadcasting Corporation (begun with radio as a monopoly in 1923) to own and operate television transmitters. The government retained the right to regulate advertising. Most of its broadcasts were prepared and presented by privately financed program contractors from their own studios. Paying the I.T.A. for the privilege of being broadcast, the contractors met their costs by selling spot announcements— seven minutes of advertising in any one hour. (This compared with eight minutes per hour in the United States, twelve minutes in prime time.) Control of program content by a sponsor was forbidden. Responsible minister for both the I.T.A. and the B.B.C. was the postmaster general.

Less than a week after the act was passed, the government appointed the members of the Independent Television Authority. Chairman was Sir Kenneth Clark, head of the Arts Council, who had also been director of the National Gallery, professor of fine art at Oxford, and an early wartime head of the Films Division of the Ministry of Information preceding Grierson's friend Jack Beddington. Among Authority members was film critic Dilys Powell. Director-general was Sir Robert Fraser, Grierson's boss during his stint at the Central Office of Information. The deputy director-general was Bernard C. Sendall, whom Grierson had more or less supplanted at the C.O.I.

The plan was to establish a nationwide network covering the main population centers and then to construct additional stations in the principal metropolitan areas. Service was begun as soon as possible with a temporary station in London on South Norwood

Hill, known officially as the Croydon Station, going on the air in September 1955. A second transmitter, near Lichfield, began broadcasting in February 1956, serving the industrial Midlands. The third, in northern England, was near Bolton and covered an area including Liverpool and Manchester. Together the three stations served some 24 million people, or about half the country's population. In the fall of 1956 a station for northeastern England was opened, followed by Scottish and Welsh stations in the fall of 1957.[2]

By the end of 1955, television had only a light and gentle impact on British life. It was still very far from being the great popular institution and all-powerful influence it had become in the United States. There were fewer than five million television sets in Britain, and only half a million or so in the London area equipped to receive the new channel.[3] But with the introduction of I.T.A., the sale of television sets reached a new high, and the economic potential opened by the competitive sights and sounds was becoming clear. Though the I.T.A. producing companies at first lost heavily, soon they were making good profits.

The Authority required each program company to produce from its own resources only 15 percent of its total program output. The other 85 percent could be taken from the national network, which linked up all the transmitting stations. Owing to the high costs of production, each company was necessarily dependent on all the other companies for a large proportion of its programs, and the network was dominated by the four big companies which among them provided service to London, the Midlands, and the North— Associated Television, Associated-Rediffusion, A.B.C. Television, and Granada T.V. Network.[4] Formed to provide programs in central Scotland, Scottish Television became the fifth largest of the broadcast companies.

It was Lord Roy Thomson, fourth-generation Canadian of Scottish ancestry, who won the television franchise for Scotland. Having started his press and broadcasting empire with one radio station at Timmins, Ontario, in the early thirties, gradually he acquired over ninety newspapers in North America, Great Britain, Africa, the Caribbean area, and Australia.[5] In 1953 he purchased the *Scotsman*[6] and moved to Scotland in 1954. In 1956 he obtained 80 percent of Scottish Television. The latter, operating on its first license through 1963 as the single I.T.A. outlet for Scotland, was phenomenally successful.[7]

At some point, Grierson evidently talked Thomson into letting him produce a series of weekly half-hour programs made up of short films and film excerpts from all over the world verbally laced together by Grierson as a sort of film jockey. It seems quite likely that he, with his constant attention to the press, would have known Thomson from Canadian days. Anyway, Grierson had once more found a "prince," a sponsor who would finance some of the things he wanted to get done in this life, successor to Tallents and King and the others.

Two months after Scottish Television went on the air in August 1957, Grierson's *This Wonderful World* appeared. The first program was aired in Scotland on October 11; a year later, on Monday evening, September 15, 1958, the series began to appear on the English network.[8]

### *This Wonderful World* (1957–66)

Fittingly, each program began with a sputnik-inspired design which faded into flowing clouds to the accompaniment of ethereal music. Turning from the universe spread before him, Grierson would look directly into the camera—"a small grey Ariel with eyes glittering enthusiastically behind his spectacles"[9]—and intone the standard opening: "I welcome you again from the Theatre Royal in Glasgow to our program *This Wonderful World*. We bring you some of the rich and strange things—the wonderful things—the camera has seen." (Standard close was "And that's all for tonight.")

Among other things, the series was roughly comparable to a global tour. Bits and pieces of film—rarely a whole one even when short—were connected with two or three brief talks by Grierson, often personal recollections of his experiences of places and persons touched upon in the films. If they were in a foreign language, he used the "international track" (music and sound effects) with narration read in English. But he tried to stick to films where no dialogue or narration was necessary. Perhaps he favored the Eastern European nations slightly—partly no doubt because of the high quality of their shorts, but one would guess, too, because of the unfamiliarity and accompanying suspiciousness of most of his audience. Grierson was conscious, Hardy said, that the urge to experiment in documentary had passed from Britain to those countries where the young filmmakers were encouraged and stimulated at film schools,[10] Poland

and Czechoslovakia as notable examples. The National Film Board of Canada was well represented, too, of course.

But in general and characteristically, he used only those films which coincided with his own notions of positive value, and was more interested in film groups and movements developing abroad than in individual films of quality.[11] Animation and abstraction—what he called "squiggly film"—also were allowed a curiously high number of samples from an old documentarian. The subjects ranged from crystal formation, a gymnasts' meeting in Prague, the Indianapolis automobile race, a dancing Negro, huge machines in the building of the city of Kitimat (Canada), drops of water, and drifting bubbles.

The commercial break could be moved around to suit him if the films weren't too long. On occasion Grierson insisted that there be no interruption during the program. The standard system was to break midway through. Sometimes he repeated particularly popular films, but he would redo the whole show with a new approach. Running throughout was Grierson's habitual educational aesthetic, if one can call it that: the recognition of excellence—whether expressed by boxer Joe Louis, artist Leonardo da Vinci, or the latest scientific achievement. "Everybody appreciates the romantic and the appeal of the far horizon," he acknowledged, sounding like a latter-day Flaherty. "You don't often change people's interests by teaching them. You do it by interesting them in new interests."[12] He was given a completely free hand by Thomson and Scottish Television. He was told to be as highbrow as he liked.[13]

Initially Grierson was merely going to produce but, he said, he got so bored with others' writing and with the intended host that he took on both jobs for the first program. Finding that he could play the MC role—which he "would have thought unlikely"—he continued to do the whole job during the ten-year run of the series.[14] Even so, it didn't absorb his still-prodigious energy—he worked at it only three weeks out of four.[15]

At first the whole show was produced in Glasgow, but Grierson's chest was bothered by the Glasgow winter, and he soon fell into a strange triangular commuting. He lived near Calne, Wiltshire, which was not far from Cardiff, where all the preparation of the material was done in an office maintained by Thomson, and then the show was taped by the technical staff in Glasgow. It was said that having developed a taste for Irish ale he used to stop off at Shannon on the way to Glasgow and back.

The actual recording took only two days a month—four programs at a time. The search for films, research, writing, and editing took the rest of the time. From near the beginning, Olwen Vaughan was Grierson's film scout, and she sought out and passed along for his review those items which seemed particularly promising. She had known Grierson for years—her father, a pastor in Liverpool, had run a film society out of his church, and Grierson had picked him up among his early converts. Ms. Vaughan had acquired a wide acquaintance with short-film producers throughout the world which gave her an advantage in competition. She did a great deal of traveling in Europe, attending film festivals and contacting producers and distributors directly. Though operating on a very small budget, Grierson was able to pay as much as the B.B.C.—usually about £10 per minute but more if he thought the film worth it; e.g., £300 for a Polish short that he particularly liked and that the B.B.C. was bidding on.[16]

Grierson himself did a lot of scouting, too, a familiar figure at European festivals, seated at a sidewalk cafe sipping gin from a coffee cup in midmorning with couriers running back and forth to report on films seen. He attended Edinburgh annually, frequently appearing on panels and the like; Brussels in 1957; was chairman of the juries in Venice (1956—no grand prize given), Cork (1958, where Frances Flaherty was also on hand for a retrospective of her husband's films),[17] Oberhausen in 1959 and 1960, and so on. He also regularly visited the main film-producing centers in Europe and farther afield.[18] Friends all over the world offered suggestions for his programs.[19] All in all, he must have seen thousands of films—an average of about twenty a week, he said.[20]

The information needed for his background remarks was researched in Cardiff by freelancers, the best available on the particular subject, and Grierson was said to be meticulous about accuracy. He did the writing and worked with an editor in excerpting the films—Harley Jones at first, who left to teach film production at a university in Wales, and then David Lewis. Grierson gave Jones a boost after he had gone by including in the series a film he had made about a boat. (At the time Grierson himself had a deep sea fishing motorboat which he very much enjoyed—a real beauty it was said to be.)

The advertising was handled in Glasgow, and Grierson didn't seem to worry about the business aspects—the amount or rate of advertising, the times the program was aired.[21] It tended to appear later and later—6:00 P.M. in Scotland (high tea time) but as late as 11:40 P.M. in London.

Though no one had expected it to achieve high audience ratings, *This Wonderful World* was a modestly substantial success. Even more surprising to those in the television industry, it held its audience of from four to seven million over the ten years of the series, as big at the end as at the beginning, according to Grierson.[22] It was the only production of Scottish Television to be shown regularly in England, and Grierson's name was listed in a *TV Times* personality contest.

It was the "capacity to surprise which gave his programme a magnetic appeal," thought Hardy. "He could and did, introduce . . . films, which, because of subject or treatment, would have been considered too difficult for showing in cinemas; but because he had gained the confidence of his audience, he was able to persuade them to accompany him on journeys into unfamiliar mental or aesthetic territories. Television had made it possible for him to reach a mass audience, composed of thousands of small family groups to whom he could talk in an intimate, persuasive way."[23] For his part, Grierson found that the special characteristics of television, its immediacy and directness, offered an unprecedented opportunity for public communication. Because of his TV job he felt like a French village curé, he said. People would come up to him and chat, discuss subjects that had been touched upon in recent "sermons," as it were. "Well Doc, you were fucking good on Leonardo the other night," one somewhat scruffy elderly gentleman remarked as he passed him on the street. It was not that he was a celebrity exactly—unlike actress Barbara Mullen, his brother-in-law John Taylor's wife, who was a star and public figure. That role was natural to her, Grierson said, and she enjoyed that; he wouldn't like it, would find it exhausting.[24]

During the television years, Grierson continued writing his book review-essays for *Scotland* magazine; they appeared in many of the issues between 1955 and 1959. His activity with the Films of Scotland Committee continued as well, and to several of its films he contributed more than advice and guidance. For a film on hydroelectric development in the Highlands, *Rivers at Work* (1960), he wrote and spoke the commentary. For *Seawards the Great Ships* (1960) he wrote the treatment and selected as director the young American experimental filmmaker Hilary Harris on the basis of some of his films Grierson had seen at festivals. It won an Academy Award as best live-action short.[25] A year later, Grierson prepared the outline for *The Heart of Scotland* (1961), about his native county, Stirlingshire, which was directed by Laurence Henson, who had worked with him on his television programs.[26]

One final bit of activity outside *This Wonderful World* did not come to fruition. He made an offer (said to be "very good") to the theatrical distributor of Eisenstein's *Ivan the Terrible, Part Two* to show it complete on a national television broadcast.[27] This harked back to Grierson's pre-documentary days and is part of considerable evidence of his sustained interest in and respect for Eisenstein's work.

## Documentary Veterans

During Grierson's Scottish Television years, the old group of documentarians were still about and pursuing more or less the earlier tradition, but with the momentum now run down and the efforts fragmented. There were still a few companies, like Realist and Anvil, which were said to maintain very much the Griersonian outlook in their work. Edgar Anstey was at British Transport; Donald Alexander at the National Coal Board; Stuart Legg and Arthur Elton at Shell.[28] It was a dwindling continuation, and it no longer had a leader. Interestingly though, working at Independent Television as Grierson was doing, was Sidney Newman, a senior producer at I.T.V. who then transferred to B.B.C.–TV as head of its drama division. One of Grierson's earliest trainees at the National Film Board, Newman would say that all he knew he had learned from Grierson.[29] If that was true, it was fitting that he would become Canadian film commissioner from 1970 to 1975.

In 1958 Sir Stephen Tallents died and Grierson wrote a tribute, published in the September 23 issue of the *Times*. A *Spectator* review of Arthur Calder-Marshall's book on Flaherty, *The Innocent Eye* (Grierson's phrase, with the biography based on research done by Rotha and Wright), was another obligation of these years that led Grierson to look at the past rather than to the future.

## Anniversaries, Honors, and Trips

Recognition came to him, too, for past achievement. In August 1959, the British Film Institute produced a film on the occasion of "The Thirty Years of British Documentary" season at the National Film Theatre. It was a filmed record of Grierson's address, in which he outlined the basic intentions of the early documentary filmmakers and the influence British documentary had since had on the rest of the world. In June 1961, he was made a Commander of the British Empire (C.B.E.). According to Stuart Legg, it wasn't until the Scots had submitted Grierson's name for an honor that the English realized that they had failed to recognize him and added his name to the Queen's Birthday Honor's List.[30]

In 1962 Grierson made his first return to the United States since he had been eased out of the country by the Department of Justice in 1946. The occasion was the establishment of a North Carolina Film Board. Apparently there was some stickiness about getting a visa even then, though the climate of Cold War and McCarthyism had changed, and it was said that Grierson insisted that the U.S. government take the initiative—that he would not humble himself to plead away the old suspicions. Evidently the person who broke the impasse and got the Department of State to issue Grierson a travel visa was Maggie Dent, a former employee of the United Nations who was well-connected in Washington, film society leader, and resident of North Carolina. According to *Variety*, Grierson's visit was sponsored jointly by a symposium on "Revolution in the Arts," the University of North Carolina–Chapel Hill Film Society, the Museum of Modern Art, and the Washington (D.C.) Film Council.[31] At the symposium, mass media critic Gilbert Seldes also spoke and both were introduced by Grierson's old friend Richard Griffith, curator of motion pictures at the Museum of Modern Art.

The patron of the film board idea was North Carolina governor Terry Sanford, who had come into office in January 1961. He appointed a fourteen-member advisory board, among whom were educators, ranging from college presidents to sociologists, and mass media representatives, including newspaper and television executives. Four members had film background and experience: Paul Green, Pulitzer Prize–winning playwright and former motion picture script writer; George Stoney, distinguished documentarist and University of North Carolina alumnus; Borden Mace, of the text-book-educational film production company Heath De Rochemont; and Grierson. The four would be named a subcommittee on production standards.[32]

Talking with N.F.B. veteran James Beveridge in Canada on his way to North Carolina, Grierson seemed excited about the documentary prospects for the state. "Make it local," he said; "keep it local; exploit the local use of each subject."[33] According to Stoney, on his arrival in Chapel Hill, Grierson handled himself beautifully, charming all and sundry. Entering the meeting room in the State House, he singled out exactly the right painting for comment and made exactly the right comments about it.[34] The planning session evidently went smoothly and expeditiously. Grierson himself seemed favorably impressed as well as being sensible of the honor paid to him. After his return to England he wrote, "Why only the other day I was invited by the Governor of North Carolina to sit in on the drafting of a Foundation for his State. We started at nine o'clock in the morning and we had it formed and financed by telephone by eleven."[35]

As for his talk at the symposium, Stoney thought him in excellent form;[36] Seldes, on the other hand, felt he didn't add much—found him much more stimulating off the platform.[37] It is curious that Seldes and Grierson had never met before, since they were contemporaries, and their common interests in mass communication were well-known to each other.

Some evidence of the respect Grierson must have commanded in the setting up of the Film Board is evident in the fact that James Beveridge, whom Grierson had once considered as his possible successor as film commissioner of Canada, was invited to become first director of the North Carolina board. Grierson may well have been supported in this choice by Stoney, who respected and liked Beveridge. In any case, the Film Board started in September 1962 with Beveridge at its head.

Though perhaps as a result of its short life, the quality of the films commissioned by the board seems to have been undistinguished, including what would become the final series—on race relations in the state. Though painstakingly mild and noncommittal, the mere choice of subject seems to have raised hackles. When the comparatively liberal Governor Sanford was defeated in his bid for reelection, his term ended in January 1965, and the Film Board ended with it (in June of that year). A member of the Institute of

Government at the University observed that "Unfortunately, the fourteen-member Advisory Board, which might have been of considerable assistance at this point, has been convened only twice and, to date, has served in a negligible role."[38]

Following that visit to North Carolina, Stoney and Grierson traveled together back to New York. Though Grierson was on good behavior in Chapel Hill, drinking only beer, Stoney sensed that he was building up to what would become a monumental celebration of nostalgic return to a city he had always enjoyed.[39] The most spectacular single event was an evening at the Museum of Modern Art, in which host, Richard Griffith, and guest and speaker, Grierson, swayed down the aisle a bit late, and the latter delivered a talk notably lacking in his usual brilliance and wit—not to mention coherence. It was cause for profound embarrassment to his many friends who attended the evening.[40]

During his brief stay in the city, he managed to talk to film classes at Columbia University. He also attempted to peddle *This Wonderful World*, or the production of an American equivalent, to commercial and then to educational television without success. Shortly he returned home by way of Canada.

In August 1964 Grierson returned to Canada for the twenty-fifth anniversary of the Film Board, a sentimental occasion with all five former commissioners on hand. According to an observer, "It started with John Grierson. Trumpeters of the Sound Track Band delivered a fanfare. And the grand old man of documentary" entered to open the celebration. "Friends, civil servants, and creative people rose and applauded. The reception was warm [with a dance in the courtyard] and a little reverent. 'Don't believe the love feast,'" Grierson is quoted as saying, "after the speeches gave way to cocktails. 'They treat me like I was. . . . [*sic*] I thought at least someone would ask me for an autograph. I feel like Hindenburg [Paul von, president of Germany, 1925–34, who turned over the reins of government to the Nazi Party]; I'd sign anything.'"[41]

Two years later, he was back in Canada for six weeks to advise the board on setting up an international center for training young filmmakers from all over the world. About this project, he said that his advice to the Canadians would be "not to run a film school as such. Poland, Italy and Spain have them, but they're too technical and high falutin' for me."[42]

## Health and Change in Lifestyle

In the fall of 1967, Grierson became seriously ill with some sort of pneumonia and was in an oxygen tent for a time. Stoney recalled Grierson saying that the doctor put it to him that if he wanted to live a while longer he would have to give up smoke and drink. He said to himself that this is ridiculous to be in this situation and quit. After decades of being a bottle and three-packs-a-day man, as Stoney put it,[43] the abstinence wasn't easy. The hardest thing about stopping the drink, according to Forsyth Hardy, was for his system—which had depended on the steady stimulant—to adjust to the withdrawal.[44] It was six months before he could work, Grierson told Stoney, but the latter felt that he somehow enjoyed the struggle in his tough, quirky Scottish way, as one more test of his will, and of course of an extraordinary constitution.[45]

By general account, the change was remarkable; certainly he looked much better. Grierson was "[t]he first reformed drunk" he had ever seen, said Stoney, who "maintained/regained his edge."[46] A year later, Grierson was "more vigorous than ever, bouncing with energy," according to Norman McLaren.[47] Whereas he formerly faded off into an alcoholic mist from time to time, said Hardy, he now was able to go a whole day keeping his mind on a problem. Mrs. Hardy added that his manners were greatly improved, that he was not nearly so aggressive. (She used to dread being in the same room with him, she confessed.)[48]

The drinking had been perhaps partly dietary, Margaret Ann Elton thought. He used it for energy. There was more drink when he was seeing people and moving about; less at home and in a settled establishment. It was also part of his boulevardier and picaresque existence. He preferred to live at cafes and pubs; liked metropolitan or country—detested suburbs and cozy dinner for six with breaded veal cutlets prepared by the little wife. Even if one can agree with Lady Elton's insistence that the drinking was *not* out of neuroticism, it did play an important part in his life; it is a recurrent source of imagery in his writing. As far as his health was concerned, the doctors apparently agreed with Arthur Elton that the smoking may have done him more harm than the drinking, and one can wonder about the gallons of coffee that substituted for gin during the years following.[49]

## *John Grierson Presents* and the Last Years in Britain (1966–68)

The television series that had begun in October 1957 as *This Wonderful World* in July 1966 became *John Grierson Presents*, a phrase that had appeared on some of the late G.P.O. title credits after Grierson had established a reputation. Its format remained the same as that of the earlier show—Grierson introducing bits of film. In fact, aside from its name, about all that changed was the new opening logo, of film unfurling and piling up accompanied by cool jazz. It was thought to be not as popular as *This Wonderful World*,[50] and Grierson was admittedly bored with it.[51] By late 1968, he had recorded five or ten programs ahead, and early in 1969 he was teaching at McGill University in Montreal. By that time he had presented nearly four hundred programs and close to two hundred hours of film miscellany from all over the world.[52]

During Grierson's last season on television, he received the Golden Thistle Award, the trophy presented annually by the Films of Scotland Committee for "outstanding achievement in the art of the cinema." The presentation was made during the Edinburgh Festival in August. The topic of his Celebrity Lecture, "The Relationship Between the Political Power and the Cinema," had a familiar ring to it, and for the festival he also selected and narrated live a succession of extracts stretching back over the history of British documentary. Entitled "I Remember, I Remember," the whole program was recorded on film in Toronto in 1970 by Grierson's protégé and friend Grant McLean for his firm, Visual Education Centre, and will be discussed in the next chapter.

# 14 ➤ MCGILL UNIVERSITY (1969–72)

## Teaching

On January 3, 1969, the *Times* (London) reported that Grierson was flying to Canada to lecture on communications at McGill University. (He flew to Montreal on January 8.) As for giving up his television career, he was quoted as saying he "should have done [it] five years ago."[1] In fact, as early as 1966, he was considering the desirability of teaching at an American university.[2] Apparently the invitation to teach at McGill began at the instigation of the then-new head of the National Film Board, Hugo McPherson, formerly professor of English at Western Ontario University. He was interested in having Grierson return to the board for consultation. According to Donald Theall, chairman of the McGill Department of English, "it was a very last minute arrangement."[3] Evidently McPherson spoke to Theall about the possibility of Grierson being brought over in connection with a new Interdisciplinary Graduate Communications Programme being developed under the administrative responsibility of the English Department, and the latter cabled Grierson on December 18. He was hired as a visiting lecturer for one term.[4] McPherson would become director of the graduate program in communications following his resignation from the N.F.B. in 1970—Grierson's boss, as it were.

Two factors seemed to influence Grierson most strongly in his decision to turn to teaching near the end of his career. One was his acknowledgment that most of his life had been devoted to education in one form or another and that classroom teaching was central to training the leaders and thus determining the directions societies would follow. His colleague Theall confirmed this: "Grierson was fond of pointing out that his life work was conceived in the university and that, therefore, it was appropriate that he return to the university. He argued that education was the most important mass medium in our society. The documentary movement itself was the transformation of the motion picture into a conscious instrument of educational policy."[5]

Second was his curiosity about what young people were like, what they were thinking and feeling in the volatile end of the sixties, when the "generation gap" had become an accepted if disturbing part of life in the West, especially in North America. He expected to find that students all wanted to be personal, avant-garde filmmakers.[6] To an old friend, Marion Michelle, then editor of *A.I.D. News*, the bulletin of the International Association of Documentary Film Makers headquartered in Paris, he expressed his feelings about this matter.

> I suppose the idea was that I should lecture about films; and certainly there is a monstrous desire among North American students to learn how to make movies. To be frank I do not like the movement at all. I suspect it. They shout to me that the 'day of the cinema has at last arrived.' They mean by that, that the 8 mm. camera now comes so cheap (for North Americans) that every babe in arms can have a go. ... [W]hat I shout back is: "Who gives a good goddamn for the 8 mm. revolution if it is going to let loose on us 'THE 8 MM. MIND.'"[7]

The other student revolution he had not anticipated but was at least equally well prepared for was the wave of student protests, strikes, sit-ins, and the like occurring on campuses throughout North America. Growing out of resistance to the Vietnam War, this loosely coordinated student activity also aimed at toppling the military-industrial-educational complex they felt had dictated what they regarded as an immoral war abroad, and which tolerated poverty, injustice, and racial discrimination at home. Much of Grierson's teaching was intended to correct or add discipline to dissent, whatever its form: to educate and enlighten students in their pursuit of personal aesthetic expression on the one hand or, on the other, to provide some intellectual underpinning for the prevalent anarchic stirrings.

He seems to have taught three courses at McGill, including large lecture classes and a smaller seminar, and also a seminar at Carleton University in Ottawa. The first lecture class started with 150 or so in attendance and would subsequently swell to over 700. The seminar seemed to be limited to about 30. In an excellent recollection of these years, Elspeth Chisholm, radio broadcaster, documentary journalist, and teacher, observed, "The titles of his courses at McGill hardly described what he taught, for it was really *himself*, his lifetime of knowledge and wisdom. . . . [M]any who had enrolled hoping to become instant filmmakers . . . were at first disappointed, for he had no intention of talking to them about craft. He said, 'I'm not interested in making filmmakers out of them. At a *university*? Teach them to run a bloody camera? No, no—not when I would like, very humbly, to be allowed to instruct them about Plato and Kant and their application to modern society.'"[8] The Thealls added, "In his teaching, as he considered the aesthetic area, he developed a broad traditional and philosophic perspective which grew out of his early training, a training which blended with the tradition that had contributed to McGill, Toronto and other older Canadian universities."[9]

As for the political radicalism, Chisholm pointed out,

> He arrived at the height of student protest. Computers [calculators surely] had been thrown out of windows at neighbouring Sir George Williams University, and on McGill's campus, political science students were doing a sit-in, barricading their building. Grierson adapted this climate of revolt to his own uses as he did all events and persons, and told the would-be revolutionaries that he was all for it. Before they could catch their breath, he went on and said he doubted if they knew anything about successful revolutions, and proceeded to tell them. Control of the essentials, like the coke and food concessions, and the washrooms, was basic, or the established powers would take over. Discipline, which he thought they lacked, was another necessary ingredient.
>
> He likened the movement to the children's crusade, "and no good came of that. How can these kids pull a revolution off the sky? They've no relationship to the workers, and how you can make progress without a knowledge of human need, I don't know." He found them woefully short on knowledge of the past, classical grounding, and of real knowledge of political positions. "When they talk of Maoism,

their political naiveté astonishes. I've got neo-Trotskyites who haven't read Trotsky, and anarchists who don't know that anarchists don't unite. There aren't many Leninists or Stalinists, I note, for that means discipline."[10]

At the same time, speaking of his students and the way in which he felt they required his teaching method and accepted it, he said:

There's no fooling them. You can't start talking about aesthetic, at least I can't, without finding yourself into the damn nonsense about the sublime and the nature of comedy. You've got to get back to the anti-mony of Kant somewhere along the line. You can't talk about free-dom without getting back to Plato. If you're going to discuss the indi-vidual artist in relation to the state you'd better take account of Trotsky's *Literature and Revolution*. You'll find yourself inevitably having to tell them to go look at Arnold's *Culture and Anarchy*. How-ever it is, you find yourself returning to the authorities and you'll find them returning with you to the authorities.[11]

The seminars were apparently largely devoid of lecturing, however. A student might be assigned to do a presentation, after which dis-cussion prevailed. Chisholm reported that "[t]hose seminars were often battlegrounds, with normally docile people screaming at each other, at Grierson's instigation and to his quiet enjoyment." "Grier-son's theory was that they were a 'hollering generation' who had been bought off by parents and teachers, who had never really lis-tened to them. He arrived at this conclusion by probing and quiz-zing everyone. . . ."[12]

George Stoney, veteran U.S. documentary filmmaker who was in charge of the Challenge for Change program at the National Film Board for two years while Grierson was there, said Grierson did not come in as a big shot. He was intent on the new job (for him) of being a good teacher, rather than the old one of traveling around the country lecturing, though he could have made much more money at the latter at several hundred dollars per lecture. Grierson said he had done that. In fact, most of the students didn't know who he was, Stoney said; thought he was just some old English teacher interested in film over from Britain. During that first term, Stoney, Tom Daly, and Guy Glover—the latter two among the first of the N.F.B. re-cruits, who had known Grierson long and well—sat in on his lec-tures. After a few sessions, Grierson asked them not to come; said he found he was talking to them rather than to the students.[13]

"In their turn," Chisholm added,

the students were astonished by Grierson's vocabulary, his talent for
turning a cliché into a conundrum, his combination of conservatism
and radicalism, and his bluntness. . . . Maoism, he told them, was a
good enough revolutionary doctrine for the peasants of China, but
hardly suitable for industrialized North America. . . . [And he] insisted
on good classroom manners, something that other professors often did
not, and got them to sit up and keep their feet down when in his class.
He spotted one young man wearing a cap, who despite Grierson's glare,
remained oblivious until his professor slowly and carefully explained
to him, "Young man, it has just occurred to me that Dostoevsky wore
his hat indoors, and nobody objected. When you can write as well as
Dostoevsky, perhaps you may too. NOW TAKE IT OFF!!"[14]

In a book that grew out of the biographical film *Grierson*, produced by the National Film Board shortly after his death, there's a
considerable collection of quotes from McGill students about Grierson as teacher that were not used in the film—outtakes, you might
say. They were responding to questions like "Did you think his ideas
were rigid?" "Did you find in his lectures that he brought in a lot of
material, a lot of references beyond your own field, beyond your
range?" "Some people said he was very authoritarian. How did
those ideas seem to sit with you, with students—the idea of ordered
freedom, responsibility to the community, of the citizens?" The responses seem not to have been in answer to specific questions but
to have come out of free-flow recollections.

One student spoke of Grierson taking "a very determined interest in our poetry," inviting student poets to the little gatherings in
his apartment. A second added that later there was a complete
change in emphasis: "He wanted people who were going to teach.
He wanted activists. He didn't want to have anything whatever to
do with the so-called artists." Another student said that when she
told Grierson she was interested in history and teaching art, "He just
completely slashed my whole future. I was practically in tears when
I walked out of class." But then he "sort of supported me later on.
. . . stood behind me all the time, encouraging me and prompting."
"It was totally contradictory." These accounts suggest a condensed
repetition of Grierson's own earlier shifts in position, from formu-
lating an aesthetic for documentary in the early thirties to concentration on propaganda in the late thirties and first half of the forties.

319

Then there is the matter of filmmakers and filmmaking—the professionalism involved; the elite cadre who were not only in command of their medium but knew the film's subject matter better than the sponsor. One student remarked: "The year before, he had said that it was a lot of nonsense to give everybody cameras and let them go out, that shooting should be kept within some sort of professional framework. But then he really changed his ideas a lot. . . ." Another added: "The very last seminar he gave, he really got into a whole new thing, decentralizing media. All the discussions were centered around the idea of people going out into the community."[15] This change came about largely because of a communication experiment in India that he took part in, and that led him from a distrust of the Challenge for Change approach to enthusiastic support of it—matters to be dealt with shortly.

Students Grierson had a particular interest in he would see outside class. One form this took was weekly evenings with students held in his bed-sitting room. Elspeth Chisholm again provided a description of these occasions.

> [H]e gave them what he called "gentle booze" and cooked delicacies like his famous shrimps in clam aspic, or wild rice, and listened to their talk. The bar was copious, and helped them to sing "like the birds in the trees," while their host drank only coffee and was never seen to eat anything. [In following terms he offered only drink, in order to avoid the cleaning up that food required.][16] He would choose a shy one to talk to, open him up, and make the evening a memorable one for him. Never in their school years had a professor paid that kind of attention to them, heightening their sense of self-value.[17]

Grierson stayed at the Crescent Hotel, at 1214 Crescent Street, an unfashionable neighborhood within walking distance of campus; accommodations were modest, not to say a bit down-at-the-heel. Grierson seems to have been comfortable and to have enjoyed himself there. The hotel staff adored him, it was said, and looked after him—the chambermaids darned his socks.[18] Margaret Grierson did not come with him to Canada; she had to stay with her mother (whom Grierson was not overly fond of).[19] He said he didn't say it very loud, but he didn't mind—he liked to be on his own. He described himself as a solitary type and hotel rooms as his natural habitat.[20] Further, he seemed to like his hotel to be in urban surroundings. (When visiting the Chicago area as a consultant to the nontheatrical film distributor Films, Inc., headquartered in suburban Wilmette, he chose to stay in a large hotel in downtown Chicago rather than in a much more convenient and probably equally comfortable one in a nearby suburb.) In Montreal he seems to have had an active social life, seeing visitors and friends as well as students and faculty, and on one remembered occasion sat up all night talking films with Dusan Makavejev, the Yugoslavian filmmaker, who may have been in town in conjunction with the production of his *Sweet Movie* (1974).

The success of Grierson's first term as visiting professor led to his permanent appointment as professor of communications in the fall of 1969. Lest there be any doubt about his satisfaction with the appointment, here is what he wrote to Marion Michelle, probably in the fall of 1970: "I had better inform you again, my dear Michelle, that I am now a professor. . . . Not here today gone tomorrow, no 'visiting' professor nonsense; the real thing."[21]

## Consulting, Reports, Interviews, Lectures

From the time he left the Film Board in 1945 until his death, Grierson remained involved with it one way or another—writing letters to the film commissioner full of advice and recommendations, making public statements about the current situation (often critical and not always appreciated by the board), being called in for consultation, issuing reports on what he found, and urging specific actions. His engagement was particularly close during his years in Montreal, of course, the Film Board's headquarters since 1956. As already noted, Hugo McPherson (film commissioner 1967–70) had initiated Grierson's being invited to McGill to have the advantage of his presence on the scene. Sydney Newman (film commissioner 1970–75), who had been one of the young producers at the wartime N.F.B., had long respected Grierson, sought out his council, and generally shared Grierson's views about what a filmmaking institution in the public service should be about and do.

Even before McGill, in 1966, under Grant McLean's acting commissionership, Grierson was invited to Canada to survey the possibility of establishing a film training center which would be open to applicants from around the world. (Grant McLean was a cousin of Ross McLean, Grierson's assistant film commissioner and subsequent commissioner.) Believing that the N.F.B. was "primarily a national information service and it is as such that it has most to teach," Grierson shunned a scholastic approach to the study of film theory and practice. He also opposed creative workers who insisted on total freedom and felt that a national information service had an obligation to teach about the combination of public duty and aesthetic expression. Contingent upon the Department of External Affairs supporting the proposal, he recommended that the N.F.B. should, if necessary, cut production in order to free up creative teaching talent. He seems to have envisioned the training center as a means for the Film Board to be reborn. The plan was never adopted,[22] but what Grierson learned about the workings of the board in the course of his survey would become the basis for his subsequent recommendations and criticisms.

Shortly after he arrived to teach at McGill, he held a press conference reported in several papers.[23] A later pair of articles, based mostly on an interview, gave his views on present N.F.B. production and distribution policies and on the National Film Board as an institution, at a time when it was being criticized by members of government and the press. Of the criticism, he said, "[It's] the best thing that could have happened to the N.F.B. Why people are not throwing up their hands with joy at this chance to review the Film Board from a national perspective, I don't know."[24]

From his lectern at McGill, he let his students know that he was disturbed by the Film Board's expansion into features. He also denounced the *auteur* principle of the director as film artist completely in control of his work that he saw being espoused there, particularly by the French Production side. "'[N]one of us can claim this total personal right in a medium where so much is at issue in the national interest.' He thought that such freedom reflected the worst and most trivial aspects of early-nineteenth-century romanticism."[25] His admonitions were ignored not only by the French N.F.B. personnel but by Film Commissioner McPherson, who liked the French features, and by the English filmmakers, who were determined to try their own hands at feature production.[26] (Grierson never acknowledged publicly the considerable friction bordering on hostility that existed between the francophone and anglophone factions at the board.)

As for the N.F.B. experimental program Challenge for Change, as mentioned earlier Grierson made a curious (but scarcely unprecedented) volte-face in regard to it. Its purpose was to provide citizens access to the media in order to express their concerns and needs, and to create a dialogue with agencies of government involved in social programs. Unlike Grierson, or any other prior filmmaker, Challenge for Change was proposing that rather than communicating *to* the people, or even *for* the people, it would attempt to make films *with* the people. Eventually this led to enabling the *people* to make their own films.[27]

Grierson's distrust of amateurs behind the cameras has already been suggested, but his interest in Challenge for Change and speculation about its methods continued unabated. Colin Low, one of its prime movers, observed that "Dr. Grierson had a love-hate relationship with the 'Challenge for Change' program. One got the feeling that he sincerely hoped it would succeed but was sure that it would fail."[28] Grierson himself, following his trip to India near the end of his life, allowed for the valuable, even necessary use of its approach in certain circumstances and for certain goals. "The sub-standard film [i.e., 8 mm] and videotape are best seen now as relatively simple tools, to be locally owned and operated within the context of local reporting, local education and democratic representation at the community level." This activity would be in conjunction with public access to local cable television, he felt. Lack of professional standards did not worry him so much in this case: they "need not be lower than standards associated with local newspapers when they were making their vital contribution to community building in, say, the twenties." In this projection, the civil-servant filmmakers would become "peripatetic teachers of film-making, moving modestly from district to district" instructing those who had public messages to send on how to use the equipment required to send them. He characterized this sort of program as "decentralizing the power of propaganda."[29]

In addition to the National Film Board, from the outset of his sojourn Grierson also focused his attention on television in Canada. He had long regretted that the relationship between the N.F.B. and the Canadian Broadcasting Corporation (C.B.C.), both government agencies, had been competitive rather than cooperative, with the C.B.C. producing its own films, and the N.F.B. refusing to let its films be aired if commercial breaks were required. "Throughout those two years [in Canada]," as Elspeth Chisholm recalled, "he was consulted by the Canadian Radio-Television Commission [CRTC] as a sort of latter-day Socrates, talking to them of matters underlying the communication bodies in Canada, of principles and policies and philosophy."[30]

The CRTC was founded in the fall of 1968, shortly before Grierson arrived at McGill. Out of his consultation came an enormous number of taped interviews conducted by Rodrigue Chiasson from 1969 to 1971. "In the beginning, we did one or two hours of taping a week," Chiasson said. "Towards the end of 1971, we taped when we felt like it, once every two or three weeks. . . ." "The angle of attack I wanted to take with him concerned the ethical aspect of communications for practitioners and agencies like the CRTC, who work in the public sector and influence the public."[31] These tapes resulted in some 650 pages of *Grierson Transcripts*.[32] In a conversation with another interviewer, Grierson estimated that "over the previous eighteen months he must have recorded half a million words on the whole nature of information."[33]

Along similar lines, he wrote a report for the administration of McGill University in the spring of 1971. Like the *Grierson Transcripts*, the conclusions it provided grew out of his retrospective thinking about media on his return to Canada. It dealt with the "special reasons why the mass media are a useful area of study at the university level," and his own "approach to the discussion of mass media." As his teaching had shown, he was "interested specifically in *what concern with the mass media came within the normal disciplines represented by political science, aesthetic, and social psychology* [Grierson's emphasis]."[34]

These two documents, the *Grierson Transcripts* and the McGill report, taken together represent a compendium of Grierson's final thinking about the media, government, and society drawn from a lifetime of analysis and leadership in the field and benefiting from the opportunity to refine and test his ideas in his classes and with his students. A vast and intricate summation, they seem a fittingly useful way for him to conclude a career based on education and intellect but spent mostly in meeting the pressing demands of immediate activity.

Another important but somewhat curious summation came about through Grierson protégé Grant McLean, who had been acting film commissioner of the Film Board. When he was not promoted to commissioner in 1967 (McPherson was appointed instead), McLean moved to Toronto where, together with two other N.F.B. alumni, he established the Visual Education Centre. Through this producer-distributor, Grierson put his Edinburgh performance of *I Remember, I Remember* into permanent film form.[35] He used the same film excerpts but rewrote the commentary, which he speaks directly to the camera—the whole very like his television series.

What Grierson chooses to remember in *I Remember, I Remember* is remarkable in the contrast it offers to his earlier position on the relationship of art to propaganda. The sequences selected from films he had helped make are those with great visual style and movement, exclusively nonverbal, of machines revolving, trains rushing, waves crashing, and the like—very few people. The narration, so firm a part of the Griersonian tradition, has been removed wherever it existed and the music and sound effects allowed to remain; even more frequently, freshly chosen symphonic music replaces the original sound track altogether. It might almost be an anthology of the avant-garde, illustrating some thesis about abstract tendencies in the cinema. In fact, he uses the word *abstract* and says not to be alarmed by it; that it means order and design, which are necessary to all modern life. Grierson continues: "Most people when they think of documentary films think of public reports and social problems and worthwhile education and all that sort of thing," but his dismissive tone serves as warning. Instead he offers as his own understanding of documentary words like "magical," "art," "beauty," and "poetry"—all with Scottish burr richly burring, and an invocation of Picasso. This seems the craziest come about in relation to the *Film and Reality* controversy of thirty years earlier (*I Remember, I Remember* going much further in regard to form, even pure form, than the Cavalcanti-Lindgren anthology) and all else that he had stood for.

Perhaps in some way this feat of intellectual prestidigitation was part of Grierson's rejuvenation and final metamorphosis into a brilliant university lecturer, who held hundreds of young Canadians at a time enthralled with paradox and Delphic cryptograms, far-ranging and free-associational erudition, looping structure decorated with occasional badinage. Having always been a teacher of one sort or another, he seems to have become a great one in the strict sense during the last two years of his life. Beating the pedagogues at their own game, which anyone who knew him never doubted he could do, he became younger in the company of young people, reinvigorated by the demands they placed on his knowledge and understanding of the world they inhabited together.

Visual Education Centre was linked with Public Media, Inc., a U.S. firm then based in Wilmette, Illinois. Owned by Charles Benton,

Public Media was an umbrella organization; its driving force was Films, Inc., purchased in 1968, the largest distributor of Hollywood feature films on 16 mm. Before becoming a part of Public Media, Films, Inc. had been acquired by Encyclopaedia Britannica Films (EBF). Charles Benton's father, William Benton, was chairman of the board of EBF. Among his many accomplishments, he had founded the Benton and Bowles advertising agency, engineered the affiliation of the *Encyclopaedia Britannica* with the University of Chicago, and become U.S. Senator (Democrat) from Connecticut. Grierson had known him when Benton was Assistant Secretary of State concerned with the establishment and early functioning of UNESCO.

Charles Benton was interested in increasing his firm's activity in the documentary and educational fields. Grierson entered into the discussions of potential projects, suggesting approaches to subjects and strategies for reaching wider audiences. As part of his consultation, Films, Inc., sponsored "A Day with John Grierson" in June 1969 in Wilmette, Illinois, for its staff and friends. It consisted of Grierson talking about his association with the development of documentary films, the use of educational films as *trampolines* which audiences could bounce off of, and screenings and discussion of some short films (including *Granton Trawler*). A festive dinner at the Bentons and an additional screening concluded the day.

Grierson's relationship with Films, Inc., and Public Media seems to have been affable. In a letter to Grant McLean written ten days before his death, Grierson concluded by saying, "You might as well tell the good Charles that I don't expect to be around at his inspired, not to say holy, meetings: not anymore. This hospital sure thinks it has got me."[36]

In addition to the full teaching load and the consulting, Grierson moved around in at least something like his old fashion. Although he published little in these last two years, he gave numerous interviews, lectured at conferences and other universities, and served as a member of juries at film festivals. The energy displayed for a man of his years was staggering.[37]

An especially significant interview, first published in the *McGill Reporter* shortly after he began teaching, was by Ronald Blumer, one of Grierson's graduate assistants. (Actually it was drawn from more than one interview, edited from some fifty pages of transcripts.)[38] The title includes a Grierson phrase explaining by what right he had become a teacher: "I derive my authority from Moses."

It contains wonderfully pungent responses to the questions put to him, ranging over art and politics, revolution and religion. This interview captures very well Grierson's mind at work and his conversational style.[39] In an interview by Darlene Kruesel, another of his McGill students, he discussed the origins of documentary and its uses as an instrument of persuasion, the artist in relation to the state, and his views of Canada and film in Canada.[40]

Then there is a statement recorded for a B.B.C.–TV *Omnibus* program on Sergei Eisenstein produced by Norman Swallow. In it Grierson expressed much appreciation and personal response to the films and to their maker. His main thesis was that Eisenstein was "the greatest master of public spectacle in the history of the cinema." He believed that "Eisenstein was most glorious, most truly himself, in his last picture, *Ivan the Terrible*."[41] There was also his eulogy to Walter Wanger at the time of Wanger's death. It, too, was a generous and personal tribute to this Hollywood producer, in which he acknowledged the ways in which Wanger had aided him and helped him to understand film.[42]

My last contact with Grierson in person was at the Midwest Film Conference held in Evanston, Illinois, in January 1971. This annual event was a combination of the screening of substantial numbers of new releases on 16 mm, presentations, and workshops. It was attended by several hundred people in the nontheatrical field, most of them associated with education in one way or another. Grierson gave the keynote address. Before he started he growled at the photographers with their flashbulbs asking them to stop; he was having enough trouble concentrating on what he wanted to say without their distraction, he explained.

The talk dealt with many of the themes sounded in his lectures at McGill. He stressed order and discipline; was against "doing your own thing," waving the camera around, the 8 mm mind, and so on. He looked to teachers to build for the future—the press had failed, as had the movies, and TV (the latter a deadening rather than a life-giving force). A few slaps at Marshall McLuhan and his ideas about the medium being the message were offered. (All this in the midst of loyal inhabitants of McLuhan's global village, who identified with their students' "now generation," and for whom "doing your own thing" was the order of the day.) Teachers can't know the word *defeat*, he said.

It was extremely rambling and quite witty—a performance, including the Chinese laundry shirt cardboards on which his notes were written. It was also a display of erudition, with quotes ranging from da Vinci and Baudelaire to Plato and Trotsky. My guess would be that the audience reaction to it varied considerably. But reaction to Grierson's public statements always had varied widely, from those who found his ideas both sensible and inspiring to those who found them anathema and dangerous, or irrelevant.

## India

Grierson's last great adventure was a trip to India in the spring of 1971. It came about when he was asked to be part of a team supplied to the Canadian International Development Agency by the National Film Board. Their mission was to assist the Indian Ministry of Health and Family Planning to devise means of communicating and educating regarding the desirability and methods of birth control. Grierson was selected to head the group. They were in India about two months.

The initial idea must have been to use the mass media, especially film and television. But what Grierson and his two colleagues (Ken McReady and Len Chatwin) determined from their research sent them off in another direction. Though Grierson met and talked with various ministers and the prime minister, Indira Gandhi herself, most of the team's time and energy were spent on extensive traveling around the country and out into the rural areas. It seemed to him that standard concepts of mass communication were of little use in relation to the huge and diverse population of the vast subcontinent: 450 million people out of a total population of 550 million were outside the range of the so-called mass media, accessible only by word of mouth.[43] Messages sent from the central government—from the top down, as Grierson put it—would have little chance of reaching audiences outside the urban areas. And there were too many cultures, too many languages for standardization; messages coming from outside the local community were not likely to be accepted in any case.

As James Beveridge summarized the report the team eventually turned in to the Indian Ministry of Health and Family Planning, and to the Canadian International Development Agency, and the National Film Board:

The major emphasis . . . was on decentralization. In essence the consultants suggested a decentralized pattern for the production of information materials, a network of local centers where such materials might be produced and used within the regional or local context, with regard to the special language and local conditions of each area. Lightweight, low-cost, easily accessible and operable equipment for making film, slides, filmstrips, and other simple visual aids was recommended. The involvement of local officials, medical personnel, teachers, and village-development workers was urged.[44]

Along with simplified visual materials—with the people themselves being taught to make filmstrips, for example (which Norman McLaren of the N.F.B. had demonstrated in China on an UNESCO mission in 1949 and again in India in 1953)[45]—Grierson addressed the problem of reaching the people of the villages from the outside in ways that would gain their attention and trust. He decided that the spoken word was the basic means of communication that must be used. What if inexpensive audio cassette players were distributed throughout the rural areas? Audio tapes could then be produced that would feature an older native woman speaking directly to female groups. The same for men: narrators were persons of the locality whose manner would identify them as the sorts of older, wiser persons whose advice was traditionally sought in dealing with matters that needed to be decided upon.[46] It was this sort of thinking that led Grierson to speculate that "we might be able to *decentralize* communication in a very vast way in India, in a way that's never been done in the world before."[47] Building on the Challenge for Change ideas, he was modifying and applying them to a new situation.

In addition to the work on family planning, Grierson was invited to review the production of the Indian government Films Division. He threw himself into this assignment with his usual energy and commitment, offering some very sharp criticism, variations on his long-term complaints about National Film Board policy and output. He felt the Films Division ought to be paying more attention to the villages, "where the heart of India beats," instead of placing its emphasis on urban concerns, which he felt it was doing in its films. Along with this he attacked the Films Division's "attempts to gain renown by competing for awards in all sorts of festivals."[48]

They win obscure prizes at obscure festivals, then talk of mass communication. They are using public money for self-indulgence. . . .
[T]here is not enough creative urge, they do no reflect the spirit of the
country lyrically and dramatically. I am tired of films on Indian music
and carvings. I think cultural India had better be forgotten. Mrs.
Gandhi talked of India on the march, going forward in terms of social
revolution. The Films Division should be more reflective of the over-
whelming story of India, its new economic and social programs, the
new life for the people.[49]

Grierson made these comments in spite of the fact that he himself
had become absorbed with Indian classical dancing.[50]

Though the Indian press seems to have been respectful of
Grierson and his criticisms, it wasn't completely supine. For example,
one journalist observed that Grierson's "scornful remarks" regarding the Films Division's "attempts to gain renown" recalled "the bad
old days," when "[a]ll that mattered was the 'content'—which
mostly meant the crudest and dullest ways of communicating a given
'message'—and aesthetic values were all but nonexistent."[51] Another
agreed, adding that Grierson's championing of "propaganda-filled
and rural-oriented product" appeared "strangely reactionary." He
concluded with the following charge: "The flickering fire of experiment has to be perpetually fanned by recognition that brings it to
public notice. In a country like India, eminently lacking in foundations and funds for research and with the private sector not touch-
ing anything useful unless it is profitable, it is only the government
that can encourage and aid experiments. To oppose it is to shut out
the last hope for its existence."[52]

At any rate, when asked for his opinion on visiting India,
Grierson replied with a chuckle: "I object on principle to visiting
great countries like India—I prefer the small ones. And, of all
things, I have come to India in the name of family planning. It all
seems surrealist."[53]

## The End

Grierson returned to Montreal to collaborate with McReady and
Chatwin, his two companions on the trip, in preparing substantial
reports for the Canadian International Development Agency and the
National Film Board. He went to England for only a brief period
during the summer, and then back to Canada.[54] In December, after

teaching the fall term at McGill, he left for London on his way to an anticipated follow-up visit to India. Before he could leave England, however, war broke out between India and Pakistan. Early in January, he went to a hospital in Bath, not far from his home in Calne, for a checkup. Cancer of the liver and of one lung was discovered. A few days later, he was admitted to the hospital and told he had a month to live.

The only visitors he permitted were his wife Margaret, who stayed in a hotel in Bath in order to be with him daily, and John Taylor (Margaret's brother; Grierson's brother-in-law) and his wife, Barbara Mullen, who came on weekends. In that last month he kept busy. His room was full of newspapers and books, television, radio, and tape recorder. He dictated many letters and was said to have been engaged in that activity when he died on February 19, 1972—two months short of his seventy-fourth birthday.[55]

He seemed content to die—in a letter to a member of the Films, Inc., staff he wrote that he was "going to the happy-happy land."[56] Perhaps he felt he had lived a full and useful life and done the best he could with it. (He didn't like the term "career" used in regard to his work.)[57] The last words of his that are heard on the sound track of the film *Grierson* seem appropriate as an end to this biography as well. They stand for the fusion of ethic and aesthetic, of propaganda and poetics, evident in his most innovative and influential contributions to public service and to film: "All things are beautiful as long as you've got them in the right order."

# 15 → POSTMORTEM: ASSESSMENTS (1972–2000)

The writing about Grierson over the past several decades has followed two main lines. One represents essentially Grierson's own views of what he had been trying to do, what he had accomplished, the importance of efforts of the sort, and the need for them to be continued and expanded. These assessments grow in large measure out of the editions of *Grierson on Documentary* (1946, 1947, 1966, 1979) edited by Forsyth Hardy. That collection combines Grierson's major writing—reviews of fiction feature films as well as essays about documentary, education, the role of communication and public opinion in the functioning of democracies—with Hardy's running biographical account of Grierson's life and career. This is the standard version, as it were—which would include this present biography, it must be acknowledged.

Writers in the second line have attempted to see Grierson's theory and practice in new ways—to penetrate what he stated the case to be in order to arrive at what he had really been trying to do. These efforts include research that intends to show that Grierson's systems of film production and distribution weren't anything like as effective as he claimed; that he and his band of followers were in fact opposed by the majority of those in political life and in the civil service; and that eventually he and his approach were in every instance removed from the body politic. Other revisionists have reinterpreted Grierson's published statements in an attempt to discover themes and arguments based on an untenable realist aesthetic and antithetical to the liberal democracy he was thought to favor.

Traditionalists and revisionists agree, however, on the importance and the extent of Grierson's influence on the way English-language documentary film and video have developed. Most of the former applaud and want to continue and extend the lines he started. Most of the latter decry some of the directions he chose and feel film development has been constrained in the documentary mold Grierson constructed.

## Traditional

### Elizabeth Sussex

The first book in the traditional line was Sussex's *The Rise and Fall of British Documentary: The Story of the Film Movement Founded by John Grierson* (1975). The term *Story* in the subtitle is apt. Sussex writes in her preface: "I set out with a tape recorder to interview as many members of the original movement as possible. . . . and that is the basis of this book. My method was to ask each interviewee to tell his story from beginning to end, and then to fit all the stories together."[1] For her interviewees, she rounded up the usual suspects. (Interviews by the author with most of them have been referred to throughout this text.) In order of appearance, she spoke to: John Grierson, Basil Wright, John Taylor, Paul Rotha, Edgar Anstey, Sir Arthur Elton, Stuart Legg, Harry Watt, Alberto Cavalcanti, Pat Jackson, W. H. Auden, and Ian Dalrymple. What is most valuable about this book is that it preserves the wonderful anecdotes, insights, and bits of humor these men had been offering and polishing with each retelling over the years. The only significant way Sussex goes beyond what they might have offered anytime earlier is by exploring the *Fall*—"The Post-War Decline" in chapter 7. The book stands as a testament to the great spirit and loyalty—to Grierson, to each other, and to the documentary idea—that bound the British documentary group together from the early thirties through the first half of the 1940s.

Harry Watt, however, was a special case, and deserves some

parenthetical comment. His memoirs, *Don't Look at the Camera*—chatty, charming, and amusing—had been published the year before. In the interview with Sussex he repeats himself almost verbatim, except for significant omissions (which may be Sussex's editing). While appreciating the opportunity he had been given to learn and practice filmmaking, and acknowledging the affection and loyalty he had felt, *Don't Look at the Camera* contains complaints about Grierson and criticisms of the Griersonian documentary. The complaints are personal and stem from "Grierson's autocratic bullying."[2] Watt was not allowed to continue working for "The March of Time"; was not credited as director of *Night Mail*; and his wife was forbidden to work on location with him.

As for the Griersonian documentary, Watt was part of the Cavalcanti heresy. He favored theatrical distribution over nontheatrical, the professionalism of features over the amateurism of early documentary shorts, funding by box office rather than sponsor, narrative rather than descriptive or expository form, character over idea, realist style rather than social program. In short, he didn't seem to understand what Grierson's goals were, and what he did understand didn't approve.

Though this might seem to place Watt in the company of the revisionists to be dealt with later, over a third of *Don't Look at the Camera* is devoted to the years working for or with Grierson. The front of the dust jacket identifies the book as "The irreverent memoirs of the maker of 'Night Mail' 'Target for Tonight' etc"; of the fifteen illustrations, twelve have to do with documentaries and only one with features, his first: *Nine Men* (1942, one of the hybrid semidocumentaries). Notwithstanding the fact that Watt spent the greater part of his career in features, he says, finally, to Sussex: "I would say quite frankly that I regret that I left documentary. As creative work it was so much more exciting, and there was so much more communal effort about it, the camaraderie, the lack basically, of jealousies."[3]

*James Beveridge*

Beveridge's *John Grierson: Film Master* (1978) is similar to Sussex's work and is useful in much the same way. As mentioned earlier, Beveridge was one of the principals—as adviser and interviewer—of the N.F.B. film biography *Grierson* (1972), and his book grew out of research and preparation for the film. It comprises transcriptions of interviews (some used in the film, others not), writings by Grierson (some not previously published) and others about him, newspaper stories, correspondence, quotes from documentary sound tracks, posters, photos, and stills. All of this is arranged chronologically, along Grierson's life and career and is stitched together with biographical notes about Grierson and accounts of the experience of making the film, including introductions of the interviewees.

Beveridge was very well qualified for his work on the film and book. Not only had he known Grierson personally since the early days of the Film Board, he knew in advance most of the persons interviewed and much about the history of documentary in Britain and, of course, Canada. At the time of publication, he was teaching film at York University, Toronto. The book remains a cornucopia of documentation useful to complement other biographical writing about Grierson.

### Forsyth Hardy

Following his long association with Grierson and editing of his writings, Hardy received Margaret Grierson's permission to write a biography of her husband after his death.[4] *John Grierson: A Documentary Biography* (1979) can thus be considered the "official biography." It has both the advantages and the shortcomings of this status. All of Grierson's papers that Margaret had saved, plus a collection of photos, were made available to Hardy. He was able to interview her and had her approval in seeking out the many Grierson friends and colleagues who contributed information and impressions to his book.

Even more helpful than this sanction was the fact that Hardy had known Grierson since 1930 and had followed and abetted his progress and that of documentary film and the documentary movement from that time. He became something of a repository for copies of speeches and articles, especially after the publication of the first edition of *Grierson on Documentary*; as he put it, "The inference was that [he] should keep the record and that a biography might emerge, although there was no formal understanding."[5]

A final qualification of Hardy's was that he was a Scot who knew and sympathized with most things Scottish and himself was a producer of films for Scottish government departments and the Films of Scotland Committee, including *Seawards the Great Ships*, based on an outline by Grierson. Promoting Grierson more than partly because he was a fellow Scot, Hardy thus had a special understanding of his early years and of the influence his background and education would have on him throughout his life.

For the biography, Hardy did a prodigious amount of research, drawing upon Grierson's papers—especially his correspondence—and extensive interviews with key people scattered around the globe who had worked with Grierson and knew him well. His research makes much less use of archival and library resources (nor does he seem to interview anyone critical of or in opposition to Grierson). Though there are extensive footnotes, Hardy's acknowledgment of sources is rather casual; there is no bibliography.

His biography is essentially the work of an excellent journalist: skilled, energetic, scrupulous enough about "getting it right," as far as he understands the matters he's investigating. The writing is first-rate—graceful, precise, and colorful—and a detailed and endearing portrait emerges with a kind of intimacy that the long and mutually supportive relationship permitted. He keeps close to his subject and doesn't take as many pains as he might or perhaps should have, given the nature of his subject, to fill out the institutional context of the career.

Hardy's biography skirts or minimizes troublesome spots. He makes no acknowledgment of the rift in British documentary—which began in the late thirties and came to a head during the war—between Grierson's loyal followers and those who followed Cavalcanti and Watt in the direction of the feature-length semi-documentaries. His failure to explore fully what might have been behind Grierson's decision to step down as film commissioner of Canada is another example. The low periods in Grierson's career, especially that between Group 3 and the beginning of *This Wonderful World*, are ignored or glossed over. Nor is there any real treatment of the people and forces trying to remove Grierson from positions of authority, or of decisions of his that moved him backwards or sideways rather than ahead towards what one would assume were his ultimate goals.

So, Hardy's book, for all the uniquely valuable information it contains, has come to be regarded in some quarters—especially among revisionists, who will be dealt with later—to be limited by the warm glow of affection and pride fueled by Grierson's acknowl-

edged charisma and persuasiveness. The term hagiography is sometimes used in reference to it. But clearly Hardy's labor of love supports his own conclusion that what Grierson managed to achieve
was of enormous importance—as far as the history of film is concerned and, even more, in the understanding of the use of modern
media in citizenship education and in government communication
with its citizens.

*Gary Evans*

*John Grierson and the National Film Board* (1984), as the subtitle
*The Politics of Wartime Propaganda* promises, is a very different
sort of book. Though biographical to an extent, covering the years
1939 to 1945 and including a considerable amount of information
that doesn't appear elsewhere, Evans's main thrust is in trying to
understand the ideological basis of Grierson's actions. This is seen
to account for the directions he took and the opposition he faced,
as well as being a basis for evaluating his successes and failures.
Evans's training is academic, his field history. The analysis he provides is extraordinarily well informed and well argued and, though
Evans may admire Grierson's ability and idealism as much as Hardy,
he does not turn away from the ultimate failure of Grierson's approach in Canada (as Grierson himself may well not have).

The central portion of the book rests on thoughtful analysis of
the propaganda strategies employed in the N.F.B. films—those produced for the nontheatrical circuits and the two theatrical series,
"Canada Carries On" and, especially, "World in Action." He notes
Grierson's (and Legg's) increasingly internationalist approach. As
Evans sees it, that, plus the spy trials, which he examines in considerable detail in the penultimate chapter ("Down the Greased Pole:
Practical Politics and Igor Gouzenko Deflate Grierson's Triumph"),
caused the undoing of what Grierson had tried to bring about.

But the final chapter does give credit to "The Grierson Legacy."
It concludes:

> He will always have the respect of those sympathetic to his ideas but
> will probably remain a dreamer to the political elites whom he sought
> to convert. Grierson's failure was not in his conception about what
> propaganda film could do, but in the questionable belief that the domi-
> nant elites in liberal democracies could be convinced to exercise their
> power and authority forever on behalf of the masses. His success was

to establish a film tradition which others have built upon, a liberal tradition which, unafraid of controversy, still affirms and celebrates human potential and dignity.[6]

The National Film Board continues to interpret Canada to Canadians and to the world; and, one must add, attempts are still being made to reduce, change, or destroy it.[7]

*Jack C. Ellis*

*John Grierson: A Guide to References and Resources* (1986) is part of a series devoted to individual filmmakers, usually directors. Its "Critical Survey," therefore, follows roughly the *auteur*-ist approach—identifying recurrent themes, forms, and techniques in the films for which this propagandist/artist was responsible.[8] Since the films over which Grierson exerted most control and to which he contributed most actively were those he produced in Britain between 1929 and 1939, concentration is on them. It was those films that established documentary as an institutionalized force in national life and gave it the forms that we in the English-speaking countries at least still think most characteristic of it.

Grierson did not think of himself as a film creator primarily; certainly not as an *auteur*. Filmmaking he regarded as a collaborative effort: you produced with others, you borrowed from others. Nonetheless, in the "Critical Survey," I argue that "[t]he ethics (social purposes) and aesthetics (formal properties) of those films are identifiable, consistent, and quite special,"[9] and describe their characteristic aspects.

*Ian Aitken*

With the exception of the present writer, the last of those who can be said to be following in the traditionalist line is Aitken. As of 1996, he was a senior lecturer in media, University of the West of England, Bristol. His *Film and Reform: John Grierson and the Documentary Film Movement* (1990) largely supports but also alters and enlarges traditional understanding with prodigious research and sophisticated philosophical analysis.

The book began as a Ph.D. dissertation at the Polytechnic of Central London. One of its most valuable aspects is its survey of the literature of the field required in such an undertaking. With an amazing command of diverse fields—corporate advertising and public relations, government propaganda, economic theory, as well as American pragmatist philosophers (such as William James and John Dewey) and social sciences—Aitken outlines fully the intellectual and cultural context within which Grierson was situated in the U.S. in the 1920s and Britain in the 1930s. He more than confirms my suspicions that Grierson's antennae were always extended, absorbing and analyzing ideas and information that would be useful to him in creating the documentary film and establishing a documentary film movement.

But the firm basis for Grierson's thinking and actions throughout his career, Aitken argues, lay in a synthesis of the idealist philosophers he studied at Glasgow University. "Grierson's ideas were derived from this synthesis of neo-hegelian and neo-kantian elements, and his general world view can be defined as a neo-kantian social-democratic version of . . . absolute idealist philosophy. His entire epistemology, aesthetic, and political philosophy was largely derived from this idealist synthesis, and it is impossible to give an accurate account of his ideas without understanding this."[10]

The other main thrust of Aitken's book is an examination of "the parallels and relations between the documentary film movement and social-democratic reformism during the inter-war period."[11] In the course of this, he investigates the ideological and intellectual currents in the United States during the years Grierson was there (1924–27), as well as the development of his aesthetic during those crucially influential years in the evolution of his ideas. Aitken then shows how these ideas were applied to the work of the Empire Marketing Board and General Post Office film units and to the documentary film movement generally (1927–39).

As for "Documentary Film and Reform," the penultimate chapter, Aitken summarizes as follows: "although Grierson believed in the need for social reform, he did not believe in the need for a socialist transformation of society. Similarly, although he believed that the State was the most important agent of reform, he did not believe that it should become too powerful." Aitken goes on to say that "[t]here was a general apprehension at the time that a strong State could turn into a fascist or a communist dictatorship."[12] Curiously, among the revisionists about to be considered, some regarded Grierson as a crypto-fascist while others as a crypto-communist (unacceptable left-wing radical at least).

It is Aitken's view that "Grierson and the documentary film movement can be identified with a demand for reform," but the identification should be "with various movements of middle opinion during the inter-war period."

> These movements were diverse and heterogeneous, but this heterogeneity concealed a core of shared beliefs and values. In the first place, there was a belief in the essential soundness of established society; in the second place, there was a belief in the need for State regulation and intervention; and, in the third place, there was a rejection of the option of a socialist or fascist transformation of society. These political and cultural parameters framed what some critics have described as a "social democratic consensus."[13]

Certainly finding areas of common or neutral ground between the party in power and the opposition was the way Grierson frequently described how it was possible to get funding for the kind of government filmmaking he was attempting—the terms "consensus" and "general sanction" appear over and over again in his writing.

Though Aitken, like others of the assessors here characterized as traditional (Sussex and Ellis), ends his study of Grierson and the documentary film movement at the end of the 1930s, before the pinnacle years of the National Film Board of Canada, his presentation of the driving forces behind Grierson's innovative contributions to film form and purpose, and to government use of film for communication, is complete and compelling. Aitken does not avoid what Grierson himself must have felt was a failure to achieve his ideal. In the final chapter, "The Influence of Idealism," Aitken concludes:

> Grierson continued to depend on an unrealistic utopian model of the relationship between documentary and the State, which he had derived from philosophical idealism, and which was incompatible with existing political circumstances. . . . In addition to being materially responsible for the documentary movement's decline, philosophical idealism was also the source of several questionable features of Grierson's ideology. His *a priori* acceptance of the "institutions of State," and the need for film-makers to work within the "general sanction," led to the production of documentary films which were of minimal critical value. . . . His theory of documentary film also implied a centralized hierarchical practice of social ideology production, in which social communication was passed down . . . to the public, and never vice-versa. . . . Beneath the rhetoric of "democracy" there was an underlying rhetoric, of a self-perpetuating bureaucratic elite.[14]

"But if," Aitken concedes, "philosophical idealism was partly responsible for the documentary movement's decline, and for authoritarian elements in Grierson's ideology, it also provided the movement with a degree of ideological coherence, and was a principal source of Grierson's reformism."[15] And finally (the book's last sentence): "it can be argued that Grierson and the documentary movement were a progressive and reformist phenomenon, in relation to the dominant Conservatism of the inter-war period."[16]

## Revisionist

### Alan Lovell

The writing of the first of those I have labeled revisionists, Lovell's "The Documentary Film Movement: John Grierson" (1972), is one of a collection of three essays by Lovell and Jim Hillier. (The other two essays are on Humphrey Jennings, maverick member of the documentary movement [by Hillier], and Free Cinema, the anti-Grierson postwar demi-movement [by Lovell].) It was published in the year of Grierson's death. The opening biographical survey leads Lovell to this conclusion: "In helping to create this complex structure [establishing government film units, training a group of filmmakers, obtaining sponsorship and nontheatrical distribution, establishing critical magazines] Grierson endowed the British cinema with a unique feature. He succeeded in linking the film culture (film as art) . . . to an instrumental use of film (film as a medium for instruction, education, propaganda)." Lovell goes on to point out that "The documentary film was Grierson's instrument. . . . Its essential function was . . . an inspirational one. It might start by giving information about the modern world but its main function was to involve the citizen in the general social process." To understand how Grierson arrived at his ideas about the uses of film, Lovell then engages in "some probing of Grierson's intellectual background."[17]

"The starting point of Grierson's position," Lovell suggests, "was a technological/collectivist account of modern society. . . . This account, with its emphasis on the effect of technology on the structure of society, has occasional marxist overtones. Grierson's identification of history as a force independent of men's wills also suggests a deterministic version of marxism."[18] "But," Lovell goes on to say, "other strands in Grierson's position are quite unmarxist. He never refers to class and seems content with the existing hierarchical order of Society. The State . . . is identified with what best serves the long-term interests of people. . . ."[19]

In trying to sort out these apparent contradictions, Lovell suggests that "It seems likely that Grierson's attitude was a combination of two different sets of ideas. The technological/collectivist emphasis probably came from sources like H. G. Wells, the Webbs and the Fabians. . . . The other source is more difficult to identify. The idea of history as an independent force and the positive attitude towards the State suggest some kind of Hegelian influence."[20] And he identifies some of the same philosophical sources that became the main basis for Aitken's interpretation of Grierson's theory and practice.

This leads Lovell to the matter that would preoccupy other revisionists: "The value Grierson placed on the State lays him open to the charge of being implicitly totalitarian," and he quotes the oft-quoted Grierson statement in defense of how totalitarian some of his conclusions might seem: "Some of us came out of a highly disciplined religion and see no reason to fear discipline and self-denial. Some of us learned in a school of philosophy which taught that all was for the common good and nothing for oneself." To this Lovell adds, "It is not, perhaps, surprising that a mixture of Calvinism and neo-Hegelianism should produce such an emphasis."[21] Thus Lovell acknowledged the two opposite poles toward which other revisionists would gravitate—Grierson as Bolshevik, Grierson as Fascist— but does not himself think either position altogether tenable.

As for the documentary films Grierson produced or inspired, Lovell sees them as growing out of an aesthetic of "naïve" realism: "that the essential nature of the cinema came from its ability to record the appearances of everyday life (this for him was 'the real world'). Through its ability to record these appearances the cinema penetrates into the nature of that life."[22] But, "If documentary film had been based only on a theory of naïve realism, it would have been close to the newsreel or the interest film. Grierson felt that his material had to be 'dramatised' or 'interpreted' if he was to achieve his ambition of using the film to involve men in the historical process."[23] Instead Grierson used narrative to dramatize social processes.[24]

Like Aitken, Lovell acknowledged the lack of artistic value in the bulk of British documentary films of the 1930s. "The importance of the documentary movement lies, not in the quality of individual films, but in the impact it had in general on the British cinema. Grierson captured the interest in film as an art that was developing in Britain in the late 1920s for the documentary movement. In effect, this meant that the documentary film became the British art film. So both film-making and critical discussion have been profoundly affected by the documentary conception."[25]

Paul Rotha made the same point, taking pride in its longevity compared to other art movements. Lovell, however, saw the documentary influence ultimately as a handicap, a limitation, and thus becomes a revisionist rather than a traditionalist.

> In general terms this [documentary influence] can be said to have produced a bias against the commercial, fiction cinema, except where that cinema has adopted documentary modes. . . . [T]he ideas that were developed in the late 1930s have never been seriously challenged; the structure of the documentary industry is still one that Grierson did so much to create. The result is that an important and influential sector of the British cinema is still shackled by a conception of the cinema developed by Grierson and his associates. . . .
>
> The best tribute that the British cinema could now pay these pioneers is to acknowledge their importance by challenging their ideas and influence. A new conception of the cinema, a different film-making structure—the task is an enormous one. But unless it is taken up, the British cinema seems likely to continue to drift, a prisoner of the past with no clear notion of its future.[26]

Lovell's general assessment is cogent and informed—without the amount of research other students of Grierson have done—and remarkably concise. He sets forth the major issues subsequent writers would deal with in more detail. Lovell demonstrates a sure sense of cultural, intellectual, and social history in Britain in the 1920s and 1930s and a disciplined intelligence applied to the subject at hand. Writers following him have drawn from and agreed with many of his insights. Not only the revisionists, like Brian Winston, to be discussed later, but the traditionalists have felt required to confront his arguments.

### Andrew Tudor

Lovell had seen that the theory of realism put forward by Grierson was "along the lines which Siegfried Kracauer was later to develop at length in his book *Theory of the Film*."[27] A second revisionist

343

would devote a whole chapter to Grierson as film theorist. Tudor, in *Theories of Film* (1974), placed Grierson ("The Problem of Context") between Eisenstein ("Great Beginnings") and André Bazin and Kracauer ("Aesthetics of Realism"). According to Tudor, Grierson "developed an aesthetic *explicitly* grounded in his more general views of society and the role of the cinema within it. In so doing he became the first major exponent of a socially derived theory of film. . . . In centring his aesthetic on a morality of social responsibility he elevated one element in the context of film to the pinnacle of aesthetic importance. It is this original claim which still makes him interesting."[28] As Tudor sees it, "his is a case for an *aesthetic* of film, not simply a justification for documentary. His views on film grow out of his analysis of twentieth century society; he thus has a practical interest in film theory. For him the cinema has a potentially great role to play in the solution of twentieth century problems. . . . The justification for one form of film as against another, for realism as opposed to fantasy, for collective ethic as opposed to the individualistic, lies in this social role."[29] In other words, what Grierson is asking for is "a purposive cinema . . . to encompass the concept of social responsibility. . . . [H]is is really a case for 'responsible propaganda.' Propaganda that is 'right.'"[30]

Thus, Tudor thinks that for Grierson

> the problem lies in providing a cultural basis . . . a system of beliefs which will make modern, democratic, industrialized societies work. . . . The one, which leads to documentary in particular and realism in general, sees the spread of information about the range of differences between man and man as a basis for social solidarity. . . . It assumes that a consensus achieved by increasing knowledge of the "real" world will bind society together. Knowing how the other half lives will enable us to recognize and hold on to our common humanity.

According to Tudor, Grierson came to feel that this first approach was inadequate to achieve his goals. "So we find a further case made for 'propaganda.' Information and realism are not sufficient. Our films must *involve* the individual in the process of creating solidarity, in the interdependence of his society, in the 'drama of his citizenship.' . . ."[31] Finally, Tudor summarizes Grierson's theory-as-theory as "context-dominant. . . . Pushed to the limit it can have no implications for our aesthetic judgments of film separate from the social function performed by the film. The measures of aesthetic taste are limited to two: the social responsibility

of the film, and its effectiveness in achieving this socially responsible aim." [32]

*Peter Morris*

The two revisionists discussed so far, Lovell and Tudor, are British
and confined themselves to Grierson's work in Britain in the thirties.
The next two are Canadian, and concentrate on his work in Canada
during the first half of the forties. First of these, and the more formidable, is Peter Morris, with two essays, one in 1986 ("Backwards
to the Future: John Grierson's Film Policy for Canada"), the other
in 1987 ("Re-thinking Grierson: The Ideology of John Grierson").
The earlier essay examines Grierson's key role in developing policies related to the feature film industry. Essentially it is a thorough
examination and refutation of Grierson's "A Film Policy for Canada" (1944) and other statements by Grierson on U.S.–Canadian film
relations. [33] "A Film Policy" goes something like this: Beginning with
the U.S. domination of the entertainment film in Canada, Grierson
moves to the difficulties that would be involved in trying to create
a Canadian feature film industry in competition with Hollywood.
This leads to a description of what the Canadian government,
through the National Film Board, was doing with the short nonfiction and nontheatrical film to give Canada and some of the rest of
the world (especially the United States) a sense of things Canadian.

Morris attacks the two parts of Grierson's presentation in two
different ways. The arguments Grierson uses against attempting to
establish a Canadian feature film industry are said to be disingenu-
ous, circular, and illusory. They advance "from: do we want to make
features? to: it would be futile to try, to, finally: those who want to
anyway will be able to on Hollywood's terms." [34] (The latter point
refers to Grierson's notions about Canadian cooperation with Hollywood to provide ideas and scripts for American films about Canada, to establish Canadian filmmakers in Hollywood to assist such
efforts, and/or to set up Hollywood production units in Canada.)
"The rationale behind 'Relations With the United States Film Industry' [a confidential memo from Grierson to the Canadian Department of External Affairs] is that cooperation with Hollywood
rather than confrontation would continue to ensure the distribution
of N.F.B. films to Canadian and U.S. theatres—the precise trade-
off spelled out in the Canadian Cooperation Project" [a postwar

agreement reached by the American film industry and the Canadian government].[35]

Morris then moves on to the second part of Grierson's position. "His arguments rest not only on a vision of the documentary film as a powerful social tool but also on the assumption that these films reached, or could reach, a large audience. Though he never makes a direct comparison, it is implicit in his 'Film Policy' that 'short films which deal with reality' could reach as many people as Hollywood features—and, of course, to greater effect."[36] Morris then proceeds to work through the conflicting, confusing, and inadequate data regarding attendance on the Film Board nontheatrical circuits and for the two monthly theatrical series with elaborate and partly conjectural computation. (In footnote 33 he adds: "I have not included details of the calculations but would be happy to provide them to anyone interested.") The bottom line, as they say in the film industry, was this: "there is good evidence to suggest that NFB audience claims during Grierson's tenure were highly exaggerated at best and knowingly false at worst."[37] This accusation is echoed by subsequent British revisionists.

Morris concludes this damning assessment as follows:

> Grierson was, of course, correct in stating that Canada did not then have the facilities necessary for a feature film industry. But . . . a start could have been made, appropriate measures taken to stimulate production, encourage investment and loosen the control of Hollywood, and, of course, train filmmakers in other skills than documentary. We might even have seen emerge a "Canadian David Selznick" who would not have needed to move to Hollywood to set up a production unit. Grierson's "Film Policy" was a failure in that it foresaw none of this but led inevitably to . . . the moribund state of the commercial film industry. . . . It was successful in that it led (as Grierson intended) to confirmation of the National Film Board as the central plank in Canada's film policy. It was, though, a policy of marginalization.
>
> It may be true, as Peter Ohlin recently argued, that "it is not a Canadian task to compete with American media, with Hollywood"; that Canadian life "is a kind of marginal existence on the outskirts of the major cultural movements." If it is true, then John Grierson was a key architect of Canada's marginalization in the film world, and events and policies since his time simply part of a self-fulfilling prophecy.[38]

Clearly a Canadian film nationalist, Morris is confronting Grierson at a time, during World War II, when internationalism—including the nascent United Nations, and his own imminent efforts to move onto a global plane with the short-lived World Today—was prominent in Grierson's thinking.

Morris's second essay is a more sweeping and profound criticism, as the title, "Rethinking Grierson: The Ideology of John Grierson," would suggest. It is also erudite, going beyond Lovell's beginnings in opening up many of the sources for Grierson's ideas subsequently explored more fully by Aitken. In fact, the bulk of this essay is devoted to an examination of these diverse sources and analogues before relating them to Grierson's writings "at the peak of his influence in the mid-thirties to mid-forties."[39] Whereas archival research for the first essay was confined to the Public Archives of Canada, here Morris makes extensive use of the John Grierson Archive at Stirling University, including correspondence and unpublished manuscripts. In sections on "Political Philosophy," "Aesthetics," and "Organization," these three aspects are interlinked and seen as being determined by Grierson's overall ideology.

Regarding Grierson's *political philosophy*, Morris contends that, though it was generally thought to be progressive, it was instead authoritarian and elitist. Numerous parallels are drawn between Grierson's ideas and those of the European neoconservatives of the 1930s—thinkers who were close to fascism—with Walter Lippmann "unquestionably a key link."[40] Grierson believed in the need for a centrally planned state and "was not at all afraid, even during the war, to use terms such as 'totalitarian' and 'authoritarian.'"[41] His "approach to propaganda, education, and the documentary film. . . . derives from the vision of a technocratic elite who could indeed know 'everything about everything' [a phrase Grierson used frequently to point out the impossibility for traditional education to equip the citizen for a democratic society] and the irrational masses who, of course, could not, but could be led, as he said, towards 'a crystallization of their sentiments and loyalties in forms useful to the people and the State alike.'"[42]

As for *aesthetics*, "Though, in later years, [Grierson] was more explicit about the basis of his aesthetic, in general he tends to prefer such apparently vague generalities as 'the creative treatment of actuality' or 'the documentary of work and workers.'"[43] Morris then puts forward the proposition that "Grierson was not a Realist (as has been assumed) but an Idealist, as much in aesthetics as he was in political philosophy."[44]

347

*Organization* refers to the system of film production and distribution developed by Grierson, and its financing. "His Hegelian Idealist conception of the state was the determining factor in his vision of the role and purpose of the documentary film. So it was logical, indeed necessary, for the state to support its production and dissemination."[45] And further, since Grierson's conception of the state was an *idealist* one, it was

> not the state of political parties, practical politics and cabinet government—the day-to-day world of liberal democracy. This Idealist vision would inevitably tend to clash with the world of practical politics, as, indeed, it did in both Britain and Canada. Grierson's sense of himself as one of the leaders "of the new forces of thought and appreciation" was bound, at some point, to conflict with the policies of his political masters, cabinet ministers who did not agree with Grierson's view that technocrats, not politicians, created policy. On the one hand, the Griersonian documentary was initially welcomed (despite well-known areas of resistance) because it celebrated the state and encouraged identification with the collectivity. On the other, it was rejected when it came too close to the political process. This is the central paradox of the Griersonian documentary approach, a paradox Grierson himself never understood.[46]

### Joyce Nelson

In *The Colonized Eye* (1988), Nelson echoes and intensifies Morris's major criticisms. The book is based upon considerable research into various fields—biography, film history, economic history, and political science. Evidence thus gathered is organized into an original, ingenious, and persuasive argument; acceptable enough, up to a point, and illuminating, too; it becomes untrustworthy in its extremes. Nelson adds to the attack on Grierson's authoritarianism and elitism his commitment to the emergent multinational economy and international capitalism, favoring the collusion of big business with big government to the detriment of the interests of the common people. She dwells on the connections both Grierson and Mackenzie King had with Standard Oil through the Rockefeller foundations as evidence of the pervasive power of corporate America.

In terms of Grierson's theory of propaganda, Nelson not only sees it as being highly manipulative, as does Morris, concerned solely with the "manufacture of consent" (a term Grierson borrowed from Lippmann), she claims to see little difference between the vision of society offered by the N.F.B. wartime films and the ideology of Nazi propaganda. She notes that *"On Guard For Thee* [(1940), one of the first compilation films made by the N.F.B.] explicitly states, 'As the first year of war runs out, to Canada comes the realization that Hitler must be beaten by his own methods.'"[47] This and other bits of evidence lead her to conclude, "The giant plan of Nazism and the master plan of democracy tended to coincide and overlap in certain areas. *This Is Blitz* (1942) claims that, under the guidance of 'military experts and scientists the world over,' democracy was building 'a war machine beyond the wildest dreams of the Nazis,' a claim that exposed similar dreams behind both ideologies."[48]

Third, and finally, regarding the Morris accusation that Grierson sold out the Canadian film industry to Hollywood, Nelson agrees. As part of her argument, she delineates (brilliantly) the internationalism in the "Canada Carries On" and "World in Action" series, and their reliance solely on stock footage fitted together to illustrate editorial points made by an authoritative voice-over commentary. In other words, there was no fresh-shot Canadian material which could have served as training for Canadian directors and cinematographers.

*Nicholas Pronay*

Though this sub-section has been entitled *Revisionists*, the next author might better be characterized as a *Destructionist*. Pronay is the only writer among all those dealt with in "Assessments," except for James Beveridge (and Harry Watt as an addendum), who actually worked with Grierson; and his appraisal ("John Grierson and Documentary—60 Years On," 1989), like Beveridge's, reflects and makes use of this singular familiarity. But it is a very different Grierson the two of them present. Pronay explains that while a postgraduate, between September 1961 and October 1964, he worked for Grierson as a member of a small team with which Grierson made *This Wonderful World* programs in the studio in Thompson House, Cardiff. He left that job for Leeds University,[49] where he subsequently became director of the Institute of Communications Studies. (He also was associate editor of the journal in which this article appeared.)

This firsthand acquaintanceship, plus archival research into public records undertaken by two of his graduate students, provided Pronay with unmatched resources with which to "swat" his subject (a term used by Grierson) in a manner different from and more thoroughgoing than any of the revisionists up to this point. If the others discussed so far (with the possible exception of Nelson) accepted Grierson's glass as half full, Pronay takes considerable pains to convince us that it was really half empty—at most. The procedure he follows is to progress through the stages of Grierson's career, giving first the "mythologised biography" offered by Grierson and his followers, then offering his own quite different account.[50]

First Pronay discounts Grierson as an innovator. He was not the first to apply the term documentary to a film, the French were; nor was *Drifters* the first British film to "put working people on the screen."[51]

Next he makes a comparison between Hitler and Nazism and Grierson and documentary: "In the autumn of 1929, with the completion of *Drifters*, Grierson acquired what the writing of *Mein Kampf* had given Hitler."[52] And from Hitler and Nazism he moves to Christ and Christianity:

> On the rock of *Drifters* he could, and he did, create a movement to which people came to belong, body and soul, and could find an ideology which was not just to be understood in the cold rational light of what was on paper, but which could be embraced in a flash of illumination through personal contact with himself, or with those filled and inspired by him, his apostles. . . .[53]
>
> . . . There is nobody else in the history of the non-written media whose influence and legacy is at once so pervasive, so much in need of re-examination in the light of the record. . . .[54]

"[T]he first step for the historian," Pronay says of the task that he is about to undertake, "is to explore the roots beneath the surface, buried in his youth and education, from which these multifarious shoots came. The second is to examine the practical forms they took when he had the chance to put them into practice."[55]

Pronay first attacks the idea of Grierson as a successful student and scholar: he says Grierson lacked academic qualifications and misrepresented his teaching experience. He started strong at Glasgow University but ended with an unimpressive degree: "Ordinary MA Unclassified." As for his first job after graduation, "he could not possibly get an academic appointment with such a poor degree. . . . Contrary to what he had always claimed by implication and by anecdotes about his 'lecturing days at Durham [University],' and what is stated in Forsyth Hardy's biography, there were no 'lecturing duties in philosophy' attached to the post of Assistant Registrars. What he did do in addition to working in the Registry was some extra-mural *adult education* work. That, as we all know, means something *quite* different!"[56]

As for the Rockefeller Research Fellowship for study in the United States, Pronay sees this as growing out of the handicap for an academic career of an inferior degree. "The route open to Grierson was to try and change subject, go to another University (which would usually mean going abroad) and take a second degree, preferably a higher degree, in a new subject. . . . Grierson, however, once again failed to continue with the expected achievement after the flying start he once again made in his second attempt at an academic career. He failed to complete his research and after 18 months dropped out altogether."[57]

But Pronay's most intense scorn is directed at Grierson's later use of "Dr. Grierson" "on the strength of a purely honorary degree" (the LL.D. conferred by Glasgow University in 1948). He doubts that Grierson knew much philosophy, especially that of Kant and Hegel, since he could not read them in their original language.[58] "How do I know? Because my first job when I went to work for him at *This Wonderful World* was to try and translate for him the script of a German *kulturfilm*."[59]

In the "second half of the mythologised biography and history" of Grierson's career, Pronay sees the same repetition of strong start, then failure and moving on, that he detected in the preparation. While the traditionalists see Grierson as moving to other, perhaps larger spheres of action at each juncture—G.P.O. to Film Centre to National Film Board to World Today to UNESCO to C.O.I. to Group 3—Pronay sees each of those moves as resulting from Grierson's being rejected and ousted. He backs this up with research by his graduate student Paul Swann (to be discussed next) into government archives which had now become accessible. The pattern begins at the G.P.O.:

> Essentially, Grierson resigned because by the end of his third year as a civil servant [the EMB years are not included in Pronay's reckoning] he had left himself no alternatives other than either to leave voluntarily, giving his own reasons, or be subject to the slow, decorous, but nevertheless merciless process with which the British Civil Service

freezes out people who had failed, in its eyes, to prove themselves fit to continue as one of their high and powerful fraternity. . . . [T]he reasons for this were that having made an excellent start he failed to build up that respect for efficiency and reliability which were the essential requirements. . . .[60]

Pronay provides considerable supporting evidence to show that by 1936 Grierson's "civil service seniors came to regard him as unreliable, and, above all, someone who broke the cardinal rule of never misleading fellow civil servants. Cooking figures, loading arguments, bringing discrete pressure by leaks to the press were perfectly alright by civil service conventions—provided it was aimed at the politicians. But to do that to your fellow civil servants broke the rules of the club."[61]

Pronay sees the same sort of thing happening again and again. He notes that Grierson was not involved or even consulted in the prewar and wartime planning and operation of British propaganda. "The disappointment engendered by London's refusal to give him a job when his country was at war was deeply felt. . . ." The National Film Board Pronay sees as second choice by far. "In the job he did not particularly want, and in Canada where he did not want to spend the war [Britain being at the center of it] he reached the apogee of his career. . . ."[62] Grierson's less-than-satisfactory achievements following his resignation from the N.F.B., with most space devoted to the C.O.I. and Group 3, are then chronicled. In them, Pronay finds the same inability to play by the rules; the only other instance of solid and sustained achievement in the latter part of his career was the ten years he worked on *This Wonderful World*, another job he did not particularly want. Of the C.O.I.: "Once again, he created his own opportunity, mesmerised and enthused people with his plans, but when it came to it he failed to carry them through."[63] Of Group 3: "For Grierson personally, it was another bitter failure over which he endlessly brooded in later days."[64]

In concluding, Pronay returns to this main theme, and his personal observation is added to what he offers as a historian.

> The contrast between the actual facts and the mythologised histories of Grierson himself and of the movement he founded—common characteristics of the charismatic leader-centered movements of the inter-war period—is a matter of historical record. . . . The statements concerning Grierson's own awareness of what really did happen, the

image of a bitter old man shaking his fist at those who has [*sic*] beaten him in the end and indeed crying up to heaven why he had been forsaken and the wicked allowed to triumph over him, rest only on personal knowledge. Quite simply, this was the Grierson I knew at *This Wonderful World*. . . .

History proved him and what he believed in wrong in his own lifetime. It was the charity of the fates which he fully deserved as a human being that there was yet more spring, or the illusion of spring, for him after that terribly long winter in which I met him. He was allowed to leave the treadmill of a weekly programme for the money and to go and become a lionised lecturer preaching his own ideology to a new generation—and to be not just 'Doctor Grierson' but 'Professor Grierson' before he died.[65]

So there it is. Pronay's indictment offers the option of believing either his "real story" or the traditionalists' "mythology."

## Paul Swann

Pronay drew to a considerable extent on evidence collected by an American who completed his doctoral dissertation, "The British Documentary Film Movement, 1926–1946," at the University of Leeds in 1979. It became a book, published in 1989, the same year as Pronay's article. At that time Swann was an associate professor of communications at Temple University in Philadelphia.

Both agree, and it seems clear from the evidence in the General Post Office Records Department, the Public Records Office, and printed government documents, that efforts were made by the Treasury and a Select Committee on Estimates to block the ambitions of Grierson and limit the activities of the Film Unit. But while Pronay sees Grierson as employing dishonesty and guile and being caught out by the regular civil service types, Swann's detailed account is of a hard-fought battle that Grierson and Tallents lost after a sustained and ingenious campaign. (Tallents left the Post Office in 1935 [Pronay says he was "fired"] to become public relations controller at the B.B.C.; Grierson left in 1937 to create Film Centre.) Acknowledging that "They were anxious that the work of the film unit and the library not be curtailed," Swann goes on to point out, "They employed two sets of tactics to circumvent the recommendations of the Select Committee and the terms of agreement with the Treasury. At times, the terms of agreement were interpreted in a manner unforeseen by the Treasury, so that the letter, if not the spirit, of the agreement was fulfilled. Alternatively, there were occasions when Tallents and Grierson chose simply to ignore it."[66]

Those opposing Grierson and Tallents wanted to confine the G.P.O. Film Unit to making films that promoted the Post Office, to use conventional commercial advertising and film production/distribution/exhibition methods and personnel. To get what they wanted, Tallents and Grierson, through various schemes, tried to increase their budget and work on a broader selection of projects, in unconventional ways (by civil service and Treasury standards), with the money available. Those in opposition kept trying to pen the Film Unit in and reduce their resources. It was this conflict which occasioned the following remark in a memo from a Treasury official to the corresponding official in the Ministry of Labour: "I should not set much store by the opinion of Grierson on a financial matter. He is a Tallents baby, and suspect accordingly in that field."[67] "Unfortunately," as Swann puts it, "the tactics they adopted did much to harm relations with the Treasury, with whom their stock soon fell quite low, which in the long run had very adverse effects upon the subsequent development of the official use of films."[68] Certainly with hindsight that can be seen to have been true.

### Brian Winston

The final revisionist to be discussed based his arguments on a number of writers preceding him—especially Lovell, Pronay, and Aitken—and built on and extended some of their views. At the time of the publication of *Claiming the Real: The Griersonian Documentary and Its Legitimations* (1995), Winston was director of the Centre for Journalism at the University of Wales in Cardiff. In his book, he is not so much after Grierson as he is after the purposes, methods, forms, contents, and means of financing Grierson conceived for documentary film that have persisted to a remarkable extent, and above all Grierson's rationale for all of these aspects—the underlying philosophy. Acknowledging Grierson's success in establishing this model, Winston attributes the success to his extraordinary skill as a publicist.

The book is structured around Grierson's definition of documentary as the *creative treatment* of *actuality*; an examination of the implications of each of the three terms comprises the book's parts.

Displaying a considerable amount of erudition—it is a veritable encyclopedia—Winston undertakes to show that each term of the definition contains uncertainties, paradoxes, and contradictions. The argument, or at least assemblage of evidence, is complex and won't be done full justice here. Fundamentally what Winston is arguing is that the whole Griersonian edifice is built on sand; that its pretensions must be abandoned and a post-Griersonian documentary arrived at.

*Creative* for Winston connotes documentary as art, and he looks at aesthetic theory relating to photography, realist painting, and social and political meaning. The attempt to enclose social and political persuasion within artistic form is what Winston sees as responsible for one of "the essential limitations of the Griersonian documentary to make good on its radical intentions, explicit and implicit."[69] As part of the efforts to make art out of social problems, or to make social problems into art, the Griersonians tended to emphasize "poor, suffering characters: victims and problem moments,"[70] and in dealing with them, to run away from the actual social meaning involved.[71]

*Treatment* Winston sees as documentary as drama. He puts forward an interesting proposition that virtually all films, including documentaries, must follow a narrative organization to connect one image or idea with another. Certain nonfiction films—travelogues, "lecture films," "anthropological and other scientific films of recording, including 'nature films' . . . [n]ewsreels, 'actualities'"— were not considered documentaries by Grierson. "These 'lower forms' of non-fiction cinema all claimed the real, as did documentary, but they did not dramatise. Fiction dramatised but did not claim the real. Ergo documentary was unique in dramatising the real." And, of course, the "fictionalising technique of dramatisation"[72] is in conflict with the documentary's claim to be an accurate and truthful account.

So, the concept of *actuality* requires considering documentary from a scientific point of view. This third part, by far the longest of the three parts, ranges over history and across various fields—optics, law, audio-visual technology, direct cinema and cinéma vérité, ethnography and visual anthropology, epistemology—to test and ultimately refute the claims of documentary films to capture the real.

Winston's concern throughout is of the relationship between the filmmaker and the subjects being filmed—the honesty of the filmmaker in that relationship. At the end of the penultimate chapter, "Towards a Post-Griersonian Documentary,"[73] he gives summary stress to the implications of his overall argument:

> For the post-Griersonian documentarist working in any mode, abandoning the all-powerful position of the artist is a necessary prerequisite for ethical filming. Once the film-maker is liberated from implications of actuality and creativity, then ethical behaviour becomes even more crucial than it was previously. Free of the need to be objective and with the amorality of the creative artist cast aside, there is no reason why such a documentarist could not put the relationship with participants on the pedestal where once these other concepts were enshrined.
>
> To hide behind science or aesthetics is not just illogical, it is unethical. The documentary needs to break free. In this way, breaking the Griersonian claim on the real brings in train a liberation from the restrictions of creativity, as the tradition conceived of it, and from the dangerous illusionism of actuality. The post-Griersonian documentarist should be constrained only by the needs of the relationship of film-maker and participant.[74]

His final, brief chapter is not so much a coda as a clincher for his argument: that the evolving technology of the visual media makes anything seem real, conflates the actual and the fabricated, and makes distinction between them impossible.

> Digitalisation destroys the photographic image as evidence of anything except the process of digitalisation. The physicality of the plastic material represented in any photographic image can no longer be guaranteed. For documentary to survive the widespread diffusion of such technology depends on removing its claim on the real.
>
> . . . in such a technological situation, Grierson's original strong claim on actuality will stand no chance at all. As it collapses, it will bring down the entire documentary edifice. The only hope is for documentary to shift to a new site where, paradoxically, because less is claimed, more might be sustained.
>
> In all this one thing only is certain—the edifice of "creative," "treatment" and "actuality" which Grierson built is going to collapse . . . Claiming the real in the old sense is rapidly becoming untenable.[75]

## Summary

Since I agree—in one way or another, to greater or lesser extent—with the other traditionalists, there seems no need to write further about their positions. The revisionists, on the other hand, have put forth salient criticisms of Grierson's theory and practice at least four of which must be dealt with.

### Film/Reality

First, and perhaps most fundamental, is Grierson's view of the relationship between film and reality, which Alan Lovell, Andrew Tudor, and especially Brian Winston consider at some length. (Grierson used the term *actuality* in his definition of documentary in hopes of bypassing the philosophical brambles surrounding *reality*.)

As for the first revisionist, Lovell, two other traditionalists have already discussed his understanding of Grierson's use of the term reality in relationship to film. Ian Lockerbie, in a paper entitled "Grierson and Realism," presented at a conference on Grierson and the National Film Board at McGill University, advanced his own conception of Grierson's aesthetic which largely followed and refuted the points put forward by Lovell.[76] Like Lockerbie, Ian Aitken also faults Lovell's understanding of Grierson's use of the term "the real." Acknowledging that Lovell was "correct to point to the origins of Grierson's ideas in the tradition of philosophical idealism," Aitken adds the qualification that Lovell "did not proceed from that starting point to investigate the substance of that philosophical tradition, or the precise nature of its influence on Grierson."[77]

Tudor's arguments are also confronted by both Lockerbie and Aitken and dismissed. Lockerbie points out that Tudor defines Grierson

> as essentially a propagandist, for whom realism was only a means to an end. He is thus able to argue that there is no reason why Grierson should have preferred a Realist aesthetic, for if the aim was essentially to change people's ways of thought, there is no case for considering Realism to be more effective for this purpose than any other film style. . . . So if Tudor's premise is correct, Grierson was confused in his aims, and hardly deserves the priviledged position Tudor himself gives him. The only way out of such an obvious paradox is to see that Tudor's premise is not correct, and that Realism was much more for Grierson than simply a means to an end.[78]

Lockerbie then proceeds to explicate what that *much more* consisted of.

About Tudor, Aitken, for his part, says simply that "Tudor misinterpreted Grierson . . . when he argued that [he] rarely considered the medium of film 'per se,' and only considered it in terms of its use as an instrument of social persuasion. Tudor also argued that Grierson's theories had no implications for an aesthetic of film. Neither of these arguments was correct."[79] Aitken's view, of course, is that Grierson's conception of film as an instrument of social persuasion was derived from an aesthetic tradition based on philosophical idealism, and that his theory of documentary film indicates that aesthetics and social purpose should have equal status.

Winston has thought long and hard about the special characteristics of the documentaries proceeding from Grierson and the theory underlying them and has acquired a vast and impressively varied amount of knowledge in the course of his investigation. Thus Winston becomes a central figure in the recent emergence of interest in documentary theory that has not been in evidence since Dziga Vertov in the 1920s and Grierson in the 1930s.[80] As his title *Claiming the Real* attests, film and reality is the main issue for him.

Though Grierson was trained in philosophy and makes a case for his aesthetic that still has to be reckoned with, I don't think he was as concerned with ontology as are Winston and other contemporary theorists. Grierson's discussion of film and actuality was framed within the context of the entertainment film of the thirties and his efforts to establish a viable documentary mode and movement distinct from it. He was simply asking that documentaries be about social matters that were part of the public life (rather than fictions about individuals), that they be shot in the locale in which those matters were important (rather than in studios and on back lots), and that the people who experienced those matters and lived and worked in those locales be shown (rather than professional actors pretending to be them while living and working somewhere else).

*Nontheatrical/Theatrical*

The second issue that concerns the revisionists is Grierson's favoring the nontheatrical film over the theatrical one. Lovell, Peter Morris, Joyce Nelson, Nicholas Pronay, Paul Swann, and Winston all deal with this. With hindsight and their own agendas, they fault Grierson for not moving along the route of the commercial entertainment film industry. The British criticize the failure to do that on the grounds that that is what the politicians, civil servants, and film industry would have understood and supported. The Canadians criticize it on the grounds that only through feature-length fiction film can a nation take pride in its film achievement and speak adequately of its culture to its own citizens and to the rest of the world. Both agree that the establishment of a nontheatrical field offered an inadequate substitute for a feature film industry, reaching only a fraction of the audience of the theaters.

It is as if the revisionists are not reading, or in any case not comprehending, the messages Grierson said over and over again that he wanted to send—the public information and persuasion (propaganda, to use his term) that would make better citizens, a better country, and perhaps even a better world. They seem variously indifferent to, suspicious of, or hostile to this program. How such a purpose could have been achieved within the theatrical film—even making the untenable assumption that American hegemony in thirties Britain and forties Canada could have been penetrated—was not evident to him, nor is it to me.

Also, the nontheatrical film was not the piddling thing the revisionists suggest. I came into film through the nontheatrical route in the late 1940s and can tell you that in North America (Canada even more than the United States, I would guess, as a result of Grierson and the Film Board), it seemed a substantial means of communication, its audience including social activists and opinion leaders—the people I sense Grierson was most interested in reaching. The nontheatrical film (again, I'm on surest ground in the United States) led to public television, community access channels, and, of course, the burgeoning video field operating quite outside the theaters on an individual rental and purchase basis. I would argue that what Grierson wanted to communicate to the public, he attempted in the only ways open to him at the time.

As for the Canadian feature films that Morris and Nelson wanted, Quebec has managed a modestly viable theatrical output because it offers French-Canadian language and culture to a loyal audience. English-language Canadian feature films, on the other hand, in spite of a Canadian Film Development Corporation established in 1964 to provide partial government funding, remain mostly pale imitations of Hollywood B-features. Then there are the few U.S. films shot in Canada because of lower production costs. Neither category offers evidence of Canadian nationality on the screen.

During World War II, Grierson was convinced that urgent and

maximum effort was needed—that it was a newsreel war, not a documentary war, let alone a fiction-feature war. Certainly this was not a time to develop Canadian feature filmmaking, which he might honestly have thought a bad idea. (He had the same opinion about prospects for Scottish feature production postwar; and the idea behind Group 3 as specifically British feature production in content and personnel didn't altogether work, though he gave it a try.) "A Film Policy for Canada" (1944) seems to me simply to state his views in terms of practicability.

### Public Servant/Operator

Third, there's the matter of Grierson's ability and trustworthiness as a civil servant, pursued by Pronay directly and vigorously and by Swann by implication. Implicit in much of Pronay's mistrust of Grierson is the same sort of antagonism of those in the government of the Conservative Party in the 1930s. For example, Pronay quotes with approval from Sir Joseph Ball, a senior civil servant, a dismissive comment about Grierson and Tallents. Ball had been director of the Conservative Research Department and was the party's film adviser.[81] According to Paul Rotha, he was one of "a small group of politicians and Film Trade men who were determined to get rid of Tallents and Grierson and their concept of the documentary film."[82] Rotha—considered its historian by those in the British documentary movement—is cited by Pronay only once. That both the politicians and Pronay distrusted Grierson's politics seems likely; Pronay's attack strikes me as coming from a conservative political position. In any case, no sympathy is apparent, and scarcely any interest, in Grierson's stated goals. Winston thinks "Pronay is to be much complimented on the fact that he is one of the very few to have worked with Grierson and remained 'unenchanted.'"[83] Perhaps so, but one wonders why this is the case.

Surely maneuvering of the sort Swann describes must be fairly common in bureaucratic territorial conflicts. Essentially what was at issue was that Tallents and Grierson wanted to expand the G.P.O. Film Unit to make films for other government departments—to become *the* government film unit—and to have it take on a broadened scope for government communication with the public via documentary film. (That is: what Tallents had posited in *The Projection of England* [1932], what Grierson largely achieved at the National

Film Board, and what even seemed to be happening when the G.P.O. Film Unit became the Crown Film Unit after the outbreak of war.) It is easy to see, given the temperaments and visions of the public servants involved, why there would be this collision. And why it was perhaps inevitable that the entrenched powers and traditional methods would ultimately triumph—but by no means destroy all that had been built.

I doubt that Grierson (and especially Tallents) failed to understand the workings and the power of the civil service. Pronay contends this, Swann does not. I think Grierson and Tallents did not want to work in the traditional ways and achieve the traditional goals any more than the senior civil servants could imagine taking the leaps into creative use of media on behalf of the sort of citizenship education to which both men were committed.

### Internationalist/Nationalist

Fourth, and finally, is the case made by Morris and Nelson that Grierson was working against the proper development of film in Canada. Since the argument is stated more strongly by Nelson let me address my remarks to hers.

My principal critique is that Nelson's neat pattern of forces lined up in a conspiracy—Mackenzie King and John Grierson, international oil, U.S. imperial power and ambitions—collapses in the denouement. If what Nelson is arguing were true, why would Grierson have left Canada at the pinnacle of his privileged position? If he was part of a cabal within the government, why did no Canadian statesman rise to defend him at the time of the spy trials? Why, during his UNESCO tenure, did he take a position directly opposed to the doctrine of the free flow of information being pushed by U.S. interests? Nelson makes no attempts to answer any of these questions.

The chief limitation of Nelson's hindsight, it seems to me, is that she does not allow sufficiently for wartime needs and pressures. Canada and the United States were truly and justifiably afraid that Britain might fall and, if it did, Germany would overrun the world. The position Grierson took from 1939 to 1945 is in relation to that threat; the ideas put forward in the much-quoted 1941 addresses— "Education and the New Order" and "Education and Total Effort"—are not matched in his writing before or after the war.

Granted that Grierson was committed to an internationalist

view. It may be, as Nelson concludes, that at the time he believed, "Through the release of corporate and mass energies, combined with full mechanization and technocratic planning, order would prevail across the planet."[84] But this scarcely makes him anti-Canadian, as she argues.

Having offered some counterarguments to the revisionists' main arguments, let me add, however, that I feel indebted to them for bringing to light through research in government archives the attitudes and forces among Grierson's employers which checked his idealism and ambition. A whole new reading of what he was trying to achieve and the reasons he didn't altogether succeed has become available in the last ten years or so. The revisionists have also questioned the traditionalists' willingness to take the word of Grierson and his associates regarding his goals, his successes, and in fact the kind of person he was. That is a useful caution that should be heeded.

# ➤ EPILOGUE

Whatever is thought or said about the life, contributions, and influence of John Grierson, there can be no question that he was the person most responsible for the documentary film as English speakers have known it. The use of institutional sponsorship, public and private, to pay for his kind of filmmaking, rather than dependence on returns from the box office, was one key Grierson innovation. A second, that complemented the first, was nontheatrical distribution and exhibition—going outside the movie houses to reach audiences in schools and factories, union halls and church basements, and eventually on television.

The three hundred or more British documentaries made between *Drifters* and Grierson's departure for Canada and the systems that spawned them became models for other countries. If many of those three hundred films were dull and transient in their significance, such an opinion would not have disturbed Grierson. His strategy involved a steady output of short films presenting a consistent social view—a constant reinforcement of certain attitudes, not unlike the strategy of today's makers of television commercials. Each film dealt with a small piece of the larger argument. It may seem ironic that conservative institutions were talked into paying for what was overall and essentially the presentation of a socialist point of view. But the desperateness of the economic situation during the Depression had to be acknowledged even by the Tories in power. Perhaps the subject matter of the films about work and workers that Grierson talked them into sponsoring was, or was made to seem, obligatory.

The attitudes of those films were always positive; problems could be solved by combined goodwill and social action. Though never acknowledged publicly, it seems to be true that the films were seen mostly by the middle and upper classes rather than by the working class whom they were mostly about. Opinion leaders were thus reached who may have been persuaded or encouraged by the films to take a Griersonian view of the world.

One of the requisites for the success of the Grierson enterprise was the idea of consensus. The documentary films did not advance partisan political positions; they stayed within what the two major political parties, Conservative and Labour, might agree upon. Nor did the documentary filmmakers attach themselves publicly to a political party. At the same time, the subjects and attitudes evident in the steady flow may have contributed to some extent to the sweeping Labour victory in 1945, at the end of the war.

In any case, Grierson once hinted that he thought the documentaries of the thirties had helped prepare the British people for the collective effort soon to be required of them in wartime. Perhaps without the documentary movement, there might have been responses other than the heroic national effort that began once the bombs started to fall. But of course Grierson himself was in Canada throughout World War II, a period that can be seen as the height of his career.

The essential point to be made about the National Film Board is that the kind of institution Grierson was able to construct in Canada was an unrivaled information system, the largest and best coordinated government film operation in the world. By 1945, the end of the war, it was producing three hundred films a year (this in contrast to three hundred documentaries produced in Great Britain in the ten years before the war). Most of the Film Board releases were said to have reached an audience of roughly four million. It had a staff of about seven hundred in production and distribution. All of this was achieved by a nation with a population of only twelve million.

Perhaps, finally, the sheer establishment of the National Film Board—which went on to other kinds of achievements, including aesthetic excellence, while the documentary movements in Britain and America faltered—is the great legacy of the wartime documentary efforts in Canada. It became a model for national film boards established in New Zealand, Australia, South Africa, India, and elsewhere. It stands as the largest and most impressive testimonial to Grierson's concepts and actions relating to the use of film by governments in communication with their citizens.

But it is, above all, for his multifaceted, innovative leadership that Grierson is most to be valued. As a theoretician, he articulated the basis for the documentary film, its form and function, its aesthetic and its ethic. As an informal teacher, he trained and, through his writing and speaking, influenced many documentary filmmakers, not only in Britain but throughout the world. As a producer, he was eventually responsible to one extent or another for thousands of films and played a decisive creative role in some of the most important of them. And for much of his life, he was an adroit political figure and dedicated civil servant. Even when not on government payroll, his central concern was always with communicating to the people of a nation and of the world the information and attitudes he thought would help them lead more useful and productive, more satisfying and rewarding lives.

# ✦ NOTES

## 1. Scotland (1898–1924)

1. According to Forsyth Hardy, in a *Scottish Life and Letters* radio broadcast, Scottish Home Service of the B.B.C., May 15, 1966.

2. Grierson, "The Course of Realism," in *Footnotes to the Film*, ed. Charles Davy (London: Lovat Dickson, 1937), pp. 137–61.

3. Grierson, *Education and the New Order*, Democracy and Citizenship Series, pamphlet no. 7 (Canadian Association for Adult Education, 1941), 15 pp.

4. Grierson, in Forsyth Hardy, *Scottish Life and Letters*.

5. Grierson, *Education and the New Order*.

6. Grierson, *Education and the New Order*. Robert Blatchford (1851–1943) was a political pamphleteer and socialist. James Keir Hardie (1856–1915) and Robert Smillie (1857–1940) were labor leaders and dedicated socialists, Hardie the first to represent the workingman in the British parliament as an independent (1892) and first to lead the Labour Party in the House of Commons (1906).

7. Grierson, *Education and the New Order*. Frederick Edwin Smith, first earl of Birkenhead, was a statesman, lawyer, and noted orator; he was lord rector of Glasgow University during 1922, while Grierson was a student there.

8. Margaret Ann Elton, interview by author, August 1966.

9. Grierson, *Education and the New Order*.

10. John Taylor, interview by author, September 1966.

11. Forsyth Hardy, in Grierson, *Grierson on Documentary*, ed. Forsyth Hardy (London: Collins, 1946; New York: Harcourt, Brace, 1947; rev. ed., Berkeley: University of California Press, 1966), p. 14. All citations are from the 1966 edition unless otherwise indicated.

12. Margaret Grierson, interview by author, September 1966.

13. Grierson, interview by author, September 1966.

14. Grierson, interview by author, September 1966.

15. Forsyth Hardy, *Scottish Life and Letters*.

16. Grierson, in Forsyth Hardy, *Scottish Life and Letters*.

17. Grierson, "The Course of Realism."

18. Grierson, interview by author, September 1966.

19. Grierson, interview by author, September 1966.

20. Grierson, quoted in Basil Wright, "The Progress of the Factual Film: 1. Grierson the Pioneer," in *Public's Progress* (London: Contact, 1948), pp. 64–71.

21. Grierson, interview by author, September 1966.

22. Grierson, interview by author, September 1966.

23. Forsyth Hardy, in Grierson, *Grierson on Documentary*, p. 14.

24. Grierson, interview by author, September 1966.

25. Grierson, "The Film at War," broadcast on the Canadian Broadcasting Corporation from Ottawa, November 30, 1939. Slightly abridged as "Broadcast to Canada," *Documentary News Letter* 1, no. 4 (April 1940): 3–4.

26. Mary Losey Field, interview by author, November 1965.

27. Grierson, *Grierson on Documentary*, p. 14.

28. Grierson, *Grierson on Documentary*, p. 14.

29. Grierson, interview by author, September 1966.

30. Grierson, interview by author, September 1966.

31. Grierson, "*Captains Courageous*: Best Release of the Month," *World Film News* 2, no. 9 (December 1937): 18–19.

32. Grierson, "Education in a Technological Society" (address to the National Conference on Adult Education, Winnipeg, May 28, 1945), *Film News* n.s., 1, no. 1 (October 1945): 12–13.

33. Grierson, "Background for the Use of Films—or Anything Else—by Rehabilitation Officers" (Ottawa: National Film Board, February, 1945), mimeographed.

34. Grierson, "The Film at War."

35. Grierson, preface to *Documentary Film*, by Paul Rotha, 3d ed. (London: Faber and Faber, 1952), pp. 15–24. James Maxton (1885–1946) was one of the leaders of left-wing socialism between World War I and II and an MP from Glasgow, 1922–46; Hardie and Smillie have already been identified; John Wheatley became Minister of Health in the first Labour government (1924)—all were leaders in the Independent Labour Party.

Walter Elliot, a longtime friend of Grierson's, became a Conservative MP (from 1918 on), Parliamentary Under Secretary of State for Scotland, Financial Secretary to the Treasury, and Minister of Agriculture and Fisheries.

36. Grierson, interview by author, September 1966.

37. Grierson, interview by author, September 1966.

38. John Taylor, interview by author, September 1966.

39. John Taylor, interview by author, September 1966.

40. Marion Grierson, interview by author, September 1966.

41. Grierson, "A Review of Reviews," *Sight and Sound* n.s. 23, no. 4 (April–June 1954): 207–8, 222.

42. Grierson, interview by author, September 1966.

43. Forsyth Hardy, in Grierson, *Grierson on Documentary*, p. 41.

44. Grierson, "Flaherty as Innovator," *Sight and Sound* n.s. 21, no. 2 (October–December 1951): 64–68.

45. Grierson, interview by author, September 1966.

46. Grierson, interview by author, September 1966.

47. Margaret Ann Elton, interview by author, August 1966.

48. Grierson, interview by author, September 1966.

49. Wright, "The Progress of the Factual Film."

50. Grierson, "Education in a Technological Society."

51. Grierson, "A Fairy Tale of Politics," *New Britain* (June 14, 1933): 110.

52. Charles Dand, letter to author, June 1967.

53. Elizabeth Sussex, "The Golden Years of Grierson," *Sight and Sound* 41, no. 3 (summer 1972): 149–53.

54. Grierson, interview by author, September 1966.

## 2. United States (1924–27)

1. Forsyth Hardy, in Grierson, *Grierson on Documentary*, p. 14.

2. Forsyth Hardy, in Grierson, *Grierson on Documentary*, p. 14.

3. Grierson, interview by author, September 1966.

4. Grierson, interview by author, September 1966.

5. Grierson, "Revolution in the Arts" (speech delivered at the University of North Carolina, Chapel Hill, April 1962), in James Beveridge, *John Grierson: Film Master* (New York: Macmillan, 1978), pp. 26–34.

6. Grierson, interview by author, September 1966.

7. Grierson, "A Day with John Grierson."

8. Grierson, "Revolution in the Arts" and "A Day with John Grierson."

9. Grierson, interview by author, September 1966.

10. Grierson, "Propaganda and Education" (address delivered to the Winnipeg Canadian Club, October 19, 1943), *Grierson on Documentary*, pp. 280–94.

11. The material in the preceding four paragraphs that relates directly to the Weisenborns was obtained in an interview, September 1963.

12. Grierson, interview by author, September 1966.

13. Rudolph Weisenborn, "Study of John Grierson," *Chicago Evening Post*, c. June 1925, Art World section.

14. Alfreda ("Fritzie") Weisenborn, interview by author, September 1963.

15. Arthur and Margaret Ann Elton, interview by author, August 1966.

16. Grierson, "Propaganda and Education."

17. Grierson, interview by author, September 1966.

18. Grierson, "Behind the Screen," *World Film News* 3, no. 1 (April 1938): 18–19.

19. Grierson, interview by author, September 1966.

20. Grierson, "Von Sternberg—and Joe," *Everyman* (April 14, 1932): 362.

21. Grierson, "The Crazy Man of the Films," *Everyman* (May 26, 1932): 554.

22. Grierson, "Criticisms—Romantic Anarchist," *World Film News* 1, no. 1 (April 1936): 11.

23. Margaret Ann Elton, letter to author, August 1968.

24. Grierson, "Two Important Films," *Clarion* (February 1930): 45.

25. According to Bosley Crowther, in Beveridge, *John Grierson: Film Master*, p. 232.

26. Forsyth Hardy, in Grierson, *Grierson on Documentary*, p. 15.

27. Grierson, "On Robert Flaherty," *Reporter* 5, no. 8 (October 16, 1951): 31–35.

28. Fritzie Weisenborn, interview by author, September 1963.

29. Richard Watts Jr., in Beveridge, *John Grierson: Film Master*, pp. 35–37.

30. Grierson, "Filming the Gospel a Dangerous Policy," *World Film News* 1, no. 2 (May 1936): 23.

31. Grierson, "The Russian Cinema Bear Awakens: The Movie Situation in the Land of the Muscovites," *Motion Picture Classic*, no. 25 (June 1927): 18–19, 74, 78.

32. Flaherty, who would have been forty-one to Grierson's twenty-seven, was living alternately in New York City and at his home in New Canaan, Conn.

33. Grierson, "Flaherty as Innovator."

34. Grierson, "On Robert Flaherty."

35. The review is quoted in full in Paul Rotha and Basil Wright, "Flaherty: A Biography" (typescript, 1959), Museum of Modern Art Library, pp. 105–7.

36. Rotha and Wright, "Flaherty," p. 120.

37. Grierson, letter to Richard Dyer MacCann, June 1968. Made available to author by Professor MacCann.

38. Grierson, *Eisenstein, 1898–1948* (London: Film Section of the Society for Cultural Relations with the U.S.S.R., 1948), 28 pp. Publication of a spoken tribute following Eisenstein's death given on May 2, 1948, by Grierson, Paul Rotha, Ivor Montagu, Marie Seton, and Herbert Marshall.

39. Grierson, letter to MacCann, June 1968.

40. Grierson, "Making a Film of the Actual: A Problem in Film Construction," *Clarion* (October 1929): 11–12.

## 3. Empire Marketing Board Film Unit (1927–33)

1. Henry Pelling, *Modern Britain: 1885–1955* (New York: W. W. Norton, 1960), pp. 90–91.

2. Sir Michael Balcon, *Michael Balcon Presents . . . A Lifetime of Films* (London: Hutchinson, 1969), p. 12.

3. Roy Armes, *A Critical History of the British Cinema* (New York: Oxford University Press, 1978), p. 73.

4. Julian Symons, *Bloody Murder* (Harmondsworth: Penguin Books, 1974), quoted in Armes, *A Critical History*, p. 12.

5. Grierson, "The E.M.B. Film Unit," *Cinema Quarterly* 1, no. 4 (summer 1933): 203–208.

6. L. S. Amery, *My Political Life* (London: Hutchinson, 1953), vol. 2, p. 347.

7. Arts Enquiry, *The Factual Film: A Survey* (London: Oxford University Press, 1947), p. 44.

8. Tallents was knighted in 1932. He died in 1958, after a distinguished career of public service.

9. Sir Stephen Tallents, "The First Days of Documentary," *Documentary News Letter* 6, no. 55 (January–February 1947): 76–77.

10. Sir Stephen Tallents, "Cinema" (1945, typescript), p. 9. The manuscript was to have been the second part of Tallents's autobiography, covering the E.M.B., kindly loaned to the author by Sir Arthur Elton. It was published as "The Birth of British Documentary," *Journal of the University Film Association* 20, nos. 1–3 (1968).

11. Forsyth Hardy, in Grierson, *Grierson on Documentary*, p. 16.

12. Tallents, "The First Days of Documentary."

13. Tallents, "The First Days of Documentary."

14. Tallents, "Cinema," p. 5.

15. Grierson, "The Story of the Documentary Film," *Fortnightly Review* 152, no. 146 (August 1939): 121–30.

16. Grierson, "The Course of Realism."

17. Grierson, "The E.M.B. Film Unit."

18. Wright, "The Progress of the Factual Film."

19. Tallents, "The First Days of Documentary."

20. Grierson, "The E.M.B. Film Unit."

21. Tallents, "Cinema," p. 6.

22. Grierson, "Notes on the Documentary Film" (Chicago: National Film Board of Canada, c. 1945), mimeographed, 10 pp. Though no author is listed, the style and other evidence strongly suggest that this is Grierson's writing.

23. Tallents, "Cinema," p. 8. He is quoting from the program notes Grierson wrote for these screenings.

24. Grierson, "The Course of Realism."

25. F. V. Millington, "Cinematograph in Agricultural Education: A Leicestershire Experiment," *Journal of the Ministry of Agriculture, London* 36 (November 1929): 739–45.

26. Tallents, "Cinema," p. 9.

27. Tallents, "Cinema," pp. 9–10.

28. Tallents, "Cinema," pp. 9–10.

29. Tallents, "Cinema," p. 10.

30. Wright, "The Progress of the Factual Film."

31. Grierson, "Making a Film of the Actual."

32. Charles Dand, manuscript enclosed with letter to author, June 1967.

33. Grierson, "The Story of the Documentary Film."

34. John Taylor, interview by author, September 1966.

35. Edgar and Daphne Anstey, interview by author, August 1966.

36. Tallents, "Cinema," pp. 14–15. As mentioned earlier, Tallents had helped plan the food rationing introduced in Britain during World War I.

37. Grierson, letter to Richard Dyer MacCann, June 1968.

38. Rotha and Wright, "Flaherty," p. 146.

39. Forsyth Hardy, "The Film Society Movement in Scotland," in *Film Society Primer: A Compilation of Twenty-Two Articles about and for Film Societies*, ed. Cecile Starr and Carolyn Henig (Forest Hills, N.Y.: American Federation of Film Societies, 1956).

40. Tallents, "Cinema," p. 15.

41. Grierson, "The Course of Realism."

42. Tallents, "Cinema," pp. 15–16.

43. Paul Rotha, *The Film Till Now: A Survey of World Cinema* (London: Jonathan Cape, 1930), p. 230.

44. Rotha, *Documentary Film*, pp. 97–98. The passage appears in the 1952 edition as it did in the 1939 one.

45. An announcement in *Close-up* 6, no. 3 (March 1930): 247.

46. Hay Chowl, "Mickey's Rival," *Close-up* 6, no. 6 (June 1930): 493–95.

47. Rotha and Wright, "Flaherty," p. 147.

48. Grierson, "The E.M.B. Film Unit."

49. Tallents, "Cinema," pp. 20–21.

50. Grierson, "The E.M.B. Film Unit."

51. Tallents, "Cinema," pp. 17–18.

52. Tallents, "Cinema," p. 18.

53. Grierson, "The E.M.B. Film Unit."

54. Tallents, "Cinema," p. 18.

55. Grierson, *A Tribute to Humphrey Jennings* (London: Olen, n.d. [1950?]). Grierson's piece is untitled and collected with other tributes by Dilys Powell, Basil Wright, and Roger Manvell.

56. Grierson, interview by author, September 1966.

57. Marion Grierson, interview by author, September 1966.

58. Forsyth Hardy, in Grierson, *Grierson on Documentary*, p. 16.

59. Tallents, "Cinema," pp. 19–20.

60. Edgar Anstey, "The Early Days of Documentary," *Cine-Technician* 7 (September–October 1941): 102–4.

61. Frank Sainsbury, "Close-Ups: No. 2—Arthur Elton," *Cine-Technician* 5 (July–August 1939): 57–58.

62. Rotha and Wright, "Flaherty," p. 148.

63. Anstey, "The Early Days of Documentary."

64. Rotha and Wright, "Flaherty," p. 148.

65. Tallents, "Cinema," p. 20.

66. Rotha and Wright, "Flaherty," p. 148.

67. Tallents, "Cinema," p. 20.

68. Tallents, "Cinema," p. 23.

69. Anstey, "The Early Days of Documentary."

70. Grierson, "The E.M.B. Film Unit."

71. Tallents, "Cinema," p. 21.

72. Forsyth Hardy, in Grierson, *Grierson on Documentary*, p. 18.

73. Basil Wright, interview by author, September 1966.

74. Great Britain. Commission on Educational and Cultural Films, *The Film in National Life* (London: Allen and Unwin, 1932), p. 73.

75. Jay Leyda, *Films Beget Films* (London: George Allen and Unwin, 1964), p. 20.

76. Tallents, "Cinema," p. 24.

77. Rotha and Wright, "Flaherty," pp. 141–42.

78. Grierson, letter to Stephen Tallents, December 1951, quoted in Rotha and Wright, "Flaherty," p. 162.

79. Rotha and Wright, "Flaherty," pp. 148–49.

80. Rotha and Wright, "Flaherty," p. 162.

81. Rotha and Wright, "Flaherty," p. 150.

82. Rotha and Wright, "Flaherty," p. 233.

83. Rotha and Wright, "Flaherty," p. 151.

84. Rotha and Wright, "Flaherty," p. 155.

85. Rotha and Wright, "Flaherty," p. 155.

86. Rotha and Wright, "Flaherty," p. 156.

87. Rotha and Wright, "Flaherty," pp. 157–58.

88. Rotha and Wright, "Flaherty," p. 158.

89. Rotha and Wright, "Flaherty," p. 159.

90. Rotha and Wright, "Flaherty," p. 162.

91. Rotha and Wright, "Flaherty," p. 162.

92. Grierson, "The Course of Realism."

93. Rotha and Wright, "Flaherty," p. 162.

94. Rotha and Wright, "Flaherty," p. 163.

95. Grierson, "The Cinema Today," in *The Arts Today*, ed. Geoffrey Grigson, 219–50 (London: Bodley Head, 1935).

96. Rotha and Wright, "Flaherty," p. 190. This incident is recounted in amusing detail but without names in Pat Mullen, *Man of Aran* (New York: E. P. Dutton, 1935), pp. 128–30.

97. Tallents, "Cinema," p. 26.

98. Tallents, "Cinema," p. 26.

99. Tallents, "Cinema," p. 27.

100. Forsyth Hardy, in Grierson, *Grierson on Documentary*, p. 19.

101. Paul Rotha, *Celluloid: The Film To-Day* (London: Longmans, Green, 1931), pp. 59–61.

102. Tallents, "Cinema," p. 23.

103. Grierson, *Grierson on Documentary*, p. 397.

104. Grierson, "Notes on the Documentary Film."

105. Rotha and Wright, "Flaherty," p. 159.

106. Arts Enquiry, *The Factual Film*, p. 57.

107. Sir Harry Lindsay, "Romance and Adventure in Real Things: The Imperial Institute and Its Film Library," *World Film News* 2 (July 1937): 19.

108. Lt.-Gen. Sir William Furse, "The Imperial Institute," *Sight and Sound* 2, no. 7 (autumn 1933): 78–79.

109. Great Britain. Commission on Educational and Cultural Films, *The Film in National Life*, p. 138.

110. Tallents, "Cinema," p. 16.

111. Tallents, "Cinema," pp. 16–17.

112. Furse, "The Imperial Institute."

113. Arts Enquiry, *The Factual Film*, p. 59.

114. Arts Enquiry, *The Factual Film*, p. 59.

115. Great Britain. Commission on Educational and Cultural Films, *The Film in National Life*, p. 129.

116. Great Britain. Commission on Educational and Cultural Films, *The Film in National Life*, p. 129.

117. Tallents, "Cinema," p. 24.

118. Basil Wright, letter to Grierson, February 1931.

119. Tallents, "Cinema," p. 25.

120. Tallents, "Cinema," p. 25.

121. Forsyth Hardy, in Grierson, *Grierson on Documentary*, p. 20.

122. Rotha and Wright, "Flaherty," p. 149.

123. Tallents, "Cinema," p. 22.

124. Grierson, "*Things to Come* by H. G. Wells," *Glasgow Herald*, October 29, 1935.

125. Grierson, *Grierson on Documentary*, p. 20.

126. Grierson, *Grierson on Documentary*, p. 394.

127. Tallents, "Cinema," p. 22.

128. Grierson, "Documentary (1)," *Cinema Quarterly* 1, no. 2 (winter 1932): 67–72.

129. Grierson, "Documentary (2): Symphonics," *Cinema Quarterly* 2, no. 3 (spring 1933): 135–39.

130. Forsyth Hardy, in Grierson, *Grierson on Documentary*, p. 21 (1947 edition).

131. Forsyth Hardy, interview by author, September 1966.

132. Grierson, "What I Look for," *New Clarion* (June 11, 1932).

133. Grierson, "Tom Mix, Man of Action," *New Britain* (August 2, 1933): 334, 342.

134. Grierson, "Flaherty—Naturalism—and the Problem of English Cinema," *Artwork* 7 (autumn 1931): 210–15."

135. Grierson, "Hitchcock: Britain's Best Director," *Clarion* (November 1930): 201–2.

136. Grierson, "The Hitch in Hitchcock," *Everyman* (December 24, 1931): 722.

137. C. A. Lejeune, *Thank You for Having Me* (London: Hutchinson, 1964), quoted in Grierson, *Grierson on Documentary*, p. 41.

138. Grierson, "Clowns of the Screen," *Everyman* (October 29, 1931): 430.

139. Grierson, "Thanks to Alistair Cooke," *World Film News* 1, no. 11 (December 1937): 89.

140. Grierson, *Grierson on Documentary*, p. x (1946 edition).

141. Tallents, "Cinema," p. 30.

142. *General Post Office Film Library Catalogue*, 1933 edition.

143. Tallents, "Cinema," p. 17.

144. Grierson, "The Story of the Documentary Film."

145. Grierson, "Notes on the Documentary Film."

146. Grierson, "Cinema of State," *Clarion* (August 1930): 235.

147. Rotha, *Documentary Film*, p. 97.

148. Grierson, "The E.M.B. Film Unit."

## 4. General Post Office Film Unit (1933–37)

1. Forsyth Hardy, in Grierson, *Grierson on Documentary*, p. 20.

2. Grierson, "The Story of the Documentary Film."

3. Grierson, "The Story of the Documentary Film."

4. Tallents, "Cinema," p. 32.

5. Tallents, "Cinema," p. 32.

6. Grierson, "Battle for Authenticity," *Documentary News Letter* (1939), reprinted in Grierson, *Grierson on Documentary*, pp. 215–17.

7. Arts Enquiry, *The Factual Film*, p. 52.

8. Great Britain. Select Committee on Estimates, *Report from a Select Committee on Estimates* (London: His Majesty's Stationery Office, July 1934).

9. Tallents, "Cinema," p. 33.

10. Paul Rotha, *Rotha on the Film: A Selection of Writings about the Cinema* (London: Faber and Faber, 1958), p. 210.

11. Grierson, "The G.P.O. Gets Sound," *Cinema Quarterly* 2, no. 4 (summer 1934): 215–21.

12. Stuart Legg, interview by author, September 1966.

13. Arthur Elton, "Barking Up the Wrong Tree," *Documentary News Letter* 7 (November–December 1948).

14. "Film of the Month—*Nine Men*," *Documentary News Letter* 4 (February 1943): 179.

15. Elton, interview by author, August 1966.

16. Quoted in "Film of the Month—*Nine Men*."

17. Elton, "Barking up the Wrong Tree."

18. Alberto Cavalcanti, "Presenting Len Lye," *Sight and Sound* 16 (winter 1947–48): 134–36.

19. Elton, interview by author, August 1966.

20. Gerald Noxon, conversation with author, April 1963.

21. Grierson, "Art and the Analysts," *Sight and Sound* 4, no. 16 (winter 1935–36): 157–59.

22. Elton, interview by author, August 1966.

23. Edgar Anstey, "The Living Story: E.M.B.–G.P.O.," *Sight and Sound* 21, no. 4 (April–June 1952): 176.

24. Rotha, *Documentary Film*, p. 169 footnote.

25. Grierson, "Book Reviews: *The Summing Up*," *World Film News* 2, no. 12 (March 1938).

26. Raymond J. Spottiswoode, *A Grammar of the Film: An Analysis of Film Technique* (London: Faber and Faber, 1935), pp. 88–89.

27. Legg, interview by author, September 1966.

28. Grierson, "The Function of the Producer: 2. The Documentary Producer," *Cinema Quarterly* 2, no. 1 (autumn 1933): 7–9.

29. Grierson, "The Story of the Documentary Film."

30. Grierson, preface to Rotha, *Documentary Film*, p. 16.

31. Roger Manvell, *Film* (Harmondsworth, Middlesex: Penguin, 1946), pp. 99, 101.

32. Rotha, *Documentary Film*, p. 162.

33. Spottiswoode, *A Grammar of the Film*, p. 90. The films of Legg that Spottiswoode is discussing are available only at the National Film Archive in London.

34. Edgar Anstey, "Some Origins of Cinéma Vérité," n.d., typescript, 7 pp. Typescript made available to the author by Anstey.

35. Spottiswoode, *A Grammar of the Film*, p. 90.

36. Spottiswoode, *A Grammar of the Film*, p. 93.

37. "Basil Wright: Close-Up," *Documentary Film News* 7 (March 1948): 34.

38. Basil Wright, "John Taylor: A Close-Up," *Documentary Film News* 7 (July 1948): 82–83.

39. Arts Enquiry, *The Factual Film*, p. 48.

40. Edgar Anstey, "The Sound-Track in British Documentary," n.d., typescript, 13 pp. Typescript made available to the author by Anstey.

41. Graham Greene, in *Garbo and the Night Watchman*, ed. Alistair Cooke, p. 210–11. London: Jonathan Cape, 1937.

42. *Time*, January 28, 1946.

43. "Basil Wright: Close-Up."

44. Anstey, "The Sound-Track in British Documentary."

45. Grierson, interview by author, September 1966.

46. Manvell, *Film*, pp. 100–101.

47. Anstey, "The Sound-Track in British Documentary."

48. Grierson, "The G.P.O. Gets Sound."

49. Spottiswoode, *A Grammar of the Film*, p. 93.

50. Rotha, *Documentary Film*, p. 362.

51. Manvell, *Film*, p. 362.

52. Anstey, "The Sound-Track in British Documentary."

53. Rotha, *Documentary Film*, pp. 194–95.

54. Anstey, "The Sound-Track in British Documentary."

55. Paul Nash, "The Colour Film," in Davy, *Footnotes to the Film*, p. 134.

56. Cavalcanti, "Presenting Len Lye."

57. Nash, "The Colour Film," p. 133.

58. Cavalcanti, "Presenting Len Lye."

59. Cavalcanti, "Presenting Len Lye."

60. J. B. Holmes, "G.P.O. Films," *Sight and Sound* 6, no. 23 (autumn 1937): 159–60.

61. Cavalcanti, "Presenting Len Lye."

62. Elton, "Barking up the Wrong Tree."

63. Tallents, "Cinema," pp. 33–34.

64. Forsyth Hardy, interview by author, September 1966.

65. Grierson, "Introduction to a New Art," *Sight and Sound* 3, no. 11 (autumn 1934): 101–4.

66. Herbert Read, "Experiments in Counterpoint," *Cinema Quarterly* 3, no. 1 (autumn 1934): 17–21.

67. Tallents, "Cinema," pp. 33–34.

68. Elton, "Barking up the Wrong Tree."

69. Anstey, "Some Origins of Cinéma Vérité."

70. Rotha, *Rotha on the Film*, p. 211.

71. Paul Rotha, "Films of Fact and the Human Element," *Times* (London), June 28, 1938; reprinted in Rotha, *Rotha on the Film*, pp. 215–16.

72. Grierson, "Propaganda: A Problem for Educational Theory and for Cinema," *Sight and Sound* 3, no. 8 (winter 1933–34): 119–21.

73. Grierson, *Grierson on Documentary*, p. 21.

74. Grierson, "The Story of the Documentary Film."

75. Arts Enquiry, *The Factual Film*, p. 48.

76. Grierson, "The Story of the Documentary Film."

77. Grierson, "Notes on the Documentary Film."

78. Basil Wright, "Ten Years of Documentary," *World Film News* 2, no. 4 (July 1937): 14–15.

79. Arts Enquiry, *The Factual Film*, p. 51.

80. Rotha, *Documentary Film*, p. 192.

81. Arts Enquiry, *The Factual Film*, pp. 58–59.

82. Arts Enquiry, *The Factual Film*, p. 57.

83. Rotha, *Rotha on the Film*, p. 227.

84. Grierson, "Notes on the Documentary Film."

85. "Notes of the Quarter," *Sight and Sound* 4 (summer 1935): 52–53.

86. J. B. Holmes, "G.P.O. Films."

87. Grierson, "Notes on the Documentary Film."

88. "For Public Relations Officers," *World Film News* 1 (November 1936): 29.

89. "G.P.O. Films on Tour," *Sight and Sound* 5 (autumn 1936): 102.

90. J. B. Holmes, "G.P.O. Films."

91. Arts Enquiry, *The Factual Film*, p. 57.

92. Grierson, "Contact," *Cinema Quarterly* 2, no. 1 (autumn 1933): 47.

93. "Perspective," *Documentary News Letter* 6, no. 54 (November–December 1946): 51, 60–63.

94. Arts Enquiry, *The Factual Film*, p. 53.

95. Anstey, "The Sound-Track in British Documentary."

96. Anstey, "Some Origins of Cinéma Vérité."

97. Grierson, "Battle for Authenticity."

98. Rotha, *Documentary Film*, p. 195.

99. Anthony Grierson, conversation with author, September 1966.

100. Forsyth Hardy, in Grierson, *Grierson on Documentary*, p. 22.

101. Anstey, "The Sound-Track in British Documentary."

102. Grierson, "Battle for Authenticity."

103. Grierson, "Notes on the Documentary Film."

104. Forsyth Hardy, in Grierson, *Grierson on Documentary*, p. 23.

105. Arts Enquiry, *The Factual Film*, pp. 59, 77.

106. Arts Enquiry, *The Factual Film*, p. 30.

107. Grierson, "In the Name of Goodness," *World Film News* 3, no. 6 (October 1938): 258–59.

108. "The Spectator," *Cinema Quarterly* 2 (autumn 1933): 3.

109. "New Documentary Group," *Sight and Sound* 4 (winter 1935–36): 174.

110. Sainsbury, "Close-Ups: No. 2—Arthur Elton."

111. Rotha, *Documentary Film*, p. 194.

112. Rotha, *Rotha on the Film*, p. 231.

113. Grierson, "The Function of the Producer."

114. "News from Film Societies," *Sight and Sound* 3 (spring 1934): 25–27.

115. "News from Film Societies," *Sight and Sound* 3 (summer 1934): 85–86.

116. Norman McLaren, interview by author, August 1962.

117. "IFMA's First Summer School at Welwyn," *Sight and Sound* 3 (autumn 1934): 59–60.

118. "What the British Film Institute Is Doing: Branches and Societies," *Sight and Sound* 4 (winter 1935–36): 195–96.

119. "London Film School," *Sight and Sound* 5 (spring 1936): 9.

120. Advertisement, *World Film News* 1 (November 1936): 36.

121. *Kine Weekly*, April 28, 1937.

122. "WFN Policy," *World Film News* 1 (April 1936): 15.

123. Marion Grierson, interview by author, September 1966.

124. Grierson, *Grierson on Documentary*, p. 173 footnote (1946 edition).

125. Arts Enquiry, *The Factual Film*, p. 190.

126. Grierson, "Documentary (1)."

127. Grierson, "John Grierson Replies," *Cinema Quarterly* 3, no. 1 (autumn 1934): 10–11.

128. Rotha and Wright, "Flaherty," p. 236.

129. Frances Flaherty, letter to author, August 1961.

130. Grierson, "The Finest Eyes in Cinema," *World Film News* 1, no. 12 (March 1937): 5.

131. Grierson, "The Course of Realism."

132. Rotha, *Documentary Film*, p. 193.

## 5. Film Centre (1937–39)

1. *Today's Cinema*, January 28, 1937.

2. Arthur Elton, interview by author, August 1966.

3. Arts Enquiry, *The Factual Film*, pp. 56–57.

4. Forsyth Hardy, in Grierson, *Grierson on Documentary*, p. 23.

5. Paul Rotha, "Correspondence," *Sight and Sound* 7 (summer 1939): 81.

6. Arts Enquiry, *The Factual Film*, p. 57.

7. Arts Enquiry, *The Factual Film*, p. 57.

8. George Audit, "Radio: News of the Month," *World Film News* 2 (October 1937): 39.

9. "Notes of the Month," *Documentary News Letter* 2 (January 1941): 1–2.

10. Anstey, "The Sound-Track in British Documentary."

11. Arts Enquiry, *The Factual Film*, p. 61.

12. Forsyth Hardy, in Grierson, *Grierson on Documentary*, p. 23.

13. Forsyth Hardy, in Grierson, *Grierson on Documentary*, p. 23.

14. Donald Alexander, "Stuart Legg: A Close-Up," *Documentary Film News* 7 (June 1948): 68.

15. Grierson, "Searchlight on Democracy," *Adult Education* 12 (December 1939): 59–70.

16. Grierson, "Films and the I.L.O." (address delivered to the International Labor Organization, Philadelphia, April 26, 1944), *Grierson on Documentary*, pp. 309–16.

17. "Perspective."

18. Grierson, "The Future of Documentary," *Cine-Technician* 3 (December 1937–January 1938): 167–68, 170.

19. Grierson, "The Film Situation," *London Mercury and Bookman* 36, no. 215 (September 1937): 459–63.

20. Davy, "Postscript," pp. 303–22.

21. Grierson, "Projection of Scotland," *Spectator* 160 (May 6, 1938): 828, 830.

22. Arts Enquiry, *The Factual Film*, p. 60.

23. Arts Enquiry, *The Factual Film*, p. 60.

24. Rotha, *Documentary Film*, p. 29.

25. "Notes of the Quarter," *Sight and Sound* 6 (winter 1937–38): 169–71.

26. Richard Griffith, "Films at the New York World's Fair," *Documentary News Letter* 1 (February 1940): 3.

27. Arts Enquiry, *The Factual Film*, pp. 61, 180.

28. Arts Enquiry, *The Factual Film*, p. 61.

29. Grierson, "Projection of Scotland."

30. Grierson, conversation with author, June 1969.

31. Pare Lorentz, conversation with author, April 1966.

32. Grierson, "Battle for Authenticity."

33. Griffith, "Films at the New York World's Fair."

34. Alberto Cavalcanti, "Correspondence," *Documentary News Letter* 1 (March 1940): 18.

35. Rotha, *Rotha on the Film*, p. 224.

36. Wright, "The Progress of the Factual Film."

37. Rotha and Wright, "Flaherty," pp. 265–66.

38. Arthur Elton, "How We Use Films in Shell," *Film User* (August 1956): 344–47.

39. Alan Field, "Ross McLean: A Close-Up," *Documentary Film News* 7 (April 1948): 45.

40. Canada. National Film Board, Information and Promotion Division, "The National Film Board of Canada" (Ottawa: National Film Board, September 1953), mimeographed, 33 pp.

41. Canada. National Film Board, Information and Promotion Division, "The National Film Board of Canada."

42. Forsyth Hardy, in Grierson, *Grierson on Documentary*, p. 25.

43. R. S. Lambert, "The Canadian Scene," *Sight and Sound* 10 (summer 1941): 23–24.

44. F. W. Harrold, "The Cinema in Canada," *Sight and Sound* 6 (winter 1937–38): 208–9.

45. Forsyth Hardy, in Grierson, *Grierson on Documentary*, p. 25.

46. Canada. National Film Board, Information and Promotion Division, "The National Film Board of Canada."

47. Donald Buchanan, "Canada on the World's Screens," *Canadian Geographical Journal* 22 (February 1941): 70–81.

48. Canada. National Film Board, Information and Promotion Division, "The National Film Board of Canada."

49. "Canadian Film Board at Work," *Documentary News Letter* 3, no. 9 (September 1942): 129.

50. Arts Enquiry, *The Factual Film*, p. 234.

51. Grierson, letter to Brooke Claxton, November 1945.

52. Grierson, "Notes on the Documentary Film."

53. Mary Losey, "Documentary in the United States," *Documentary News Letter* 1 (May 1940): 9.

54. Rotha and Wright, "Flaherty," p. 277.

55. Arts Enquiry, *The Factual Film*, p. 60.

56. Grierson, "Notes on the Documentary Film."

57. Forsyth Hardy, in Grierson, *Grierson on Documentary*, pp. 24–25.

58. Grierson, "Notes on the Documentary Film."

59. Grierson, "The Film at War."

60. Forsyth Hardy, in Grierson, *Grierson on Documentary*, p. 26.

61. Marjorie McKay, interview by author, August 1962.

62. Forsyth Hardy, in Grierson, *Grierson on Documentary*, p. 26.

63. Basil Wright, "Documentary To-Day," *Penguin Film Review*, no. 2 (January 1947): 37–44.

64. Grierson, "The Story of Documentary Film."

65. Grierson, "A Time for Enquiry."

## 6. National Film Board of Canada (1939–45)

1. H. Reginald Hardy, *Mackenzie King of Canada* (London: Oxford University Press, 1949), p. 128.

2. Gudrun Bjerring Parker, conversation with author, August 1962.

3. H. Reginald Hardy, *Mackenzie King*, p. 309.

4. Forsyth Hardy, in Grierson, *Grierson on Documentary*, p. 20.

5. Grierson, "The Documentary Idea 1942," *Documentary News Letter* 3, no. 6 (June 1942): 83–86.

6. "New Documentary Films," *Documentary News Letter* 1, no. 5 (May 1940): 7.

7. "Films Across Canada," *Documentary News Letter* 1, no. 1 (January 1940): 9–11.

8. Donald Slesinger, "War: First Reactions of U.S.A. Documentary to the Entrance of the United States into the War," *Documentary News Letter* 3, no. 2 (February 1942): 20.

9. Stuart Legg, letter to Wright, February 1940. (This and all subsequent letters cited were made available to author by Basil Wright or Sir Arthur Elton.)

10. Winifred Holmes, "British Films and the Empire," *Sight and Sound* 5 (autumn 1936): 72–74.

11. E. Stanhope Andrews, "Letter from New Zealand," *Documentary News Letter* 4, no. 1 (January 1943).

12. Andrews, "Letter from New Zealand."

13. Grierson, letter to Arthur Elton, March 1940.

14. Cranstone, "Government Film-Making in Australia," *Documentary News Letter* 6 (October 1947).

15. Malcolm Otton, "Film Society Movement in Australia," *Documentary Film News* 8, no. 1 (January 1949): 5, 11.

16. Rotha, *Documentary Film*, p. 298.

17. Canada. National Film Board, Information Section, "The National Film Board: A Survey" (Ottawa: National Film Board, June 1945), mimeographed, 22 pp. This and subsequently listed unpublished materials were consulted at the N.F.B. archive.

18. Grierson, "Notes on the Documentary Film."

19. James Beveridge, interview by author, September 1962.

20. Legg, interview by author, September 1966.

21. Julian Roffman, interview by author, August 1962.

22. "Who's Who in Filmmaking," *Sightlines* 1 (November–December 1967): 4–5.

23. McKay, interview by author, August 1962.

24. Grierson, "The Documentary Idea 1942."

25. Beveridge, interview by author, September 1962.

26. "Australia," *Film News* 20, no. 4 (1963): 6–7.

27. Roffman, interview by author, August 1962.

28. McLaren, interview by author, August 1962; and Alan Phillips, "The Inspired Doodles of Norman McLaren," *McLean's: Canada's National Magazine*, c. 1952.

29. Canada. National Film Board, Information and Promotion Division, "The National Film Board of Canada."

30. Rotha, *Documentary Film*, p. 327.

31. McKay, interview by author, August 1962.

32. Roffman, interview by author, August 1962.

33. Roffman, interview by author, August 1962.

34. Guy Glover, interview by author, August 1962.

35. Grierson, "The Documentary Idea 1942."

36. Tom Daly, interview by author, August 1962.

37. Glover, interview by author, August 1962.

38. Forsyth Hardy, in Grierson, *Grierson on Documentary*, p. 26.

39. Raymond J. Spottiswoode, "Developments at the National Film Board of Canada, 1939–44," *Journal of the Society of Motion Picture Engineers* 44, no. 5 (May 1945): 391–400.

40. Canada. National Film Board, Information and Promotion Division, "The National Film Board of Canada."

41. Grierson, letter to Wright, October 1940.

42. Donald Fraser, interview by author, August 1962.

43. McKay, interview by author, August 1962.

44. Grierson, letter to Wright, October 1940.

45. Grierson, "The Eyes of Canada," in Beveridge, *John Grierson: Film Master*, 143–44. Publication of a broadcast talk on the Canadian Broadcasting Corporation, January 21, 1940.

46. Legg, letter to Wright, December 1940.

47. Margaret Grierson, letter to Wright, February 1941.

48. "News from Canada," *Documentary News Letter* 2, no. 4 (April 1941): 76.

49. McKay, interview by author, August 1962.

50. Canada. National Film Board, Information and Promotion Division, "The National Film Board of Canada."

51. "Canadian Film Board at Work," *Documentary News Letter* 3, no. 9 (September 1942): 129.

52. Spottiswoode, "Developments at the National Film Board of Canada."

53. "Canadian Film Board at Work."

54. Spottiswoode, "Developments at the National Film Board of Canada."

55. Canada. National Film Board, Information and Promotion Division, "The National Film Board of Canada."

56. Grierson, "A Film Policy for Canada," *Canadian Affairs* 1, no. 11 (June 1944): 3–15.

57. Rotha, *Documentary Film*, p. 331.

58. Grierson, "A Film Policy for Canada."

59. McKay, in Grierson, *Grierson on Documentary*, p. 28.

60. Canada. National Film Board, "The National Film Board" (Ottawa: National Film Board, c. 1944), mimeographed, 8 pp.

61. Canada. National Film Board, Information Section, "The National Film Board: A Survey."

62. Grierson, "Tomorrow the Movies II: Pictures Without Theaters," *Nation* 160, no. 1 (January 13, 1945): 37–39.

63. Legg, interview by author, September 1966.

64. Spottiswoode, "Developments at the National Film Board of Canada."

65. Spottiswoode, "Developments at the National Film Board of Canada."

66. Daly, interview by author, August 1962.

67. Daly, interview by author, August 1962.

68. Canada. National Film Board, Information and Promotion Division, "The National Film Board of Canada."

69. Theodore Strauss, "Canada's Camera on the War Clouds," *Documentary News Letter* 3, no. 5 (March 1942): 38–39.

70. Canada. National Film Board, "National Film Board Annual Report, Fiscal Year 1944–45" (Ottawa: National Film Board, 1945), mimeographed, 30 pp.

71. Canada. National Film Board, "National Film Board Annual Report, Fiscal Year 1944–45."

72. Griffith, in Rotha, *Documentary Film*, pp. 332–33.

73. Canada. National Film Board, Information and Promotion Division, "The National Film Board of Canada."

74. Rotha, *Documentary Film*, p. 332.

75. Anstey, "The Sound-Track in British Documentary."

76. Margaret Ann Elton, conversation with author, August 1966.

77. *Time*, June 15, 1942.

78. Rotha, *Documentary Film*, p. 333.

79. *New York Times*, December 5, 1943.

80. Grierson, interview by author, September 1966.

81. Grierson, "A Film Policy for Canada."

82. Daly, interview by author, August 1962.

83. Beveridge, interview by author, September 1962.

84. Griffith, in Rotha, *Documentary Film*, pp. 334, 335.

85. Grierson, "The Documentary Idea 1942."

86. Canada. National Film Board, Information Section, "The National Film Board: A Survey."

87. Canada. National Film Board, Information and Promotion Division, "The National Film Board of Canada."

88. All of the following information on distribution comes from the N.F.B. Information and Promotion Division's September 1953 report, "The National Film Board of Canada."

89. Leonard L. Knott, "Inside Information," *Canadian Business* (October 1943): 24–27, 134, 136, 138.

90. ZAB, "Men o' War: Grierson a Go-Getter," *Montrealer* (December 1943): 15.

91. Legg, interview by author, September 1966.

92. Grierson, "Wartime Information Board: It Is Not Done with Mirrors," c. December 1943. Typescript.

93. ZAB, "Men o' War."

94. Knott, "Inside Information."

95. ZAB, "Men o' War."

96. Knott, "Inside Information."

97. Grierson, "Wartime Information Board."

98. Knott, "Inside Information."

99. McKay, interview by author, August 1962.

100. Grierson, "Films as an International Influence," address to the Vancouver Advertising and Sales Bureau, December 1944, nimeographed, 6 pp.

101. Gordon Weisenborn, interview by author, September 1963.

102. Gordon Weisenborn, interview by author, September 1963.

103. Legg, interview by author, September 1966.

104. Michael Spencer, "John Grierson," *Canadian Film Institute Bulletin* 3, no. 3 (March 1957): 1–2.

105. ZAB, "Men o' War."

106. McKay, interview by author, August 1962.

107. *Ottawa Journal*, May 20, 1949.

108. Legg, interview by author, September 1966.

109. ZAB, "Men o' War."

110. Legg, interview by author, September 1966.

111. Gordon Weisenborn, interview by author, September 1963.

112. King, quoted in H. Reginald Hardy, *Mackenzie King*, p. 285.

113. King, quoted in J. W. Pickersgill, *The Mackenzie King Record* (Toronto: University of Toronto Press, 1960), pp. 222–23.

114. Legg, interview by author, September 1966.

115. Beveridge, interview by author, September 1962.

116. Grierson, "The Film in International Relations" (typescript). This manuscript in two parts, labeled "Article 1" and "Article 2," accompanied a letter to Basil Wright dated November 21, 1944, and was made available to the author by Wright.

117. McKay, interview by author, August 1962.

118. Grierson, letter to Brooke Claxton, November 1945.

119. Michael Spencer, interview by author, August 1962.

120. McKay, interview by author, August 1962.

121. Roffman, interview by author, August 1962.

122. Canada. National Film Board, "The National Film Board."

123. McKay, as quoted in Grierson, *Grierson on Documentary*, p. 28.

124. Spottiswoode, "Developments at the National Film Board of Canada."

125. Daphne and Edgar Anstey, interview by author, August 1966.

126. Roffman, interview by author, August 1962.

127. McLaren, interview by author, August 1962.

128. Glover, interview by author, August 1962.

129. Donald Fraser, interview by author, August 1962.

130. Fritzie Weisenborn, interview by author, September 1963.

131. Fraser, interview by author, August 1962.

132. Forsyth Hardy, interview by author, September 1966.

133. Fritzie Weisenborn, interview by author, September 1963.

134. Anstey, interview by author, August 1966.

135. Legg, interview by author, September 1966.

136. Daly, interview by author, August 1962.

137. Anstey, interview by author, August 1966.

138. Grierson, interview by author, September 1966.

139. Margaret Grierson, letter to Wright, February 1941.

140. Grierson, letter to Wright, April 1941.

141. Grierson, letter to Wright, September 1942.

142. ZAB, "Men o' War."

143. Fraser, interview by author, August 1962.

144. Grierson, letter to Wright, October 1940, and other sources.

145. McKay, interview by author, August 1962.

146. McKay, interview by author, August 1962.

147. Margaret Ann Elton, interview by author, August 1966.

148. Beveridge, interview by author, September 1962.

149. Legg, interview by author, September 1966.

150. Grierson, quoted in Zechariah Chafee Jr., *Government and Mass Communications: A Report from the Commission on Freedom of the Press* (Chicago: University of Chicago Press, 1947).

151. Forsyth Hardy, in Grierson, *Grierson on Documentary*, p. 227 in 1947 edition.

152. Margaret Ann Elton, interview by author, August 1966.

## 7. Reaching Out from Canada (1939–45)

1. Forsyth Hardy, in *Grierson on Documentary*, p. 227 in 1947 edition.

2. Grierson, interview by author, September 1966. See Laurence Stallings, "Hitler Did Not Dance that Jig," *Esquire* 50, no. 4 (October 1958): 280, 284.

3. Grierson, "Tomorrow the Movies II."

4. Grierson, "The Future of the Films," address to the Conference of the Arts, Sciences, and Professions in the Post–War World, at the Waldorf-Astoria Hotel, New York City, June 23, 1945. Published as "Documentary: Post-War Potential," *Film News* 6, no. 6 (June 1945): 6–8.

5. Grierson, *Education and the New Order.*

6. Grierson, "The Nature of Propaganda," *Documentary News Letter* 2, no. 5 (May 1941): 90–93.

7. Grierson, *Education and the New Order.*

8. Grierson, "The Film at War."

9. Grierson, "The Necessity and Nature of Public Information" (Ottawa: National Film Board, c. 1942), mimeographed, 8 pp.

10. Grierson, "Notes on the Psychological Factor in Administration and the Relations of Public Information to Public Morale" (Ottawa: National Film Board, January 1943), mimeographed, 4 pp. Labeled "Ottawa Papers (internal circulation)," this seems to be a press release. No author is listed but it is surely Grierson's writing, probably from his new post at the War Information Board.

11. Grierson, "Letter to Roly Young." *Globe and Mail* (Toronto), January 16, 1945.

12. Grierson, *Education and the New Order.*

13. Bosley Crowther, "Word to the Wise: A Searching Comment by

John Grierson on the Responsibilities of Films," *New York Times*, July 1, 1945, sec. 2, p. 1, cols. 7–8.

14. Grierson, "The Documentary Idea 1942."

15. Mary Losey, "Documentary in the United States," *Documentary News Letter* 1 (May 1940): 9.

16. *Documentary News Letter* 2 (March 1941): 50.

17. Gloria Waldron, *The Information Film* (New York: Columbia University Press, 1949), pp. 99, 146, 148–49.

18. Rotha, *Documentary Film*, p. 309.

19. Irving Jacoby, "Film School," *Documentary News Letter* 3 (July 1942): 102–5.

20. Jacoby, "Film School."

21. Waldron, *The Information Film*, pp. 99, 146, 148–49.

22. Grierson, "Notes on the Documentary Film."

23. Grierson, "The Future of the Films."

24. Grierson, "On Robert Flaherty."

25. Legg, interview by author, September 1966.

26. Glover, interview by author, August 1962.

27. Letter from Richard Griffith, September 1959, to Rotha and Wright, quoted in their "Flaherty," p. 32.

28. Chafee, *Government and Mass Communications*, p. 744.

29. Chafee, *Government and Mass Communications*, pp. 744–45.

30. Chafee, *Government and Mass Communications*, pp. 745–46.

31. Chafee, *Government and Mass Communications*, p. 790.

32. Chafee, *Government and Mass Communications*, p. 789.

33. Rotha, *Rotha on the Film*, p. 230.

34. Forsyth Hardy, "The British Documentary Film," in Michael Balcon, Ernest Lindgren, Forsyth Hardy, and Roger Manvell, *Twenty Years of British Film 1925–1945* (London: Falcon, 1947), pp. 48–80.

35. Wright, interview by author, September 1966.

36. "Notes of the Month," *Documentary News Letter* 3 (March 1942): 34.

37. Charles Barr, "War Record," *Sight and Sound* 58 (autumn 1989): 260–65. The article describes the establishment of the Films Division within the Ministry of Information and is the clearest and most accurate account to date of the G.P.O. Film Unit into the Crown Film Unit.

38. Grierson, conversation with author, June 1969.

39. Arthur Elton, conversation with author, November 1965.

40. "Ruby Grierson," *Documentary News Letter* 1, no. 10 (October 1940): 2.

41. "News from Canada," *Documentary News Letter* 2 (January 1941): 15; (April 1941): 76.

42. Grierson, letter to Arthur Elton, January 1941.

43. Grierson, "The Documentary Idea 1942."

44. Grierson, letter to Elton, March 1940.

45. Michael Spencer, interview by author, August 1962.

46. Anstey, interview by author, August 1966.

47. Grierson, letter to Wright, October 1941.

48. Wright, interview by author, September 1966.

49. "Grierson, Mr. J. (Canada)—arrives in London, July 13 [1944], 2e (4*)," (London) *Times Index*.

50. Grierson, "Talk on a Visit to Normandy and Brittany" (radio broadcast on the Canadian Broadcasting Corporation, August 20, 1944), *Documentary News Letter 5*, no. 4 (1944): 44.

51. "The Other Side of the Atlantic," *Documentary News Letter 1*, no. 9 (September 1940): 3–4. The article is anonymous, but it appears likely that Grierson is the author.

52. American Correspondent, *Documentary News Letter 1* (October 1940).

53. Grierson, letter to Elton, January 1941.

54. Grierson, letter to Wright, December 1940.

55. Grierson, letter to Arthur Elton, January 1941.

56. Grierson, letter to Wright, October 1941.

57. Wright, interview by author, September 1966.

58. Anstey, interview by author, August 1966.

59. Grierson, "Grierson Asks for a Common Plan," *Documentary News Letter 5*, no. 5 (1944): 49–51.

60. See A. M. Sperber, *Murrow: His Life and Times* (New York: Freundlich Books, 1986), p. 174.

61. Quoted in Paul Rotha, "Correspondence," *Documentary News Letter 1* (December 1940): 19.

62. "Film of the Month: *Foreign Correspondent*," *Documentary News Letter 1* (November 1940): 6.

63. Rotha, "Correspondence," December 1940.

64. Rotha, "Correspondence," December 1940.

65. Brian Smith, "Correspondence: Foreign Correspondent," *Documentary News Letter 2* (January 1941): 13–14.

66. R. McNaughton, *Cine-Technician 6* (August–September 1940): 81.

67. Wright, *Documentary News Letter 3* (March 1942): 40–42.

68. Ernest H. Lindgren and Basil Wright, "Propaganda or Aesthetics?" *Documentary News Letter 3*, no. 4 (April 1942): 56–58.

69. "Notes of the Month," *Documentary News Letter 3*, no. 4 (April 1942): 50.

70. Grierson, "The Documentary Idea 1942."

71. Glover, interview by author, August 1962.

72. Alberto Cavalcanti, foreword to *Sound and the Documentary Film*, by Ken Cameron (London: Sir Isaac Pitman & Sons, 1947), pp. vii–viii.

73. Cavalcanti, *Sound and the Documentary Film*.

74. Forsyth Hardy, "John Grierson and the Documentary Idea," in *Films in 1951: A Special Publication on British Films and Film-Makers for the Festival of Britain* (London: British Film Institute, 1951), pp. 55–56.

75. Legg, interview by author, September 1966.

76. Tom Daly, interview by author, August 1962.

77. Grierson, letter to Stuart Legg, October 1945.

78. Ben Kerner, *Camera Close Up*, March 16, 1946.

79. Gordon Weisenborn, interview by author, September 1963.

80. "Grierson Confirms Resignation from Film Board," *Ottawa Journal*, August 9, 1945.

81. Canada. National Film Board, "Memorandum to Mr. Salisbury. . . .," July 1944, N.F.B. archive.

82. Rotha, *Documentary Film*, p. 298.

83. Grierson, "Films as an International Influence."

84. Julian Roffman, interview by author, August 1962.

85. McKay, interview by author, August 1962.

86. Beveridge, interview by author, September 1962.

87. Grierson, letter to Brooke Claxton, November 1945.

## 8. International Film Associates (1945–47) and World Today (1946–47)

1. "Grierson Confirms Resignation from Film Board," *Ottawa Journal*, August 9, 1945.

2. Grierson, letter to J. P. R. Golightly, July 1945. (Copies of this and all subsequent letters cited were made available to author by either Sir Arthur Elton or Basil Wright.)

3. A. J. Arnold, "Canada's Film Future Has Wealth and New Careers," *Saturday Night* (January 5, 1946): 5.

4. Grierson, letter to Stuart Legg, November 1945.

5. Grierson, letter to Legg, November 1945.

6. Grierson, letter to Mary Losey, December 1945.

7. Grierson, letter to Legg, November 1945.

8. Grierson, letter to Losey, December 1945.

9. Grierson, letter to Losey, December 1945.

10. Grierson, *Grierson on Documentary*, p. 30.

11. Rotha, *Documentary Film*, p. 313.

12. Legg, interview by author, September 1966.

13. Grierson, letter to Legg, November 1945.

14. Legg, interview by author, September 1966.

15. Glover, interview by author, August 1962.

16. Gordon Weisenborn, interview by author, September 1963.

17. Mary Losey Field, interview by author, November 1965.

18. Gordon Weisenborn, interview by author, September 1963.

19. "Post-War Student Film," *UNESCO Courier* 1 (August 1948): 2.

20. Roffman, interview by author, August 1962.

21. Thomas Brandon, "Survival List: Films of the Great Depression," *Film Library Quarterly* 12, nos. 2/3 (1979): 33–40.

22. Grierson, *Grierson on Documentary*, p. 30.

23. Grierson, *Grierson on Documentary*, p. 30.

24. Grierson, preface to Rotha, *Documentary Film*, pp. 15–24.

25. Grierson, letter to Golightly, July 1945.

26. Margaret Ann Elton, interview by author, August 1966.

27. Mary Losey Field, interview by author, November 1965.

28. Gordon Weisenborn, interview by author, September 1963.

29. Rotha, *Documentary Film*, p. 314.

30. Cecile Starr, ed., *Ideas on Film: A Handbook for the 16 mm Film User* (New York: Funk & Wagnalls, 1951), p. 54.

31. Ruth A. Inglis, *Freedom of the Movies* (Chicago: University of Chicago Press, 1947), p. 222.

32. Grierson, "Postwar Patterns," *Hollywood Quarterly* 1, no. 2 (January 1946): 159–65.

33. Grierson, "America's Most Vital Medium: The Documentary Film," *Library Journal* 71 (May 1, 1946): 630–34.

34. Grierson, "Tolerance Is a Law," *Junior League Magazine* 32, no. 10 (June 1946): 8.

35. Grierson, "The Library in an International World" (address before the American Library Association, Buffalo, New York, June 17, 1946), *Grierson on Documentary*, pp. 295–305.

36. Grierson, "Film Horizons," *Theatre Arts* 30, no. 12 (December 1946): 698–701.

37. Grierson, "Notes on 'The Tasks of an International Film Institute,'" *Hollywood Quarterly* 2, no. 2 (January 1947): 192–96.

38. Margaret Ann Elton, interview by author, August 1966.

39. Len Deighton, *The Ipcress File* (Greenwich, Conn.: Fawcett, 1965), p. 167.

40. Fritzie Weisenborn, interview by author, September 1963.

41. Margaret Ann Elton, interview by author, August 1966.

42. Gordon Weisenborn, interview by author, September 1963.

43. H. Reginald Hardy, *Mackenzie King*, p. 267.

44. Canada. Royal Commission, *Report of the Royal Commission to Investigate the Facts Relating to and Circumstances Surrounding the Communication, by Public Officials and Other Persons in Positions of Trust, of Secret and Confidential Information to Agents of a Foreign Power* (Ottawa: Edmond Cloutier, June 27, 1946).

45. Canada. Royal Commission. *Report of the Royal Commission,* p. 482.

46. Canada. Royal Commission. *Report of the Royal Commission,* p. 486.

47. Canada. Royal Commission. *Report of the Royal Commission,* p. 489.

48. Canada. Royal Commission. *Report of the Royal Commission,* pp. 489–90.

49. McKay, interview by author, August 1962.

50. Margaret Ann Elton, interview by author, August 1966.

51. Canada. Royal Commission. *Report of the Royal Commission.*

52. Legg, interview by author, September 1966.

53. "Head of Film Board Ousted, Magazine Editor Gets Post," *Montreal Gazette*, December 19, 1949.

54. Legg, interview by author, September 1966.

55. Donald Taylor, interview by author, September 1966.

56. Donald Taylor, interview by author, September 1966; also Richard Griffith, conversation with author, March 1963.

57. Michael Spencer, interview by author, August 1962.

58. Margaret Ann Elton, interview by author, August 1966.

59. Richard Griffith, conversation with author, March 1963.

60. Legg, interview by author, September 1966.

61. Margaret Ann Elton, interview by author, August 1966.

62. Grierson, conversation with author, June 1969.

63. Margaret Ann Elton, interview by author, August 1966.

64. James Beveridge, interview by author, September 1962.

65. McKay, interview by author, August 1962.

66. Beveridge, interview by author, September 1962.

67. "Only One N.F.B. Film Withheld from Quebec," *Montreal Gazette*, April 4, 1946.

68. "Film Board Needs 'Fumigating,'" *Ottawa Citizen*, July 12, 1946.

69. "Charges Against Film Board Denied," *Ottawa Citizen*, July 18, 1946.

70. "Taxies for Grierson Cost Gov't $2,460 in Five Years," *Ottawa Journal*, August 1, 1946.

71. "Mr. Fraser's Pachyderm," *Ottawa Citizen*, May 8, 1947.

72. "Sellar Explains Film Board Appropriations," *Ottawa Citizen*, July 3, 1947.

73. "MP Calls for 'Clean-Up' of Film Board," *Ottawa Evening Citizen*, February 26, 1948.

74. "MP Calls for 'Clean-Up.'"

75. McKay, interview by author, August 1962; and Mary Losey Field, interview by author, November 1965.

76. A. R. Sykes, "Believe Suspicion Will Kill Film Board's Bid for Independence," *Ottawa Journal*, November 25, 1949.

77. Basil Wright, "Documentary: Flesh, Fowl, or . . . ?" *Sight and Sound* 19 (March 1950): 43, 47.

78. "Head of Film Board Ousted."

79. Beveridge, interview by author, September 1962.

80. McKay, interview by author, August 1962.

81. Beveridge, interview by author, September 1962.

82. Daly, interview by author, August 1962.

83. Legg, interview by author, September 1966.

84. Gordon Weisenborn, interview by author, September 1963.

85. Donald Taylor, interview by author, September 1966.

86. Legg, interview by author, September 1966.

87. Pare Lorentz, conversation with author, April 1966.

88. Donald Taylor, interview by author, September 1966.

89. John Taylor, interview by author, September 1966.

90. Anstey, interview by author, August 1966.

91. Legg, interview by author, September 1966, and Margaret Ann Elton, interview by author, August 1966.

92. Grierson, interview by author, September 1966.

93. Grierson, "Tolerance Is a Law."

94. Grierson, "O Canada! We Stand on Guard for Thee," *Documentary Film News* 7, no. 3 (March 1948): 28, 35.

## 9. UNESCO (1947–48)

1. Grierson, interview by author, September 1966.

2. Margaret Ann Elton, interview by author, August 1966.

3. Grierson, interview by author, September 1966, and Mary Losey Field, interview by author, November 1965.

4. Margaret Ann Elton, interview by author, August 1966.

5. "UNESCO Appoints Canadian," *New York Times*, February 21, 1947, p. 7, col. 1.

6. Wright, "Documentary."

7. Sinclair Road, "In the Minds of Men," *Documentary News Letter* 6 (1946).

8. UNESCO, *Conference for the Establishment of UNESCO*, June 1946.

9. UNESCO, *Report of the Director General*, September 1947.

10. UNESCO, *The Programme of UNESCO Proposed by the Executive Board* (Paris: UNESCO, 1950).

11. UNESCO, *Report of the Director General*, p. 5.

12. Grierson, "Notes on 'The Tasks of an International Film Institute.'"

13. Sinclair Road, "UNESCO Reports," *Documentary News Letter* 6 (October 1947).

14. Basil Wright, "Films and UNESCO," in *Informational Film Year Book 1947* (London: Albyn Press, 1947), pp. 38–41.

15. *Informational Film Year Book 1948* (Edinburgh: Albyn Press, 1948), p. 117.

16. *Documentary News Letter* 6 (August–September 1947): 120.

17. UNESCO, *Report of the Director General*, p. 6.

18. Road, "UNESCO Reports."

19. William Farr, letter to Basil Wright, September 1947, in which he is quoting Grierson in regard to this assignment. This and all other letters cited were made available to author by Wright.

20. Ernest Borneman, "Canada, Unesco, and the Movies," *Ottawa Evening Citizen*, September 10, 1948.

21. UNESCO, *Report of the Director General*, p. 93.

22. UNESCO, *Records of the General Conference* 2 (April 1948): 32.

23. Grierson, *Grierson on Documentary*, p. 30.

24. French, "UNESCO Confers in Mexico City," January–February 1948. This is all the information I have available on this source.

25. "February Filldyke," *Documentary News Letter* 7 (February 1947): 13.

26. Mary Losey Field, interview by author, November 1965.

27. UNESCO, *Press, Film, Radio (Report of the Commission on Technical Needs)* (Paris: UNESCO, September 1948).

28. "Overseas News," *Documentary News Letter* 7 (February 1948): 16–17.

29. Grierson, interview by author, September 1966.

30. Mary Losey Field, interview by author, November 1965.

31. Grierson, "A Day with John Grierson."

32. Grierson, interview by author, September 1966.

33. UNESCO, *Report of the Director General*, p. 67.

34. Grierson, interview by author, September 1966, and UNESCO, *Report of the Director General*, p. 71.

35. *Film Today: An Occasional Miscellany Devoted to the Contemporary Cinema.*

36. "Edinburgh in Review," *Documentary News Letter* 6 (November–December 1947): 152–54, 160.

37. *Film Today.*

38. *Documentary News Letter* 6 (October 1947): 135.

39. Grierson, "A Time for Enquiry."

40. "Edinburgh in Review." During the UNESCO period, late 1947 or early 1948, there appeared in *Theatre Today* an "Imaginary Conversation." Internal evidence strongly suggests that this amusing fantasy is by Grierson, though the author's name is given as A. D. Macklay. The conversation takes place between King James VI (of Scotland, who became James I of England), the playwright James Barrie (of Scotland), and John Grierson. The subject of their conversation is how to represent Scotland in the arts. Grierson, of course, plumps for documentary.

41. "Notes of the Month," *Documentary News Letter* 7 (February 1948): 14.

42. "Notes of the Month," *Documentary News Letter* 7 (January 1948): 2.

43. Grierson, "The Film in British Colonial Development," *Sight and Sound* 17, no. 65 (spring 1948): 2–4.

44. Grierson, interview by author, September 1966.

45. Forsyth Hardy, interview by author, September 1966.

46. Mary Losey Field, interview by author, November 1965.

47. Grierson, interview by author, September 1966; and Forsyth Hardy, interview by author, September 1966.

48. Grierson, letter to Wright, July 1947.

49. Forsyth Hardy, interview by author, September 1966.

50. Grierson, letter to Wright, July 1947.

51. Forsyth Hardy, interview by author, September 1966.

52. Arthur Elton, interview by author, August 1966; Forsyth Hardy, interview by author, September 1966; Stuart Legg, interview by author, September 1966.

53. Grierson, "Notes on 'The Tasks of an International Film Institute.'"

54. Grierson, "Notes on 'The Tasks of an International Film Institute.'"

55. UNESCO, *Report of the Director General*, p. 69.

56. UNESCO, *Report of the Director General*, p. 45.

57. "Overseas News."

58. Anstey, interview by author, August 1966.

59. Grierson, "Notes on 'The Tasks of an International Film Institute.'"

60. UNESCO, *Press, Film, Radio.*

61. Grierson, "Prospect for Documentary: What Is Wrong and Why," *Sight and Sound* 17, no. 66 (summer 1948): 55–59.

## 10. Central Office of Information (1948–50)

1. Wright, letter to Grierson, January 1946. This and other letters cited were made available to author by Wright.

2. "What Is to Be Done?" *Documentary News Letter* 6, no. 1 (1946): 1–2.

3. "Financial Notes: Government Films," *Penguin Film Review* no. 3 (August 1947): 88–89.

4. "Financial Notes."

5. Basil Wright and Alexander Shaw, interview by author, September 1966.

6. Arts Enquiry, *The Factual Film*, p. 66.

7. Paul Rotha, interview by author, September 1966.

8. Irmgard Schemke, "Documentary To-day," *Sequence* no. 3 (spring 1948): 12–14.

9. Sinclair Road, "The Influence of the Film," *Penguin Film Review* no. 1 (August 1946): 57–65.

10. Rotha, *Documentary Film*, p. 216.

11. Grierson, "Reporting Progress," *Documentary 49: Film Festival* (Edinburgh: Albyn, 1949).

12. Roger Manvell, "The Cinema and the State: England," *Hollywood Quarterly* 2 (April 1947): 289–93.

13. Rotha, *Documentary Film*, pp. 34–35.

14. Forsyth Hardy, in Grierson, *Grierson on Documentary*, p. 32.

15. Grierson, "Prospect for Documentary: What is Wrong and Why."

16. Legg, interview by author, September 1966.

17. Rotha, interview by author, September 1966.

18. C. A. Oakley, *Where We Came In: Seventy Years of the British Film Industry* (London: George Allen and Unwin, 1964), p. 217.

19. Legg, interview by author, September 1966.

20. Rotha, *Documentary Film*, p. 34.

21. *Cine-Technician* (July–October 1945).

22. Oakley, *Where We Came In*, p. 217.

23. Grierson, *Grierson on Documentary*, p.180 in 1946 edition.

24. Rotha, *Documentary Film*, p. 34.

25. Rotha, *Documentary Film*, p. 31.

26. "Cripps at ASFP," *Documentary News Letter* 6 (November–December 1947).

27. Grierson, "Prospect for Documentary."

28. Edgar Anstey, "The Year's Work in the Documentary Film," in *The Year's Work in the Film: 1949*, ed. Roger Manvell (London: Longmans Green, 1950), pp. 30–36.

29. Stuart Legg, "The Sulky Fire (2)." *Sight and Sound* n.s. 22 (July–September 1952): 38, 48.

30. Grierson, "Prospect for Documentary."

31. Grierson, "The Relationship Between the Political Power and the

Cinema" (Celebrity Lecture, Edinburgh International Film Festival, August 24, 1968) *Grierson on Documentary*, pp. 191–205.

32. Grierson, "Prospect for Documentary."

33. Rotha, "Extracts from a privately circulated Memorandum, August 9, 1946," *Rotha on the Film*, p. 235.

34. Anstey, "The Year's Work in the Documentary Film."

35. Legg, "The Sulky Fire (2)."

36. Rotha, "Extracts from a privately circulated Memorandum, August, 1947," *Rotha on the Film*, p. 238.

37. Rotha, *Documentary Film*, p. 31.

38. Rotha, *Documentary Film*, p. 32.

39. Rotha, "Memorandum, August, 1947," *Rotha on the Film*, p. 239.

40. Grierson, "A Time for Enquiry."

41. Grierson, "Extract from Grierson," *Documentary News Letter* 6 (November–December 1947).

42. Rotha, "Memorandum, August, 1947," *Rotha on the Film*, p. 240.

43. "Financial Notes."

44. Philip Mackie, "Production History of a COI Film," *Documentary News Letter* 6 (November–December 1947): 157.

45. "Open Letter from a Schoolteacher," *Documentary News Letter* 7 (January 1948): 10; "Correspondence," *Documentary News Letter* 7 (February 1948): 24.

46. *Informational Film Year Book 1948*.

47. R. E. Tritton, "The Government and the Cinema," in *The British Film Yearbook 1949–50*, ed. Peter Noble (London: Skelton Robinson, 1949), pp. 56–60.

48. R. K. Neilson Baxter, "The Structure of the British Film Industry," *Penguin Film Review* no. 7 (September 1948): 83–90.

49. Tritton, "The Government and the Cinema."

50. John Taylor, interview by author, September 1966.

51. Wright, interview by author, September 1966.

52. John Taylor, interview by author, September 1966.

53. "Government Films: Mr. John Grierson's New Appointment," *Times* (London), February 20, 1948, p. 6, col. e.

54. Kenneth Gordon, "Cinema Log," *Cine-Technician* 14 (March–April 1948): 48.

55. Forsyth Hardy, in Grierson, *Grierson on Documentary*, p. 31.

56. Donald Taylor, interview by author, September 1966.

57. Forsyth Hardy, in Grierson, *Grierson on Documentary*, p. 31.

58. John Taylor, interview by author, September 1966.

59. *The British Film Yearbook 1949–50*, p. 279.

60. Tritton, "The Government and the Cinema."

61. Grierson, interview by author, September 1966.

62. John Taylor, interview by author, September 1966.

63. Schemke, "Documentary To-day."

64. Legg, interview by author, September 1966.

65. Robert Katz and Nancy Katz, "Documentary in Transition, Part II: The International Scene and the American Documentary," *Hollywood Quarterly* 4, no. 1 (fall 1949): 51–64.

66. Donald Taylor, interview by author, September 1966.

67. *The British Film Yearbook 1949–50*, p. 278.

68. *The British Film Yearbook 1949–50*, p. 278.

69. Great Britain. Central Office of Information, *Annual Report 1948–49*, p. 31.

70. Great Britain. Central Office of Information. *Annual Report 1948–49*, p. 37.

71. Katz and Katz, "Documentary in Transition."

72. *The British Film Yearbook 1949–50*, p. 289.

73. Great Britain. Central Office of Information. *Annual Report 1948–49*, p. 20.

74. Great Britain. Central Office of Information. *Annual Report 1948–49*, p. 13.

75. Great Britain. Central Office of Information. *Annual Report 1948–49*, pp. 5–7.

76. Great Britain. Central Office of Information. *Annual Report 1948–49*, p. 13.

77. Forsyth Hardy, in Grierson, *Grierson on Documentary*, p. 32.

78. Katz and Katz, "Documentary in Transition."

79. Grierson, preface to Rotha, *Documentary Film.*

80. Rotha, *Documentary Film*, p. 260.

81. Rotha, *Documentary Film*, p. 260.

82. Donald Taylor, interview by author, September 1966.

83. Great Britain. Central Office of Information. *Annual Report 1948–49*, p. 14.

84. Great Britain. Central Office of Information. *Annual Report 1948–49*, p. 14.

85. Great Britain. Central Office of Information. *Annual Report 1948–49*, p. 3.

86. Grierson, interview by author, September 1966.

87. Great Britain. Central Office of Information. *Annual Report 1949–50*, p. 31.

88. John Taylor, interview by author, September 1966.

89. Great Britain. Central Office of Information. *Annual Report 1948–49*, p. 43; *1949–50*, pp. 34–35.

90. Great Britain. Central Office of Information. *Annual Report 1948–*

*49*, p. 45; Great Britain. Central Office of Information. *Annual Report 1949–50*, pp. 34–35.

91. Great Britain. Central Office of Information. *Annual Report 1949–50*, p. 21.

92. Rotha, *Documentary Film*, p. 32.

93. Rotha, *Documentary Film*, pp. 32–33.

94. Rotha, *Documentary Film*, p. 223.

95. Rotha, *Documentary Film*, p. 32.

96. Rotha, *Documentary Film*, p. 223.

97. Grierson, "The Front Page," *Sight and Sound* n.s. 21, no. 4 (April–June 1952): 143.

98. Grierson, "The Front Page."

99. Grierson, "The Front Page."

100. Grierson, interview by author, September 1966.

101. Grierson, interview by author, September 1966.

102. Wright, interview by author, September 1966.

103. John Taylor, interview by author, September 1966.

104. Donald Taylor, interview by author, September 1966.

105. Grierson, "The Front Page."

106. Grierson, interview by author, September 1966.

107. Grierson, interview by author, September 1966.

108. Anstey, interview by author, August 1966.

109. Wright, interview by author, September 1966.

110. Forsyth Hardy, interview by author, September 1966.

111. John Taylor, interview by author, September 1966.

112. Glover, interview by author, August 1962.

113. John Taylor, interview by author, September 1966.

114. Grierson, interview by author, September 1966.

115. Legg, "The Sulky Fire (2)."

116. John Taylor, interview by author, September 1966.

117. "Film Corner," by Ronald Strode, editor: 'Film Sponsor,' *World's Press News*, c. January 1951.

118. Strode, "Film Corner."

119. "Summary of the Debate," *Cine-Technician* 14 (May–June 1948). See also "Grierson on Documentary," *Cine-Technician* 14 (July–August 1948): 123–24, 126–28.

120. *New York Times*, June 9, 1949, sec. 1, p. 8, and sec. 3, p. 5.

121. Grierson, "Edinburgh 1948," *Documentary Film News* 7, no. 8 (August 1948): 87.

122. John Maddison, "International Scientific Film Congress: London 1948," *Documentary Film News* 7 (September–October 1948): 98.

123. "New London Film Society," *Sight and Sound* 17 (autumn 1948): 150.

124. Grierson, *Eisenstein, 1898–1948.*

125. Rotha, *Documentary Film*, p. 303.

126. Grierson, "Prospect for Documentary."

127. Advertisement, *Sequence*, no. 12 (autumn 1950): back cover.

128. "The Front Page," *Sight and Sound* 19 (December 1950): 309.

129. Forsyth Hardy, interview by author, September 1966.

130. Lindsay Anderson, "A Possible Solution," *Sequence*, no. 3 (spring 1948): 7–10.

131. Schemke, "Documentary To-day."

132. Winifred Holmes, "What's Wrong with Documentary?" *Sight and Sound* 17, no. 65 (spring 1948): 44–45.

133. Grierson, "Prospect for Documentary."

134. Jack Beddington, "Off With Their Heads!" *Documentary Film News* 7, no. 67 (July 1948): 77.

135. "Government PRO (name and address supplied)" [*sic*], *World's Press News*, September 7, 1951.

136. Anstey, "The Living Story."

137. B. Charles-Dean, "Correspondence: Crown Film Unit," *Sight and Sound* n.s. 22, no. 1 (July–September 1952): 46.

138. Peter Price, "The Sulky Fire (3): The Light that Failed," *Sight and Sound* n.s. 22 (January–March 1953): 139.

139. Grierson, interview by author, September 1966.

140. Rotha, *Documentary Film*, p. 35.

141. Forsyth Hardy, in Grierson, *Grierson on Documentary*, p. 33.

## 11. Group 3 (1951–55)

1. Oakley, *Where We Came In*, p. 199.

2. "Points of Reference," in *Films of 1951* (London: Sight and Sound for the British Film Institute, 1951).

3. Grierson, "The Relationship Between the Political Power and the Cinema."

4. Margaret Ann Elton, interview by author, August 1966.

5. Arthur Elton, interview by author, August 1966.

6. Anstey, interview by author, August 1966.

7. Grierson, interview by author, September 1966.

8. Oakley, *Where We Came In*, p. 199.

9. "Cut in Information Services; Crown Film Unit to Close Down," *Times* (London), January 30, 1952.

10. Rotha, *Rotha on the Film*, p. 241.

11. Rotha, *Documentary Film*, p. 39.

12. Rotha, *Rotha on the Film*, p. 28.

13. Oakley, *Where We Came In*, p. 206.

14. Glover, interview by author, August 1962.

15. Oakley, *Where We Came In*, p. 206.

16. Grierson, "The Front Page."

17. Grierson, interview by author, September 1966.

18. Paul Rotha, Basil Wright, Lindsay Anderson, and Penelope Houston, "The Critical Issue," *Sight and Sound* 27, no. 6 (autumn 1958): 271–75.

19. Lindsay Anderson, "British Cinema: The Descending Spiral," *Sequence*, no. 7 (spring 1949): 6–11.

20. Sir Michael Balcon, "The Feature Carries on the Documentary Tradition," *UNESCO Courier* 4 (September 1951): 5.

21. Rotha, *Rotha on the Film*, p. 29 n.

22. "British Feature Directors: An Index to Their Work," *Sight and Sound* 27 (autumn 1958): 289–304.

23. Grierson, interview by author, September 1966.

24. Forsyth Hardy, in Grierson, *Grierson on Documentary*, p. 34.

25. Gavin Lambert, "Reviews: . . . Brandy for the Parson," *Sight and Sound* n.s. 21, no. 4 (April–June 1952): 171.

26. James Morgan, "People and Films: London," *Sight and Sound* n.s. 21, no. 3 (January–March 1952): 103.

27. Forsyth Hardy, in Grierson, *Grierson on Documentary*, p. 34.

28. Morgan, "People and Films."

29. Edgar Anstey, "The Current Cinema: Films from Group 3," *Sight and Sound* n.s. 22, no. 2 (October–December 1952): 78–79.

30. Anstey, "The Current Cinema."

31. Grierson, interview by author, September 1966.

32. Rotha, interview by author, September 1966.

33. Grierson, "A Review of Reviews," *Sight and Sound* n.s. 24, no. 2 (October–December 1954): 101–3.

34. Rotha, *Rotha on the Film*, p. 310.

35. Forsyth Hardy, in Grierson, *Grierson on Documentary*, p. 34.

36. Lindsay Anderson, "In the Picture: Perspectives at Cannes," *Sight and Sound* n.s. 24 (July–September 1954): 6–8.

37. John Taylor, interview by author, September 1966.

38. Morgan, "People and Films."

39. Forsyth Hardy, in Grierson, *Grierson on Documentary*, p. 33.

40. Grierson, interview by author, September 1966.

41. Anstey, "The Current Cinema."

42. Donald Taylor, interview by author, September 1966.

43. Gavin Lambert, "Edinburgh," *Sight and Sound* n.s. 21, no. 2 (October–December 1951): 90.

44. Irene A. Wright and Floyd E. Brooker, *Sixth International Edinburgh Film Festival, 1952: Report* (Washington, D.C.: Department of State, 1952): 36–37.

45. "Documentaries 'Still Alive,'" *Edinburgh Evening News*, September 1, 1954; "Hope for the Future of 'Documentary,'" *Glasgow Herald*, September 1, 1954.

46. *Daily Mail*, September 1, 1954.

47. Grierson, "A Review of Reviews," *Sight and Sound* n.s. 24, no. 3 (January–March 1955): 157–58.

48. Grierson, "*Grierson on Documentary.*"

49. Grierson, "British Documentary," *Documentary 51* (Edinburgh: Edinburgh Film Festival, 1951).

50. Grierson, "Book Reviews: *Documentary Film* by Paul Rotha," *Sight and Sound* n.s. 22, no. 2 (October–December 1952): 92, 93.

51. Grierson, "Work of Australian Film Board," *Times* (London), June 5, 1954, p. 7, col. e.

52. Grierson, "A Review of Reviews," *Sight and Sound* n.s. 23, no. 4 (April–June 1954): 207–8, 222; n.s. 24, no. 1 (July–September 1954): 143–44; no. 2 (October–December 1954): 101–3; no. 3 (January–March 1955): 157–58.

53. Margaret Ann Elton, interview by author, August 1966.

54. Grierson, "John Barleycorn," *Scotland* no. 58 (December 1951): 69–73.

55. Grierson, "Nature in the Raw," *Scotland* no. 61 (March 1952): 72–76.

56. Grierson, "The B.B.C. and All That," *Quarterly of Film, Radio, and Television* 9, no. 1 (fall 1954): 46–59.

57. "In the Picture: Cavalcanti in Brazil," *Sight and Sound* n.s. 22, no. 4 (April–June 1953): 152.

58. "British Feature Directors."

59. Gavin Lambert, "Edinburgh."

60. David Robinson, "Looking for Documentary, Part Two: The Ones that Got Away," *Sight and Sound* 27, no. 2 (autumn 1957): 70–75.

61. Paul Rotha, "Television and the Future of Documentary," *Quarterly of Film, Radio, and Television* 9 (summer 1955): 366–73.

62. David Robinson, "In the Picture: Edinburgh," *Sight and Sound* n.s. 24, no. 2 (October–December 1954): 59.

63. Rotha, "Television and the Future of Documentary."

64. Oakley, *Where We Came In*, p. 208.

65. Grierson, "Robert Flaherty: An Appreciation," *New York Times*, July 29, 1951, sec. 2, p. 3, col. 4.

66. Grierson, "On Robert Flaherty."

67. Grierson, "Flaherty as Innovator."

68. Grierson, "Robert Flaherty: An Appreciation."

69. Grierson, "Portrait of Robert Flaherty," radio broadcast produced

by Oliver Lawson Dick for the B.B.C. Third Programme, September 2, 1952. Grierson was one of many paying tribute.

70. A. William Bluem, *Documentary in American Television* (New York: Hastings, 1965), p. 243.

71. Forsyth Hardy, in Grierson, *Grierson on Documentary*, p. 35.

72. "The Front Page," *Sight and Sound* 24, no. 4 (spring 1955): 169.

73. Rotha et al., "The Critical Issue."

74. Elton, interview by author, August 1966.

75. Grierson, "The Relationship Between the Political Power and the Cinema."

76. Penelope Houston, "Time of Crisis," *Sight and Sound* 27 (spring 1958): 166–75.

77. Grierson, interview by author, September 1966.

78. Grierson, "A Review of Reviews," *Sight and Sound* n.s. 24, no. 2 (October–December 1954): 101–3.

79. Grierson, interview by author, September 1966.

80. Donald Taylor, interview by author, September 1966.

81. John Taylor, interview by author, September 1966.

82. Grierson, interview by author, September 1966.

83. Grierson, interview by author, September 1966.

84. Forsyth Hardy, in Grierson, *Grierson on Documentary*, p. 35.

85. Forsyth Hardy, in Grierson, *Grierson on Documentary*, p. 35.

86. Grierson, "The Relationship Between the Political Power and the Cinema."

87. Margaret Ann Elton, interview by author, August 1966.

88. Sheet in British Film Institute Library, no author or date. Typescript.

89. Biography Service: Reference Division: Central Office of Information, July 7, 1960. Mimeographed handout.

90. John Taylor, interview by author, September 1966.

## 12. Interim (1955–57)

1. Grierson and Philip Mackie, "Welcome Stranger!" *Sight and Sound* 18, no. 69 (spring 1949): 51.

2. "Free Cinema: A portfolio of information and background material" (Canadian Federation of Film Societies, Portfolio No. 1, June 1958). Mimeographed, 7 pp.

3. Grierson, "A Review of Reviews," *Sight and Sound* n.s. 23, no. 4 (April–June 1954): 207–8.

4. Lindsay Anderson, "Correspondence: Straight Questions," *Sight and Sound* n.s. 24, no. 2 (October–December 1954): 207–8.

5. Grierson, "A Review of Reviews," *Sight and Sound* n.s. 24, no. 3

(January–March 1955): 157–58. Olwen Vaughan was an old friend who would become Grierson's film scout and procuress for his television series, *This Wonderful World*, in a couple years.

6. Grierson, "A Review of Reviews," *Sight and Sound* n.s. 24, no. 3 (January–March 1955): 157–58.

7. Paul Rotha, Basil Wright, Lindsay Anderson, and Penelope Houston, "The Critical Issue," *Sight and Sound* 27, no. 6 (autumn 1958): 271–75.

8. David Robinson, "Looking for Documentary, Part Two: The Ones that Got Away," *Sight and Sound* 27, no. 2 (autumn 1957): 70–75.

9. Grierson, interview by author, September 1966.

10. Peter Davis, "Lindsay Anderson Views His First Feature Film," *Panorama—Chicago Daily News*, July 28, 1963, p. 21. (The film would have been *This Sporting Life* [1963].)

11. Davis, "Lindsay Anderson."

12. Grierson, "Documentary: A World Perspective," *Grierson on Documentary*, 365–71. Written much earlier than its publication date of 1966; author received a typescript from Grierson in summer 1961.

13. Davis, "Lindsay Anderson."

14. Grierson, interview by author, September 1966.

15. Beveridge, interview by author, September 1962.

16. McLaren, interview by author, August 1962.

17. Grierson, "A Time for Inquiry," *Documentary* 47 (Edinburgh: Albyn, 1947).

18. Wright, interview by author, September 1966.

19. John Taylor, interview by author, September 1966.

20. Margaret Ann Elton, interview by author, August 1966.

21. Forsyth Hardy, letter to author, January 1971.

22. Colin Neil MacKay, "John Grierson—Expert on the Poetry of Living," *TV Times*, no. 566 (September 1, 1966): 4.

23. MacKay, "John Grierson—Expert on the Poetry of Living."

24. Elton, interview by author, August 1966.

25. Iain Crawford, "Entertaining Scotland," *Scottish Field* 103, no. 630 (June 1955): 57.

26. Forsyth Hardy, interview by author, September 1966.

## 13. Scottish Television (1957–68)

1. Grierson, "The B.B.C. and All That."

2. All of the information on the I.T.A. was drawn from Burton Paulu, "Britain's Independent Television Authority (Part I)," *Quarterly of Film, Radio, and Television* 10 (summer 1956): 325–36.

3. Winston Burdett, "TV Commercials Come to Britain," *Quarterly of Film, Radio, and Television* 10 (winter 1955): 180–85.

4. "Television Topics: T.V.'s Soaring Profits," *Film Teacher* no. 16 (February 1959): 20–22.

5. "Thomson Outlines African Radio-TV Plans," *Broadcasting*, January 15, 1962, p. 67.

6. Roy Thomson, "Scotland Today: Like it Here," *Spectator*, May 29, 1959.

7. "Thomson Outlines African Radio-TV Plans."

8. Maurice Richardson, "Wreath for Homo Sapiens," *Observer*, September 21, 1958.

9. "A Mass Medium Addressed to Individuals: Mr. John Grierson's Way with Television," *Times* (London), January 28, 1960, p. 3, col. e.

10. Forsyth Hardy, in Grierson, *Grierson on Documentary*, p. 37.

11. Grierson, "A Day with John Grierson."

12. Some of the above drawn from "A Mass Medium Addressed to Individuals"; the rest from personal viewing.

13. Grierson, "*This Wonderful World*," *TV Times*, February 6, 1959.

14. Grierson, "A Day with John Grierson."

15. Olwen Vaughan, interview by author, September 1966.

16. Vaughan, interview by author, September 1966.

17. Francis Koval, "Cork Film Festival" (letter to the editor), *Films in Review* 9 (November 1958): 539–40.

18. Forsyth Hardy, in Grierson, *Grierson on Documentary*, p. 37.

19. MacKay, "John Grierson—Expert on the Poetry of Living."

20. MacKay, "John Grierson—Expert on the Poetry of Living."

21. Vaughan, interview by author, September 1966.

22. Grierson, "A Day with John Grierson."

23. Forsyth Hardy, in Grierson, *Grierson on Documentary*, pp. 36–37.

24. Grierson, interview by author, September 1966.

25. Stanley Russell, "Shooting the Great Ships," *Film User* 16 (June 1962): 266–67.

26. Forsyth Hardy, in Grierson, *Grierson on Documentary*, p. 37.

27. Derek Hill, "Defense through FIDO," *Sight and Sound* 28 (summer–autumn 1959): 183–84.

28. David Robinson, "Looking for Documentary, Part Two: The Ones that Got Away," *Sight and Sound* 27, no. 2 (autumn 1957): 70–75.

29. Donald Taylor, interview by author, September 1966.

30. Legg, interview by author, September 1966; "Grierson, Daubeny Honored by Queen," *Variety*, June 21, 1961.

31. "Seldes, Grierson Talks on the Arts at N. Car. U.," *Variety*, April 11, 1962.

32. Elmer Oettinger, "The North Carolina Film Board: A Unique Program in Documentary and Educational Film Making," *Journal of the Society of Cinematologists* 5 (1965): 55–65.

33. Oettinger, "The North Carolina Film Board."

34. George Stoney, conversation with author, summer 1962.

35. Grierson, "A Mind for the Future" (Saint Andrew's Day Lecture, November 30, 1962, Scottish Home Service of the B.B.C.), *Grierson on Documentary*, pp. 382–93.

36. Stoney, conversation with author, summer 1962.

37. Gilbert Seldes, conversation with author, spring 1963.

38. Oettinger, "The North Carolina Film Board."

39. Stoney, conversation with author, summer 1962.

40. Accounts from a number of people who were present.

41. Howard Junker, "The National Film Board of Canada: After a Quarter Century," *Film Quarterly* 18, no. 2 (winter 1964): 22–29.

42. MacKay, "John Grierson—Expert on the Poetry of Living."

43. Stoney, conversation with author, summer 1962.

44. Forsyth Hardy, conversation with author, November 1968.

45. Stoney, conversation with author, summer 1962.

46. Stoney, conversation with author, summer 1962.

47. Norman McLaren, conversation with author, November 1968.

48. Forsyth Hardy, conversation with author, November 1968.

49. Margaret Ann and Arthur Elton, interview by author, August 1966.

50. Marion Grierson, interview by author, September 1966.

51. Grierson, interview by author, September 1966.

52. *Scotland on the Screen*. Printed program for an occasion honoring Grierson, recipient of the Golden Thistle Award, Caley Picture House, Edinburgh, August 25, 1968.

## 14. McGill University (1969–72)

1. "Old Campaigner Prepares," *Times* (London), January 3, 1969.

2. Grierson, interview by author, September 1966.

3. "Grierson to Teach Film Art at McGill," *Montreal Star*, January 6, 1969.

4. See Forsyth Hardy, *John Grierson: A Documentary Biography* (London: Faber and Faber, 1979), pp. 232–33, for a fuller account of reasons for and events of the hiring.

5. Grierson, "John Grierson on Media, Film and History," ed. Donald F. and Joan B. Theall, in *Studies in Canadian Communications*, ed. Gertrude Joch Robinson and Donald F. Theall (Montreal: Graduate Programme in Communications, McGill University, 1975).

6. "Old Campaigner Prepares."

7. Grierson, "Letter to Michelle," *A.I.D. News* no. 1 (January): 6–7.

8. Elspeth Chisholm, "The Canadian Indian Summer of John Grierson," *Motion* 4, no. 5 (November 1975): 6–8.

9. Grierson, "John Grierson on Media, Film and History."

10. Chisholm, "The Canadian Indian Summer."

11. Grierson, "The 35mm Mind," *McGill News* 52, no. 2 (March 1971): 12–15. Interview by Darlene Kruesel.

12. Chisholm, "The Canadian Indian Summer."

13. Stoney, conversation with author, May 1969.

14. Chisholm, "The Canadian Indian Summer."

15. Beveridge, *John Grierson: Film Master*, p. 323.

16. Marjorie Saldanha, one of Grierson's teaching assistants, interview by author, May 1972.

17. Chisholm, "The Canadian Indian Summer."

18. Conversations of author with Crescent Hotel employees, October 1981.

19. Author's inference from a conversation with Grierson, in June 1969; confirmed by Marjorie Saldhana.

20. Grierson, conversation with author, June 1969.

21. Grierson, "Letter to Michelle."

22. Gary Evans, *In the National Interest: A Chronicle of the National Film Board of Canada from 1949 to 1989* (Toronto: University of Toronto Press, 1991).

23. See, for example, Dick MacDonald, "NFB's Founder Grierson Back as McGill Visiting Lecturer," *Montreal Star*, January 16, 1969, p. 41; MacDonald, "John Grierson Still a Niagara of Ideas," *Montreal Star*, January 25, 1969; Luc Perreault, "Le 'père du cinéma canadien,' John Grierson, se fait professor," *La presse* (Montreal), January 17, 1969, p. 29.

24. Dusty Vineburg, "Father of Film Board Urges Re-examination of Charter," *Montreal Star*, November 22, 1969, sect. 2, p. 15.; and Vineburg, "Grierson Says Film Board Over-Mechanized," *Montreal Star*, November 22, sect. 2, p. 20.

25. Evans, *In the National Interest*, p. 155.

26. Evans, *In the National Interest*, p. 157.

27. For a discussion of Challenge for Change, see Jack C. Ellis, *The Documentary Idea: A Critical History of English-Language Documentary Film and Video* (Englewood Cliffs, N.J.: Prentice Hall, 1989), pp. 273–75.

28. Colin Low, "Grierson and Challenge for Change," in the John Grierson Project, McGill University, *John Grierson and the NFB* (Toronto: ECW Press, 1984), pp. 111–19.

29. Grierson, "Memo to Michelle about Decentralizing the Means of Production," *A.I.D. News* no. 2 (November 1971): 5–7.

30. Chisholm, "The Canadian Indian Summer."

31. Rodrigue Chiasson, "The CRTC Tapes," in the John Grierson Project, McGill University, *John Grierson and the NFB*, pp. 42–49.

32. *Grierson Transcripts: Interviews Recorded with John Grierson, February 1969–July 1971,* transcribed by Sandra Gathercole, 4 vols. (Ottawa: Canadian Radio and Television Commission, 1973).

33. Elizabeth Sussex, "The Golden Years of Grierson," *Sight and Sound* 41, no. 3 (summer 1972): 149–53.

34. As quoted in "John Grierson on Media, Film and History."

35. Grierson, *I Remember, I Remember,* 16 mm color film, 58 minutes; produced by the Visual Education Centre, Toronto, in association with Films of Scotland and Scottish Television, 1970.

36. Grierson, letter to Grant McLean, February 1972.

37. I have record of only a few of these additional special occasions; a fuller account is available in Forsyth Hardy, *John Grierson: A Documentary Biography,* pp. 241–45.

38. Ronald Blumer, conversation with author, March 1971.

39. "John Grierson: 'I derive my authority from Moses,'" *McGill Reporter,* February 24, 1969, 4–5. Grierson interviewed by Ronald Blumer.

40. Grierson, "The 35mm Mind."

41. Grierson, a statement recorded for a B.B.C.–TV *Omnibus* program on Eisenstein, March 1971; produced by Norman Swallow. In Grierson, *Grierson on Documentary,* pp. 180–84.

42. Grierson, "Mr. Walter Wanger," *Times* (London), November 21, 1971.

43. Sussex, "The Golden Years of Grierson."

44. Beveridge, *John Grierson: Film Master,* p. 300.

45. *McLaren* (Montreal: National Film Board of Canada, 1980), p. 12.

46. Saldanha, interview by author, May 1972. Saldanha reported that she was with Grierson for a month in India, replacing Rashmi Sharma, another of Grierson's teaching assistants at McGill. (She also said that among Grierson's teaching assistants there was a "bad Indian girl and a good Indian girl," leaving me to infer which she was.)

47. Grierson, "Address to the National Institute of Design, Ahmedabad, India," in *John Grierson: Film Master,* by James Beveridge (New York: Macmillan, 1978), pp. 311–13.

48. Bikram Singh, "Cultural Causerie," *Evening News of India,* May 26, 1972; reprinted in Beveridge, *John Grierson: Film Master,* pp. 304–5.

49. Quoted in "John Grierson: The Reluctant but Angry Guru, by Our Delhi Film Critic," *Sunday Statesman* (Delhi), May 9, 1971; reprinted in Beveridge, *John Grierson: Film Master,* pp. 305–9.

50. Saldanha, interview by author, May 1972.

51. Singh, "Cultural Causerie."

52. "Keeping Alive the Spirit of Experimenting," *Star and Style,* September 9, 1971.

53. Quoted in "John Grierson: The Reluctant but Angry Guru."

54. Forsyth Hardy, *John Grierson: A Documentary Biography*, p. 249.

55. The information on Grierson's final days is drawn primarily from a conversation with Marjorie Saldanha (she was in touch with John and Margaret Grierson by phone), and from Forsyth Hardy, *John Grierson: A Documentary Biography*, pp. 251–52. The Hardy account is more detailed than this one.

56. Gale Livengood, conversation with author, c. May 1972.

57. Grierson, conversation with author, January 1971.

## 15. Postmortem: Assessments (1972–2000)

1. Elizabeth Sussex, *The Rise and Fall of British Documentary: The Story of the Film Movement Founded by John Grierson* (Berkeley: University of California Press, 1975).

2. Harry Watt, *Don't Look at the Camera* (London: Elek, 1974), p. 46.

3. Sussex, *The Rise and Fall of British Documentary*, p. 188.

4. Forsyth Hardy, *John Grierson: A Documentary Biography*, p. 263.

5. Forsyth Hardy, *John Grierson: A Documentary Biography*, p. 263.

6. Gary Evans, *John Grierson and the National Film Board: The Politics of Wartime Propaganda* (Toronto: University of Toronto Press, 1984), p. 283.

7. An excellent history of the N.F.B. is D. B. Jones's *Movies and Memoranda: An Interpretive History of the National Film Board of Canada* (Ottawa: Canadian Film Institute and Deneau, 1981), which chronicles not only the wartime years but deals with Grierson before he came to Canada and his continuing influence after he left.

8. Jack C. Ellis, *John Grierson: A Guide to References and Resources* (Boston: G. K. Hall, 1986), pp. 17–28.

9. Ellis, *John Grierson: A Guide*, p. 19.

10. Ian Aitken, *Film and Reform: John Grierson and the Documentary Film Movement* (London: Routledge, 1990), p. 12.

11. Aitken, *Film and Reform*, p. 15.

12. Aitken, *Film and Reform*, p. 168.

13. Aitken, *Film and Reform*, p. 168.

14. Aitken, *Film and Reform*, p. 194.

15. Aitken, *Film and Reform*, p. 194.

16. Aitken, *Film and Reform*, p. 195.

17. Alan Lovell, "The Documentary Film Movement: John Grierson," in *Studies in Documentary*, ed. Alan Lovell and Jim Hillier (New York: Viking, 1972), p. 18.

18. Lovell, "The Documentary Film Movement," p. 18.

19. Lovell, "The Documentary Film Movement," p. 19.

20. Lovell, "The Documentary Film Movement," p. 19.

21. Lovell, "The Documentary Film Movement," pp. 22–23.

22. Lovell, "The Documentary Film Movement," p. 24.

23. Lovell, "The Documentary Film Movement," p. 25.

24. Lovell, "The Documentary Film Movement," p. 28.

25. Lovell, "The Documentary Film Movement," p. 35.

26. Lovell, "The Documentary Film Movement," p. 35.

27. Lovell, "The Documentary Film Movement," pp. 23–24.

28. Andrew Tudor, "The Problem of Context: John Grierson," in *Theories of Film* (New York: Viking, 1974), p. 62.

29. Tudor, "The Problem of Context," p. 66.

30. Tudor, "The Problem of Context," p. 73.

31. Tudor, "The Problem of Context," p. 74.

32. Tudor, "The Problem of Context," p. 75.

33. Grierson, "A Film Policy for Canada."

34. Peter Morris, "Backwards to the Future: John Grierson's Film Policy for Canada," in *Flashback: People and Institutions in Canadian Film History*, ed. Gene Walz, vol. 2 of *Canadian Film Studies* (Montreal: Médiatexte Publications, 1986), p. 23.

35. Morris, "Backwards to the Future," p. 26.

36. Morris, "Backwards to the Future," p. 26.

37. Morris, "Backwards to the Future," p. 27.

38. Morris, "Backwards to the Future," p. 31.

39. Peter Morris, "Re-thinking Grierson: The Ideology of John Grierson," in *Dialogue: Canadian and Quebec Cinema*, ed. Pierre Vérronneau, Michael Dorland, and Seth Feldman, vol. 3 of *Canadian Film Studies* (Montreal: Médiatexte Publications and La Cinématheque Québécoise, 1987), p. 26.

40. Morris, "Re-thinking Grierson," p. 33.

41. Morris, "Re-thinking Grierson," p. 34.

42. Morris, "Re-thinking Grierson," pp. 37–38.

43. Morris, "Re-thinking Grierson," p. 39.

44. Morris, "Re-thinking Grierson," p. 42.

45. Morris, "Re-thinking Grierson," p. 44.

46. Morris, "Re-thinking Grierson," p. 45.

47. Joyce Nelson, *The Colonized Eye: Rethinking the Grierson Legend* (Toronto: Between the Lines, 1988), p. 105.

48. Nelson, *The Colonized Eye*, p. 105.

49. Nicholas Pronay, "John Grierson and the Documentary—60 Years On," *Historical Journal of Film, Radio and Television* 9, no. 3 (1989): 246, n. 3.

50. Pronay, "John Grierson and the Documentary," p. 231.

51. Pronay, "John Grierson and the Documentary," p. 227.

52. Pronay, "John Grierson and the Documentary," pp. 227–28.

53. Pronay, "John Grierson and the Documentary," p. 228.

54. Pronay, "John Grierson and the Documentary," p. 229.

55. Pronay, "John Grierson and the Documentary," p. 230.

56. Pronay, "John Grierson and the Documentary," p. 231.

57. Pronay, "John Grierson and the Documentary," p. 232.

58. Pronay, "John Grierson and the Documentary," p. 233.

59. Pronay, "John Grierson and the Documentary," p. 234.

60. Pronay, "John Grierson and the Documentary," p. 234.

61. Pronay, "John Grierson and the Documentary," p. 235.

62. Pronay, "John Grierson and the Documentary," p. 238.

63. Pronay, "John Grierson and the Documentary," p. 241.

64. Pronay, "John Grierson and the Documentary," p. 244.

65. Pronay, "John Grierson and the Documentary," p. 245.

66. Paul Swann, *The British Documentary Film Movement, 1926–1946* (Cambridge: Cambridge University Press, 1989), p. 59.

67. Swann, *British Documentary Film Movement*, p. 61.

68. Swann, *British Documentary Film Movement*, p. 57.

69. Brian Winston, *Claiming the Real: The Griersonian Documentary and Its Legitimations* (London: British Film Institute, 1995), p. 79.

70. Winston, *Claiming the Real*, p. 40.

71. Winston, *Claiming the Real*, p. 35.

72. Winston, *Claiming the Real*, p. 103.

73. Winston, *Claiming the Real*, pp. 251–58.

74. Winston, *Claiming the Real*, p. 258.

75. Winston, *Claiming the Real*, p. 259.

76. Ian Lockerbie, "Grierson and Realism," in the John Grierson Project, McGill University, *John Grierson and the NFB*, pp. 86–101.

77. Aitken, *Film and Reform*, p. 11.

78. Lockerbie, "Grierson and Realism," pp. 86–87.

79. Aitken, *Film and Reform*, p. 10.

80. Most notably (and preceding Winston) are Bill Nichols, *Representing Reality: Issues and Concepts in Documentary* (Bloomington: Indiana University Press, 1991), and Michael Renov, ed., *Theorizing Documentary* (New York: Routledge, 1993). I am grateful to Carolyn Anderson for suggesting this connection.

81. Paul Rotha, *Documentary Diary: An Informal History of British Documentary Film, 1928–1939* (New York: Hill and Wang, 1973), p. 122.

82. Rotha, *Documentary Diary*, p. 233.

83. Winston, *Claiming the Real*, p. 265, n. 7.

84. Nelson, *The Colonized Eye*, p. 167.

# ✦ BIBLIOGRAPHY

## Works by John Grierson

"Address to the National Institute of Design, Ahmedabad, India." In Beveridge, *John Grierson: Film Master*, 311–13.

"America's Most Vital Medium: The Documentary Film." *Library Journal* 71 (May 1, 1946): 630–34.

"Art and the Analysts." *Sight and Sound* 4, no. 16 (winter 1935–36): 157–59.

"Background for the Use of Films—or Anything Else—by Rehabilitation Officers." Ottawa: National Film Board, February, 1945. Mimeographed.

"Battle for Authenticity." *Documentary News Letter* (1939). Reprinted in Grierson, *Grierson on Documentary*, 215–17.

"The B.B.C. and All That." *Quarterly of Film, Radio, and Television* 9, no. 1 (fall 1954): 46–59.

"Behind the Screen." *World Film News* 3, no. 1 (April 1938): 18–19.

"Better Popular Pictures." *Transactions of the Society of Motion Picture Engineers* 11 (August 1927): 227–49.

"Book Reviews: *Documentary Film* by Paul Rotha." *Sight and Sound*, n.s., 22, no. 2 (October–December 1952): 92, 93.

"Book Reviews: *The Summing Up.*" *World Film News* 2, no. 12 (March 1938).

"British Documentary." *Documentary 51*. Edinburgh: Edinburgh Film Festival, 1951.

"*Captains Courageous*: Best Release of the Month." *World Film News* 2, no. 9 (December 1937): 18–19.

"Cinema of State." *Clarion* (August 1930): 235.

"The Cinema Today." In *The Arts Today*, edited by Geoffrey Grigson, 219–50. London: Bodley Head, 1935.

"Clowns of the Screen." *Everyman* (October 29, 1931): 430.

"Constructive Criticism." *American Cinematographer* (January 1929): 28, 29, 31.

"Contact." *Cinema Quarterly* 2, no. 1 (autumn 1933): 47.

"The Course of Realism." In *Footnotes to the Film*, edited by Charles Davy, 137–61. London: Lovat Dickson, 1937.

"The Crazy Man of the Films." *Everyman* (May 26, 1932): 554.

"Criticisms—Romantic Anarchist." *World Film News* 1, no. 1 (April 1936): 11.

"Documentary (1)." *Cinema Quarterly* 1, no. 2 (winter 1932): 67–72.

"Documentary (2): Symphonics." *Cinema Quarterly* 2, no. 3 (spring 1933): 135–39.

"Documentary: A World Perspective." *Grierson on Documentary*, 365–71.

"The Documentary Idea 1942." *Documentary News Letter* 3, no. 6 (June 1942): 83–86.

"Edinburgh 1948." *Documentary Film News* 7, no. 8 (August 1948): 87.

*Education and the New Order*. Democracy and Citizenship Series, pamphlet no. 7, Canadian Association for Adult Education, 1941. 15 pp.

"Education in a Technological Society." Address to the National Conference on Adult Education, Winnipeg, May 28, 1945. Mimeographed, 6 pp. In *Film News* n.s., 1, no. 1 (October 1945): 12–13.

*Eisenstein, 1898–1948*. London: Film Section of the Society for Cultural Relations with the U.S.S.R., 1948. 28 pp.

"The E.M.B. Film Unit." *Cinema Quarterly* 1, no. 4 (summer 1933): 203–208.

"Extract from Grierson." *Documentary News Letter* 6 (November–December 1947).

"The Eyes of Canada." In Beveridge, *John Grierson: Film Master*, 143–44.

*Eyes of Democracy*. Edited by Ian Lockerbie. Stirling, Scotland: John Grierson Archive, University of Stirling, 1990.

"A Fairy Tale of Politics." *New Britain* (June 14, 1933): 110.

"The Film at War." Broadcast on the Canadian Broadcasting Corporation from Ottawa, November 30, 1939. Slightly abridged as "Broadcast to Canada." *Documentary News Letter* 1, no. 4 (April 1940): 3–4.

"Film Horizons." *Theatre Arts* 30, no. 12 (December 1946): 698–701.

"The Film in British Colonial Development." *Sight and Sound* 17, no. 65 (spring 1948): 2–4.

"Filming the Gospel a Dangerous Policy." *World Film News* 1, no. 2 (May 1936): 23.

"A Film Policy for Canada." *Canadian Affairs* 1, no. 11 (June 1944): 3–15.

"Films and the I.L.O." Address delivered to the International Labor Organization, Philadelphia, April 26, 1944. *Grierson on Documentary*, 309–16.

"Films and Universities: Two Viewpoints." In *The Relation Between Universities and Films, Radio and Television*, edited by Glynne Wickham. London: Butterworths Scientific Publications, 1953. (coauthored with Basil Wright)

"Films as an International Influence." Address to the Vancouver Advertising and Sales Bureau, December 1944. Mimeographed, 6 pp.

"The Film Situation." *London Mercury and Bookman* 36, no. 215 (September 1937): 459–63.

"The Finest Eyes in Cinema." *World Film News* 1, no. 12 (March 1937): 5.

"First Things First at UNESCO." In *Film To-day Books: Screen and Audience*, edited by John E. Cross and Arnold Rattenbury, p. 79. London: Saturn Press, 1947.

"Flaherty." *ACT Journal* 16 (July–August 1951).

"Flaherty as Innovator." *Sight and Sound* n.s. 21, no. 2 (October–December 1951): 64–68.

"Flaherty—Naturalism—and the Problem of English Cinema." *Artwork* 7 (autumn 1931): 210–15.

Foreword to *The Cinema in School*, by W. H. George. London: Isaac Pitman, 1935.

"The Front Page." *Sight and Sound* 21, no. 4 (April–June 1952): 143.

"The Function of the Producer: 2. The Documentary Producer." *Cinema Quarterly* 2, no. 1 (autumn 1933): 7–9.

"The Future of Documentary." *Cine-Technician* 3 (December 1937–January 1938): 167–68, 170.

"The Future of the Films." Address to the Conference of the Arts, Sciences, and Professions in the Post–War World, at the Waldorf-Astoria Hotel, New York City, June 23, 1945. Published as "Documentary: Post-War Potential," *Film News* 6, no. 6 (June 1945): 6–8.

"The G.P.O. Gets Sound." *Cinema Quarterly* 2, no. 4 (summer 1934): 215–21.

"Grierson Asks for a Common Plan." *Documentary News Letter* 5, no. 5 (1944): 49–51.

"Grierson on Documentary." *Cine-Technician* 14 (July–August 1948): 123–24, 126–28.

*Grierson on Documentary.* Edited by Forsyth Hardy. London: Collins, 1946. New York: Harcourt, Brace, 1947. Rev. ed., Berkeley: University of California Press, 1966. Abr. ed., London: Faber and Faber, 1979. All citations are from the 1966 edition unless otherwise indicated.

*Grierson Transcripts: Interviews Recorded with John Grierson, February 1969–July 1971.* Interviews by Rodrigue Chiasson, transcribed by Sandra Gathercole. 4 vols. Ottawa: Canadian Radio and Television Commission, 1973.

"Hitchcock: Britain's Best Director." *Clarion* (November 1930): 201–2.

"The Hitch in Hitchcock." *Everyman* (December 24, 1931): 722.

"In the Name of Goodness." *World Film News* 3, no. 6 (October 1938): 258–59.

"Introduction to a New Art." *Sight and Sound* 3, no. 11 (autumn 1934): 101–4.

*I Remember, I Remember.* 16 mm color film, 58 minutes. Produced by the Visual Education Centre, Toronto, in association with Films of Scotland and Scottish Television, 1970.

"Is the Free Film Show a Menace?" *Kine Weekly* (October 17, 1935): 13.

"John Barleycorn." *Scotland* no. 58 (December 1951): 69–73.

"John Grierson on Media, Film and History," selected and edited by Donald F. and Joan B. Theall. In *Studies in Canadian Communications,* edited by Gertrude Joch Robinson and Donald F. Theall. Montreal: Graduate Programme in Communications, McGill University, 1975.

"John Grierson Replies." *Cinema Quarterly* 3, no. 1 (autumn 1934): 10–11.

"Letter to Michelle." *A.I.D. News* no. 1 (January): 6–7.

"The Library in an International World." Address before the American Library Association, Buffalo, New York, June 17, 1946. In Grierson, *Grierson on Documentary,* 295–305.

"Louisiana Story." *Documentary Film News* 7 (September–October 1948): 108.

"Making a Film of the Actual: A Problem in Film Construction." *Clarion* (October 1929): 11–12.

"Memo to Michelle about Decentralizing the Means of Production." *A.I.D. News* no. 2 (November 1971): 5–7.

"A Mind for the Future." Saint Andrew's Day Lecture, November 30, 1962, Scottish Home Service of the B.B.C. In Grierson, *Grierson on Documentary,* 382–93.

"Nature in the Raw." *Scotland* no. 61 (March 1952): 72–76.

"The Nature of Propaganda." *Documentary News Letter* 2, no. 5 (May 1941): 90–93.

"The Necessity and Nature of Public Information." Ottawa: National Film Board, c. 1942. Mimeographed, 8 pp.

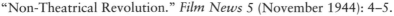

"Non-Theatrical Revolution." *Film News* 5 (November 1944): 4–5.

"Notes on the Documentary Film." Chicago: National Film Board of Canada, c. 1945. Mimeographed, 10 pp.

"Notes on the Psychological Factor in Administration and the Relations of Public Information to Public Morale." Ottawa: National Film Board, January 1943. Mimeographed, 4 pp.

"Notes on 'The Tasks of an International Film Institute.'" *Hollywood Quarterly* 2, no. 2 (January 1947): 192–96.

"O Canada! We Stand on Guard for Thee." *Documentary Film News* 7, no. 3 (March 1948): 28, 35.

"On Robert Flaherty." *Reporter* 5, no. 8 (October 16, 1951): 31–35.

"The Other Side of the Atlantic." *Documentary News Letter* 1, no. 9 (September 1940): 3–4.

"Portrait of Robert Flaherty." Radio broadcast produced by Oliver Lawson Dick for the B.B.C. Third Programme, September 2, 1952.

"Postwar Patterns." *Hollywood Quarterly* 1, no. 2 (January 1946): 159–65.

Preface to *Documentary Film*, by Paul Rotha. 3d ed. London: Faber and Faber, 1952.

"Projection of Scotland." *Spectator* 160 (May 6, 1938): 828, 830.

"Propaganda and Education." Address delivered to the Winnipeg Canadian Club, October 19, 1943. *Grierson on Documentary*, 280–94.

"Propaganda: A Problem for Educational Theory and for Cinema." *Sight and Sound* 3, no. 8 (winter 1933–34): 119–21.

"Prospect for Documentary: What Is Wrong and Why." *Sight and Sound* 17, no. 66 (summer 1948): 55–59.

"The Relationship Between the Political Power and the Cinema." Celebrity Lecture, Edinburgh International Film Festival, August 24, 1968. *Grierson on Documentary*, 191–205.

"Reporting Progress." *Documentary 49: Film Festival*. Edinburgh: Albyn, 1949.

"A Review of Reviews." *Sight and Sound* n.s. 23, no. 4 (April–June 1954): 207–8, 222; n.s. 24, no. 1 (July–September 1954): 143–44; no. 2 (October–December 1954): 101–3; no. 3 (January–March 1955): 157–58.

"Revolution in the Arts." Speech delivered at the University of North Carolina, Chapel Hill, April 1962. In *John Grierson: Film Master*, by James Beveridge, 26–34.

"The Russian Cinema Bear Awakens: The Movie Situation in the Land of the Muscovites." *Motion Picture Classic*, no. 25 (June 1927): 18–19, 74, 78.

"Searchlight on Democracy." *Adult Education* 12 (December 1939): 59–70.

"The Story of the Documentary Film." *Fortnightly Review* 152, no. 146 (August 1939): 121–30.

"Talk on a Visit to Normandy and Brittany." Radio broadcast on the Canadian Broadcasting Corporation, August 20, 1944. Mimeographed, 6 pp. *Documentary News Letter* 5, no. 4 (1944): 44.

"Thanks to Alistair Cooke." *World Film News* 1, no. 11 (December 1937): 89.

"*Things to Come* by H. G. Wells." *Glasgow Herald*, October 29, 1935.

"The 35mm Mind." *McGill News* 52, no. 2 (March 1971): 12–15. Interview by Darlene Kruesel.

"A Time for Enquiry." *Documentary* 47. Edinburgh: Albyn, 1947.

"Tolerance Is a Law." *Junior League Magazine* 32, no. 10 (June 1946): 8.

"Tom Mix, Man of Action." *New Britain* (August 2, 1933): 334, 342.

"Tomorrow the Movies II: Pictures Without Theaters." *Nation* 160, no. 1 (January 13, 1945): 37–39.

*A Tribute to Humphrey Jennings*. London: Olen, n.d. [1950?].

"Two Important Films." *Clarion* (February 1930): 45.

"Von Sternberg—and Joe." *Everyman* (April 14, 1932): 362.

"What I Look for." *New Clarion* (June 11, 1932).

"Why Produce Films by Rule of Thumb?" *Kine Weekly* (January 9, 1936): 35.

"World's Fair and Royal Visit Are Our Greatest Opportunities in 1939." *Kine Weekly* (January 12, 1939): 44.

"Welcome Stranger!" *Sight and Sound* 18, no. 69 (spring 1949): 51. (co-authored with Philip Mackie)

## Other Sources

Aitken, Ian. *Film and Reform: John Grierson and the Documentary Film Movement*. London: Routledge, 1990.

———. "John Grierson, Idealism and the Inter-war Period." *Historical Journal of Film, Radio, and Television* 9, no. 3 (1989): 247–58.

Amery, L. S. *My Political Life*. 2 vols. London: Hutchinson, 1953.

Anstey, Edgar. "The Early Days of Documentary." *Cine-Technician* 7 (September–October 1941): 102–4.

———. "The Living Story: E.M.B.–G.P.O." *Sight and Sound* 21, no. 4 (April–June 1952): 176.

———. "Some Origins of Cinéma Vérité." N.d., typescript, 7 pp.

———. "The Sound-Track in British Documentary." N.d., typescript, 13 pp.

———. "The Year's Work in the Documentary Film." In *The Year's Work in the Film: 1949*, edited by Roger Manvell, 30–36. London: Longmans Green, 1950.

Anstey, Edgar, Stuart Hood, Claire Johnston, and Ivor Montagu. "The Grierson Influence." *Undercut,* no. 9 (summer 1983).

Armes, Roy. *A Critical History of the British Cinema.* New York: Oxford University Press, 1978.

———. *Film and Reality: An Historical Survey.* London: Penguin, 1974.

Arts Enquiry. *The Factual Film: A Survey.* London: Oxford University Press, 1947.

Balcon, Sir Michael. *Michael Balcon Presents . . . A Lifetime of Films.* London: Hutchinson, 1969.

Barrot, Olivier, et al. *L'Angleterre et Son Cinéma: le Courant Documentaire 1927/1965.* Paris: Filmeditions, 1977.

"Basil Wright: Close-Up." *Documentary Film News* 7 (March 1948): 34.

Bertrand, Ina, and Diane Collins. *Government and Film in Australia.* Sydney: Currency Press and Australian Film Institute, 1981.

Beveridge, James. *John Grierson: Film Master.* New York: Macmillan, 1978.

Bluem, A. William. *Documentary in American Television.* New York: Hastings, 1965.

British Film Institute. *The Film in National Life: Being the Proceedings of a Conference Held by the British Film Institute in Exeter, April 1943.* London: British Film Institute, 1943.

*The British Film Yearbook 1949–50.* Edited by Peter Noble. London: Skelton Robinson, 1949.

Buchanan, Andrew. *The Art of Film Production.* London: Pitman, 1934.

Campbell, Andrew. "John Grierson's Rhetoric, A Movement Study of British Documentary Film 1929–1939." Ph.D. diss., Northwestern University, 1989.

Canada. National Film Board. "Memorandum to Mr. Salisbury. . . ." July 1944. N.F.B. archive.

———. National Film Board. "The National Film Board." Ottawa: National Film Board, c. 1944. Mimeographed, 8 pp.

———. National Film Board. "National Film Board Annual Report, Fiscal Year 1944–45." Ottawa: National Film Board, 1945. Mimeographed, 30 pp.

———. National Film Board, Information and Promotion Division. "The National Film Board of Canada." Ottawa: National Film Board, September 1953. Mimeographed, 33 pp.

———. National Film Board, Information Section. "The National Film Board: A Survey." Ottawa: National Film Board, June 1945. Mimeographed, 22 pp.

———. Royal Commission. *The Report of the Royal Commission to Investigate the Facts Relating to and Circumstances Surrounding the Communication, by Public Officials and Other Persons in Positions of Trust, of Secret and Confidential Information to Agents of a For-*

*eign Power*. Ottawa: Edmond Cloutier, Printer to the King, His Most Excellent Majesty, June 27, 1946.

Cavalcanti, Alberto. Foreword to *Sound and the Documentary Film*, by Ken Cameron. London: Sir Isaac Pitman & Sons, 1947.

———. "Le Mouvement néo-réaliste en Angleterre." *Le Rôle intellectuelle du cinéma*, 235–41. Paris: Institute international de coopération intellectuelle, 1937. Excerpts reprinted in translation in *French Film Theory and Criticism*, by Richard Abel, 2:233–38. Princeton, N.J.: Princeton University Press, 1988.

———. "Presenting Len Lye." *Sight and Sound* 16 (winter 1947–48): 134–36.

Chafee, Zechariah, Jr. *Government and Mass Communications: A Report from the Commission on Freedom of the Press*. Chicago: University of Chicago Press, 1947.

Chiasson, Rodrigue. "The CRTC Tapes." In the John Grierson Project, McGill University, *John Grierson and the NFB*. Toronto: ECW Press, 1984.

Chittock, John, ed. *Researchers' Guide to John Grierson: Films, Reference Sources, Collections, Data*. London: Grierson Memorial Trust, 1990.

Chowl, Hay. "Mickey's Rival." *Close-up* 6, no. 6 (June 1930): 493–95.

*Cinéma D'Aujourd'hui* no. 11 (February–March 1977). Issue devoted to the British documentary.

Clandfield, David. *Canadian Film*. Toronto: Oxford University Press, 1987.

Colls, Robert, and Philip Dodd. "Representing the Nation—British Documentary Film, 1930–1945." *Screen* 26, no. 1 (1985): 21–33.

Corner, J., and K. Richardson. *Documentary in the Mass Media*. London: Edward Arnold, 1986.

Curran, James, and Vincent Porter, eds. *British Cinema History*. London: Weidenfeld & Nicolson, 1983.

Davy, Charles. "Postscript: The Film Marches On." *Footnotes to the Film*. London: Lovat Dickson, 1937.

Dawson, Jonathon. "The Grierson Tradition." In *The Documentary Film in Australia*, edited by Ross Lansell and Peter Beilby. Melbourne: Cinema Papers and Film Victoria, 1981.

Deighton, Len. *The Ipcress File*. Greenwich, Conn.: Fawcett, 1965.

Dickinson, Margaret, and Sarah Street. *Cinema and State: The Film Industry and the British Government, 1927–1984*. London: British Film Institute, 1985.

Elder, R. Bruce. *Image and Identity: Reflections on Canadian Film and Culture*. Waterloo, Ontario: Wilfrid Laurier University Press, 1989.

Ellis, Jack C. "Changing of the Guard: From the Grierson Documentary to Free Cinema." *Quarterly Review of Film Studies* 1 (February 1976): 70–78.

———. *The Documentary Idea: A Critical History of English-Language*

*Documentary Film and Video*. Englewood Cliffs, N.J.: Prentice Hall, 1989.

———. "The Final Years of British Documentary as the Grierson Movement." *Journal of Film and Video* 36 (fall 1984): 41–49.

———. "Grierson at University." *Cinema Journal* 12 (spring 1973): 24–35.

———. *John Grierson: A Guide to References and Resources*. Boston: G. K. Hall, 1986.

———. "John Grierson's First Years at the National Film Board." *Cinema Journal* 10 (fall 1970): 2–14. Reprinted in *Canadian Film Reader*, edited by Seth Feldman and Joyce Nelson, 37–47. Toronto: Peter Martin, 1977.

———. "John Grierson's Relations with British Documentary During World War Two." In the John Grierson Project, McGill University, *John Grierson and the NFB*, Toronto: ECW Press, 1984.

———. "The Young Grierson in America, 1924–1927." *Cinema Journal* 8 (fall 1968): 12–21.

Elton, Arthur. "Barking Up the Wrong Tree." *Documentary News Letter* 7 (November–December 1948).

Evans, Gary. *In the National Interest: A Chronicle of the National Film Board of Canada from 1949 to 1989*. Toronto: University of Toronto Press, 1991.

———. *John Grierson and the National Film Board: The Politics of Wartime Propaganda*. Toronto: University of Toronto Press, 1984.

———. "John Grierson's Final Advice to the National Film Board of Canada, 1966–1971." *Historical Journal of Film, Radio and Television* 9, no. 3 (1989): 291–300.

Feldman, Seth. *Take Two: A Tribute to Film in Canada*. Toronto: Irwin, 1984.

Fetherling, Douglas, ed. *Documents in Canadian Film*. Peterborough: Broadview, 1988.

Furse, Lt.-Gen. Sir William. "The Imperial Institute." *Sight and Sound* 2, no. 7 (autumn 193): 78–79.

Great Britain. Central Office of Information. *Annual Report 1948–49*.

———. Commission on Educational and Cultural Films. *The Film in National Life*. London: Allen and Unwin, 1932.

———. Select Committee on Estimates. *Report from a Select Committee on Estimates*. London: His Majesty's Stationery Office, July 1934.

*Grierson*. 16 mm color film, 59 minutes. Produced by the National Film Board of Canada, 1972.

Hardy, Forsyth. "The British Documentary Film." In *Twenty Years of British Film 1925–1945*, by Michael Balcon, Ernest Lindgren, Forsyth Hardy, and Roger Manvell, 48–80. London: Falcon, 1947.

————. "The Film Society Movement in Scotland." In *Film Society Primer: A Compilation of Twenty-Two Articles about and for Film Societies*, edited by Cecile Starr and Carolyn Henig. Forest Hills, N.Y.: American Federation of Film Societies, 1956.

————. "Final Word on Documentary Maker's Philosophy." *Scotsman* (January 18, 1991): 15.

————. "Grierson's Pioneer Film Set to Music." *Scotsman* (May 5, 1986).

————. *John Grierson: A Documentary Biography*. London: Faber and Faber, 1979.

————. "John Grierson and the Documentary Idea." In *Films in 1951: A Special Publication on British Films and Film-Makers for the Festival of Britain*, 55–56. London: British Film Institute, 1951.

————. *Scotland in Film*. Edinburgh: Edinburgh University Press, 1990.

————. *Scottish Life and Letters* radio broadcast. Scottish Home Service of the B.B.C., May 15, 1966.

Hardy, H. Reginald. *Mackenzie King of Canada*. London: Oxford University Press, 1949.

Hawes, Stanley. "Grierson in Australia." In *Australian Film Reader*, edited by Albert Moran and Tom O'Regan. Sydney: Currency Press, 1985.

Higson, Andrew. "'Britain's Outstanding Contribution to Film': The Documentary-Realist Tradition." In *All Our Yesterdays: Ninety Years of British Cinema*, edited by Charles Barr, 72–97. London: British Film Institute, 1986.

*Historical Journal of Film, Radio and Television* 9, no. 3 (1989). Special issue: "John Grierson: A Critical Retrospective," edited by I. C. Jarvie and Nicholas Pronay.

Hogenkamp, Bert. "The British Documentary Movement in Perspective." In *Image, Reality, Spectator: Essays on Documentary Film and Television*, edited by Willem De Greef and Willem Hesling. Louvain: Acco, 1989.

Holmes, J. B. "G.P.O. Films." *Sight and Sound* 6, no. 23 (autumn 1937): 159–60.

Hood, Stuart. "John Grierson and the Documentary Film Movement." *Sight and Sound* 17, no. 65 (spring 1948): 44–45.

*Informational Film Year Book 1948*. Edinburgh: Albyn Press, 1948.

Inglis, Ruth A. *Freedom of the Movies*. Chicago: University of Chicago Press, 1947.

Jarvie, Ian, and Robert L. Macmillan. "John Grierson on Hollywood's Success, 1927." *Historical Journal of Film, Radio and Television* 9, no. 3 (1989): 309–26.

"John Grierson Archive." *Historical Journal of Film, Radio and Television* 9, no. 3 (1989): 327.

John Grierson Project, McGill University. *John Grierson and the NFB.* Conference at McGill in October 1981 that opened the Grierson Project. Toronto: ECW Press, 1984.

"John Grierson: The Reluctant but Angry Guru, by Our Delhi Film Critic." *Sunday Statesman* (Delhi), May 9, 1971. Reprinted in Beveridge, *John Grierson: Film Master*, 305–9.

Jones, D. B. "Assessing the National Film Board, Crediting Grierson." *Historical Journal of Film, Radio and Television* 9, no. 3 (1989): 301–8.

———. *The Best Butler in the Business: Tom Daly of the National Film Board of Canada.* Toronto: University of Toronto Press, 1996.

———. "Book Reviews: *The Colonized Eye: Rethinking the Grierson Legend.*" *Historical Journal of Film, Radio and Television* 10, no. 1 (1990): 107–9.

———. *Movies and Memoranda: An Interpretive History of the National Film Board of Canada.* Ottawa: Canadian Film Institute and Deneau, 1981.

Klingender, F. D., and Stuart Legg. *Money Behind the Screen: A Report Prepared on Behalf of the Film Council.* London: Lawrence and Wishert, 1937. 79 pp.

Lee, J. M. "The Dissolution of the EMB, 1933: Reflections on a Diary." *Journal of Imperial and Commonwealth History* 1, no. 1 (1972): 49–57.

Lee, Rohama. *Master of the Film Medium: John Grierson Pioneered the Documentary Film in Britain and Canada.* Ames, Iowa: American Archives of Factual Film, Iowa State University, 1984.

Lerner, Loren R. *Canadian Film and Video: A Bibliography and Guide to the Literature.* Toronto: University of Toronto Press, 1996.

Leyda, Jay. *Films Beget Films.* London: George Allen and Unwin, 1964.

Lindsay, Sir Harry. "Romance and Adventure in Real Things: The Imperial Institute and Its Film Library." *World Film News* 2 (July 1937): 19.

Lockerbie, Ian. "Grierson and Realism." In the John Grierson Project, McGill University, *John Grierson and the NFB.* Toronto: ECW Press, 1984.

———. "Thoughts on the Re-thinking of Grierson." A paper delivered at the 1989 Conference of the Association for the Study of Canadian Radio and Television.

Lovell, Alan. "The Documentary Film Movement: John Grierson." In *Studies in Documentary,* edited by Alan Lovell and Jim Hillier, 9–61. New York: Viking, 1972.

Lovell, Terry. *Pictures of Reality: Aesthetics, Politics and Pleasure.* London: British Film Institute, 1979.

Low, Colin. "Grierson and Challenge for Change." In the John Grierson Project, McGill University, *John Grierson and the NFB*. Toronto: ECW Press, 1984.

Macmillan, Robert. "A Note Concerning John Grierson and the National Gallery of Canada, 1939–1943." *Historical Journal of Film, Radio and Television* 9, no. 3 (1989): 283–90.

MacPherson, Don, and Paul Willemen, eds. *Traditions of Independence: British Cinema in the Thirties*. London: British Film Institute, 1979.

Manvell, Roger. *Film*. Harmondsworth, Middlesex: Penguin, 1946.

———. *Films and the Second World War*. New York: Dell, 1976.

McArthur, Colin. *Scotch Reels: Scotland in Cinema and Television*. London: British Film Institute, 1981.

Millington, F. V. "Cinematograph in Agricultural Education: A Leicestershire Experiment." *Journal of the Ministry of Agriculture, London* 36 (November 1929): 739–45.

Morris, Peter. "Backwards to the Future: John Grierson's Film Policy for Canada." In *Flashback: People and Institutions in Canadian Film History*, edited by Gene Walz, 17–35. Vol. 2 of *Canadian Film Studies*. Montreal: Médiatexte Publications, 1986.

———. "'Praxis into Process': John Grierson and the National Film Board of Canada." *Historical Journal of Film, Radio and Television* 9, no. 3 (1989): 269–82.

———. "Re-thinking Grierson: The Ideology of John Grierson." In *Dialogue: Canadian and Quebec Cinema*, edited by Pierre Vérronneau, Michael Dorland, and Seth Feldman, 21–56. Vol. 3 of *Canadian Film Studies*. Montreal: Médiatexte Publications and La Cinématheque Québécoise, 1987.

Mullen, Pat. *Man of Aran*. New York: E. P. Dutton, 1935.

Nash, Paul. "The Colour Film." In *Footnotes to the Film*, edited by Charles Davy. London: Lovat Dickson, 1937.

Nelson, Joyce. *The Colonized Eye: Rethinking the Grierson Legend*. Toronto: Between the Lines, 1988.

Nichols, Bill. *Representing Reality: Issues and Concepts in Documentary*. Bloomington: Indiana University Press, 1991.

Oakley, C. A. *Where We Came In: Seventy Years of the British Film Industry*. London: George Allen and Unwin, 1964.

Parsons, Brenda M. "A Dramatic Interpretation of Reality for Democratic Purposes: John Grierson's *Drifters*." Master's thesis, McGill University, 1983.

Pelling, Henry. *Modern Britain: 1885–1955*. New York: W. W. Norton, 1960.

"Perspective." *Documentary News Letter* 6, no. 54 (November–December 1946): 51, 60–63.

Pickersgill, J. W. *The Mackenzie King Record*. Toronto: University of Toronto Press, 1960.

"Points of Reference." In *Films of 1951*. London: Sight and Sound for the British Film Institute, 1951.

Pratley, Gerald. *Torn Sprockets: The Uncertain Projection of the Canadian Film*. Cranbury, N.J.: Associated University Presses, 1987.

Read, Herbert. "Experiments in Counterpoint." *Cinema Quarterly* 3, no. 1 (autumn 1934): 17–21.

Renov, Michael, ed. *Theorizing Documentary*. New York: Routledge, 1993.

Rodger, Andrew. "Some Factors Contributing to the Formation of the National Film Board of Canada." *Historical Journal of Film, Radio and Television* 9, no. 3 (1989): 259–68.

Rotha, Paul. *Celluloid: The Film To-Day*. London: Longmans, Green, 1931.

———. *Documentary Diary: An Informal History of the British Documentary Film, 1928–1939*. New York: Hill and Wang, 1973.

———. *Documentary Film*. New York: Hastings House, 1952.

———. *The Film Till Now: A Survey of World Cinema*. London: Jonathan Cape, 1930.

———. *Robert J. Flaherty: A Biography*, edited by Jay Ruby. Philadelphia: University of Pennsylvania Press, 1983.

———. *Rotha on the Film: A Selection of Writings about the Cinema*. London: Faber and Faber, 1958.

Rotha, Paul, and Basil Wright. "Flaherty: A Biography." 1959. Typescript. Museum of Modern Art Library.

Sainsbury, Frank, ed. "Close-Ups: No. 2—Arthur Elton." *Cine-Technician* 5 (July–August 1939): 57–58.

Schemke, Irmgard. "Documentary To-day." *Sequence* no. 3 (spring 1948): 12–14.

Sherman, John. "The Grierson Influence." *Undercut* no. 9 (summer 1983): 16–17.

Sperber, A. M. *Murrow: His Life and Times*. New York: Freundlich Books, 1986.

Spottiswoode, Raymond J. *A Grammar of the Film: An Analysis of Film Technique*. London: Faber and Faber, 1935.

Starr, Cecile, ed. *Ideas on Film: A Handbook for the 16 mm Film User*. New York: Funk & Wagnalls, 1951.

Sussex, Elizabeth. "Basil Wright and Edgar Anstey." *Sight and Sound* 57 (winter 1987): 17.

———. "The Golden Years of Grierson." *Sight and Sound* 41, no. 3 (summer 1972): 149–53.

———. *The Rise and Fall of British Documentary: The Story of the Film Movement Founded by John Grierson*. Berkeley: University of California Press, 1975.

Swann, Paul. "The British Documentary Film Movement 1926–1946." Ph.D. diss., University of Leeds, 1979.

———. *The British Documentary Film Movement, 1926–1946.* Cambridge: Cambridge University Press, 1989.

———. "John Grierson and the G.P.O. Film Unit, 1933–1939." *Historical Journal of Film, Radio and Television* 1, no. 1 (1983): 19–32.

———. "The Selling of the Empire: The EMB Film Unit." *Studies in Visual Communication* 9, no. 3 (1983): 15–24.

Tallents, Sir Stephen. *British Documentary.* London: Film Centre, 1968.

———. "Cinema." 1945. Typescript. Published as "The Birth of British Documentary." *Journal of the University Film Association* 20, nos. 1–3 (1968).

———. "The First Days of Documentary." *Documentary News Letter* 6, no. 55 (January–February 1947): 76–77.

Taylor, Donald F. "In the Service of the Public." *Sight and Sound* 2 (winter 1933–34): 128–31.

Toeplitz, Jerzy. *A Few Lectures on Documentary Film.* North Ryde, Sydney: Australian Film & Television School, 1972.

Tritton, R. E. "The Government and the Cinema." In *The British Film Yearbook 1949–50,* edited by Peter Noble, 56–60. London: Skelton Robinson, 1949.

Tudor, Andrew. "The Problem of Context: John Grierson." In *Theories of Film,* 59–76. New York: Viking, 1974.

UNESCO. *Conference for the Establishment of UNESCO.* June 1946.

———. *Press, Film, Radio (Report of the Commission on Technical Needs).* Paris: UNESCO, September 1948.

———. The Programme of UNESCO Proposed by the Executive Board. Paris: UNESCO, 1950.

———. *Records of the General Conference* 2 (April 1948): 32.

———. *Report of the Director General.* September 1947.

Vaughan, Dai. *Portrait of an Invisible Man: The Working Life of Stewart McAllister, Film Editor.* London: British Film Institute, 1983.

Waldron, Gloria. *The Information Film.* New York: Columbia University Press, 1949.

Ward, Kenneth. "British Documentaries of the 1930s." *History,* no. 62 (October 1977): 426–31.

Watt, Harry. *Don't Look at the Camera.* London: Elek, 1974.

———. "NFT Programme Notes." *Screen* 13 (summer 1972).

Weisenborn, Rudolph. "Study of John Grierson." *Chicago Evening Post,* c. June 1925, Art World section.

Winston, Brian. *Claiming the Real: The Griersonian Documentary and Its Legitimations.* London: British Film Institute, 1995.

————. "Great Artist or Fly on the Wall: The Griersonian Accommodation and Its Destruction?" In *Visual Explorations of the World: Selected Papers from the International Conference on Visual Communication*, edited by Jay Ruby and Martin Taureg, 190–204. Aachen, GDR: Herodet im Rader Verlag, 1987.

Woods, D. L. "John Grierson: Documentary Film Pioneer." *Quarterly Journal of Speech* 57 (1971): 221–28.

Wright, Basil. "Documentary: Flesh, Fowl, or . . . ?" *Sight and Sound* 19 (March 1950): 43, 47.

————. "Documentary To-Day." *Penguin Film Review*, no. 2 (January 1947): 37–44.

————. "Films and UNESCO." In *Informational Film Year Book 1947*, 38–41. London: Albyn Press, 1947.

————. "John Taylor: A Close-Up." *Documentary Film News* 7 (July 1948): 82–83.

————. *The Long View.* London: Secker & Warburg, 1974.

————. "The Progress of the Factual Film: 1. Grierson the Pioneer." In *Public's Progress*, 64–71. London: Contact, 1948.

Yentob, Alan. *Arena: The GPO Story.* Television program. Production company: B.B.C.–TV; prod./dir. Alan Yentob; telecast December 14, 1983.

ZAB. "Men o' War: Grierson a Go-Getter." *Montrealer* (December 1943): 15.

# ✦ INDEX

Titles in **boldface** are some of the films John Grierson was most closely involved with.

JACK C. ELLIS established the film program at Northwestern University and was chair of the Department of Radio/Television/Film. A founding member of the Society for Cinema Studies, he served as its president and as editor of *Cinema Journal*. He is the author of *The Documentary Idea: A Critical History of English-Language Documentary Film and Video* and *A History of Film*.